GODLY KI
RESTORATI

The position of English monarchs as supreme governors of the Church of England profoundly affected early modern politics and religion. This innovative book explores how tensions in church–state relations created by Henry VIII's Reformation continued to influence relationships between the crown, parliament, and common law during the Restoration, a distinct phase in England's 'long Reformation'. Debates about the powers of kings and parliaments, the treatment of Dissenters, and emerging concepts of toleration were viewed through a Reformation prism where legitimacy depended on godly status. This book discusses how the institutional, legal, and ideological framework of supremacy perpetuated the language of godly kingship after 1660, and how supremacy was complicated by an ambivalent Tudor legacy. This was manipulated by not only Anglicans, but also tolerant kings and intolerant parliaments, Catholics, Dissenters, and radicals like Thomas Hobbes. Invented to uphold the religious and political establishments, supremacy paradoxically ended up subverting them.

JACQUELINE ROSE is a lecturer in Modern British History at the University of St Andrews. She researches and teaches extensively on early modern political, religious, and intellectual history.

Cambridge Studies in Early Modern British History

This is a series of monographs and studies covering many aspects of the history of the British Isles between the late fifteenth century and the early eighteenth century. It includes the work of established scholars and pioneering work by a new generation of scholars. It includes both reviews and revisions of major topics and books which open up new historical terrain or which reveal startling new perspectives on familiar subjects. All the volumes set detailed research within broader perspectives, and the books are intended for the use of students as well as of their teachers.

For a list of titles in the series go to
www.cambridge.org/earlymodernbritishhistory

GODLY KINGSHIP IN RESTORATION ENGLAND

The Politics of the Royal Supremacy, 1660–1688

JACQUELINE ROSE

University of St Andrews

CAMBRIDGE
UNIVERSITY PRESS

The Edinburgh Building, Cambridge CB2 8RU, UK

Published in the United States of America by Cambridge University Press, New York

Cambridge University Press is part of the University of Cambridge.

It furthers the University's mission by disseminating knowledge in the pursuit of education, learning and research at the highest international levels of excellence.

www.cambridge.org
Information on this title: www.cambridge.org/9781107689886

First published 2011
First paperback edition 2013

A catalogue record for this publication is available from the British Library

Library of Congress Cataloguing in Publication data
Rose, Jacqueline, 1982–
Godly kingship in Restoration England : the politics of the royal supremacy, 1660–1688 / Jacqueline Rose.
p. cm. – (Cambridge studies in early modern British history)
Includes bibliographical references and index.
ISBN 978-1-107-01142-7 (hardback)
1. Church and state – Great Britain – History – 16th century. 2. Church and state – Great Britain – History – 17th century. 3. Henry VIII, King of England, 1491–1547 – Influence. 4. Great Britain – Church history – 16th century. 5. Great Britain – Church history – 17th century. 6. Great Britain – History – Restoration, 1660–1688. 7. Great Britain – History – Stuarts, 1603–1714. I. Title.
BR757.R67 2011
261.7′3094109032–dc22 2011013373

ISBN 978-1-107-01142-7 Hardback
ISBN 978-1-107-68988-6 Paperback

Contents

Acknowledgements

So-called monographs are only produced with the support of many scholars and friends, and this book is no exception. I would like to express my thanks to the staff of Cambridge University Library, the British Library, the Bodleian Library, The National Archives, The Queen's College, Oxford, the Forbes-Mellon Library at Clare College, and Newnham College Library for assistance in accessing material. The Master and Fellows of Gonville and Caius College and their Library kindly allowed the reproduction of images. I am grateful to the Arts and Humanities Research Council for financial support throughout my doctorate, and to Geoffrey Elton's family and Clare College for the honour of holding the Geoffrey Elton Studentship in History. I owe thanks too to Newnham College for sabbatical leave, which expedited the process of converting thesis into book form, and to Clare College for having provided a beautiful and congenial setting for undergraduate and postgraduate study.

My greatest intellectual debt is to Mark Goldie, for his unstinting support in exemplary supervision of my doctoral work, for his guidance on all the extra accoutrements which Ph.D students have to acquire in addition to their thesis, and for his confidence both in the viability of a huge project and my ability to bring it to completion on time while holding a college lectureship. Fortunately, the fact that a significant number of our interests overlapped proved a source of fruitful exchange rather than of competition. Richard Serjeantson provided not only guidance in a stimulating term of supervision but also a sense of pure intellectual enjoyment of research, which renewed my enthusiasm for learning. John Guy's support was vital: I thank him for offering guidance on the sixteenth-century aspects of the thesis, as well as for proving that Tudor scholars would have an interest in what happened to the supremacy in the seventeenth century – and for his confidence that I could manage to discuss both of them. I am also immensely grateful to John Morrill for providing significant help both in the shape of comments on recalcitrant chapters and in the form of cheerful cups of tea, and to Alex Walsham for her advice on the final form of the book. I was fortunate in having two examiners, Stephen Taylor and John Spurr, who made a viva an enjoyable discussion. I would like to thank my editors and production team at Cambridge University Press: Michael Watson, Liz Friend-Smith, Chloe Howell, and Joanna Breeze, for providing helpful and friendly guidance on the publishing process, and my copy-editor, Caroline Drake. All errors, naturally, remain my own.

Conversations with Stephen Alford, Justin Champion, Alexander Courtney, Eoin Devlin, Kenneth Fincham, Ludmilla Jordanova, Hunter Powell, Richard Rex, Roly Tyler, and Ian Williams assisted my understanding of particular aspects of early modern religion and philosophy. Further thoughts arose from questions and comments at the Cambridge seminar in Early Modern British History and the Religious History seminar at the Institute of Historical Research. I am grateful, too, for wider support from Richard Partington and Gill Sutherland. And for planting a love of history, expressing confidence in my work, offering doses of sanity, and providing a necessary escape from the Cambridge bubble, I thank my parents, to whom this book is dedicated.

Abbreviations and conventions

All works were published in London unless otherwise stated. For ease of reference, roman numerals used as page numbers in sixteenth-century works have been converted to arabic numerals. All biblical citations are from the Authorized Bible. Dates given are Old Style, but the year has been taken to begin on 1 January. In quotations, original spelling and orthography have been preserved. In manuscript sources, *italics* denote expansions, words in <angled brackets> authorial insertions, and ~~struck-through~~ text deletions.

BL	British Library, London
Bodl.	Bodleian Library, Oxford
CJ	*Journals of the House of Commons*
CSPD	*Calendar of State Papers, Domestic*
CUL	University Library, Cambridge
EB	Mark Goldie et al., eds., *The Entring Book of Roger Morrice* (6 vols., Woodbridge, 2007). Cited by original volume and page number.
HMC	Royal Commission on Historical Manuscripts
LEP	Richard Hooker, *The Laws of Ecclesiastical Polity.* Cited by book, chapter, and paragraph, with page references to the Folger Library Edition of the Works of Richard Hooker, ed. W. Speed Hill (7 vols., Cambridge, MA, 1977–98) in parentheses.
LJ	*Journals of the House of Lords*
ODNB	H. C. G. Matthew and Brian Howard Harrison, eds., *Oxford Dictionary of National Biography* (61 vols., Oxford, 2004)
SP	State Papers
TNA	The National Archives, Kew, London

Depiction of Charles II, from the frontispiece of William Prynne, *An Exact Chronological Vindication and Historical Demonstration of our British, Roman, Saxon, Danish, Norman, English Kings Supreme Ecclesiastical Jurisdiction over all Prelates, Persons, Causes* (1666). Reproduced by kind permission of the Master and Fellows of Gonville and Caius College, Cambridge.

INTRODUCTION

The Restoration, the Reformation, and the royal supremacy

The idea of the godly magistrate was common parlance in Restoration England. The depiction of Charles II on the frontispiece of William Prynne's *An Exact Chronological Vindication and Historical Demonstration of our British, Roman, Saxon, Danish, Norman, English Kings Supreme Ecclesiastical Jurisdiction* of 1666 (see plate 1, opposite) was an exemplary illustration of the godly ruler. The Church quite literally rests on the royal sword, around which are entwined the words 'Carol[us] D[ei] G[ratia] fidei et ecclesiae defensor': Charles by the grace of God defender of the faith and church. Power flows from a heavenly hand to Charles, who wears a closed imperial crown, symbol of his Constantinian sovereignty. And above the Church is a banner referring to Isaiah 49:23, the proof-text for royal supremacy: 'kings shall be thy nursing fathers, and their queens thy nursing mothers'. This reflected a widespread language of godly kingship in Restoration England. This book provides the first account of the significance of this rhetoric.

The relationship between the crown and the Church in Restoration England has never been fully analysed until now. This is peculiar, because that relationship – formally embodied in the king's position as supreme governor on earth of the Church of England – involved fundamental questions about early modern religion and politics. What was the nature of royal authority – was it absolute, or tempered by parliament? How much power did the king, as a layman, have over the direction of national religion? Was the Church a holy catholic society constituted by its clergy and merely allied with the temporal polity, or was it established, and thus governed, by English law? What was the best response to the Dissenters and Catholics who wished to worship outside the national Church – might they be tolerated, or did church and crown have a holy duty to persecute them? The politics of the royal supremacy were affected by, and had an impact on, these questions. Supremacy provides an unexpectedly fruitful route into understanding critical issues of kingship, toleration, and Reformation history.

No sixteenth-century historian would doubt the centrality of supremacy to Tudor kingship; the surprise is how large a role it played after the Civil Wars. That Charles II and James II were supreme governors of their Church was not a polite fiction or an empty titular appendage. It mattered. It was important for anyone interested in the relationship between crown, parliament, and common law and for those concerned with the spectrum of attitudes ranging from persecution to toleration. Indeed, it mattered for all Englishmen when James II tried to use it to reverse the Reformation between 1685 and 1688. This book demonstrates how often debate on Restoration religion and politics involved debate on the royal supremacy.

Discussion of supremacy was not merely more prevalent than has previously been thought; it was also more complicated, because the exact meaning of supremacy was remarkably unclear. Lack of clarity about the location of supremacy in England's undefined constitution led to conflict between crown and parliament, especially in 1663, 1673, and 1685. Uncertainty about how far bishops were subordinate to their royal supreme governor rendered reactions to James II's Catholicism problematic and fuelled the first Anglican schism in 1689. The difficulty of ascertaining whether kings could choose the direction of religious worship led to the paradox of nonconformist praise for, and episcopal criticism of, the earthly head of the Church of England. This study explains how Restoration polemicists exploited the legacy of an ambiguous Reformation for their own purposes. The Civil Wars might appear to be a natural break in historical time, and have been assumed so in many books ending in 1642 or beginning in 1660. This study shows, firstly, that ecclesiastical developments between 1530 and 1660 continued to be central to the politics of religion in Restoration England. *Apropos* episcopacy and divine right monarchy, persecution and toleration, crown and parliament, a good case can be made for the Restoration as part of a long Reformation, albeit a distinct phase within this.

Secondly, this book emphasises the potential – and often very real – conflict between Restoration kings and the Church over which they presided. There were major rifts between Charles II's and James II's willingness to tolerate Catholics and Dissenters and the intolerance of the dominant strand of Restoration churchmanship. Religious views had a significant impact on political alignments, but royal policies could push these in unexpected directions. Dissenters who favoured civil liberties might praise the ecclesiastical prerogative in order to gain toleration. Conversely, Anglicans, who usually favoured royal absolutism and denounced 'fanatic sedition', constantly frustrated the king's decisions when they saw them as undermining their church-state. Invented to uphold the establishment, supremacy paradoxically ended up subverting it.

Thirdly, this book demonstrates how frequently Restoration political thinking took place in a religious framework. Political ideology was often shaped by an ecclesiological prism; that is, one of church–state relations. Since the Church of England was established, it was a political as well as a spiritual entity. Because the monarch headed the Church, discourse about the rights and duties of kingship involved discussion of how rulers should govern a godly polity. After 1660, Anglicans and Dissenters wrestled with the dual problematic central to Reformation political thought: how to make the magistrate godly, and what to do if he turned ungodly. To secularise Reformation Europe's political thought is to distort it, for the 'legitimacy' or 'tyranny' of rulers was determined by their 'godly' or 'ungodly' status. The question of the circumstances in which an ungodly tyrant could be resisted, and by whom, drove Catholic and Calvinist political thought. The absolutist response depended on showing that the Bible ordained obedience of subjects. God, not the people, punished evil kings – but monarchs ought to be no less careful for that. These European debates took on a distinct form in England because of the royal supremacy, which entrenched the idea of godly kingship in an elaborate legal and constitutional framework. Neither church nor state could be altered without disrupting the supremacy. Thus this book shows how the political thought of the Restoration phase of the long Reformation was naturally deeply concerned with the godly magistrate. As John Pocock has argued, 'it is in the consequences of Henry VIII's Reformation that we find the enduring problematics of English political thought for the next three centuries'.[1]

The idiosyncrasies of England's magisterial Reformation created an institutional, legal, and intellectual framework for church and state which lasted late into the seventeenth century. The royal supremacy did not dwindle into a mere cipher between 1660 and 1688. Rather, its powers were debated and manipulated by kings, parliaments, bishops, and Dissenters, each of whom were able to point to Reformation precedents

[1] J. G. A. Pocock, 'A Discourse of Sovereignty: Observations on the Work in Progress', in Nicholas Phillipson and Quentin Skinner, eds., *Political Discourse in Early Modern Britain* (Cambridge, 1993), p. 381.

for their claims. Studying the politics of supremacy helps dissect the complexities of attitudes to monarchy, Anglican and Dissenting ideologies, and the interweaving of political, ecclesiological, and legal languages in Restoration England. It also raises awareness of just how ambiguous, varied, and muddled Tudor *imperium* was. This book shows how the royal supremacies of Restoration England were multivalent and creative developments of Henry VIII's legacy in the circumstances of later Stuart kingship.

REFORMATION AND RESTORATION: CONTEXTS FOR SUPREMACY

Restoration religious debates took place in two contexts. One was the continuance of the legal and mental worlds of pre-Civil War England. The other was a novel set of experiences and royal policies. The interaction between the two provides the framework for this study. Restoration monarchs enjoyed the ecclesiastical prerogatives of their Tudor predecessors, but they put those powers to very different uses.

As Chapter 1 of this study shows, Restoration kings inherited a panoply of ecclesiastical powers from the Tudor Reformations. The royal supremacy founded by Henry VIII in the 1530s meant monarchical control of church law and the Church's legislative body, convocation. The Act of Submission of the Clergy (1534) decreed that convocation needed a royal licence to meet, separate permission to debate new canons, and ratification of these before they became legally binding. Henry VIII finally eliminated papal claims to appoint English bishops; instead he told cathedral chapters whom to elect, although episcopal succession was maintained by the need for other bishops (nominated by the king) to consecrate the royal candidate. The fiscal and juridical powers of the papacy were similarly transferred to the crown, with ecclesiastical appeals now heard in English courts, clerical 'First Fruits' harvested by the monarch, and the monasteries dissolved. Through the supremacy, Henry and his successors could regulate English worship by royal proclamations known as injunctions, and they could prosecute religious dissent by ecclesiastical commissions made up of laity and clergy. Although, as will be seen, these prerogatives were complex and ambiguous, they could largely be wielded (and certainly be claimed) by later Stuart monarchs. Charles II, James II, and their subjects worked within a legal framework over a century old.

As an extreme version of the magisterial Reformation, the English Reformation rested on the idea that the monarchy and the established Church were invariably allied. The Civil Wars of the middle of the seventeenth century shattered this assumption. The outburst of sectarian pluralism that emerged from the fragmentation of the puritan–Parliamentarian movement taught some Englishmen that religious diversity could never be prevented again. Others learned the anarchic dangers which stemmed from attacking the monarchy. More crucially, the Civil Wars divided the Church of England from the crown. Although Charles I professed that he died a martyr for both, in 1648 he had agreed to a three-year trial of Presbyterianism, and his son forged an alliance with Scottish Presbyterians. Bereft of a supportive supreme head, the (formerly) established Church bewailed its fate – but got on with surviving, even when Charles refused to appoint new bishops when the old ones died. Shorn of legal establishment, in the 1650s Anglicans found new intellectual bases, in particular the pre-imperial Christianity of the third century. Constantine was useful but he was not, after all, necessary.

The Restoration combined, therefore, the experience of the Interregnum with an antebellum legal framework. Many of the ideas associated with the Tudor and early Stuart polity also survived. Anglicans[2] insisted that their Church was perfect because it was established by divine and by human law.[3] Both they and many Dissenters believed in a national church, not in toleration, still less in the separation of church and state. And kings still used their ecclesiastical supremacy. The fundamental change after 1660 was the purposes to which supremacy was put: no longer just to uphold bishops and the Prayer Book, but to aid Catholics and Dissenters. This peculiar combination made the years 1660 to 1688 a distinct phase in England's 'long Reformation'.

Restoration monarchs swung, sometimes with alarming rapidity, between upholding the Church and undermining it. Charles II opened his reign by seeking religious reconciliation, imposed a harsh settlement in 1662, and subverted it in the late 1660s and early 1670s. From 1673, with the rise of the Anglican royalist Earl of Danby, he backed the Church, and it backed him and the presumptive succession of his Catholic brother in the

[2] This term seems acceptable for the Civil War era onwards. For comments on its use, see John Morrill, 'The Church in England, 1642–9', in Morrill, ed., *Reactions to the English Civil War, 1642–1649* (London and Basingstoke, 1982), p. 231, n. 2 (meaning those conforming to the 1559 Settlement); and John Spurr, *The Restoration Church of England, 1646–1689* (New Haven, 1991), pp. xiii–xiv (meaning a distinct outlook). I have preferred alternative epithets for the period before 1642; and it should be clear when Anglican refers to those conforming or to those with a political and religious agenda.

[3] Jacqueline Rose, 'By Law Established: The Church of England and the Royal Supremacy', in Grant Tapsell, ed., *The Later Stuart Church* (Manchester, forthcoming).

Restoration crisis of 1678–82. In the final three years of Charles's reign and the first of his brother (1682–6), Anglican royalism, absolutist and intolerant, flourished, before James abandoned it for a Catholic–Dissenting alliance. Even he briefly jettisoned this in the autumn of 1688. If this was the broad pattern, there were many short-term fluctuations. For example, in 1667 and 1668 Charles negotiated with Dissenters. In 1670 he passed the Second Conventicles Act, more vicious than any before it. During 1672 and 1673 a Declaration of Indulgence offered prerogative toleration to Dissenters and Catholics. Its withdrawal provoked the First Test Act against Catholics, to which Charles consented. In this situation, no one group could *rely* on royal support, but all could *hope* for it. This encouraged Catholics and nonconformists to be more positive about the supremacy than before, and Anglicans to variously uphold or distance themselves from it.

Charles and James were able to pursue their ecclesiastical policies with vigour in part because they retained a large prerogative over the church. If the Tudor legal inheritance and the experience of the Civil Wars helped create this, a third ingredient was the legacy of the mismatch between the ecclesiastical and political restorations. That the monarchy would be restored was clear by 1660. What was not apparent was that this restitution would be unconditional. Charles II was returned through the machinations of Presbyterian royalists who had sought to impose limitations on his father in the 1640s but who opposed the regicide and radicalisation of the Parliamentarian cause.[4] These men were puritans who wanted a national church, shorn of 'popish' remnants, but were intolerant of sects. They were not Presbyterians *stricto sensu* (the word came to denote more a political view than a model of church government), but they desired a 'moderated' or 'reduced' episcopacy which would work with other clergy for pastoral ends. While such figures could find common ground with the 'constitutional royalists' who had fought for Charles I but wanted a negotiated settlement to curb abuses of the prerogative,[5] they were anathema to Laudian churchmen and hardline royalists. These latter scorned negotiations but had divided over Civil War strategy. Royalists around Henrietta Maria had urged an alliance with Catholics in order to secure victory. Staunch churchmen urged both Stuarts, father and son, to adhere to the Church of England, and they felt secret relief when Presbyterian alliances (by Charles I in 1648 and Charles II in 1650–1) failed.

[4] George R. Abernathy, jr, 'The English Presbyterians and the Stuart Restoration, 1648–1663', *Transactions of the American Philosophical Society*, n.s. 55 (1965), number 2.

[5] On these, see David L. Smith, *Constitutional Royalism and the Search for Settlement, c. 1640–1649* (Cambridge, 1994).

It was the political Presbyterians who restored Charles, but it was a tide of relief at the return of stability which swept away any chance of imposing limitations in 1660. Charles's masterly Declaration of Breda carefully disdained revenge, offered liberty to tender consciences, and deposited the tricky question of restitution of property in parliament's lap. The temporal aspects of the Restoration continued such compromises. Those exempted from pardon were only a handful of regicides. Charles was granted £1.2m in exchange for giving up the feudal dues which his father had so unpopularly extorted, and he confirmed the legislation of 1641. There was even a Triennial Act, albeit a toothless one which Charles would ignore after 1681. His privy council contained political Presbyterians and constitutional royalists, and local government was placed in the hands of socially prominent men, whatever their Civil War allegiances. If any group was irked by the political aspects of Restoration, it was the loyal royalists who moaned that they were ignored in favour of Charles's enemies.

Wholly at odds with this political reconciliation was the church settlement of 1662. The Act of Uniformity ordered, firstly, that all clergy swear their 'unfeigned assent and consent' to a Prayer Book that had not been reformed in line with puritan concerns. The rites, gestures, ceremonies, and vestments which had annoyed puritans since the 1560s were retained: kneeling to receive Communion, signing the cross in baptism, and wearing the surplice would thus remain Restoration complaints. In addition, all clergy had to have episcopal ordination.[6] This outlawed the ministry of foreign Reformed divines in England, and it dismayed Civil War puritan appointees who had not received episcopal ordination by seemingly invalidating their ministry. Deciding between tacitly admitting such invalidity by seeking episcopal ordination (*re*ordination?) and giving up their pastoral work was not easy. The West Country Presbyterian John Humfrey wavered, complied, and recanted.[7] Throughout the Restoration, negotiations between the Church and Dissenters would try repeatedly to find a formula to solve this problem. Finally, the clergy were required to abjure the Solemn League and Covenant. Few adhered to its sentiments, but many were unwilling to repudiate an oath solemnly sworn. In

[6] This was newly inserted into the 1662 Act of Uniformity (13 & 14 Chas. II c. 4, clause 10) and newly emphasised in the Ordinal, the preface to which stated that none could be ordained 'except he be called, tryed, examined, and admitted thereunto, according to the Form hereafter following <or hath had formerly Episcopall consecration or Ordination>' (*Facsimile of the Original Manuscript of The Book of Common Prayer Signed by Convocation December 20th, 1661, and Attached to the Act of Uniformity, 1662* (1891), p. 510. The Ordinal was also rewritten to emphasise bishops as a distinct order: Spurr, *Restoration Church*, pp. 140, 145.

[7] E. C. Vernon, 'John Humfrey', *ODNB*.

August 1662 approximately 2,000 ministers were ejected for not complying with the Act of Uniformity, as compared with fourteen bishops being deprived (but the majority of lower clergy conforming) in 1559, perhaps 3,600 suffering in the Civil Wars and Interregnum, and the deprivation of six bishops and 400 nonjurors in 1689.[8] The 1662 'Bartolomeans', so called because they were deprived on St Bartholomew's Day, often conformed to Anglican worship as lay communicants, offering supplementary sermons and pastoral care outside the Church. For these practices they could be prosecuted as Dissenters, and were – much to their chagrin – legally equated with Independents, Baptists, and Quakers under the Clarendon Code of the early 1660s. Even more insultingly, those who did not attend church could be prosecuted under Elizabethan acts against recusancy.

The political and the ecclesiastical restorations thus differed significantly, and to understand why this is so it is necessary to return to the two years between 1660 and 1662. How could a king who had proclaimed (*promised*, Dissenters said) liberty to tender consciences sign into law such a severe statute? Charles had spent much of the intervening two years seeking alternatives. He promoted meetings between Anglican bishops and Presbyterian representatives (with some of the latter offered bishoprics) at Worcester House in October 1660 and at the Savoy Conference in April 1661.[9] He attempted to insert provisos in the Act of Uniformity allowing him to bypass the enforcement of Anglican rites. And he tried to delay the enforcement of the Act in the summer of 1662. Dissenters were not wrong in looking back to 1660–2 as the best missed opportunity to purify the church, nor in considering Charles their ally.

Four reasons prevented the relaxation of Uniformity before and after 1662: Anglican power, Dissenting divisions, fears of Catholicism, and constitutional concerns. Firstly, a significant proportion of the Anglican hierarchy opposed concessions. Even if a Laudian clique were not merely pretending to talk in 1660,[10] plenty of churchmen thought Dissenters were guilty of schism, were prone to sedition, and ought to be made to conform. Secondly, Dissenters could not agree on what to demand. The

[8] David Appleby, *Black Bartholomew's Day: Preaching, Polemic, and Restoration Nonconformity* (Manchester, 2007); on 1559, see Eamon Duffy, *Fires of Faith: Catholic England under Mary Tudor* (New Haven, 2009), pp. 195, 197, 199; on the Civil Wars, see Spurr, *Restoration Church*, p. 6; on 1689, see Spurr, *Restoration Church*, p. 104.

[9] Anne Whiteman, 'The Restoration of the Church of England', and Roger Thomas, 'Comprehension and Indulgence', both in Geoffrey F. Nuttall and Owen Chadwick, eds., *From Uniformity to Unity, 1662–1962* (1962).

[10] As suggested by Robert S. Bosher, *The Making of the Restoration Settlement: The Influence of the Laudians, 1649–1662* (1951). For a reply, see I. M. Green, *The Re-Establishment of the Church of England, 1660–1663* (Oxford, 1978).

more conservative amongst them, the Baxterian Presbyterians, continued earlier calls for a national but fully reformed church. If popish rites and vestments could not be banned, they might at least be made optional. If bishops were to exist, could they not ordain and exercise jurisdiction in conjunction with presbyters rather than alone? These divines wanted to broaden the church to include or 'comprehend' the Bartolomeans and their lay followers, and they might have succeeded had Richard Baxter not overplayed his hand at the Savoy Conference.[11] But in pushing for comprehension they alienated themselves from the sects whose only hope of relief was toleration outside the pale of the established church. Independents were not interested in comprehension. Nor would Catholics be – and if the king was ultimately seeking toleration for Catholics, but willing to grant it to Dissenters in return, he would not be committed to comprehension. Arguments between Presbyterians and Independents, comprehension versus toleration, derailed negotiations in the late 1660s in particular. And, over time, a younger generation of Presbyterians who were more mentally attuned to their place outside the Church began to tire of seeking comprehension. One sign of this was their increasing willingness to hold conventicles at the same time as Anglican services, rather than practising partial conformity. In Ernst Troeltsch's language, these became 'sect-type', not 'church-type', Christians.[12]

The law assumed a clear divide between conformists and Dissenters, but in practice this was far from the case. Some churchmen were rigid upholders of an unreformed establishment. Others were open to comprehension but not to toleration (a classic 'latitudinarian' position). Few bishops argued for toleration, but there were lay and clerical conformists who supported Dissenters. Hence the repeated pursuit of comprehension in the Restoration: in 1660, 1661, 1667–8, 1675, 1680, and 1689. Toleration was secondary, a poor substitute – 'the product of an unedifying mixture of ecclesiastical backtracking and political horse-trading' in 1689.[13]

[11] E. C. Ratcliff, 'The Savoy Conference and the Revision of the Book of Common Prayer', in Nuttall and Chadwick, eds., *Uniformity to Unity*, pp. 114, 125–6, but cf. pp. 127–8 on the unlikelihood of parliament passing a comprehensive settlement.

[12] Ernst Troeltsch, *The Social Teaching of the Christian Churches*, trans. Olive Wyon (2 vols., 1931), I.331–43. For the themes of this paragraph, see Thomas, 'Comprehension and Indulgence'; Mark Goldie, *Roger Morrice and the Puritan Whigs* (Woodbridge, 2007); John D. Ramsbottom, 'Presbyterians and "Partial Conformity" in the Restoration Church of England', *Journal of Ecclesiastical History*, 43 (1992), pp. 249–70; Robert Beddard, 'Vincent Alsop and the Emancipation of Restoration Dissent', *Journal of Ecclesiastical History*, 24 (1973), pp. 161–84.

[13] John Miller, 'James II and Toleration', in Eveline Cruickshanks, ed., *By Force or by Default? The Revolution of 1688–1689* (Edinburgh, 1989), p. 23. For historiography on these episodes, see Chapter 4.

Both intellectually and practically, Anglicans and Dissenters overlapped, divided only by a porous boundary.[14]

The split between Anglicans and Catholics was easier to discern, as recusants were willing to seclude themselves from the established Church. The phenomenon of church papistry has not been traced after 1660. But this does not mean that Catholics retreated into their manor houses; many vigorously participated in pamphlet debates. Nevertheless, Catholics being a minority did not preclude fear of popery infusing political life, particularly in the 1670s with the prospect of a Catholic successor, in the context of the rising power of Louis XIV.[15] Charles as well as his brother wanted toleration for Catholics. He, unlike his brother, realised after 1673 that this was impossible – perhaps, the reason why he stopped issuing declarations of indulgence. (Comprehension proposals after 1673 did not come with royal sponsorship.) The third reason for the failure to relax uniformity was fear of Catholicism: plain in response to the Declarations of 1662 and 1672. James's Declarations were also stymied because he fatally combined absolutism with Catholicism. The fourth reason for the failure of indulgences to relax uniformity was constitutionalist concern about prerogative power overriding statute.

Many of the themes outlined above have become commonly accepted features of Restoration historiography: the unimportance of toleration, the prevalence of comprehension and ideas of a national church, the fear of popery. All add up to a sense of the interplay of politics and religion which has provided the foundations of the latest generation of Restoration historiography. As the following section shows, this study accepts this foundation whilst raising awareness of the complex associations between religious and political positions after 1660. It furthermore shows the Restoration to be part of the 'long Reformation' and ecclesiastical powers to be a vital element of the political thought of early modern England.

RESTORATION RELIGION, HISTORY, AND IDEOLOGY

'That which … hath been the great Occasion of our Trouble, and is still of our Fears … is *Religion*', reflected the popular preacher Edward Stillingfleet in a sermon of 1678.[16] Over recent decades, Restoration

[14] Goldie, *Puritan Whigs*, p. 230; Mark Goldie and John Spurr, 'Politics and the Restoration Parish: Edward Fowler and the Struggle for St Giles Cripplegate', *English Historical Review*, 109 (1994), pp. 572–96, at p. 595.

[15] John Miller, *Popery and Politics in England, 1660–1688* (Cambridge, 1973).

[16] Edward Stillingfleet, *A Sermon Preached on the Fast-Day at St Margaret's Westminster, Novemb. 13 1678*, in *Ten Sermons* (1697), p. 226.

historians have increasingly concurred with Stillingfleet's diagnosis of religion as the basis for politics after, as well as before, the Civil Wars. In so doing, they have pulled the Restoration back into the milieu of Reformation and Civil War politics, loosening any sense of it as the prelude to modern party politics or, in J. H. Plumb's famous formulation, the 'growth of political stability'.[17] Three interconnected themes in recent historiography are especially pertinent for this study: the nexus of politics and religion, the use of history, and the ideological dimensions of politics. This book develops but also complicates these areas. It shows how religious needs fostered unusual political alignments, how the Restoration both reflected on and participated in Reformation politics, and how late seventeenth-century political thinking was heavily infused with ecclesiological and legal language. It also contributes to our understanding of the later Stuart Church by showing how the legacy of an ambiguous Reformation was still being fought over until the Revolution of 1688.

The significance of religion to Restoration politics is now a historiographical truism. Heralded in a volume of collected essays published in 1990, the interplay of religious and political positions has been well studied.[18] Charles II and James II no longer preside over an increasingly secularised and tolerant society purged of its pious rage by the Puritan Revolution, but govern a world in which 'popery' and 'fanaticism' were as dominant as the (twinned) fears of arbitrary government and anarchy. When political parties emerged in the late 1670s and early 1680s, they did so under religious guises: hierarchists and tantivies, fanatics and Presbyterians.[19] The two great crises of the Restoration, that of 1678–82 and that of 1688–9, were to a significant extent about fears of a Catholic ruling the English Protestant polity and of Francophile popery creeping into royal government. The greatest thinker of the age, John Locke, attacked *iure divino* clericalism as well as unconstitutional rule, while the

[17] J. H. Plumb, *The Growth of Political Stability in England, 1675–1725* (Harmondsworth, 1967). See *Albion*, 25 (1993), pp. 237–77, 565–651. Endeavours to deny this have generally failed, although for two attempts see Alan Houston and Steve Pincus, 'Introduction: Modernity and Later-Seventeenth-Century England', in Houston and Pincus, eds., *A Nation Transformed: England After the Restoration* (Cambridge, 2001); C. John Sommerville, *The Secularization of Early Modern England: From Religious Culture to Religious Faith* (Oxford, 1992).

[18] Tim Harris, Paul Seaward, and Mark Goldie, eds., *The Politics of Religion in Restoration England* (Oxford, 1990); Tim Harris, 'What's New About the Restoration?' *Albion*, 29 (1997), pp. 187–222; Grant Tapsell, '"Weepe Over the Ejected Practice of Religion": Roger Morrice and the Restoration Twilight of Puritan Politics', *Parliamentary History*, 28 (2009), pp. 266–94, at p. 286.

[19] Mark Goldie, 'Danby, the Bishops and the Whigs', in Harris, Seaward, and Goldie, eds., *Politics of Religion*, pp. 79–80; Gary De Krey, *London and the Restoration, 1659–1683* (Cambridge, 2005), ch. 6.

deposition of James II was 'an act of the Reformation'.[20] Restoration politics was less the hedonistic life of Pepys than the 'darker', altogether more serious, concern of Roger Morrice.[21]

This historiography rests on taking seriously the religious language in which politics was often conducted, and it presents a set of general politico-religious alignments. Strongest among these was the alliance of an indefeasible hereditary divine-right monarchy with the established episcopal Church of England, united in preventing any repetition of the Civil Wars. The Church supported James's succession during the Exclusion Crisis, and it constantly preached the need for loyalty and obedience to a powerful ruler. Locke accurately stated that the 'Drum Ecclesiastick' rendered Filmerian absolute monarchy 'the Currant Divinity of the Times'.[22] Anglican royalists positively revelled in their claims to be the *only* upholders of true Christian obedience, unlike Catholics and Dissenters.[23] Conversely, nonconformists joined whigs in decrying such rhetoric as erecting 'popery and arbitrary government' (both sides, revealingly, denouncing the other as 'popish'). By pursuing constitutional limits through parliament, radical insurrection outside it, or republican modes of rule (these last much emphasised by recent historians), Dissenters petitioned for a less absolute monarchy.[24] The group tellingly labelled 'puritan whigs' wanted a restored monarchy along the lines of the Newport negotiations of 1648; they sought to exclude a popish successor and they overthrew a Catholic king in 1688.[25]

Both sides of this equation, the 'Anglican royalists' and the 'puritan whigs', tended to present their alliances as a natural fact of Restoration politics. For significant parts of the period they were, particularly between 1678 and 1685 and to an extent between 1660 and 1662. These tropes,

[20] Mark Goldie, 'John Locke and Anglican Royalism', *Political Studies*, 31 (1983), pp. 61–85; Mark Goldie, 'The Political Thought of the Anglican Revolution', in Robert Beddard, ed., *The Revolutions of 1688* (Oxford, 1991), p. 111.

[21] Mark Goldie, 'A Darker Shade of Pepys: The *Entring Book* of Roger Morrice' (Friends of Doctor Williams's Library, 61st Annual Lecture, read 25 Oct. 2007, publ. 2009); Goldie, *Puritan Whigs*; Tapsell, 'Roger Morrice'.

[22] John Locke, *Two Treatises of Government*, ed. Peter Laslett (Cambridge, 1988), preface, p. 138; Goldie, 'Anglican Royalism'.

[23] Jacqueline Rose, 'Robert Brady's Intellectual History and Royalist Antipopery in Restoration England', *English Historical Review*, 122 (2007), pp. 1287–1317.

[24] For a republican emphasis, see Jonathan Scott, *Algernon Sidney and the Restoration Crisis, 1677–1683* (Cambridge, 1991). For a reply, see De Krey, *London and the Restoration*.

[25] Goldie, *Puritan Whigs*; Douglas R. Lacey, *Dissent and Parliamentary Politics in England, 1661–1689* (New Brunswick, NJ, 1969). The Treaty of Newport, based on the Newcastle Propositions of 1646, would have restrained royal authority over the militia and over appointments to state offices, and introduced Presbyterianism or modified episcopacy for three years.

begun by Restoration actors, have become embedded in modern accounts, perhaps because historians of 'the Restoration' have tended to focus on the process of restoration (1660–2) and on crises (1678–82, 1688–9), and because recent historiography has quarried print culture, more to uncover images and stereotypes that political groups constructed than to elucidate their organisation or even ideologies.[26] Studying image-creation is helpful, for cultural historians have rightly shown how representation not only reflects mentalities but also affects behaviour. But this study questions whether such alliances were always so strong: were Anglicans necessarily absolutist? Were Dissenters invariably whiggish about the prerogative? Anglican royalism and puritan whiggery often accurately capture political positions, especially regarding the king's *temporal* prerogative. But the royal *ecclesiastical* supremacy, as used by Restoration monarchs, muddled such tidy taxonomies. Anglicans were not 'royalist' in the sense of supporting the king's wishes when the will of the king was to tolerate Catholics and Dissenters.[27] And Dissenters were sometimes quick to seize on indulgence granted by the royal prerogative rather than tarry for parliamentary statute. Shaftesburian whigs, too, exalted royal authority in order to crush clerical aggrandisement.[28]

As Mark Goldie and Gary De Krey have shown, whigs' anticlerical motivations could override their desire for constitutional niceties.[29] This book reflects on the implications of this for both Dissenters and Anglicans. Clerical independence of the supreme governor and Dissenting support for prerogative overriding statute were especially manifest between 1667 and 1673 and during 1686–8. They were hard to maintain because, as stated above, kings rarely adhered to their promises of indulgence, and so such associations rapidly alternated with 'natural' Restoration alignments. Seeking justification for their accounts of why kings either must support the episcopal Church or had the power to depart from it, all groups naturally turned to Reformation history for precedents for their actions.

Restoration writers felt a pressing need to understand the Reformation. A tory lawyer advising Archbishop Sancroft reflected that 'a clear, &

[26] Representative of this work and its achievements is Mark Knights, *Representation and Misrepresentation in Later Stuart Britain* (Oxford, 2005).

[27] The meaning of royalist in the Restoration and even in the Civil Wars was fluid. One genre of royalism included allegiance to the Church, another favoured constitutional monarchy, a third might constitute obedience to royal wishes.

[28] Goldie, 'Danby'; Mark Goldie, 'Priestcraft and the Birth of Whiggism', in Phillipson and Skinner, eds., *Political Discourse*.

[29] Goldie, 'Priestcraft', esp. p. 214; Gary S. De Krey, 'Reformation in the Restoration Crisis, 1679–1682', in Donna B. Hamilton and Richard Strier, eds., *Religion, Literature, and Politics in Post-Reformation England, 1540–1688* (Cambridge, 1996), p. 241.

full Collection of Ecc*lesiastica*ll Transactions since *the* Reform*ati*on (if it could be had) were of great use', whilst Stillingfleet longed to 'clear the most important *Difficulties* of *Ecclesiastical History*', despite thinking 'a *General Church-History* too heavy a Burthen to be undergone by any Man'.[30] Such accounts would be acceptable only if they were polemically useful. While late seventeenth-century historians strove for an aura of credibility, increasingly including transcripts of documents in their published works, and would be criticised for factual errors, they also worked within a partisan context. Mistakes were dangerous because they empowered one's opponents, not simply because they misled readers as to *wie es eigentlich gewesen ist*.[31] Defending the Reformation against Catholic challenge was a *sine qua non*, but how to present sixteenth-century religious change divided English Protestants. Asserting the legality of reform because of parliamentary consent was a matter of pride to the whig cleric Gilbert Burnet and of shame to Laud's *quondam* chaplain Peter Heylin.[32] Restoration historians did believe that a correct account of Reformation and royal supremacy could and should be established. But this would prove impossible because, as Chapter 1 shows, the events of the sixteenth century were susceptible to a variety of interpretations.

The Reformation provided Restoration groups with various models for conduct and argument. Thus puritan divines could see Marian martyr-bishops as a model for a reforming episcopate, while conformists were advantaged by the lack of a strong puritan refutation of Richard Hooker's *Laws of Ecclesiastical Polity* of the 1590s. The Reformation also offered important precedents, intellectual and legal. A basic working knowledge of Reformation statutes was needed for bishops to avoid *praemunire* and helped nonconformists evade prosecution.[33] This study will show repeatedly how Tudor and early Stuart repeal and counter-repeal of laws, and their interpretation in the courts, could help both sides of a case. Awareness of royal injunctions and proclamations, correspondence between English and European reformers, and parliamentary bills would provide support for those who wished to argue that Elizabeth I or James

[30] [Roger North], 'A*nim*adu*er*sions upon *th*e Vindic*aci*on of *th*e Eccl*esiast*icall Com*mission*', Bodl.,Tanner MS 460, fo. 32v; Edward Stillingfleet, *Origines Britannicae* (1685), p. lxxii.

[31] See, for example, Chapter 5, pp. 221–8.

[32] See J. A. I. Champion, *The Pillars of Priestcraft Shaken: The Church of England and its Enemies, 1660–1730* (Cambridge, 1992); Andrew Starkie, 'Gilbert Burnet's *Reformation* and the Semantics of Popery', in Jason McElligott, ed., *Fear, Exclusion, and Revolution: Roger Morrice and Britain in the 1680s* (Aldershot, 2006).

[33] *Praemunire*: the crime of clerical subversion of royal power. Initially propounded in fourteenth-century statures against the papacy, it was employed against Rome in the 1530s, and thereafter it might be wielded against English bishops seen to limit the supremacy.

I, or Jewel or Cranmer, were really on 'their' side. Prior polemical literature was also useful because the fundamentals of the disagreements between Anglicans and Catholics, conformists and nonconformists, had hardly changed.

Restoration authors wrote histories of the Reformation, but that did not preclude them from a feeling of participation in it. In ecclesiological politics, the Restoration was part of Nicholas Tyacke's 'long Reformation', not the 'long eighteenth century'.[34] Dissenters might see, in comprehension proposals, a chance finally to complete the reformation of the national church and fulfil the desires of their Elizabethan ancestors. Anglicans did not think that the Civil Wars had ended the era of uniformity, and they sought to purify the church of secular interference in Laudian vein. Nothing symbolises better the Reformation mindset of 1680s Englishmen than the *re*publication (organised by Dissenters) of John Foxe's *Acts and Monuments*, perhaps as a warning against a popish successor, and the *re*translation (by an Anglican royalist) of John Jewel's *Apology for the Church of England* when such a king came to the throne.[35] The royal supremacy was still governed by Elizabethan, Edwardian, and Henrician laws, and continuing developments of and within this sixteenth-century framework made the politics of Restoration supremacy a distinct phase in England's long Reformation, not a 'post-Reformation'.[36]

This book is an important reminder of the world we may lose if we subject the history of early modern political thought to modern secular analysis. If Pocock is right that 'English political debate is recurrently subordinate to English political theology', then defining the sphere of 'political thought' by its modern, secular, scope is problematic.[37] Interest

[34] Nicholas Tyacke, ed., *England's Long Reformation, 1500–1800* (1998).

[35] John Jewel, *The Apology of the Church of England*, trans. Edmund Bohun (1685); for Foxe, see Goldie, *Puritan Whigs*, p. 50.

[36] Cf. John Spurr, *The Post-Reformation: Religion, Politics and Society in Britain, 1603–1714* (Harlow, 2006); John Spurr, 'The English "Post-Reformation"?', *Journal of Modern History*, 74 (2002), pp. 101–19.

[37] Pocock, 'Discourse of Sovereignty', p. 381; Mark Goldie, 'The Civil Religion of James Harrington', in Anthony Pagden, ed., *The Languages of Political Theory in Early-Modern Europe* (Cambridge, 1987), esp. pp. 198–9; Alister Chapman, John Coffey, and Brad Gregory, eds., *Seeing Things Their Way: Intellectual History and the Return of Religion* (Notre Dame, 2009), arising from the conference 'Seeing Things Their Way: Studying the History of Religious Ideas' (Selwyn College, Cambridge, 1–3 July 2004). The lack of space dedicated to the theory of Tudor *imperium* in the standard volumes on early modern political thought is striking, although see Quentin Skinner, *The Foundations of Modern Political Thought* (2 vols., Cambridge, 1978), II.86–9 (a rare engagement with Elton); Francis Oakley, 'Christian Obedience and Authority, 1520–1550', in J. H. Burns and Mark Goldie, eds., *The Cambridge History of Political Thought, 1450–1700* (Cambridge, 1991), pp. 176–82; J. H. M. Salmon, 'Catholic Resistance Theory, Ultramontanism, and the Royalist Response, 1580–1620', in Burns and Goldie, eds., *Cambridge History of Political Thought*, pp. 244–53.

in theorists of resistance often focuses on their ideas of social contract and rights, rarely evoking their language – so ubiquitous in studies of their medieval forebears – of *regnum* and *sacerdotium*. Yet the images of the Keys and the swords survived alongside those of godly Israelite iconoclasm and the *ius zelotarum* of tyrannicide. As this study embeds the Restoration in the Reformation, it considers questions about the relationship between church and polity with which Tudor (or even medieval) historians are more familiar than with Stuart ones: the politics of godly rule, *regnum* and *sacerdotium*, *praemunire*, and counsel. 'A mind attuned to the struggle against *imperium in imperio* did not suspend this mode of explanation with the Henrician Reformation', Goldie comments.[38] In fact, the legacy of the 1530s intensified such discourse.

Since supremacy was a simultaneously political, jurisdictional, and theological construct, a study of it necessitates moves between sources, contexts, and historiographical debates in religious, political, and intellectual history. Religious and political as well as linguistic contexts are necessary to explain why different ideas about supremacy sometimes coexisted and sometimes clashed. It was royal policies which, for example, forced *iure divino* episcopacy and supremacy into open conflict at points during the Restoration, and which encouraged Dissenters to praise the ecclesiastical prerogative. Yet ideas of supremacy were not merely epiphenomenal froth on the surface of 'practical' politics, nor masks for writers' 'real' motivations. Instead, those ideas themselves had motive force in constraining and enabling certain policies. Elizabeth I authorised her Ecclesiastical Commission to punish nonconformists, but discussion about its basis in statute law or prerogative would constrain James II's attempt to resurrect an equivalent. Thus ideas and policies existed in a symbiotic relationship, both influencing behaviour. This study therefore agrees with Quentin Skinner that ideologies make an impact on politics.[39] But it suggests that Skinner's emphasis on the primacy of linguistic context, and the distinction between 'convention' and linguistic innovation, need adjustment.[40] Here, for example, the claim that supremacy was monarchical and jurisdictional, upholding the Church of England and its bishops, came close to being the 'official' 'convention'. Those who dissented from it might be the heterodox Hobbes or religious nonconformists, but they were also bishops, Cavalier Anglican MPs, and even monarchs themselves. If

[38] Goldie, 'Priestcraft', p. 214.

[39] Quentin Skinner, 'The Principles and Practice of Opposition: The Case of Bolingbroke versus Walpole', in Neil McKendrick, ed., *Historical Perspectives* (1974), esp. pp. 127–8.

[40] Quentin Skinner, *Visions of Politics*, vol. 1, *Regarding Method* (Cambridge, 2002).

threatened by nonconformists or Catholics, the Church clung to its royal nursing parents. If endangered by royal policies, it defiantly asserted its own independence. The latter situation, so frequently the case during the Restoration, made Anglican royalist theories as diverse and even potentially subversive as those of puritan whigs. Anglican 'royalists' tried to tweak the supremacy to their own purposes, while puritan 'whigs' were able to cite it and undermine the religious 'establishment' while ostensibly upholding its political counterpart. All these divergences took place within the framework of Tudor supremacy. Thus it was the ambiguities of the conventional discourse which permitted disagreement, arguments between individual members of the political and religious elites opening intellectual spaces for more radical thinkers.[41] Supremacy could provide Restoration nonconformists (for example) with that rarest of early modern languages, a rhetoric of loyal opposition,[42] since Tudor precedents could be cited for many differing purposes. Intellectual proximity as well as linguistic revolution could endanger conventions.

Anglican political thought has perhaps been relatively neglected because it appears nothing more than an 'Erastian' surrender to lay state control. The political theory of passive obedience has been reduced to passivity. In fact, withdrawing cooperation (active assistance) was extremely effective in a pre-modern state, as 1688 proved. More importantly, Anglicans were dedicated to distinguishing absolute from arbitrary government. This book shows how the idea of *imperium* did not constitute a supine submission to royal whim. Rather, modelling their conduct on prophets rebuking kings and Bishop Ambrose reproving the emperor Theodosius, Anglicans aggressively counselled their supreme governors in order to determine the direction of religious policy.[43] Although hedged by the legal framework of lay patronage, and reliant on the secular arm to effectively enforce uniformity legislation, Restoration churchmen often conceived of their church as having fundamental rights which kings should never violate. Bishop Carleton of Bristol, for example, ignored royal licences allowing Dissenters to worship and prosecuted them anyway.[44]

[41] As Noel Malcolm comments: '*Leviathan*, the Pentateuch, and the Origins of Modern Biblical Criticism', in Tom Sorell and Luc Foisneau, eds., *Leviathan after 350 Years* (Oxford, 2004), pp. 247–8.

[42] This parallels Bolingbroke's strategy of turning whig ideas against themselves: see Skinner, 'Bolingbroke versus Walpole', p. 126.

[43] Jacqueline Rose, 'Kingship and Counsel in Early Modern England', *Historical Journal*, 54 (2011), pp. 47–71; Patrick Collinson, 'If Constantine, then also Theodosius: St Ambrose and the Integrity of the Elizabethan *Ecclesia Anglicana*', *Journal of Ecclesiastical History*, 30 (1979), pp. 205–29.

[44] Victor D. Sutch, *Gilbert Sheldon: Architect of Anglican Survival, 1640–1675* (The Hague, 1973), p. 120.

But Anglicans did not think with a single homogeneous mind, a fact which has led to differing perceptions of the Restoration Church. For John Spurr, it was fundamentally dependent on lay support, whereas for Mark Goldie and Jeffrey Collins it was vigorous and persecutory.[45] This division rests partly on whether one considers the Church's adamantine rhetoric or the practicalities of enforcement. But even if persecution was patchy, its unpredictability was no warrant for Dissenters' security. Furthermore, even if the process of restoring a narrow and intolerant church in 1662 derived less from Laudian machinations than a popular desire for security and the old order, the Restoration establishment contained distinctly 'Laudian' elements. Its clergy shared a largely Arminian theology and parishes put into practice 'Laudian' modes of worship such as railed altars.[46]

As the leading historian of the Restoration Church, John Spurr, has argued, Restoration Anglican ecclesiology was rooted in the experiences of the Interregnum. Defending themselves against Catholic attacks at a time when they were unable to call royal authority to their aid, divines such as Henry Hammond and John Bramhall argued that their Church maintained Catholic unity and episcopal independence against papal usurpations – more catholic than Rome. Hammond in particular emphasised the mutual correspondence between equal bishops, an ecclesiology drawn from the third-century African bishop Cyprian.[47] After 1660, Spurr rightly notes, this shift continued, tilting the Church of England away from its Reformed towards its catholic pole. Spurr depicts this change as reconciling the early Stuart division between catholic and Reformed elements, creating a distinctly Anglican phase which was only shattered in 1689 by the nonjuring schism.[48] Whilst Spurr does note the variety of positions

[45] Spurr, *Restoration Church*, pp. 55–6, 188–9; John Spurr, *England in the 1670s* (Oxford, 2000), pp. 231, 234–5; Claire Cross, *Church and People: England, 1450–1660*, 2nd edn (Oxford, 1999), ch. 10; Mark Goldie, 'The Theory of Religious Intolerance in Restoration England', in Ole Peter Grell, Jonathan I. Israel, and Nicholas Tyacke, eds., *From Persecution to Toleration: The Glorious Revolution and Religion in England* (Oxford, 1991); Mark Goldie, 'The Hilton Gang and the Purge of London in the 1680s', in Howard Nenner, ed., *Politics and the Political Imagination in Later Stuart Britain* (Rochester, NY, 1997); Jeffrey R. Collins, 'The Restoration Bishops and the Royal Supremacy', *Church History*, 68 (1999), pp. 549–80.

[46] On theology, see Nicholas Tyacke, 'Arminianism and the Theology of the Restoration Church', in Simon Groenveld and Michael Wintle, eds., *The Exchange of Ideas* (Zutphen, 1994); on altars, see Kenneth Fincham, '"According to Ancient Custom": The Return of Altars in the Restoration Church of England', *Transactions of the Royal Historical Society*, 6th ser., 13 (2003), pp. 29–54.

[47] Spurr, *Restoration Church*, ch. 1 and pp. 116–19; John Spurr, 'Schism and the Restoration Church', *Journal of Ecclesiastical History*, 41 (1990), pp. 408–24, at pp. 413–14.

[48] Spurr, *Restoration Church*, pp. 112–13 (the early Stuart division), xiii (Anglican), xiv, 376, 379, 391 (nonjurors). For the two poles, see Anthony Milton, *Catholic and Reformed: The Roman and Protestant Churches in English Protestant Thought, 1600–1640* (Cambridge, 1995).

amongst churchmen, he overemphasises the consensus which he sees as being maintained despite this diversity. 'The history of the Restoration Church of England is essentially a tale of clerical coherence and unity.'[49] For Spurr, claims about episcopacy were 'ill-defined', pragmatic, and evasive; few churchmen were willing to realise the consequences of *iure divino* arguments for the supremacy, and those who did were suppressed.[50] But as Spurr occasionally hints, churchmen quarrelled over how to deal with Dissent, arguments which he sees occurring between the Popish Plot and Tory Reaction in particular.[51] Thus, although it is true that there was no schism before 1689, there were divisions. The ideas that the nonjurors made *explicit* after the Revolution were being *thought* (and preached and published) beforehand.

Most significantly for this study, there was greater tension between the supremacy and episcopacy than allowed for by Spurr, who denies that the Church challenged the supremacy before 1689.[52] Bishops could see themselves as agents of a godly monarch, but they also challenged the ecclesiastical prerogative when it was employed to dispense with uniformity – for they saw the king and his supremacy as the agent of their godly ideals.[53] This is not to argue that there was an inevitable clash between *iure divino* episcopacy and supremacy, but that tension could become conflict in particular circumstances, for example when comprehension and indulgence were mooted: 1662–3, 1667–8, 1672–3, and 1686–8. Jeffrey Collins therefore correctly describes the 1660s as witnessing 'a degree of hostility between the royal court and the English episcopate unprecedented since the Reformation'.[54] This did not mean that the Restoration Church wished to jettison the supremacy; used 'rightly', it was a defensible and powerful weapon against Dissent. But Spurr's account of an ideal of an 'autonomous national church'[55] obscures the extent to which a particular church was now depicted as constituted by its bishops and metropolitan rather than by the borders of monarchical sovereignty. More accurately,

49 Spurr, *Restoration Church*, pp. xvi, 104 (qu.), 106–7; compare Starkie, 'Burnet's *Reformation*', pp. 140–1.

50 Spurr, *Restoration Church*, pp. 149, 160, 146, 391.

51 Spurr, *Restoration Church*, pp. 82–3; John Spurr, '"Latitudinarianism" and the Restoration Church', *Historical Journal*, 31 (1988), pp. 61–82, at p. 67; Goldie and Spurr, 'Politics and the Restoration Parish', p. 576.

52 Spurr, *Restoration Church*, pp. 132, 164, 106–7.

53 As Goldie, 'Danby', p. 77.

54 Collins, 'Restoration Bishops', p. 549.

55 John Spurr, '"A Special Kindness for Dead Bishops": The Church, History, and Testimony in Seventeenth-Century Protestantism', *Huntington Library Quarterly*, 68 (2005), pp. 313–34, at p. 324. Spurr, 'Schism', p. 415, hints at more of a change, but still tends to conflate national and episcopal.

Spurr speaks of how the 'ideal of a national church constituted by a godly prince was wearing dangerously thin' by the late seventeenth century.[56]

If in practice lay assistance, whether of the monarch or the local magistrate, was needed to enforce uniformity, some churchmen were nevertheless willing to defend prosecution of nonconformity in forthright terms, Augustinian as well as Erastian.[57] They defended the principle of uniformity not just because English law demanded it, but also because divine law damned schism. But Restoration Anglicans' desire to uphold uniformity affected their energetic political thought. This was an unreconciled mixture of obedience to God's deputies on earth (Romans 13) and the need to obey God rather than man (Acts 5:29). How to combine the two was a classic Reformation problematic. When kings acted as God's lieutenants for Anglican uniformity, supremacy and episcopacy provided a powerful partnership. But Restoration monarchs apostatised as often as they conformed to their role in Anglican utopias, and the resulting questions forced all groups to re-examine their ecclesiologies. The consequent instability was intensified by the mental and legal framework which the Reformation had bequeathed to the Restoration.

THE ROYAL SUPREMACIES

Thus far this study has spoken of 'the' royal supremacy, but pluralising the term may be more appropriate, for almost every aspect of royal ecclesiastical prerogative was contested. No homogeneous entity, royal supremacy was conceived in many different models, which might be more or less monarchical, and more or less absolute. To apply David Armitage's analysis of empire (drawn from Ronald Dworkin's of rights), the 'concept' of royal supremacy existed in a variety of 'conceptions'.[58] As Tudor and early Stuart historians have shown, royal supremacy was the object of debate and, because of its fluidity and ambiguity, an arena for argument. This book applies that view of supremacy to the Restoration era.

Such ambiguity was present from the inception of supremacy in the 1530s. Henry VIII held ecclesiastical authority which descended from God, as English kings (it was said) had done from time immemorial, but those powers were declared and codified in statutes which could not be changed except by further parliamentary legislation. Matters were further complicated when Henry delegated what he saw as a personal

[56] Spurr, *Restoration Church*, p. 399.
[57] Goldie, 'Theory of Intolerance'; Spurr, 'Schism'.
[58] David Armitage, *The Ideological Origins of the British Empire* (Cambridge, 2000), pp. 7–8.

supremacy to a lay vicegerent, Thomas Cromwell. The monarch was normally treated as supreme in jurisdictional governance, not doctrine, but this was denounced by Catholics and Calvinists as entrenching on the spiritual sphere of priestly action. Could the *potestas jurisdictionis* melt into the *potestas ordinis*? If supremacy only regulated ecclesiastical jurisdiction and simply *enforced* the doing of clerical duties, was it limited? Supremacy looked rather less absolute when it became a tool to enforce the true religion as declared by clergy; problematic since, from the 1520s onwards, what 'true religion' meant was contested. And Henry used his supremacy to create an idiosyncratic mixture of evangelical and traditional ideas, supported (and opposed) by men from all parts of the theological spectrum. Henry's Tudor and Stuart successors would prove that supremacy could be wielded on behalf of almost any religious position. The location, powers, and purposes of royal supremacy were all subject to what might be positively deemed creative tension or negatively derided as incoherent fudge.

Tudor historians are well attuned to the ambiguities of supremacy, whether as debated by elites or, in Ethan Shagan's terms, 'negotiated' by the populace.[59] As Shagan and Karl Gunther put it, supremacy was contested by 'the king himself, court humanists, Oxbridge dons, amateur theologians, parish priests, and precocious peasants … support for the royal supremacy became … not an ideology in itself but a site where ideological differences of many sorts were canvassed'.[60] John Guy has richly demonstrated the bifurcation of Henrician supremacy into the 'thesis' of imperial monarchy and 'counter thesis' of crown-in-parliament. These two interpretations, Guy posits, were represented in the 1530s by Henry VIII and the lawyer Christopher St German respectively, and continued to clash for decades afterwards.[61] Whilst these two views were perhaps the most important division in how the supremacy was conceived, other interpretations of its nature and extent were also rooted in Henrician ambiguity.

Claire Cross, Conrad Russell, and William Lamont have extended accounts of royal supremacy and its ambiguities into the late sixteenth and early seventeenth centuries. Cross's book, which remains the leading work on the Elizabethan supremacy, outlined how supremacy was

[59] Ethan H. Shagan, *Popular Politics and the English Reformation* (Cambridge, 2003).

[60] Karl Gunther and Ethan H. Shagan, 'Protestant Radicalism and Political Thought in the Reign of Henry VIII', *Past and Present*, 194 (2007), pp. 35–74, at p. 35.

[61] John Guy, 'Thomas Cromwell and the Intellectual Origins of the Henrician Revolution', and 'Tudor Monarchy and its Critiques', in Guy, ed., *The Tudor Monarchy* (1997); John Guy, 'The "Imperial Crown" and the Liberty of the Subject: The English Constitution from Magna Carta to the Bill of Rights', in Bonnelyn Young Kunze and Dwight D. Brautigam, eds., *Court, Country and Culture* (Rochester, NY, 1992).

established in parliament, theorised by clergy, and implemented in the localities.[62] Cross importantly noted that supremacy was not merely upheld by the Church and denied by its opponents; rather, Presbyterians favoured a national church enforced by a godly magistrate, while bishops such as Edmund Grindal circumscribed Elizabeth's authority.[63] However, Cross left unclear the exact location of supremacy, tending to conflate monarchical, parliamentary, lay, and 'Erastian' as labels for it. Her remark that 'Elizabethan laymen implicitly believed that the royal supremacy meant the government of the church by the crown and parliament' left confused the two theses which Guy identified for the 1530s, and she did not explore, although she identified, the tension between Hooker's account of supremacy which gave parliament a role and Elizabeth's more imperial view of her prerogative.[64] Even if Elizabethans did not notice the potential tension between these types of supremacy, it is important for historians to recognise, in order to ask why sometimes they coexisted and sometimes clashed. The present study sharpens Cross's distinctions, albeit recognising that this is partly because their conflict had become more apparent by the later-seventeenth century.

Cross rightly noted a change in tone in the Elizabethan church-state in the queen's 'second reign'. The growing rhetoric of *iure divino* episcopacy had, she discerned, the potential to 'emancipate the clergy from the Erastian interpretation of the royal supremacy'.[65] The realisation of that potential was explored in William Lamont's *Godly Rule*, published in the same year as Cross's book. Lamont emphasised the centrality of millenarianism in the early seventeenth century, showing how it encouraged many alternative models of godly rule (which could be translated into accounts of supremacy): monarchical, episcopal, parliamentary, and popular.[66] Lamont especially emphasised the conflict between *iure divino* episcopacy and imperial monarchy, their logical incompatibility providing a fund of puritan argument.[67] His vision of millenarianism as a blank

62 Claire Cross, *The Royal Supremacy in the Elizabethan Church* (1969).

63 Cross, *Royal Supremacy*, pp. 47–67.

64 Cross, *Royal Supremacy*, pp. 68 (perhaps meaning crown-*in*-parliament) and pp. 34–6. Her main division was into 'theoretical' and 'practical' workings of supremacy.

65 Cross, *Royal Supremacy*, pp. 90, 67 (qu., using Erastian to mean a jurisdictional supremacy); for a 'second reign', see John Guy, ed., *The Reign of Elizabeth I: Court and Culture in the Last Decade* (Cambridge, 1995).

66 William Lamont, *Godly Rule: Politics and Religion, 1603–60* (1969) – not always explicitly speaking of supremacy, but employing ideas which clearly map onto it.

67 Lamont, *Godly Rule*. This does not mean that they *actually* clashed: Johann P. Sommerville, 'The Royal Supremacy and Episcopacy "Jure Divino", 1603–1640', *Journal of Ecclesiastical History*, 34 (1983), pp. 548–58, posits greater coexistence.

sheet on which conservative or 'radical magisterial' thought could be inscribed recalls Shagan and Gunther's view of supremacy.[68] But, in addition to overstating the role of millenarianism, Lamont wrongly implied a progression between models of godly rule: a godly monarch under James I, godly bishops under Charles I, a godly parliament in the 1640s. But these versions could be proposed simultaneously, disappearing and reviving in different debates over time. Furthermore, Lamont wrongly deemed such language to have ceased under Cromwell, and did not continue his account into the Restoration – a decision which his later book on Richard Baxter retracted.[69]

Where Lamont spoke of bishops and puritans, Conrad Russell considered early Stuart kings and parliaments through the lens of parliamentary bills and common law, a mode more akin to Guy's. Russell, too, saw an increase in tension from late Elizabethan times, and also sourced this to the ambiguities of Henry's Reformation. Early Stuart ecclesiology had to contend with two versions of supremacy: that of the Act of Appeals (1533), which depicted a dualist model of separate spiritual and temporal jurisdictions; and that of the Act of Submission of the Clergy (1534), which subordinated convocations and canons to the crown, and perhaps to parliament and common law.[70] Until it was clear whose authority supremacy rested on, what powers it entailed could not be decided.[71] Yet Russell sees this as solved when parliament voted down the canons of 1640, for this enabled

> the triumph of one version of the Royal Supremacy over another ... of Christopher St German over Bishop Stephen Gardiner, of Sir Francis Knollys over Queen Elizabeth I, of Chief Justice Coke over Lord Chancellor Ellesmere, and of John Pym over Archbishop Laud.[72]

This study brings together the debates between crown, convocation, and parliament noted by Guy and Russell, and those of church, crown, and nonconformity highlighted by Cross and Lamont. It analyses their continued existence, and the perpetuation of tension between them, for the

[68] Gunther and Shagan, 'Protestant Radicalism', p. 72; Lamont, *Godly Rule*, pp. 23, 25, 31.

[69] Lamont, *Godly Rule*, pp. 20, 26, 70, 126, ch. 6; cf. William Lamont, *Richard Baxter and the Millennium: Protestant Imperialism and the English Revolution* (1979).

[70] Conrad Russell, 'Parliament, the Royal Supremacy, and the Church', in J. P. Parry and Stephen Taylor, eds., *Parliament and the Church, 1529–1960* (Edinburgh, 2000) (*Parliamentary History*, 19), pp. 28–9; Conrad Russell, 'Whose Supremacy? King, Parliament and the Church, 1530–1640', *Ecclesiastical Law Journal*, 4 (1996–7), pp. 700–8.

[71] Russell, 'Whose Supremacy?', p. 701.

[72] Russell, 'Whose Supremacy?', pp. 707, 700 (describing his own ability, though an atheist, to vote in parliament on the church).

period after 1660. Two other models were also added in the Restoration: a radically sacerdotal version of supremacy, and Catholic exploitation of its powers. As Guy has suggested, but not fully detailed, it was only after 1689 that imperial supremacy was 'emasculated'.[73] Between 1660 and 1688 whether supremacy was royal or parliamentary, whether jurisdictional or spiritual, whether indelibly tied to the Church of England or manipulable by other religious groups, remained open questions.

The amount of discussion of the supremacy after 1660 is obscured by the need to approach it obliquely. Few works on ecclesiology announce themselves as being about the supremacy. William Falkner's *Christian Loyalty: Or, A Discourse wherein is Asserted that just Royal Authority and Eminency, which in this Church and Realm of England is Yielded to the King, especially Concerning Supremacy in Causes Ecclesiastical* is a rare exception.[74] Instead, historians must sidle up to views of royal ecclesiastical prerogative as it was invoked in debates over comprehension and toleration, *iure divino* episcopacy, and popery. These discussions took place in parliament and the pulpit as well as the press, and this study consequently draws on scribal treatises and sermons, parliamentary speeches and legal discourse, as well as (predominantly) printed tracts. These all contributed to perennial Restoration questions about supremacy, negotiating the Tudor inheritance in a world where Dissent was growing and kings were disinclined to unquestioningly uphold uniformity, and in which Anglicans might therefore constrain the prerogative.

Chapter 1 of this study outlines the contours of supremacy from 1530 to 1660, demonstrating how it was claimed by a variety of groups, each of which had a slightly different view of what it meant. Chapters 2 to 5 consider how a specific group responded to supremacy during the Restoration, often linked to a question about a particular aspect of the supremacy, such as royal rights over convocation, or bishops, or the nature of the national church of which the king was supreme governor. Chapter 2 describes how MPs and lawyers could (but did not always) restrain the prerogative by statute and common law, especially regarding convocation, church law, and the dispensing power. Chapter 3 explores how far churchmen submitted to the supremacy, and whether this correlated to thinking episcopacy *iure humano* or *iure divino*. Anglican divines restrained supremacy when they saw kings dispensing with uniformity; conversely, such policies encouraged Dissenters to praise the prerogative,

[73] Guy, 'Imperial Crown', p. 86.

[74] Conversely, works indexed under 'the royal supremacy' may discuss only royal temporal prerogative.

as Chapter 4 demonstrates. Dissenting imperialism or supremacism exploited the jurisdictional possibilities of royal suppression of bishops by insisting that prelates subverted supremacy. Such rhetoric was shared with the writers discussed in Chapter 5, who, however, went further in making the supremacy a sacerdotal power – causing Anglicans to return to Reformation history to deny such a supremacy was intended. Finally, Chapter 6 considers the actions of and reactions to a Catholic supreme governor. James II's reign brought together many questions about supremacy as the king dispensed with statutes, attacked the Church more openly than Charles II had done, and provoked an episcopal counterblast which aimed to defend the Church without overthrowing the crown. Under James, tensions between crown, parliament, and the Church over supremacy turned into open conflict to such an extent that they significantly contributed to revolution.

In the aftermath of 1688, questions of supremacy echoed on in the non-juring schism, the Convocation controversy, the bishoprics crisis of 1707, and in the works of Benjamin Hoadley in the 1710s and Edmund Gibson in the 1730s. In 1850 the 'Gorham Judgment', wherein a bishop's decision about the doctrinal unsuitability of a candidate for a benefice was overruled by the privy council, intensified debate over the relationship of a national episcopal church with the state. But after 1689 the provision of a Protestant king, the allowance of nonconformist worship, and a less aggressive use of the royal prerogative marked a change from the Restoration. Constitutional monarchy was not, of course, simply imported with William of Orange and imperial kingship expelled with James II, but ecclesiastical *imperium* had changed. The years between 1660 and 1688 had not, however, witnessed the dying breaths of an outdated prerogative, but one of the most contested and creative phases of exploration of a multivalent supremacy. Within a framework of Reformation prerogatives, there were distinct Restoration questions, the most fundamental shift being the attitudes of monarchs to the established Church. The willingness of Charles II and James II to use their dispensing power converted latent tensions between different (and long-established) notions of the supremacy into open conflict. Such actions created the issues explored in each chapter of this study, which tells the story of how the Restoration reflected on, reinvented, and eventually revolutionised the royal supremacies of Reformation kingship.

CHAPTER I

Foundations and legacies: the Reformation and the royal supremacies, 1530–1660

In the records of parliament, the revolutionary is intermingled with the mundane. In 1533, parliament found time, between making a statute to pave the streets of London and passing an act to prevent 'excess in apparel', to redefine the relationship between the king and the church in England. The Act in Restraint of Appeals was not the first assertion of royal independence from clerical jurisdiction, for such claims had been made by medieval kings against popes. But 1533 marked something qualitatively new. It began a process of reconstituting the English church and crown which would fuel debate for the next 150 years.

This chapter surveys the institutional framework and arguments for the supremacy from 1530 to 1660, paying particular attention to statutes, texts, themes, and ambivalences which would become significant in the Restoration. The following is, therefore, not a full account of Tudor and early Stuart supremacy, for that would be a book in itself, and it may even distort the relative significance of certain events and writers because of its ultimate focus on Restoration uses of this tradition. Thus the 1559 Injunctions will be found to be as important as the Acts of Supremacy and the Edwardian Act for the Election of Bishops will be shown to have had a vibrant Restoration afterlife. The origins both of legal discourse about crown, parliament, and canon law and those of the idea of *iure divino* episcopacy will be outlined, to show how ideas which would later cause conflict over supremacy were not created with the intent of challenging royal power. Most important of all, there was no one Reformation interpretation of supremacy which could validate or invalidate a single Restoration view of it. If the dominant rhetoric (intended by Henry) was of monarchical jurisdiction over an episcopal church, the method of the 1530s revolution left crucial questions unanswered. A supremacy enforced by statute implied parliament had a role in church government. Henry's theological idiosyncrasies and the reform and counter-reform undertaken by his successors created a hybrid and fudged reformation. What status did it leave bishops? Could any religious group use supremacy or was it fundamentally Protestant? Differing versions of supremacy were not invariably present, but were always latent, between the 1530s and 1660. Nor were they necessarily conflicting: only particular events or aims caused monarchical and parliamentary, or royal and episcopal, authority to clash. Crucially, however, Restoration writers had to work within, and were able to exploit, a rich legacy of ecclesiological argument.

ESTABLISHMENT: 1530–1547

In the 1530s, statutes dismantled papal authority in England and transferred Rome's fiscal and juridical powers to the crown. Payment of annates, first fruits, and Peter's Pence was banned. Appeals to Rome were outlawed. The monasteries were dissolved and their revenues administered by the Court of Augmentations. Most famously of all, the Act in Restraint of Appeals of 1533 (24 Hen. VIII c. 12) outlined two complementary spiritual and temporal legal systems which both operated under royal jurisdiction.[1] Describing England as an empire, presided over by a king with 'plenarie hole and intiere power ... and jurisdiccion to render and yelde Justice and final det*er*mynacion ... in all causes', this outlined in the highest degree what would come to be known as sovereignty. It also asserted the jurisdictional self-sufficiency of the English church under the king (and indeed this act made the archbishop of Canterbury the judge of final appeal, changed in 1534 to the king or chancery). The Act of Appeals was the most famous statement of Henrician *imperium*, but other statutes would prove equally significant in the long run. The Act Restraining the Payment of Annates (25 Hen. VIII c. 20) set down that it was *praemunire* for an archbishop to refuse to consecrate the king's nominee to a bishopric, a law which would worry clergy opposed to James II's catholicising programme in the 1680s. This followed the Act of Submission of the Clergy (25 Hen. VIII c. 11), which ordered that convocation needed a royal writ to assemble, separate permission to debate new canons, and that draft canons became legally binding only with royal assent. Royal ratification ordained by statute opened a loophole for later claims that parliament could and should ratify canons. In 1682, the royal paper office contained some unspecified manuscripts about the Submission.[2] All these acts were

[1] G. R. Elton, 'The Evolution of a Reformation Statute', *English Historical Review*, 64 (1949), pp. 174–97.

[2] Bodl., Tanner MS 271, fo. 58v.

repealed by Mary and revived by Elizabeth. Two others were repealed and not revived: the Act Extinguishing the Authority of the Bishop of Rome (28 Hen. VIII c. 10), which set out an oath to 'utterly renounce' papal jurisdiction and accept the royal supremacy; this was in effect replaced by the Elizabethan Oath of Supremacy, still in force in the Restoration. And the Act of Supremacy itself (26 Hen. VIII c. 1), not revived because Elizabeth changed her title, was a brief law notable mainly for how it 'corroborates' and 'confirms', i.e. did not create, supremacy.

What parliament legislated, Henry practised. The visual culture of English worship was supposed to change: mentions of the pope and Thomas Becket expunged; royal coats of arms painted in churches. The Great Bible of 1540 depicted Henry handing down the Word of (a rather tiny) God to his people. In 1538 he sat in judgement on the radical John Lambert. In 1536 he delegated his supremacy to Thomas Cromwell, his vicegerent in spirituals. This, perhaps intended to intimidate the bishops, would inspire later anticlerical authors such as William Prynne before the Civil Wars, and the Earl of Shaftesbury after them. And the royal injunctions of 1536, drafted by Cromwell, ordered that supremacy be preached four times a year. If bemused priests wondered how to do this, they could find plenty of arguments for supremacy spewing from the press.[3]

Understandings of royal government of the church rested on how the church itself was conceived. The visible church on earth included both the saved (the invisible church) and the reprobate, the wheat and the tares (Matt. 13:29). As an earthly society, it was a corporation which needed hierarchy and government, but did it need universal government? The bishops' formulary of faith of 1537 noted that the catholic church was geographically unbounded, a spiritual unity and mystical body headed by Christ. But this entity was composed of 'particuler churches', which were 'all equall in power and dignitie', none ruling over the others. Rome was not of itself the catholic church but only a member of the same, along with the churches of England, France, and Spain. The revised formulary of faith authorised by the king in 1543 concurred. Both texts went on to explain how each particular church was governed by its own rulers. For

[3] Henrician supremacy is more fully dissected in Graham David Nicholson, 'The Nature and Function of Historical Argument in the Henrician Reformation' (Ph.D thesis, University of Cambridge, 1977); John Guy, 'Thomas Cromwell and the Intellectual Origins of the Henrician Revolution', and 'Tudor Monarchy and its Critiques', in Guy, ed., *The Tudor Monarchy* (1997); Walter Ullmann, '"This Realm of England is an Empire"', *Journal of Ecclesiastical History*, 30 (1979), pp. 175–203; Shelley Lockwood, 'Marsilius of Padua and the Case for the Royal Ecclesiastical Supremacy', *Transactions of the Royal Historical Society*, 6th ser., 1 (1991), pp. 89–119.

churches in diuers contreies seuerally called … for theyr most necessary gouernement, as they be distinct in places, so they haue distinct ministers & diuers heades in earth, gouernours, and rulers.[4]

Such claims justified jurisdictional independence from Rome, but did not of themselves argue for royal as opposed to archiepiscopal supremacy. They did, however, mark a shift not only away from papal authority but also from the ecclesiastical supremacy of a general council. As Reformation divisions became entrenched, papalism was refuted not by conciliarism but provincial self-determination – or, perhaps more accurately, by the version of conciliarism that had emphasised national over general councils.

The King's Book did explain that Christian kings 'be the head gouernours vnder [Christ], in the particular churches'.[5] But it was the theologically conservative bishop of Winchester, Stephen Gardiner, who offered the fullest case for *royal* supremacy over these provincial-cum-national churches. In 1532 Gardiner had seemed to be a staunch defender of the church against the supremacy, penning the 'Answer of the Ordinaries' which insisted on the clerical, rather than royal, right to rectify religious grievances. But in 1535 Gardiner appears to have experienced a change of heart, an alteration of view which his tract began by characterising as a Damascene conversion. (The Protestant annotator of the edition republished to embarrass Gardiner under Mary I dubbed him 'Doctor dubbleface'.)[6] Gardiner too argued that Christ headed the universal church, but added that as a 'communion of christen people' a group of people were named a 'church', and 'to be named the churche of Englande as is the churche of Fraunce the churche of Spayne *and* the churche of Rome'. The king, as head of the body politic, must logically head the Church of England, based on a nominalist claim that church and commonwealth were two names for the same thing:

seing the churche of Englande consisteth of the same sortes of people at this daye that are comprised in this worde realme of whom the kinge his [*sic*] called the headde: shall he not beinge called the headde of the realme of Englande be also the headde of the same men whan they are named the churche of Englande?

[4] *The Institvtion of a Christen Man* (1537, citing STC 5164), fos. 14v–15v; *A Necessary Doctrine and Ervdition for any Christen Man* (1543, citing STC 5168), fos. 15v–17v.

[5] *Necessary Doctrine*, fo. 17v.

[6] Stephen Gardiner, *De vera obedientia oratio*, in Pierre Janelle, ed., *Obedience in Church and State: Three Political Tracts by Stephen Gardiner* (Cambridge, 1930), pp. 70–3, 169 (marg.). See Glyn Redworth, *In Defence of the Church Catholic* (Oxford, 1990), p. 66, n. 59, for a defence (*contra* Janelle) of Gardiner's sincerity.

This bishop found it impossible to conceive of the king as head of his subjects but not supreme head over the church of English Christians.[7] Throughout the early modern period, defenders of supremacy would continue this dual argument, firstly showing the independence of provincial churches and secondly proposing royal headship over the same as logically following. Crucially, however, the two prongs could be separated to argue for episcopal government of the church on the model of pre-Constantinian Christianity. But the assumption that all the members of the polity were (or ought to be) of one religion reinforced and underlay the logic of royal civil and ecclesiastical headship. This assumption was the bedrock of the Restoration Anglican drive for uniformity.

Defending royal jurisdiction over ecclesiastical affairs was facilitated by the idea that the details of worship practised by the members of the English church-state were not specified by divine law. The catholic universal church shared doctrine, but worship differed over space and time, because significations of decency and reverence varied in different societies. Rites and ceremonies were thus unspecified in the Bible, but governed by the need to worship 'decently and in order' (I Cor. 14:40), interpreted to require uniformity in a single state. It was such *adiaphora* which kings decreed, explained Thomas Starkey's *Exhortation to the People*, written in 1535 and published the following year. This outlined how 'all suche thynges, whiche by goddis worde are nother prohibyted nor commaunded' were 'lefte to worldly polycie, wherof they take their ful authoritie'.[8] For Starkey it was the king whose 'worldly policy' determined *adiaphora*, those items in which the *Institution* thought provincial churches to 'moche differe, and be discrepant the one from the other'. This theory was particularly advantageous for the supremacy, since it outlawed papal impositions of universal standards, and yet barred challenges from dissent within the realm: it was 'conuenie*n*t' for each province to have a head, but 'playne foly' to think that a single head could govern diverse nations, languages, and laws.[9] Henry's polemicists here described what their king practised in his Injunctions of 1536. That monarchs decided ceremonial details but did not interfere with doctrine would become another classic defence of supremacy. Restoration clergy attacked Dissenters for refusal to obey national decisions on *adiaphora*.[10]

The pre-modern distaste for anything innovatory was potentially problematic for defending the supremacy. Writers thus manipulated history

[7] Gardiner, *De vera obedientia*, pp. 115, 93–5 (qu.).
[8] Thomas Starkey, *An Exhortation to the People* (1536), fo. 6v.
[9] *Institvtion*, fo. 15r; Starkey, *Exhortation*, fos. 66v–67r. [10] See Chapter 3, p. 146.

to assert papal power was a novelty which usurped royal and episcopal rights. Supremacy theorists struck at the root of papal claims when they insisted that all the apostles had held equal authority. Simon Matthew preached that 'the substance of the church was equally builded vpon them all'. Reflecting this state of apostolic equality, bishops in the early church were also noted to have held 'lyke meryte … lyke prelacy', each supreme in their own diocese, free from earthly headship or Roman interference.[11] Henry's polemicists denied the antiquity of papal claims, pointing to Nicene canons which spoke of the ancient custom of episcopal equality, and to evidence that the pope had interpolated canons advantageous to himself. A hundred and fifty years later, the great Restoration antipapal polemicist Isaac Barrow would repeat these ideas.[12] Renaming the pontiff the bishop of Rome thus bore ideological weight, for it implied that his jurisdiction (or lack thereof) over England was the same as any other foreign bishop's.[13]

The origins of papal power were thus deemed *iure humano*. A common history was constructed of clerical jurisdiction being a legacy of innocent gifts made by emperors to early pious clergy, or powers which cunning papal ambition had extorted from naïve rulers, later falsely claimed as *iure divino*.[14] Henry's *Epistle* to Christian princes, rejecting participation in the Council of Trent, castigated the pope's 'pretended honour fyrste gotten by superstition, after encreased by violence … borne by the ignorancie of the worlde, nouryshed by the ambition of byshops of Rome, defended by places of Scripture, falsely understande[d]'.[15] The royal almoner Edward Foxe blamed the seventh-century Byzantine emperor Phocas for ceding imperial powers.[16] Foxe's narrative is worth quoting at length since it would be echoed and subverted in the seventeenth century:

[11] Simon Matthew, *A Sermon made in the Cathedrall Churche of Saynt Paule at London, the XXVII day of June, Anno 1535* (1535), sig. C4r–v; *Institvtion*, fo. 48r; *Necessary Doctrine*, fos. 37v–38r; Edward Foxe, *The True Dyfferens Between the Regall Power and the Ecclesiasticall Power*, trans. Henry Lord Stafford (1548), fos. 21v, 31v, 15r; Cuthbert Tunstall, *A Sermon of Cvthbert Bysshop of Duresme made vpon Palme Sondaye last past* (1539), sig. [C6]; Thomas Swinnerton, *A Mustre of Scismatyke Byshoppes of Rome* (1534), sigs. [C6]v–[C7]r; [Thomas Swinnerton], *A Litel Treatise Ageynste the Mutterynge of some Papistis in Corners* (1534), sig. A3r.

[12] Tunstall, *Sermon*, sigs. D5v–[D6]v; *Institvtion*, fos. 47v–48r; *Necessary Doctrine*, fos. 38v–39r. For Barrow, see below, Chapter 6, pp. 244–51.

[13] Gardiner, *De vera obedientia*, pp. 127–9; Matthew, *Sermon*, sig. B2v; Swinnerton, *Mustre*, sigs. [C4]v, D3r.

[14] Starkey, *Exhortation*, fos. 61v–62r.

[15] *An Epistle of the Most Myghty & Redouted Prince Henry the VIII … to all Christen Princes* (1538), sig. A4r–v.

[16] Anon., *A Treatise Provynge … the Byshops of Rome had Neuer Ryght to any Supremitie within this Realme* (1534), sig. [A4]r; Foxe, *True Differens*, fo. 30r; Gardiner, *De vera obedientia*, p. 149.

grette was the police and subteltye of the byshoppes of rome for whome [bishops] dyd fyste go oboute to abtayne *th*e chefe Empyre and supremyte, thei dyd deuyde the power and iurisdiction with kinges with verye louinge and gentle termes or titles, and so that they might be made lordes in spirituall thinges they dyd permyt to kinges all temporall thinges … And the swerde (whiche they haue sharpened by the the gentilnes and permission of prynces & endewed with worldly riches and possessions by the gentle and lyberall gifte of princes) they exercice & drawe it out agaynst them whe*n* they thinke best.[17]

A good mark of a writer's religious attitude would be whether they applied such a narrative to popes, papal clergy, English bishops, or all churchmen. Dissenters might argue that all prelates played such tricks; anticlerical writers that it was a fault of any cleric – priestcraft *avant la lettre*. The *iure humano* origins of papal or episcopal authority were important to demonstrate because emperors and kings could reverse their ancestors' grants.

Complementing the idea of papal novelty in the 1530s was an insistence on the ancient nature of the royal supremacy, evident in sacred Israelite history, imperial Christian Rome, and defended despite papal incursions during the medieval era. These examples would prove axiomatic for decades, especially those from the Bible and the fourth-century church. (Early modern authors would differ as to whether they emphasised medieval papal hegemony or royal defiance of it.) Henry's polemicists insisted that the royal supremacy was, contrary to appearances, not a new invention, though perhaps a newly clear title. His ancestors, it was asserted, had 'the self same power and supremitie' which was 'vnited and knytte to the imperiall crowne … though they dydde not vse to wryte the same in their style'.[18] David, Solomon, Hezekiah, and Jehosaphat had appointed priests and Levites, deposed the same, purged God's people of idolatry, and purified the Temple. 'The byshoppes of the Hebrewes' – the anachronism is telling – 'were subiectes to kynges, and the kynges deposed the bysshoppes'.[19] Such histories were embodied in the *Collectanea satis copiosa*, the 'sufficiently copious' documentary dossier assembled in the early 1530s on the historical practice of royal supremacy.

The two key eras which bore witness to royal *imperium* – Israelite and Constantinian – also provided a store of examples of the limits as well as powers of supremacy. If royal ecclesiastical authority undoubtedly

[17] Foxe, *True Differens*, fos. 41r–42r. See below, p. 280.

[18] *Treatise Provynge … the Byshops of Rome had Neuer Ryght to any Supremitie*, sig. A3r; Gardiner, *De vera obedientia*, pp. 91–3, 121.

[19] Gardiner, *De vera obedientia*, pp. 107–13; Anon., *A Dialogve Betwene a Knyght and a Clerke* (1533), fos. 6r (qu.), 13r; Foxe, *True Differens*, fos. 59v–67v (from fo. 64 the facing rectos and versos share a folio number).

included expelling papal jurisdiction, it was not deemed unbounded. This, not surprisingly, was made clear by Henry's more conservative supporters. Gardiner said the king was supreme 'albeit not in all thinges yet in most thinges' and Tunstall's letter to Pole insisted that supremacy did not involve the king preaching.[20] The evangelically minded Foxe was more ambiguous. When describing the ecclesiastical supremacy of Anglo-Saxon princes, Foxe pointed to their laws for 'the ordering & reseruing of Sacramentes & spirituall thinges', for such monarchs 'had grete authorite i*n* spiritual thinges'. Foxe never suggested that kings could actually administer the sacrament, and he, unlike the translator of his work, Lord Stafford, described them as investing not consecrating bishops, even when forbidden by popes. As Francis Oakley has shown, Stafford consistently mistranslated this as consecration (although a careful reading of even the translation hints that investiture is what is meant).[21] The Bishops' Book of 1537 more clearly adhered to a limited supremacy, saying:

> we maye not thinke, that it doth apperteyne vnto thoffice of kynges and princis, to preache and teache, to administre the sacramentes, to absoyle, to excommunicate, and suche other thynges, belongynge to thoffice and admynistration of byshops and priestes.

The status of kings as 'chiefe heedes and ouerlokers' was to ensure that priests were carrying out their functions, and enforce their duties on them if they disobeyed.[22] The statement was pithy, clear, and unambiguous. It also disappeared from the revised version of 1543, a rare instance where the King's Book looked less traditional than the Bishops' Book. That supremacy was jurisdictional, not priestly, was the most important defence of it throughout the early modern period.

The two formularies did concur, however, in characterising the supremacy as empowering the monarch primarily so that he could carry out certain duties. Supremacy was limited by the moral duty to defend true religion more than by earthly constitutionalist constraints. The royal duty to uphold religious truth was a common line amongst men who would doubtless have fundamentally disagreed as to what true religion was. The humanist Richard Morison argued that it was 'a princis dede' to expel the

[20] Gardiner, *De vera obedientia*, p. 119; Cuthbert Tunstall and John Stokesley, *A Letter written … vnto Reginald Pole* (1540), sig. C4r.

[21] Foxe, *True Differens*, fos. 80r, 83r, 85v–r [*sic*]. The translation's hint is where it speaks of consecration by 'a ryng and a crowche'. See Francis Oakley, 'Edward Foxe, Matthew Paris, and the Royal *Potestas Ordinis*', *Sixteenth Century Journal*, 18 (1987), pp. 347–53.

[22] *Institvtion*, fo. 49v.

pope, and commendable to restore true religion; the conservative Bishop Tunstall that to enforce the doing of their duties on the clergy was what 'the chiefe and the best of the kynges of Israell did, and as all goode christiane kinges *oughte* to doe'.[23] One tract of 1534 argued that kings and parliaments not only had power to redress defaults, but were bound in conscience so to do.[24] This type of rhetoric powerfully authorised the king to make sweeping changes under the guise of reforming abuses, and the ambiguity of 'true religion' allowed support to be drawn from groups otherwise opposed. Yet it also opened up the supremacy to pressure from a variety of quarters – inevitably someone was going to be disillusioned with royal policies – and would, in the reigns of Henry's successors, permit 'counselling' the monarch as to what true religion was to slide into a contest as to who could manipulate the supremacy into upholding their own aims.

The majority of those who wrote on supremacy in the 1530s were clergy, but one of the lay minority is crucial to consider: the Middle Temple utter-barrister Christopher St German. Fairly conservative in his theology and piety, St German came to the supremacy after a career in common law practice, which had been under attack from the equitable jurisdiction of Chancery as well as perennial clashes with ecclesiastical courts.[25] From his most famous work on English laws, *Doctor and Student*, in use until the 1870s, to his printed tracts on lay–clerical relationships (some against Thomas More), to his unprinted discussions on the sacraments and soteriological fundamentals, St German attacked clerical meddling with anything construed as property. Mortmain, sanctuary, benefit of clergy, mortuaries, and diriges were all to be regulated by the laity, not the clergy. For churchmen to claim tithes *iure divino* was an error. Justices of the peace ought to be able to enquire into, though not judge, heresy.[26] Prelates wrongly made laws independently of parliament, so many extant canons clashed with English laws and the royal prerogative. St German's visceral anticlericalism led him to propose penalties of treble damages on clergy who failed to use the king's laws when handling property, and

[23] Richard Morison, *A Lamentation ... what Ruyne and Destruction cometh of Seditious Rebellyon* (1536), sig. B2v; Tunstall, *Letter*, sigs. D4v–D5r (my emphasis).

[24] *Treatise Provynge ... the Byshops of Rome had Neuer Ryght to any Supremitie*, sig. Dr.

[25] On the context, see Alan Cromartie, *The Constitutionalist Revolution* (Cambridge, 2006), ch. 2; J. H. Baker, ed., *The Reports of Sir John Spelman* (2 vols., 1977–8), vol. II; Christopher W. Brooks, *Law, Politics and Society in Early Modern England* (Cambridge, 2008), chs. 2–3.

[26] Christopher St German, *Doctor and Student*, ed. T. F. T. Plucknett and J. L. Barton (1974), pp. 320–3; Christopher St German, *A Treatise Concernynge the Diuision Between the Spirytualtie and Temporaltie*, in Thomas More, *Complete Works*, vol. IV, ed. J. B. Trapp (New Haven, 1979), pp. 175–212, at pp. 190, 195; Christopher St German, *The Addicions of Salem and Byzance* (1534), fo. 14r.

tenfold requital if they charged fees for visitations.[27] Historians have generally agreed that St German located supremacy not in the king alone, but in king-in-parliament, most clearly in *An Answere to a Letter* (1535).[28] The following account confirms that St German had a rather different concept of *imperium* to his monarch. But despite the underlying continuities across his works, looking in detail at his illustrative examples demonstrates that he spoke interchangeably and loosely of king, parliament, and king and parliament. St German would thus bequeath both the idea that parliament had a role in the supremacy and frustrating imprecision in expressing this.[29]

Whilst limiting the sphere of clerical jurisdiction by removing from it anything which might be deemed property, St German attacked the distinction between laity and clergy. Almost every one of his tracts insists that the 'church' includes all Christian people, not just the clergy. 'Al the people of Engla*n*de make the churche of Engla*n*de', he wrote in 1534, echoing the arguments for royal supremacy discussed above.[30] Such language would be developed by later critics to undermine clerical privileges and powers, such as that of excommunication. If contemporary definitional laxity wrongly employed church for churchmen, it erred even more badly by treating the see of Rome and the church as synonymous.[31] This was not the only aspect of St German's thought which cohered with wider Henrician argument. He offered his own story of the rise of clerical power through pious princes granting early churchmen powers 'which they might haue done themselfe if they hadde lyste'. The long practice of such activities had led to the mistaken idea that they were held by the clergy *iure divino* – and thus to the decay of royal authority. The emperor Phocas, St German tartly pointed out, would never have granted popes

[27] Christopher St German, *A Treatise Concernynge Diuers of the Constitucyons Prouyinciall and Legantines* (1535), sig. [A5]v; Christopher St German, *A Treatyse Concerninge the Power of the Clergye and the Lawes of the Realme* (n.d.), sig. C2r; St German's parliamentary draft of 1531 in John Guy, *Christopher St German on Chancery and Statute* (1985), pp. 130, 132.

[28] John Guy, 'Thomas More and Christopher St German: The Battle of the Books', in Alistair Fox and John Guy, eds., *Reassessing the Henrician Age* (Oxford, 1986); Guy, *Chancery and Statute*, pp. 39–40. Cromartie dissents, but on his account, see below.

[29] Bequeath in a loose sense: it is exceedingly difficult to trace the direct legacy of anything beyond *Doctor and Student*. Nevertheless, later writers clearly participated in the same sentiments.

[30] St German, *Addicions of Salem and Byzance*, fo. 49v (qu.); St German, *Power of the Clergye*, sig. D4r; St German, *Constitucyons*, sig. [A8]v; Christopher St German, *An Answere to a Letter* (1535), sig. B2v; Christopher St German, *A Treatise Concernynge Generall Councilles, the Byshoppes of Rome, and the Clergy* (1538), sig. C5v. On the authorship of the last, see Richard Rex, 'New Additions on Christopher St German: Law, Politics, and Propaganda in the 1530s', *Journal of Ecclesiastical History*, 59 (2008), pp. 281–300.

[31] St German, *Addicions of Salem and Byzance*, fo. 24v.

authority over himself.[32] Where in 1532 St German had urged reform of clerical pride in general, in 1538 he applied this specifically to popes. Only one tract really engaged in a discussion of Peter's authority (or lack of it) over the other apostles, perhaps because St German had no wish to elevate general apostolic – and thus episcopal – powers.[33] He paid only lip-service to the other alternative to popes – general councils – repeatedly denouncing them as not binding because they had not been called by kings and did not include representatives of the laity. In two unprinted pieces of the later 1530s, at a time when Henry's government was attempting to extricate itself from conciliar jurisdiction, St German argued that councils could not legislate for the church until properly representative of it.[34]

If a truly general council was not feasible – and St German may have deliberately described an impossible scenario – who governed the church? St German was capable of monarchist comments. His account of *The Power of the Clergye and the Lawes of the Realme* opened with a series of biblical proof-texts for royal authority – just like the (rather repetitive) *Treatise Concernynge Generall Councilles*. Israelite kings appointed priests. The Bible showed that 'longe before the comyng of Cryste … king*es* were the heddes over the people'. If a general council kept up 'oon catholique feithe thorough all christen realms … as for ceremonyes every king in his contrye may order theym'.[35] Whereas *Doctor and Student* had initially announced that 'temporall rewlers' had care of the souls as well as the bodies of their subjects, later in that work and in the 1535 *Answere to a Letter* this was applied specifically to kings.[36] St German noted again and again the idea that kings had a duty to recover their true rights from clerical usurpation – indeed, he spoke only rarely of parliaments having the same obligation.[37] Perhaps this was what he perceived the Henrician Reformation to be doing, and thus what he defended in 1535 using the two cases fast becoming classic. Firstly, statutes declared long-established

32 St German, *Power of the Clergye*, sigs. D8r–E1r (qu.); St German, *Answere*, sigs. B8v–C1r, B1r–v.

33 St German, *Generall Councilles*, sigs. B2v–B4v, C3v–[C8]v. The date of this tract is signified by its deeming papalism heresy (at C3v, C4r, [C8]r), a rarity in the English Reformation. See Peter Marshall, 'Papist as Heretic: The Burning of John Forest, 1538', *Historical Journal*, 41 (1998), pp. 351–74.

34 Christopher St German, 'A Discourse of the Sacraments', TNA, SP 6/8, p. 11; Christopher St German, '<A Dyalogue shewinge> What we be bounde to byleve as thing*es* necessary to Salvac*i*on and what not', TNA, SP 6/2, pp. 121–3.

35 St German, *Power of the Clergye*, sig. A7r; St German, 'Dyaloge', pp. 129, 123.

36 St German, *Doctor and Student*, pp. 172, 258; St German, *Answere*, sig. G4r.

37 St German, *Diuision*, p. 202; St German, 'Dyaloge', pp. 124, 133, 166; St German, *Generall Councilles*, sig. [D7]v. For parliament's duty: St German, *Diuision*, p. 191.

royal powers rather than creating new ones. Secondly, kings did not assert spiritual authority (rightly defined): absolution, orders, sacramental powers. 'And if percase the parlyamente & conuocacyon also had expressely graunted to the ki[n]g with the seyd name of the supreme heed: such sp*irit*ual auctorityes it is no dout but that *tha*t graunt had be*en* voyde: for they haue no auctorite to change the lawe of god.' St German did not think parliament was omnicompetent but rather that it was in effect infallible, for it was unthinkable that it would legislate *ultra vires*.[38]

Just as frequently, St German spoke of parliament's authority over ecclesiastical matters. Indeed, he often began by mentioning kings and concluded by invoking parliament. In a discussion about pruning the number of holy days, he insisted that 'princes … are bounde also to put to their hands for reformacyon', for if there are excess holy days 'the parlyament hath good authorite to reforme it'. A few pages later, this was inverted in a discussion of abolishing the writ *de excommunicado capiendo*, which parliament might put away, and whose unjust use king and parliament were bound to rectify.[39] If a customary right is abused by the clergy, parliament may change it, 'a dede that the kynge is bounde to at his coronacion'.[40] *Doctor and Student*, describing the care of souls as well as bodies, spoke firstly of temporal rulers, secondly of kings, and thirdly of 'the kynge in his parlyament' so doing. King and parliament decide who is the true pope in a schism and they can inquire about heresies. St German said his proposed great standing council would not question suspected heretics, but banned any churchman from interrogating them until the council had certified them obstinate. Heresy was also in effect defined as what the council thought contrary to faith.[41]

The idea that the laity were an integral part of the church was married to the notion that king and parliament interpreted scripture in the *Answere to a Letter*. Agreeing that the catholic church expounds scripture, St German then subtly changed who constituted this body – laity as well as clergy, so that 'the emperoure kynges and pri[n]ces with their people expounde it'. Given that this is impracticable, those 'who*m* the people haue chosen' their rulers 'with theire counsell spirytuall & temporall' expounde it 'for the p*ar*liament so gathered togyther ~~the people~~ representeth the estate of al the people within this realme that is to say

[38] St German, *Answere*, sig. B3r (qu.); St German, *Doctor and Student*, p. 300; see Mark D. Walters, 'St German on Reason and Parliamentary Sovereignty', *Cambridge Law Journal*, 62 (2003), pp. 335–70.

[39] St German, *Power of the Clergye*, sigs. E1r–v, [E3]v–[E5]r.

[40] St German, *Diuision*, p. 202.

[41] St German, *Doctor and Student*, p. 327; Guy, *Chancery and Statute*, pp. 127–8.

of the whole catholyque churche therof'.[42] Alan Cromartie has recently suggested that St German saw interpretation of scripture as a matter for the king alone, since when St German introduced the Fortescuean distinction between *dominicum regale* and *dominicum politicum et regale* (broadly, mere versus mixed monarchy), he said scriptural exegesis was done by the first.[43] But Cromartie ceases his citation too soon, for on the following page, apropos *ius regale politicum*, St German insisted that 'this power hathe the kynges grace in this Realme'.[44] Following this he stated 'and why shulde nat the parlyament than whiche representeth the whole catholyke churche of Englande expounde scrypture rather than the convocacyon whiche representeth onely the state of the clergy'.[45] If the king was supreme, he shared this position with parliament.

St German's slippage between king and parliament is complicated by his occasional introduction of a third group: lawyers. It is his professional colleagues who should adjudicate which laws on ecclesiastical affairs are valid, and who 'enstructe the parliament ... what they may laufully do concernynge the spirituall iurisdiction'.[46] In 1534 he explained that 'specially they that were lerned in the laws of the realme' helped parliament decide on papal provisions of bishops and told the king's council what was and was not ruled by the Keys of the church. Sanctuary was decided by 'the kinges lawes', which parliament set down.[47] Lawyers might pretend ignorance of scriptural exegesis, but they had to advise kings and parliaments on church law, otherwise the clergy could intrude any interpretation.[48] The prevalence of lawyers in guiding reform of clerical jurisdiction was partly a function of practical experiences such as tithe disputes, perhaps with an admixture of professional empire-building. But it was also an early indication of how often those who wanted parliament to have a role in the royal supremacy would also find a part for lawyers to play: Edward Coke and Edward Bagshaw in the early Stuart period, Matthew Hale in the Restoration.[49]

St German's terminological slippage aptly demonstrates the inability of Henrician writers to think that imperial supremacy declared by parliament might contain an inherent contradiction. His version of supremacy *included* parliament without *excluding* the king: a sort of mixed

[42] St German, *Answere*, sigs. G4v–G6v. On this question, see John Guy, 'Scripture as Authority: Problems of Interpretation in the 1530s', in Fox and Guy, eds., *Henrician Age*.
[43] St German, *Answere*, sig. G5v; Cromartie, *Constitutionalist Revolution*, p. 56.
[44] St German, *Answere*, sig. G6r.
[45] St German, *Answere*, sig. G6v.
[46] St German, *Doctor and Student*, pp. 309, 332 (qu.).
[47] St German, *Addicions of Salem and Byzance*, fo. 60r–v; St German, *Constitucyons*, sig. [D3]r.
[48] St German, *Power of the Clergye*, sigs. Iv–[I2]r.
[49] See below, Chapter 2.

monarchical supremacy. *Doctor and Student* noted that parliament was the highest court of the realm, but also that the king was the 'hede and most chyef & pryncipall parte of the Parlyament'.[50] The practicalities of Henry's use of statute led more than the aging lawyer to slide into emphasising consent.[51] Even the Act of Appeals, by speaking of the imperial crown, allowed *imperium* to be abstracted from the king and translated into the sovereign independence of the realm rather than its ruler. In the 1530s, of course, concepts of the state and the decline of personal monarchy were far in the future. It would take a civil war in the next century to establish parliamentary supremacy independently of the crown, and that was reversed at the Restoration. But in Henry's supremacy – royal and parliamentary, catholic and evangelical – lay the seeds of ecclesiological discord which germinated, sometimes slowly, sometimes rapidly, between the 1530s and 1680s.

REFORMATION AND COUNTER-REFORMATION: 1547–1553

Whatever details Henrician supremacy left undefined, it was undoubtedly intended for an adult male monarch. Such a king would not be seen again for fifty-six years. The fact of *imperium* dominated Tudor politics, but much of that politics was shaped by negotiating supremacy in the circumstances of evangelising minority rule, Catholic married queenship, and unwedded female Protestant monarchy. Whilst Edward VI's supremacy was in many ways a natural progression from his father's, it also broke with Henry's by welding itself to evangelism. Between 1547 and 1553, Reformation and kingship became inseparable.[52] A close-knit regime patronised printers such as John Day (future publisher of Foxe's *Actes and Monuments*) and William Seres (joint publishers of Bishop Latimer's court sermons), and Walter Lynne (who wrote his own attack on papalism and published Bernando Ochino's, which was translated by Bishop John Ponet and owned by the king and his second regent, Northumberland).[53]

[50] St German, *Doctor and Student*, pp. 159–60.

[51] Popular consent is mentioned in *Institvtion*, fo. 45v; Anon., *Dialogve Betwene a Knyght and a Clerke*, fo. 25r–v; Anon., *Treatise Provynge … the Byshops of Rome had Neuer Ryght to any Supremitie*, sig. Dr.

[52] Stephen Alford, *Kingship and Politics in the Reign of Edward VI* (Cambridge, 2002), pp. 33, 112, 115.

[53] Peter Blayney, 'William Cecil and the Stationers', in Robin Myers and Michael Harris, eds., *The Stationers' Company and the Book Trade, 1550–1990* (Winchester, Hants., 1997), pp. 15, 26–30; Alford, *Kingship and Politics*, pp. 116–19, 101.

Edward himself abstracted arguments against the pope in a work which was published in 1682. 'Neither the Pope, or any on Earth, can be our Head', but only Christ, the supreme head of the English Church pronounced.[54] Under Edward, old arguments against the pope were reiterated: the equality of apostles and early church patriarchs, the dubious inheritance of Petrine power by Rome. In Ochino's *Tragoedie*, the character Pseudologus cited forged documents for papal supremacy.[55] Lynne depicted the rise of papal power over kings pictorially. The main Edwardian addition to earlier anti-papal rhetoric was a sense of the papacy as a diabolical tool subverting true religion, linking to a rhetoric of the pope as antichrist.[56] If the pope was antichrist, Edward was characterised as a godly Israelite ruler reforming the nation. As Nicholas Udall wrote in a preface to Erasmus's *Paraphrases* – supposed to be placed in every parish church – if Henry was Moses freeing the Israelites, Edward was Joshua, leading them into Canaan. If Henry was Moses translating the Bible, Edward was Josiah, rediscovering the Law and leading a covenanted nation. And if Henry was David, his son was Solomon building the Temple.[57] Citing Josiah, Hezekiah, and Jehosaphat was especially pertinent for a king who was a minor, for these examples legitimated iconoclastic reformation by a youthful king. Edward, unlike his Protestant half-sister, proved willing to play such a role. In his 'Chronicle', reporting his answer to the imperial ambassador's criticism of arresting Mary's servants for saying mass, he declared he did but do 'according to a king's office herein, in observing the laws that were so godly and in punishing the offenders'. His Restoration editor praised this piety as exceeding not only that of Edward's lay but also his clerical counsellors: he 'made his *Bishops* weep … to see their tardy Zeal rebuk'd by the King[']s' – for the editor, perhaps an implicit critique of the tardy zeal of some later Stuart churchmen.[58]

If the evangelical clique in authority constructed the king they wanted, we might expect Edward's reign to have been six years of golden fulfilment of godly expectations, celebrated in court sermons. But of course

[54] Bernando Ochino, *A Tragoedie or Dialoge of the Vniuste Vsurped Primacie of the Bishop of Rome*, trans. John Ponet (1549), sigs. O2r–v; *K. Edward VI his own Arguments Against the Pope's Supremacy* (1682), pp. 39–42.

[55] Ochino, *Tragoedie*, sigs. [G4]v–H1r, Q1r–v, Q3v–[Q4]r; *Edward VI his own Arguments*, pp. 69, 73. Pseudology: false speaking, the art of lying (*Oxford English Dictionary*).

[56] Walter Lynne, *A most necessarie Treatise, declaring the Beginning and Ending of all Poperie* (1548); *Edward VI his own Arguments*, pp. 3, 44, 58.

[57] Nicholas Udall, *The First Tome … of the Paraphrases of Erasmus* (1551), ep. ded., sig. [*6]r.

[58] *Edward VI his own Arguments*, pp. 116–17; W. K. Jordan, ed., *The Chronicle and Political Papers of King Edward VI* (1966), p. 80.

reformation was neither easy nor unchallenged, either by overt rebellion or by silent non-compliance. Latimer complained of a nation of backsliding Israelites baulking at godly leadership.[59] Even court preachers urged the regime on to further, faster reformation with amazing urgency. Latimer told Edward that kings, unlike other men, were particular officers of God with special duties. What else should a preacher do in a court sermon but remind the king of these heavy responsibilities?[60] Expounding Deuteronomy 17:18–19, Latimer emphasised that it was the duty of the king to see God's Law faithfully copied out, doing so himself if necessary, for 'readynge the boke of God ... is the kings pastime by goddes appoyntemente'.[61] Latimer certainly endorsed royal supremacy, but only as 'a dygnity wyth a charge'.[62] Lever and Latimer complained of social ills, lack of financial support to godly preachers, and delays in purging corrupt priests.[63] It was the government's fault that these went unremedied, and their hands were 'full of bloude, not so muche by doyng, as by sufferynge all these euyls'.[64] Again, Edward listened. The lengthy list of religious matters needing attention in Edward's memorandum of 1552 to the council – catechising, uniformity of doctrine, discipline, diligence, reorganising the bishopric of Durham, homilies, more injunctions, and amending (altered to abrogating) canon law – suggests that he, unlike his half-sister Elizabeth, was favourably inclined to motions for further reformation.[65] His 'Discourse on the Reform of Abuses in Church and State' of spring 1551 condemned impropriations. 'I would wish no authority given generally to all bishops', but only a 'commission' to 'those that be of the best sort of them, to exercise [discipline] in their dioceses'; to bishops (he wrote in 1552) 'grave, learned, wise, sober, and of good religion'.[66]

59 Hugh Latimer, *The Fyrste Sermon of Mayster Hughe Latimer which he Preached before the Kynges Maiest[ie]* (1549), sigs. B4v–[B5]r; Hugh Latimer, *The Seconde[-Seventh] Sermon ... Preached before the Kynges Maiestie* (1549), sig. B2r.

60 Latimer, *Seconde Sermon*, sigs [F6]r–[F7]r; Latimer, *Fyrste Sermon*, sig. Br.

61 Latimer, *Seconde Sermon*, sigs. B1r–v, [C6]r–[C8]v, [D5]r–v, qu. sig. F2r. On the importance of Deuteronomy 17 ('when he sitteth upon the throne ... he shall write him a copy of this law in a book ... and it shall be with him, and he shall read therein all the days of his life'), see Margaret Aston, *The King's Bedpost* (Cambridge, 1993), pp. 37–48; and on its radical implications, Alford, *Kingship and Politics*, pp. 180–2.

62 Latimer, *Seconde Sermon*, sig. [K3]v.

63 Thomas Lever, *A Sermon Preached the Thyrd Sondaye in Lent* (1550), sigs. [C6]r, E5v; Latimer, *Firste Sermon*, passim; Latimer, *Seconde Sermon*, passim.

64 Hugh Latimer, *A moste faithfull Sermon* (1550), sigs. D2r–v; Latimer, *Seconde Sermon*, sig. [S6]v; Lever, *Sermon*, sigs. E2r–v, C2r (qu.).

65 Jordan, ed., *Chronicle*, p. 179; p. 110 carefully listed those involved in the *reformatio legum ecclesiasticarum*.

66 Jordan, ed., *Chronicle*, pp. 165, 159–60, 179.

The idea of needing a commission to exercise episcopal authority echoed a statute little noticed by modern historians, but often cited in the Restoration. The Act for Election of Bishops (1 Edw. VI c. 2) removed the fiction of cathedral chapters electing bishops in favour of simple appointment by letters patent. It went on to declare that since all jurisdiction originated from the king, and all ecclesiastical courts were held by his authority, ecclesiastical process was to be made 'in the name, and with the Style of the King', as in common law courts. All bishops were to 'use no other Seale of Jurisdiction but wherein his Ma*jesti*es armes be ingraven'. Impressing royal authority on clerical minds as well as on ecclesiastical documents, the statute of 1547 was beloved by later antiprelatical writers such as Prynne, Edmund Hickeringill, and Henry Care in the 1680s – even, astonishingly, echoing in James II's ecclesiastical commission. The paper office at Whitehall in 1682 contained a document, dating from 1609, entitled 'Reasons propounded by Mr Serle why all processes of Jurisdiction ecclesiasticall should proceed in the Kings name and style, and to be sealed with his Ma*jes*ties Armes'.[67] The 1547 Act symbolised the Edwardian regime's willingness to break with traditional clerical authority and thus annoyed conservatives like Gardiner who had supported Henrician supremacy. Gardiner's case against Edwardian reform, however, significantly exploited Henry's parliamentary Reformation. Removed from the Regency Council in the closing weeks of Henry's reign, Gardiner subjected the Council to a barrage of letters on the illegitimacy of non-parliamentary Reformation, especially during minority. He admitted that the Council substituted for the king, but thought it should realise the 'difference … to direct and order things established and to make in the highest innovations', the latter illegitimate during minority.[68] The final confrontation came over the new book of homilies authorised by royal prerogative but which did not cohere with the King's Book of 1543. In a revealing letter of 30 August 1547, Gardiner elaborated the supremacy of statute over mere monarchical power. Since a statute (34, 35 Hen. VIII c. 1) forbade teaching contrary to the King's Book, Gardiner argued that the visitation to enforce Edward's homilies was at risk of *praemunire*. For he had

> hard the lerned men of the Commen [Law] say that if any, although he be deputed by th[e] King, do, in execution of spirituall jurisdiction, extend the same contrary to Commen Law or act of Parliament, it is a premunire both

[67] Bodl., Tanner MS 271, fo. 69v. See Chapter 4, pp. 194–6, and Chapter 6, pp. 254–6.

[68] J. A. Muller, ed., *The Letters of Stephen Gardiner* (Cambridge, 1933), no. 124 (to Cranmer, just after 12 June 1547), at p. 313.

to the judge and the parties, althogh it be done in the Kings Majesties name; bicause they say the Kinges Majesties supremac[ie] in visiting and ordring of the Churche is reserved to spirituall jurisdiction.

Gardiner professed willingness to cite this against any visitation to his diocese to enforce the homilies.[69] In October, whilst imprisoned in the Fleet, Gardiner wrote directly to Somerset recalling how Henry's Lord Chancellor Audley had warned Gardiner against committing *praemunire*, which the bishop thought 'straung that a man autorised by the King (as, sence the Kings Majesty hath taken upon him the supremacy, every bishop is such one) could fall in a premunire'. In response, Audley cited the Act of Supremacy which 'restrayned' the king to spiritual jurisdiction, and pointed out that other statutes 'provided that no Spirituall Lawe shall have place contrary to a Common Lawe or Acte of Parliament'. In order to prevent the bishops and king dominating the laity, Audley threatened, 'we wil provide … that the premunire shall ever hang over your heads'.[70]

Gardiner's true motive – to preclude religious innovation – is fairly clear, but Henry's use of parliament nevertheless provided a loophole to exploit. And for all the regime's insistence that Edward held the same authority as an adult king, the circumstances of minority meant a more collaborative view of Reformation kept creeping in. Was Reformation enacted by a godly king advised by godly counsellors *royal* supremacy or collective authority? Court sermons were preached to king and counsellors. John Cheke, tutor to Edward, spoke of reformation by 'the king's majesty etc'. The final dialogues of Ochino's book depicted Henry VIII expelling the pope, but Edward and a 'Christian protectour' eliminating superstition. Ochino's Christian protector, however, morphed into the council in the aftermath of Northumberland's coup.[71] When crown and counsellors agreed, this worked; when they dissented, as under Elizabeth, cracks began to show.

Reformation came to a jarring halt in 1553 because of Edward's death, not because of minority. Short though it was, Edward's reign added to religious and political ambiguities surrounding *imperium*. A Reformation more radical than any before (or after), it provided an ideal for future Protestant critics of a backsliding establishment, alongside a political elite

[69] Gardiner, *Letters*, nos. 127 (to the Privy Council, 30 Aug. 1547) (qu. p. 370), 128 (to Sir John Mason, 30 Aug. 1547); see also no. 129 (to Sir John Godsalve, between 12 and 25 Sept. 1547): it is treason to act against parliament even when ordered by the king.

[70] Gardiner, *Letters*, no. 130 (to Somerset, 14 Oct. 1547), qu. p. 392.

[71] Alford, *Kingship and Politics*, pp. 62–3, 116; Ochino, *Tragoedie*, sigs. [X4]v–Y1r, Bb4v; the epistle dedicated to Edward praises the council as well.

willing to resist ungodly monarchy or to challenge kings only partially committed to Protestantism.[72]

Mary I was not merely uncommitted to Protestantism; she fervently favoured Catholic restoration. Insofar as this process was driven by Cardinal Pole, it may well have been one of the earliest attempts at Catholic Reformation on Tridentine lines.[73] Given Pole's earlier opposition to Henrician supremacy, and given the increasingly Roman (papal) emphasis of the Council of Trent's view of Catholicism, it is hardly surprising that Mary overtly rejected the title of supreme head.[74] Yet Mary's royal will was inhibited by the fact that supremacy had been enshrined in statute. Her attempt to bypass this by substituting 'etc.' for 'supreme head' in writs summoning parliament was thought by some to invalidate the acts of her parliaments. John Hales told Elizabeth that Mary 'could not' decide to omit supreme head, because

> this title and style more touched the commonwealth and realm of England, than the king. For … it was ordained for the conservation of the liberty of the whole realm, and to exclude the usurped authority of the bishop of Rome. And no king nor queen alone could renounce such title: but it ought … [to] be taken away orderly, and formally by act of parliament sufficiently called and summoned.[75]

One of William Cecil's earliest memos noted the need to look into the question of etceteration and parliamentary writs. Nevertheless, at a discussion at Serjeants Inn the writs were deemed valid by a majority of lawyers. They judged that Mary could not add to her royal style, but she did not have to write it out in full.[76] A parallel problem was Mary's desire to restore church lands, to which some of her council replied that 'what by the consent of Parliament had been assigned to the Crown could not be renounced by the Queen without the Parliament's consent'.[77]

Despite her professed distaste for the title of supremacy, Mary was not above using its powers. She held Edwardian deprivations of bishops

[72] Alford, *Kingship and Politics*, ch. 6; Diarmid MacCulloch, *Tudor Church Militant: Edward VI and the Protestant Reformation* (1999), ch. 4.

[73] As Eamon Duffy argues: *Fires of Faith: Catholic England under Mary Tudor* (New Haven, 2009). For Mary's Church, see also Eamon Duffy and David Loades, eds., *The Church of Mary Tudor* (Aldershot, 2006); and for Pole's career, see Thomas F. Mayer, *Reginald Pole: Prince and Prophet* (Cambridge, 2000).

[74] As urged by Pole: *Calendar of State Papers Venetian, 1534–1554*, pp. 447–8 (1 Dec. 1553).

[75] Quoted in Norman L. Jones, *Faith by Statute: Parliament and the Settlement of Religion, 1559* (1982), p. 87.

[76] Jones, *Faith by Statute*, pp. 85–6; TNA, SP 12/1, fo. 5; William Dalison, *Les reportes des divers special cases* (1689), p. 14; a fuller report, which identifies the opinions of individual judges, is in James Dyer, *Cy ensouont ascuns novel cases* (1585), fo. 98r.

[77] *Calendar of State Papers Venetian, 1555–1556*, p. 154 (9 Aug. 1555).

by royal commissions to be invalid. But she herself deprived Edwardian appointees by deeming the inclusion of *quamdiu se bene gesserint* in their patents to invalidate their appointment – in effect, another deprivation under the aegis of the royal supremacy.[78] In January 1554 Mary restored the see of Durham, dissolved under Edward, and reappointed its bishop, Cuthbert Tunstall, deprived by an Edwardian commission. That action was only later ratified by parliament – with Tunstall voting on his own restoration![79] Ecclesiastical officers were banned from using *regia auctoritate fulcitus* in the *royal* injunctions of 4 March 1554.[80] Although Mary got Pole to secretly authorise her new episcopal nominations, this was technically *praemunire*. And if her belief in her royal authority and the rectitude of her actions initially appeared in her overriding statutory limitations, they later manifested themselves in a bitter argument with the pope.[81] James II would show a similar willingness to exploit royal ecclesiastical prerogatives to benefit Catholics. Paradoxically, though, while the debate in his reign about supremacy drew on Henrician, Edwardian, and Elizabethan statutes, there was strikingly little discussion of Marian rule.

RE-ESTABLISHMENT: 1558–1603

In 1559, the restoration of royal supremacy and Protestantism was high on a very full monarchical agenda. The Act of Supremacy which finally resulted (1 Eliz. c. 1) provided the jurisdictional framework of supremacy not just for Elizabeth, but also for her Stuart successors. It revived, *inter alia*, the Henrician Acts of Appeals, Annates, Submission, and consecrating bishops, all of which were to apply to Elizabeth 'as fully and lardgely' as to Henry. It abolished the ecclesiastical jurisdiction of any 'forreine Prynce P*er*son Prelate State or Potentate'. Renouncing such jurisdiction was included in the Oath of Supremacy to be taken by all clergy and spiritual and temporal officeholders. These men were to swear that Elizabeth was 'thonelye supreme Governour of this Realme … as well in all Sp*irit*uall or Ecclesiasticall Thinges or Causes as Temporall'. A second conviction for maintaining foreign jurisdiction was *praemunire*; a

[78] *Calendar of Patent Rolls, 1553–1554*, pp. 74–5, 76, 175–6 (22, 23 Aug. 1553, 15 Mar. 1554); D. M. Loades, *The Oxford Martyrs* (1970), p. 113.

[79] D. M. Loades, 'The Last Years of Cuthbert Tunstall, 1547–1559', *Durham University Journal*, n.s. 35 (1973), pp. 10–21, at pp. 14–19.

[80] Gerald Bray, ed., *Documents of the English Reformation* (Minneapolis, 1994), p. 315. *Fulcitus*: sanctioned.

[81] Partly over her use of *defensor fidei*: Edward Coke, *The Fourth Part of the Institutes of the Lawes of England*, 4th edn (1669), p. 344.

third, high treason. Parliament pre-emptively defended its own actions by enacting that nothing it did was to be deemed heresy, and that ecclesiastical judges could only deem matters heretical if they were so judged by scripture, the first four general councils,[82] or by parliament and convocation. The Act furthermore stated that ecclesiastical powers to correct 'all maner of Errours Heresies Scismes Abuses Offences Contemptes and Enormities, shall for ever by auctorite of this p*resen*t P*arlia*m*en*t be united and annexed to the Imperiall Crowne' and that monarchs could appoint commissioners by letters patent to exercise such authority. The significance of this statute is hard to overstate. The Oath of Supremacy would remain in force until it was modified in 1689. Parliament claimed the right not only to ban foreign jurisdiction, but also in effect to oversee the determination of heresy. And the ability to appoint an Ecclesiastical Commission would be a contentious issue, involving discussion of the 1559 Act, for decades: under James I, in parliament in 1641 and 1661, and in print between 1686 and 1688. When Edward Coke famously descanted on Elizabeth's imperial prerogative in Caudrey's Case in 1593, he cited the Act of Supremacy.[83]

All this had been painfully won. In spring 1559, the government had begun by initiating a bill which combined the restoration of supremacy and uniformity (i.e. the Book of Common Prayer). It had been thwarted not by zealous Protestants in the Commons but by Catholics in the Lords.[84] Elizabeth's regime only forced new, separate, supremacy and uniformity bills through parliament by sleight of hand. The Act of Supremacy was passed, by twenty-one votes to eighteen, in the Lords when the bishops were prevented from attending.[85] Viscount Montague and Archbishop Heath attacked the first supremacy bill on a number of fronts, most emphatically denouncing it as a novelty unique to England, which would renew schism not only from the pope, but also from the ancient catholic faith, laws, general councils, and the church universal. Heath asked bitterly 'whether this House maye graunt' such powers to Elizabeth and whether she 'bee an apte person to receave them or not'.[86] Both these speeches were proleptic of later Catholic condemnation of the supremacy *in toto*. The distinction between supreme head and governor, which historians have emphasised, meant nothing to these men, and Elizabeth's gender

[82] Nicæa (325), Constantinople (381), Ephesus (431), and Chalcedon (451).

[83] 77 Eng. Rep. 1, 1 Co. Rep. 1 (1593). See John Guy, 'The Elizabethan Establishment and the Ecclesiastical Polity', in Guy, ed., *The Reign of Elizabeth I* (Cambridge, 1995).

[84] Jones, *Faith by Statute*, chs. 4–5. [85] Jones, *Faith by Statute*, p. 150.

[86] T. E. Hartley, ed., *Proceedings in the Parliaments of Elizabeth I* (3 vols., 1981–95), I.11–17, at pp. 12 (qu.), 16.

(another historiographical keynote) was merely another stick with which to beat supremacy.[87] Montague did not mention queenship. Heath said that 'her Highnes, being a woman[,] by birthe and nature, is not qualefied by God's wordes to feede the flocke of Christe'. But neither were kings. Montague similarly insisted that 'to teache me Christes true religion in this his Churche … God hath … appoynted neither emperour, kynge or temporall governour'. Heath insisted that Christ could not have left His church without government until Constantine, therefore he must have entrusted it to the apostles and priests.[88] Male ecclesiastical supremacy was unpalatable to these men, for they saw it as indelibly tied to the exercise of sacerdotal functions, and therefore as illegitimate. Heath cited the biblical example which would appear time and again in Tudor and Stuart polemic to demonstrate the error of royal priestly powers: that of King Uzziah. Uzziah, with the best of intentions, had attempted to burn incense in the Temple, had ignored warnings from his priests to stop, and been smitten with leprosy. When Uzziah burned the incense, Heath noted:

> The priest Azarias did resiste him, and expelled him out of the temple, and sayd unto him … *Non est officij tui, Ozia, ut adoleas incensum Domino, sed est sacerdotum et filiorum Aaron, ad huiusmodi enim officium consecrati sunt* [… if] he spake the truthe, then King Ozias was not the supreme head of the churche of the Jewes [if he did not] whye did God then plage the king withe a leprosye, and not the prieste? … it is moste manifeste Ozias, in that he was a kinge, could not be supreme head of the Churche.[89]

In fact no defender of the Church of England would question this; they merely asserted that supremacy did not involve sacerdotal functions. It was *this* debate, between jurisdictional and spiritual powers, which proved crucial to Elizabethan and later argument. It was the newly Roman emphasis of Tridentine Catholicism alongside (especially) the Protestantisation of supremacy under Edward, not its feminisation under Elizabeth, which left a bitter taste in the mouths of Catholics who had swallowed it under Henry VIII.

Newly surveying Elizabethan defences of supremacy against Catholicism in the 1560s is necessary, partly because historians have been remarkably disinclined to look at much of the polemical literature,

[87] Claire Cross, *The Royal Supremacy in the Elizabethan Church: England, 1450–1660*, 2nd edn (Oxford, 1999), pp. 20–1; Anne McLaren, *Political Culture in the Reign of Elizabeth I* (Cambridge, 1999), ch. 1.

[88] Hartley, ed., *Proceedings*, 1.16, 8, 14.

[89] Hartley, ed., *Proceedings*, 1.14. The Authorized Bible renders 2 Chron. 26:18 as 'it appertaineth not unto thee, Uzziah, to burn incense unto the Lord, but to the priests the sons of Aaron, that are consecrated to burn incense'.

especially those works dealing specifically with supremacy, and partly to demonstrate the crucial arguments about it. Robert Horne, bishop of Winchester; Alexander Nowell, dean of St Paul's; and John Bridges, future bishop of Oxford, spoke not of titles and gender but of the antiquity of supremacy, its jurisdictional not sacerdotal nature, and the role of clerical advice in complementing royal authority. These themes were not only reiterated in the latter part of the reign against Presbyterian opponents, but echoed throughout the seventeenth century. Under the Stuarts, the most frequently cited document on supremacy was the 'Admonition to Simple Men, deceyued by Malicious' appended to the royal Injunctions of 1559. This explained that Elizabeth did not

> chalenge auctoritie and power of ministrie of divine offices [but only] the souer-aigntie & rule ouer all maner persons borne within these her realms ... of what estate either ecclesiasticall or temporall so euer they be.[90]

This section therefore notes early Elizabethan arguments for an ancient, purely jurisdictional, counselled royal supremacy before turning to consider echoes of St German's supremacy of crown-in-parliament. It then discusses Presbyterian accounts of supremacy and the later Elizabethan Church's response to them, crucial to consider because that response involved claims for episcopacy *iure divino*.[91] Contemporaries and historians debated whether divine right episcopacy undermined supremacy. The complex answer to that question will feature prominently not only in the rest of this chapter but throughout this book.

Early Elizabethan writers deconstructed papal power in well-established ways. Peter's faith, not his person, was the foundation of the church. Both the apostles and early bishops, supreme rulers in their provinces, were equal. 'Ancient Learned fathers ... euermore ... limitted the Pope within his own particulare Iurisdiction.'[92] Horne, Bridges, and Walter Haddon explored the collapse of imperial authority due to papal powers granted by lackadaisical monarchs who neglected their godly duties.[93] The Church of England was thus presented as recovering early Christian organisation and lack of papal jurisdiction as well as pure original doctrine. Royal

[90] 'An Admonition to Simple Men, deceyued by Malicious', in *Iniunctions geven by the Quenes Maiestie* (1559), sigs. D2v–[D3]r.

[91] I take the Admonition Controversy of 1572 as impelling a shift towards anti-puritan argument, although anti-Catholic discourse obviously continued.

[92] John Jewel, *A Defense of the Apologie of the Churche of Englande* (1571), pp. 559 (qu.), 43, 114–15, 121, 193–4, 462; Alexander Nowell, *The Reprovfe of M. Dorman ... continued* (1566), fos. 52v, 58v, 63r, 136v, 151r–v; Walter Haddon, *A Sight of the Portugall Pearle*, trans. Abraham Hartwell (1565), sig. C3r; Walter Haddon, *A Dialogue Agaynst the Tyrannye of the Papistes* (1562), sig. [A8]v.

[93] Robert Horne, *An Answeare ... to a Booke Entituled, The Declaration of Svche Scruples ...* (1566), fos. 47r, 67v, 70r–v; John Bridges, *The Supremacie of Christian Princes* (1573), pp. 735–8.

supremacy was not new, although Tudor kings had newly recovered it. 'We flatter not our Prince with any newe imagined extraordinarie power, but onely geue him that Prerogatiue and Chieftie, that euermore hath benne dewe vnto him by the ordinance & Worde of God', wrote Jewel in 1571.[94] Israelite kings were widely invoked as exemplars of royal supremacy over churchmen: Moses, Joshua, David, Josiah, and Hezekiah – mapping male examples on to a queen seemed unproblematic.[95] King Solomon had deposed the high priest Abiathar, so Tudor princes could expel popes. This example would remain in use for many decades, although it proved problematic in the nonjuring schism of the 1690s.[96]

Examples from sacred history were complemented by those from church history. A full description of 'the fathers and of the histories' was just too much for Bridges to fit in his (already exceedingly long) book, and his promised volume on them never appeared. But he had already made clear a parallel between Israelite and Christian emperors and Elizabeth, for his queen's 'authoritie, in renuing such orders as long haue bene decayed or abolished, is no lesse than was theirs, in the first ordering and commaunding of them'.[97] Horne insisted that no matters were considered to be beyond imperial jurisdiction, and his account of emperors outlawing private chapels, non-resident clergy, and ignorant priests bore an uncanny, and doubtless not entirely coincidental, resemblance to the Tudor Reformations.[98] He painted a picture of early Christian bishops importuning emperors to resolve their disputes, deferential to kings and their delegates in councils.[99] Constantine, Theodosius, and Justinian were all cited along with king Lucius, who 'gaue the onsette, and shapte a patern for Constantine to followe'.[100] Imperial authority over church councils was especially emphasised, perhaps because of the looming threat of Trent.[101] For Horne, Elizabethan-style supremacy 'was practised continually by the Emperours: and approued, praysed and highly commended by thousandes of the best Bishoppes & most godly

94 Jewel, *Defense of the Apologie*, p. 14.

95 Horne, *Answeare*, fo. 109v; Jewel, *Apologie*, fo. 57v; Bridges, *Supremacie of Christian Princes*, pp. 199–200, 216, 296–7, 282–3; Nowell, *Reprovfe*, fos. 146v–168v, 177v–179r; John Jewel, *An Apologie or Aunswer in Defence of the Church of England* (1562), fos. 57v–58r. Only Aylmer, given his response to Knox, sought specifically female models, but he used male ones too.

96 Nowell, *Reprovfe*, fo. 181r; Bridges, *Supremacie of Christian Princes*, pp. 250–1, 254–6, 316.

97 Bridges, *Supremacie of Christian Princes*, pp. 309, 1113, 287 (qu.).

98 Horne, *Answeare*, fos. 22r, 42v–43r.

99 Horne, *Answeare*, fos. 30v, 25r, 24r.

100 Horne, *Answeare*, fos. 93v–94v (qu.), 15r, 17r–v; Nowell, *Reprovfe*, fos. 225v–226r, 258v, 260v–263r; Jewel, *Defense of the Apologie*, p. 12; Jewel, *Apologie*, fos. 58r, 59v.

101 Nowell, *Reprovfe*, fos. 212r–217v, 74r–v, 208v, 243v; Jewel, *Defense of the Apologie*, pp. 710–11; Horne, *Answeare*, fos. 22r, 51r–v, 53r, 117r.

Fathers that hath beene'.[102] Unlike during the Restoration, the era before Christian emperors was little analysed, although Cyprian's opposition to papal authority was mentioned. Nowell explained that Ignatius had not argued for royal supremacy because he lived under heathen monarchs – but surely would have supported Elizabeth's governance had he been born in her reign.[103]

What, apart from the antiquity of supremacy, did these examples demonstrate? The most crucial point was that supremacy did not permit the monarch to wield sacerdotal powers to administer the sacrament, consecrate bishops, or ordain clergy. Endless citations could be given of repeated denials that royal supremacy meant priestly monarchy. Uzziah was a model that English clergy had to prevent their Catholic opponents mapping on to the queen: 'our Princes doo no suche thinges', exclaimed Nowell.[104] Careful distinctions were made between Elizabeth having 'gouernment over spirituall and ecclesiasticall matters' but not 'spirituall gouernment'. Royal 'Ecclesiastical government' was denied by Bridges; Jewel used the epithet but denied Elizabeth 'Ecclesiasticall correction'.[105] Horne barred monarchs from jurisdiction 'not cohibitive' and from excommunication, only giving them authority over the external public court – like Bridges's 'outwarde setting forth and publique direction'. George Carleton in 1610 and John Bramhall in the 1650s would closely echo Horne's taxonomy.[106] Despite the variances in verbal casuistry, in essence the argument was the same: that supremacy was a jurisdictional and not sacerdotal matter. It might, and indeed should, force corrupt priests to do their duties, but this was a matter of direction and enforcement, not exercise, of such powers.[107]

Preventing supremacy from invading the sacerdotal sphere was the most important refutation of Catholic criticisms. Elizabeth's gender was relatively insignificant. Aylmer's response to Knox's gynocratic attack cohered with general discourse on supremacy when he argued that 'she hath thauthority and ouersight but not the function and practise' of ministry. His discussion – headed 'how the Quene may ouersee the churche

[102] Horne, *Answeare*, fo. 36r (qu.); Jewel, *Apologie*, fo. 60r.

[103] Nowell, *Reprovfe*, fos. 62r–63v, 233v, 61r; Jewel, *Apologie*, fo. 10v; Jewel, *Defense of the Apologie*, pp. 124–7, 380, 467.

[104] Bridges, *Supremacie of Christian Princes*, p. 1094; Jewel, *Defense of the Apologie*, sig. [A3]r; Nowell, *Reprovfe*, fo. 101r.

[105] Bridges, *Supremacie of Christian Princes*, pp. 95, 230 (qu.), 765, 783, 794 (qu.), 123; John Jewel, *A Sermon Preached Before Q. Elizabeth* (1641), sig. G2v.

[106] Bridges, *Supremacie of Christian Princes*, p. 626; Horne, *Answeare*, fo. 105r–v.

[107] Horne, *Answeare*, fos. 95v–96r; Jewel, *Defense of the Apologie*, p. 678; Nowell, *Reprovfe*, fos. 26v, 23r, 133v–134r; Bridges, *Supremacie of Christian Princes*, pp. 104–7, 119, 135, 256, 787, 802–3, 888.

and yet be no priest' – cited Moses as an example of oversight without function.[108] The limitation of the prince's sacerdotal power to the equivalent of that held (or not held) by any lay figure was an important refutation of Catholic attacks on Elizabeth, but it also usefully applied to any male supreme head.[109] There was also minimal concern about Elizabeth's new title. Cecil, Jewel, and Nowell did note the change, but briefly. Criticising Elizabeth for being supreme head was, Cecil wrote, 'a manifest lie and vntrueth'.[110] Nowell and Jewel both insinuated that Catholics had dubbed Henry supreme 'head' in order to slander him and incite opposition. Royal headship, Jewel wrote to Harding (a supporter of Henrician supremacy) was 'your fathers inuention, and not ours', 'wee diuised it not … wee vse it not … our Princes at this present claime it not'. And yet even Jewel allowed the title 'Heade of the Churche' to 'sometimes … be applied in sober meaninge, and good sense, not onely vnto *Princes*, but also vnto others, far inferiour vnto *Princes*'.[111] Furthermore, when the change of title was discussed, it was not in the context of female monarchy. Nowell came closest, since after he attributed headship to Henrician Catholic theorists he insisted 'the same right and authoritie hath an absolute Queene, as hath a kinge'. He went on to explain that

> some simple men mistooke the title of supreame head of the Church [so] it was afterwarde, for their sake mollified by these woords, chiefe gouernour &c. and an admonition also to the simple by the malitio[u]s deceiued, was to the same added.[112]

At no point did Nowell make an explicit link between queenship and the need for supreme 'governance' rather than 'headship'. Indeed, the 'admonition' to which he refers was that appended to the Injunctions of 1559, i.e. an explanation not that royal supremacy was permissible for a queen, but that it did not involve sacerdotal powers. If queens had equal rights to kings, Bridges was certain that kings had the same limitations on priestly actions as queens.[113] Not only Elizabeth, but also her brother and father were maligned by Catholic claims of a sacerdotally intrusive supremacy: 'as though [Edward] or his father toke vpon him, any *ecclesiastical*

[108] John Aylmer, *An Harborowe for Faithfull and Trewe Subiectes* (Strasbourg [London], 1559), sig. [I4]v.

[109] Here there is a parallel to Aylmer's famous assertion of mixed government at *Harborowe*, sigs. H2v–[H3]r, which applied to kings as well as queens, as his praise for those who opposed Henry VIII's desire to make his proclamations as important as statutes shows.

[110] William Cecil, *The Execution of Iustice in England* (1583), sig. B2r.

[111] Nowell, *Reprovfe*, fos. 125r–127r; Jewel, *Defense of the Apologie*, pp. 676–8.

[112] Nowell, *Reprovfe*, fos. 127v, 129v.

[113] Bridges, *Supremacie of Christian Princes*, pp. 809–11.

primacie, bicause they toke vpon them *a supreme gouernement in all ecclesiasticall matters*'.[114]

Clerical authority, it was argued, was not swamped by supremacy; indeed, it actually partnered royal power by providing counsel on true religion and doctrinal matters. Clerical counsel should never slip into papal powers to decree to, denounce, and depose kings. Uzziah had been warned off touching the Ark by his priests, but it was God who struck him with leprosy. Bishop Ambrose had forcefully criticised Theodosius, but not deposed him. Advice from godly clergy ought to be heard. 'All Princes learned and vnlearned, godlie and vngodlie, should learne of the Bishoppes, rather than teache them: and so learned and godly should the Bishoppes be, that Learned Lay men (not onely vnlearned) might be gladde to learne of them.' Jewel argued that wise kings were inferior to the humblest priest in spirituals.[115] An asymmetrical relationship existed between the spiritual superiority of the clergy and the jurisdictional supremacy of the monarch, as Bridges clearly explained. 'In their spirituall ministration [churchmen] are higher ministers: but in governing them, ouerseeing them, directing, punishing, maynteyning, placing, or displacing them, as they shall do their dueties well or yll, the Prince therein is higher than they.'[116] In treatises and sermons, members of the established Church told Elizabeth that her supremacy involved duties as well as rights, excellently outlined by Nowell:

> [Christian princes have] a speciall care to mainteine true Religion, to reforme it decaied, to restore it fallen downe, to ouersee all the Bishoppes and Cleargie, that they did their duetie, to call vppon them, to com*m*aunde them to doo their duetie, to punishe them beyng slacke … or otherwise offendinge, and to depriue and depose them vppon their iust deserte, to summon them to Synodes and Councelles, to ordre and gouerne them assembled, to know, allow, and confirme by their authoritie, lawes, and rites Ecclesiasticall, in such Synodes, for the outwarde Regiment of the Churche.[117]

The underlying purpose of supremacy was to foster godly rule.

Counsel derived from clergy: in convocation, in sermons, in private advice-giving. Did the Great Council of the realm have a role to play in this? The legitimation of supremacy occasionally slid towards a rhetoric of consent. This was used in the Lord Keeper's speech to the House of

[114] Bridges, *Supremacie of Christian Princes*, p. 854.
[115] Bridges, *Supremacie of Christian Princes*, pp. 920, 930–1, 919, 1004, 1077, 1032–3; Nowell, *Reprovfe*, fo. 110r; Jewel, *Defense of the Apologie*, p. 433.
[116] Bridges, *Supremacie of Christian Princes*, pp. 765 (qu.), 985, 845–6, 672–3.
[117] Nowell, *Reprovfe*, fo. 68r.

Commons on 25 January 1559, against the Northern Rebels of 1569, by Walter Haddon against Jerome Osório, and by Jewel.[118] In fact, Jewel began by speaking of clerical consent to supremacy and ended by invoking parliament, used by Anglo-Saxon kings to determine religious matters.[119] Catholic opponents of the supremacy were quick to scornfully deride the English Church as a 'Parlamente Religion, Parlamente Gospel, Parlamente Faithe'. Bridges and Jewel denied this to be so, the latter not only arguing that episcopal consent was not needed for statutes to be valid (important because of the exclusion of the bishops from parliament in 1559), but also sarcastically asking whether pre-Reformation England had enjoyed a 'Parlamente Faithe a Parlamente Masse, and a Parlamente Pope'.[120]

Parliament had been vital to Elizabeth's partial restoration of Henrician supremacy. In 1559 statutes unpicked Marian acts which had repealed early Tudor legislation, in 1563 the Act for the Assurance of the Queens Majesties Royal Power imposed the Oath of Supremacy on all officeholders, and throughout the reign legislation attempted to deal with recusants and (in the 1590s) sectaries. In addition, there was a steady flow of bills pursuing further reform of religion, precluded from enactment by a combination of the increasing amount of parliamentary business and royal opposition. Certain MPs, and not a few privy councillors, considered parliament had a role in governing religion and bringing abuses to royal attention. Other members, and the queen herself, disagreed. From the Alphabetical Bills of the 1560s, through puritan petitions of the 1570s and 1580s, to James Morice's attack on High Commission in the 1590s, there was tension between crown and MPs over the method as well as extent of reformation. The queen clearly felt that reforms should be considered by the bishops and convocation, and parliament brought in only if temporal legislation was needed; and some MPs, such as Francis Alford, concurred.[121] But other members loudly disagreed. In 1571 Fleetwood stated that Anglo-Saxon monarchs made ecclesiastical laws 'in their parliamentes'. He, like Peter Wentworth in 1576, insisted that the laity as well as clergy had a role in governing religion. After all, Wentworth argued, the expulsion of the pope and the restoration of true religion 'had there begining from this Howse'.[122] Calls for further reformation via parliament

[118] Hartley, ed., *Proceedings*, I.33–4; *An Aunswere to the Proclamation of the Rebels in the North* (1569), sig. A5v; Haddon, *Sight of the Portugal Pearle*, sigs. F2v, Cr, A2v.

[119] Jewel, *Apologie*, fo. 51v; Jewel, *Defense of the Apologie*, pp. 31, 621.

[120] Jewel, *Defense of the Apologie*, pp. 619–21; Bridges, *Supremacie of Christian Princes*, p. 56.

[121] Hartley, ed., *Proceedings*, I.82, 372, 256, 362.

[122] Hartley, ed., *Proceedings*, I.202, 430–2. For Restoration equivalents, see below, Chapter 2.

enraged the queen, who sent furious messages to cease such demands. These were received in varying ways. In 1572 such instructions 'semed mutch to impugne the libertie of the House, but nothinge was saied'. In November 1584, Sir William Fitzwilliam recorded that the queen's restriction of religious debate was 'thought verye straunge' since 'by searching of the recordes it appearethe that from xxi^{mo} Henry 8 … when the Pope first begann to stagger in England all ~~or the more parte~~ <vearie manie> of <the> Church matters tooke theire beginning from the Nether House'. In March 1585 the royal message that Elizabeth 'knowes and thinkes you know she ys suprem governor of this Churche next under God … by law of the crowne as by law posityve by statute', followed by a disdainful comment that reformation 'pertayned least unto them being the lowest of the iij estates', riled the Commons. Fitzwilliam recorded that the House was 'greatlie moved and deeplye wounded'.[123]

Not the least of Elizabeth's problems in restraining parliament's role in the supremacy was the fact that several of her privy councillors clearly agreed with the Houses. When James Morice attacked *ex officio* process used by the High Commission, he was praised by Knollys and protected by Burghley. Some counsellors, indeed some lawyers, were perfectly able to support an imperial account of the prerogative, along with Whitgift's crackdown on puritanism. Christopher Hatton, Elizabeth's somewhat historiographically elusive Lord Chancellor, was one such man. But others felt sympathy for a more Reformed church. For these men, like the puritans with whom they sympathised, attacking Elizabeth's authority was impossible. They therefore suggested instead that the clergy breached the royal prerogative, statute, and common law. Such claims, redolent of later Dissenting attacks on bishops, were posited by the puritan William Stoughton, both in his petitions to parliament for reform of the ministry and in his *Abstract … of Certaine Acts of Parliament* of 1583. They were pursued by Knollys, when he was nearly eighty years old, in a series of letters in 1589 moaning that *iure divino* arguments for episcopacy were in effect *praemunire*. And they appeared, perhaps with a more cynical motivation, in the Marprelate tracts of the later 1580s.[124] Having seen how early Elizabethan churchmen defended supremacy against Catholics, it

[123] Hartley, ed., *Proceedings*, I.331, II.129, 54–6, 183.

[124] Knollys to Burghley in BL, Lansdowne MS 61, nos. 47 (5 July 1589), 54 (4 Aug. 1589), 57 (15 Aug. 1589), 66 (18 Sept. 1589); see also no. 27 (Rainoldes to Knollys, 19 Sept. 1589); TNA, SP 12/221/23 (Knollys to Walsingham, 20 Mar. 1588/9). See W. D. J. Cargill Thompson, 'Sir Francis Knollys' Campaign Against the *Jure Divino* Theory of Episcopacy', in C. Robert Cole and Michael E. Moody, eds., *The Dissenting Tradition* (Athens, OH, 1975).

is therefore useful to turn to how they and their counterparts defended it against puritans in the 1580s and 1590s. Since it was these decades in which the idea of *iure divino* episcopacy emerged, a brief account of its relationship to the supremacy will also demonstrate whether or not the two were inherently incompatible.

Elizabethan Presbyterians claimed to believe in the royal supremacy. They did so in part of necessity, to appear loyal to Elizabeth while attacking the bishops. They professed, perhaps sincerely, that *iure divino* episcopacy detracted from the supremacy, being *praemunire* and treason in its introduction of a foreign government and in inciting God's wrath against England's fudged Reformation. Henry Barrow insisted that his fellow forward Protestants prayed for the queen's safety before the prelates did.[125] Stoughton urged Elizabeth to a visitation of the bishops, to 'take the entier dominion … into hir own handes'.[126] Nevertheless, the Presbyterian godly magistrate differed from the conformist one. For Cartwright and his allies, the queen should establish Presbyterianism because it was decreed in scripture, and she ought to enact what godly ministers told her to. She was a member or perhaps chief governor of the church, not its head; a nursing parent who (as Isaiah said) would 'lick up the dust' at the feet of the church. The godly ruler punished vice, banished blasphemy, and compelled all subjects to the true religion – but deferred to divines on the details on this.[127] As Peter Lake has stated, this allowed a claim to obey supremacy. But it meant presiding over Reformation and then stepping aside, not the quotidian supremacy advocated by conformists.[128] Although criticism of bishops as reprehensibly and illegally thwarting godly rule was shared by work which Lake characterises as 'moderate'

[125] Henry Barrow, *A Petition Directed to Her Most Excellent Maiestie* (S.I., 1591), p. 20 and passim; Thomas Cartwright, *A Second Admonition to the Parliament* ([Hemel Hempstead?], 1572), sig. [*4]v; Martin Marprelate, *Hay any Work for Cooper* ([Coventry, 1589]), pp. 13, 29, 37; Martin Marprelate, *Oh read ouer D. John Bridges* ([East Molesey, Surrey, 1588]), pp. 12–15, 21; Martin Marprelate, *Theses Martinianae* ([Wolston, 1589]), thesis 109; John Penry, *Th'Appellation of Iohn Penri, vnto the Highe Court of Parliament* ([La Rochelle, 1589]), p. 9; William Stoughton, *An Abstract of Certain Acts of Parliament* (1583), pp. 224, 227, 232. On divine wrath, see John Penry, *A Treatise wherein is manifestly proved …* ([Edinburgh, 1590]), sig. Þr; Penry *Th'Appellation*, pp. 14, 16.

[126] Stoughton, *Abstract*, pp. 65–6, 140 (qu.).

[127] Cartwright, *Second Admonition*, p. 8; Thomas Cartwright, *The Second Replie … against Maister Doctor Whitgiftes Second Answer* ([Heidelberg], 1575), pp. 100, 234; Marprelate, *Theses*, thesis 22; John Penry, *An Hvmble Motion with Svbmission* ([Edinburgh], 1590), pp. 43, 61–3; John Penry, *A Briefe Discouery of the Vntrvthes and Slanders (against the Trve Gouernement of the Church of Christ)* ([Edinburgh], 1590), pp. 36, 41; John Udall, *A New Discovery of Old Pontificall Practises* (printed 1643), p. 38; Stoughton, *Abstract*, pp. 92–3. Isaiah 49:23: [monarchs] 'shall bow down with their face toward the earth, and lick up the dust of thy feet'.

[128] Peter Lake, *Anglicans and Puritans? Presbyterianism and English Conformist Thought from Whitgift to Hooker* (1988), pp. 75–6, 51–2.

and 'radical', he notes that the conformist drive of the 1580s often forced off the Presbyterians' 'respectable mask'.[129] Nevertheless, attacking the bishops for undermining supremacy would remain a feature of Stuart nonconformist argument.

In response to arguments that Presbyterianism was ordained by scripture, late Elizabethan writers on episcopacy shifted their claims on to higher, *iure divino*, grounds.[130] What exactly constituted a divine right case is actually far from clear. Episcopacy might be apostolic, as the Acts and Epistles described James, bishop of Jerusalem, Timothy, and Titus (Acts 15, Gal. 1:19, 1 Tim. 1:3, Titus 1:5). But this showed God's approval more than Christ's institution. The latter (dominical episcopacy) was a stronger but harder case, resting on Christ's distinction between the Twelve Apostles (bishops) and Seventy Disciples (presbyters), in Luke 6 and 10. Even this argument was totally watertight only if it could be shown that this distinction was decreed as perpetual, to make episcopacy the *esse*, not just *bene esse*, of the church.

When Whitgift attacked Cartwright, he still treated government along with rites as *adiaphorous*, necessarily changing over time and space, and to be obeyed because of civil decrees. But he also cited the early church to show episcopacy was the best church government. In the early 1580s Richard Bancroft agreed, arguing (perhaps in a rather backwards manner) that church government must be changeable because otherwise a Christian magistrate lost their 'authoritie in causes ecclesiasticall'. Yet in a sermon of 1589 he said bishops were apostolic and it was heretical to deny it.[131] John Bridges's doorstopping *Defence of the Government Established* began by similarly denying 'any perpetual forme' was ordained, and saying civil authority chose episcopacy. But he also showed episcopacy to be settled in apostolic times, or even earlier. Augustine said Christ 'instituted Bishops'; Paul had divine warrant to ordain Titus.[132] Tortuously, Bridges argued that although episcopacy was 'not expresly, *so much the ordinaunce of God as of man*: yet bicause it is not forbidden but allowed of God, it is in a sorte euen the *ordinaunce of God* also'. He repeated this

[129] Lake, *Anglicans and Puritans*, p. 82. [130] Lake, *Anglicans and Puritans*, p. 96.

[131] John Whitgift, *An Answere to a certain Libell intituled, An Admonition to the Parliament* (1573), pp. 103, 108ff, 162, 74; *Tracts Ascribed to Richard Bancroft*, ed. Albert Peel (Cambridge, 1953), p. 112 (an almost verbatim rendition of John Whitgift, *The Defense of the Aunswere to the Admonition against the Replie of T[homas] C[artwright]* (1574), p. 660); Richard Bancroft, *A Sermon Preached at Paules Crosse the 9 of Februarie 1588* ([1589], citing STC 1347), pp. 69, 99, 102, 98.

[132] John Bridges, *A Defence of the Government Established in the Church of England for Ecclesiasticall Matters* (1587), pp. 336, 413, 388, 78–9.

in private exchanges with Knollys.[133] The seventh book of Hooker's *Lawes* allowed episcopacy to have 'either Divine appointment beforehand, or Divine approbation afterwards, and is in that respect to be acknowledged the Ordinance of God'.[134] Episcopacy as ecclesiological *esse*? Not quite. Albeit the institution was divine, its perpetuation might not be so. 'The absolute and everlasting continuance of [episcopacy], [bishops] cannot say that any Commandment of the Lord doth injoyn; And therefore must acknowledge that the Church hath power by universal consent upon urgent cause to take it away.'[135] Only three theologians, the Dutch exile Hadrian Saravia, the future bishop of Winchester, Thomas Bilson, and the dean of Exeter, Matthew Sutcliffe, argued for apostolic and dominical episcopacy as 'not to bee repealed'.[136] But if Whitgift had fallen silent by the 1590s, his patronage of Saravia and Sutcliffe hinted at his approbation of their writings, whilst Bilson's book was produced by the deputies of the royal printer Christopher Barker. In the seventeenth century, their divine right view would gain increasing hegemony.

Church government was therefore moved, to varying degrees, out of the realm of *adiaphora*, thus in theory restricting royal power over church polity. But this seems to have had only limited impact on the way supremacy was treated. Hooker repeated the well-worn argument for supremacy: the members of church and commonwealth were the same, not 'two severall [individual] impaled societies'. Hooker did not wish to dissolve the church into the polity; they are 'names which import thinges really different. But those thinges are accidentes and such accidentes as may and should alwayes lovingly dwell together in one subject.' That one subject was the territorial Church of England, Elizabeth's 'own precinctes and territories'.[137] This combination of provincial self-determination with a shared civil and ecclesiastical headship (Gardiner's argument), was also advocated by Bridges. 'Though diuersity may be in diuers states of Churches, yet in one state one vniformity.'[138] Royal supremacy was also justified as a purely juridical power; it was 'grosse error' to attribute sacerdotal supremacy to kings. Bridges

[133] Bridges, *Defence*, p. 280; BL, Add. MS 48064, fos. 229v–234r.

[134] *LEP*, VII.i.4 (p. 147), VII.v.3 (p. 161), VII.v.10 (p. 170).

[135] *LEP*, VII.v.8 (p. 168). Who constitutes the church thus becomes crucial.

[136] Hadrian Saravia, *Of the Diuerse Degrees of the Ministers of the Gospell* (1592), sig. C3r, pp. 4, 55; Thomas Bilson, *The Perpetval Gouernement of Christes Chvrch* (1593), pp. 235, 290, and 245 (bishops are needed to perpetuate the church); Matthew Sutcliffe, *A Treatise of Ecclesiasticall Discipline* (1591, citing STC 23472), pp. 43, 51.

[137] *LEP*, VIII.i.4–5 (pp. 323–5), VIII.ii.1 (pp. 332–3).

[138] Bridges, *Defence*, p. 320.

reiterated that Elizabeth wielded '(not *Ecclesiasticall Gouernment*, but) *supreame Gouernment*'.[139] So too did Bilson insist that 'Princes cannot authorize Pastours to preach the worde, administer the Sacraments, remitte sinnes, and impose handes', though they could 'see that Pastours doe their dueties'.[140] Whitgift defended calling his queen head of the church; Hooker, also refuting Cartwright, insisted that Christ's invisible headship was so clearly different from his monarch's headship of extern matters that a child could understand it.[141]

Defending royal supremacy, authors spoke of more than monarchs. Whitgift decried puritan criticism of a church settlement which had 'the common consent of the whole realme in Parliament': opposing such legislation thus meant attacking one's own decisions![142] The ecclesiastical lawyer Richard Cosin spoke of High Commission as part of the 'ancient right' of royal supremacy, but '(in trueth) a *preheminence* vnited and annexed to the *Imperiall crowne* of this realme, by *Parliament*', a 'prerogatiue roiall, and supreme gouernment (that was yeelded vnto her highnesse by statute)'.[143] For Cosin, statutes (25 Hen. VIII cc.19, 21; 5 Eliz. c. 25) legitimated and domesticated canons and archiepiscopal Faculties, and empowered royal letters patent to grant High Commissions powers of jailing and fining.[144] In Hooker the 'royal' supremacy is one according to law, parliament, and convocation, tempered by the consent of all. Hooker stressed the value of collective over individual reason, the need for the 'whole intire body' of the church to consent to ecclesiastical law, and that parliament was more than a 'meer temporall *Court*'. 'To define of our own *Churches* regiment, the *Parlament* of *England* hath competent authoritie.'[145] Sutcliffe described a supremacy 'by Gods law due and by act of Parliament vnited to the crowne, and by generall consent of the Realme … giuen'.[146] Even Saravia spoke, albeit without expansion as to whom exactly he meant, of 'the place, power, and authoritie, it hath

139 Bridges, *Defence*, pp. 1042, 93 (qu.), 710, 98–102, 1329–33, 1189, 1193. See Lake, *Anglicans and Puritans*, p. 126; *LEP*, VIII.iii.5 (p. 352), pref. vii.6 (p. 36).

140 Bilson, *Perpetval Gouernement*, pp. 149–51.

141 *LEP*, VIII.iv.5 (pp. 362–3), VIII.iv.7 (p. 370), VIII.iv.9 (pp. 377–8).

142 Whitgift, *Defense*, pp. 377 (qu.), 542, 680.

143 Richard Cosin, *An Apologie for Svndrie Proceedings by Iurisdiction Ecclesiasticall* (1593, in three parts), I.102.

144 Cosin, *Apologie*, I.103, I.106.

145 *LEP*, VIII.vi.1 (p. 386), VIII.vi.10–11 (pp. 401–4). See Lake, *Anglicans and Puritans*, pp. 208–9, 211; p. 220 places Hooker nearer Whitgift than 1590s polemicists.

146 Sutcliffe, *Treatise*, p. 128. Cf. James E. Hampson, 'Richard Cosin and the Rehabilitation of the Clerical Estate in late Elizabethan England' (Ph.D thesis, University of St Andrews, 1997), p. 264, n. 24, who sees parliamentary warrant as an insurance policy.

pleased her Maiestie *and the rest of the states*, the Bishops should reteine in this kingdome'.[147]

Despite their deference to civil authority, theorists fretted at lay intrusion into the church. Cosin's defence of ecclesiastical jurisdiction argued that civil courts committed *praemunire* if they encroached on ecclesiastical territory. Echoing the Act of Appeals, he presented temporal and ecclesiastical authority as 'both ... in their seuerall kindes supreme ... the one of them is not to be abridged, restrained, or controlled by the other'.[148] Saravia argued that one must render to God as well as to the king in proportionate measure to the extent to which God exceeds man, a comment fraught with unavoidably clericalist strains.[149] His complaints about royal seizure of church goods cannot have rung happily in English monarchical ears, since Elizabeth kept bishoprics vacant and gained the temporalities *sede vacante*.[150]

The proper relationship between kings and clergy was thus monarchs hearing clerical advice.[151] Despite their changing ecclesiology, here again late Elizabethan writers repeated the examples and ideas of their earlier counterparts. Hooker's eighth book opened with Simon, David, Jehosaphat, Hezekiah, and Josiah as the 'patterne' and 'example' of English royal supremacy.[152] Bishops' civil coercive authority derived from monarchical delegation, and they were jurisdictionally subordinate to kings. But spiritually they were superior, giving advice about piety and religious affairs. Counsel did not damage supremacy, but counsel on the church ought to, and did, come from divines.[153] Bridges, Whitgift, and Sutcliffe praised Ambrose for defying Theodosius. This was distinct from Presbyterian arguments because conformists stated that if kings erred, they could and should be admonished but they could not be excommunicated. The concept of defying kings did not stem from *iure divino* ecclesiology, but from the spiritual superiority of any pastor. 'Any priest', wrote Sutcliffe, might act like Ambrose, for every minister was 'bound to declare to princes their duties, out of the word of God, although he haue no superior iurisdiction by the word of God'.[154] Bridges concurred.[155]

147 Saravia, *Diuerse Degrees*, sig. B3r (my emphasis).

148 Cosin, *Apologie*, III.225–6 (qu.), I.120, I.130. Writs of consultation were issued in such cases.

149 Saravia, *Diuerse Degrees*, pp. 130–1.

150 Saravia, *Diuerse Degrees*, pp. 109, 220, 227.

151 For the themes of this paragraph, see Jacqueline Rose, 'Kingship and Counsel in Early Modern England', *Historical Journal*, 54 (2011), pp. 47–71.

152 *LEP*, VIII.i.1 (pp. 316–17).

153 Whitgift, *Defense*, pp. 699, 701; *LEP*, VII.xviii.5 (p. 256), VIII.vi.11 (p. 403), VIII.iii.5 (p. 353), see also VII.xviii.9 (pp. 259–60); Bridges, *Defence*, pp. 1339, 103–4, 114–16.

154 Sutcliffe, *Treatise*, p. 148.

155 Bridges, *Defence*, pp. 452, 177.

These authors grappled less with resistance to ungodly monarchy than with judicious management of a recalcitrantly godly queen. They had no notion that their ecclesiological claims or argument about counsel would disadvantage supremacy. Duties to God and the commonwealth could not conflict, Saravia wrote, 'when the Church is the Common-wealth'.[156]

Divine right episcopacy theoretically restricted the monarch's supremacy, for it removed the ability to abolish the entirety of the English church structure. That prospect was least of all likely during the late sixteenth and early seventeenth centuries – Restoration kings would prove somewhat less reliable. Those who argued for divine right bishops were in the vanguard of the late Elizabethan campaign to strengthen the crown. Whitgift crossly rejected Cartwright's account of England as a mixed monarchy.[157] Saravia wrote one of the earliest accounts of absolute monarchy. Bancroft denounced Presbyterian and Catholic resistance theory. Divine right episcopacy and divine right monarchy grew up together, not least because they shared the same enemies (papalism and Presbyterianism). This is not to argue that bishops always agreed with kings over religious policy. Elizabeth quarrelled with her early bishops over the ornaments in her Chapel Royal. She disagreed with Whitgift's Lambeth Articles on predestination. And, most famously of all, she deprived Archbishop Grindal for refusing to suppress the prophesyings. Grindal told the queen she ought not to decree ecclesiastical affairs 'so resolutely and peremptorily, *quasi ex auctoritate*, as ye may do in civil and extern matters'.[158] He did not excommunicate her. He did not need, and probably did not have, any theory of divine right episcopacy in order to defy his monarch. Divine right would be useful, therefore, in quarrels about ecclesiastical policy, in which the Grindal episode was tactfully omitted. But it was the (ab)use rather than fact of supremacy which provoked clerical claims about restricting royal power so it could not damage true religion. But if discerning true religion was difficult in the late Elizabethan period, it would become even more highly charged in the early Stuart polity. Henry VIII had not left his crown to the Scottish Stuarts, but he did inadvertently bequeath a still ambiguous ecclesiological legacy. After 1603, kings, parliaments, bishops, and nonconformists continued to argue over who held supremacy, and what they could and should do with it.

[156] Saravia, *Diuerse Degrees*, pp. 190, 191.

[157] Peter Lake, '"The Monarchical Republic of Queen Elizabeth I" (and the Fall of Archbishop Grindal) Revisited', in John F. McDiarmid, ed., *The Monarchical Republic of Early Modern England* (Aldershot, 2007).

[158] Patrick Collinson, 'If Constantine, then also Theodosius: St Ambrose and the Integrity of the Elizabethan *Ecclesia Anglicana*', *Journal of Ecclesiastical History*, 30 (1979), pp. 205–29, at p. 217.

REASSERTION: 1603–1642

The accession of James VI to the English throne in 1603 marked the restoration of the adult male monarchy for which Henrician supremacy was designed, albeit by a king whose family Henry had excluded from the succession. James I and Charles I remained supreme governors (not heads) of their English and Irish Churches, and the circumstances of their reigns required the reassertion of justifications of supremacy against both Catholic and Presbyterian opponents. The years between 1603 and 1642 witnessed explosive debates over religion, the ecclesiological dimensions of which have attracted much historiographical debate. Alongside questions of the theology of grace and practices of worship lay ones about who enforced uniformity and under what warrant: issues about the relative roles of crown, parliament, and convocation in governing English religion.[159] Early Stuart monarchs had problems with their churches and they had problems reflected in their churches, not least the dynamics of multiple monarchy and the congruity of the churches of the Three Kingdoms.[160] Royal supremacy affected these debates, for it was in their capacity as supreme governors that James and Charles presided over religious conferences, appointed bishops, and authorised new canons, articles, and prayer books. Conversely, wider quarrels infected discussions of supremacy. Puritan objections to the content of ecclesiastical policy were bolstered by the ability to claim that the mechanisms which enforced that content, High Commission and ecclesiastical canons, were of dubious legality because they were not authorised by common law and parliament. Heightened political tension manifested itself ecclesiologically in claims that bishops who claimed authority *iure divino* committed *praemunire*, and assertions that common lawyers and MPs who questioned royal policy subverted supremacy.

The case for supremacy was reiterated both institutionally and polemically. The second canon of 1604 excommunicated anyone who denied the king's supremacy. The thirty-sixth canon required subscription to Whitgift's Three Articles, the first of which upheld supremacy. In the

159 On ecclesiology, see Nicholas Tyacke, 'Puritanism, Arminianism and Counter-Revolution', in Conrad Russell, ed., *The Origins of the English Civil War* (Basingstoke, 1975); Julian Davies, *The Caroline Captivity of the Church: Charles I and the Remoulding of Anglicanism, 1625–1641* (Oxford, 1992); Anthony Milton, *Catholic and Reformed: The Roman and Protestant Churches in English Protestant Thought, 1600–1640* (Cambridge, 1995); Charles W. A. Prior, *Defining the Jacobean Church: The Politics of Religious Controversy, 1603–1625* (Cambridge, 2005).

160 John Morrill, 'A British Patriarchy? Ecclesiastical Imperialism under the Early Stuarts', in Anthony Fletcher and Peter Roberts, eds., *Religion, Culture and Society in Early Modern Britain* (Cambridge, 1994).

aftermath of the Gunpowder Plot, the European controversy over the Oath of Allegiance provoked treatments of the rise of papal depositions of kings, and stimulated attention to medieval history.[161] Early Stuart defenders of supremacy included more discussion of high medieval papalism and of Catholic divisions between conciliarists and papalists than their Tudor predecessors had. This section first demonstrates how the examples, powers, and limits of royal supremacy were reiterated, before showing how divine right episcopacy and supremacy cohered for divines like George Carleton and William Laud. Finally, the increasingly bitter spats between crown, parliament, and lawyers over ecclesiastical jurisdiction will be outlined; quarrels more oppositional than they had been under Elizabeth, but which did not necessarily follow a simple trajectory of increasing challenges between 1603 and 1640.

During his entry to London in 1604, James I was greeted with representations of himself as David, Solomon, and that staple of godly kingship, Josiah. In a sermon *coram rege* that same year, Anthony Rudd urged James to model himself on Solomon but shun Uzziah's example, while a generation later John Donne urged Charles I to take Josiah as his pattern.[162] Donne described James's supremacy as based 'upon the steps of the *Kings of Judah*, of the *Christian Emperours* … of all the *Kings of England* that embraced the Reformation'. Constantine remained an important model as well. The historian John Hayward was atypical in drawing on non-Christian models for sovereign supremacy in religion, but even he mentioned Constantine.[163] As under the Tudors, Israelite and Christian imperial examples had a twofold meaning, demonstrating both the powers of kings and their duties. The royal chaplain Richard Eedes praised Theodosius for thinking his membership of the church better than his headship of the world. The Irish prelate Malcolm Hamilton warned Charles I that he had a duty to compel Catholics to come into the true church, for a pious king could not choose when to be godly. Negligent Israelite kings had, after all, been punished by God.[164] Such

161 J. P. Sommerville, 'Jacobean Political Thought and the Controversy over the Oath of Allegiance' (Ph.D thesis, University of Cambridge, 1981).

162 Graeme Murdock, 'The Importance of being Josiah: An Image of Calvinist Identity', *Sixteenth Century Journal*, 29 (1998), pp. 1043–59, at p. 1051; Anthony Rudd, *A Sermon Preached at the Covrt at Whitehall before the Kings Maiesty … the 13 of May 1604* (1604), pp. 3–4; John Donne, *Sermons*, ed. George R. Potter and Evelyn M. Simpson (10 vols., 1953–62), VIII.180.

163 Donne, *Sermons*, IV.201 (qu.), VIII.183; John Hayward, *Of Supremacie in Affaires of Religion*, 2nd edn (1624), p. 44.

164 Richard Eedes, *Six Learned and Godly Sermons* (1604), fo. 9r; Alan Ford, 'Criticising the Godly Prince: Malcolm Hamilton's *Passages and Consultations*', in Vincent P. Carey and Ute Lotz-Heumann, eds., *Taking Sides? Colonial and Confessional Mentalités in Early Modern Ireland* (Dublin, 2003), pp. 136, 123, 135.

warnings were entirely compatible with a belief in divine right kingship, because they insisted on God's sole right to punish kings, neatly denying papal deposing. This did not mean that the English Church became a supine source of flattery. Agreeing that Catholics were wrong in permitting the deposing power, William Goodwin preached to the king in 1614 that 'wee may reproue, not chastise, reprehend not punish, depresse not depose: to vs your soules, to you our Bodies are committed'. God – not David – deposed Saul. James himself used the same example in 1615, alongside a denial that Uzziah's priests had removed him.[165]

Alongside continuing assertions that the Church submitted to kings' supremacy but counselled them against abuses of it came repeated insistence that supremacy was not sacerdotal. Kings, Donne explained,

> are supreame heads of the Church; But they minister not the Sacraments of the Church. They give preferments; but they give not the capacity of preferment. They give order who shall have; but they give not orders, by which they are enabled to have, that have.[166]

Donne saw the Church as regulating fundamental doctrinal truths and kings governing *adiaphora*. Imperial moderation of synods, James commented, did not mean that emperors judged questions of faith.[167] The careful balancing of episcopal authority with kingly power would allow divine right bishops and kings to coexist before 1660. They might continue to complement each other when Restoration monarchs leaned towards the established Church.

A cynosure of Jacobean argument was the tract published by George Carleton, later bishop of Chichester, in 1610. The first three chapters of *Ivrisdiction Regall, Episcopall, Papall* justified supremacy on well-worn lines (despite Carleton's claim of novelty).[168] The universal catholic church was headed by Christ, but particular churches were jurisdictionally self-sufficient 'for many Churches, many gouernours', either spiritual (bishops) or temporal (kings). The church's royal governor was emphatically not to meddle with sacramental functions, nor with internal jurisdiction over conscience, only with external jurisdiction.[169] This accorded with the 1559 Injunctions, with the *external* episcopate of Constantine, and prevented

165 William Goodwin, *A Sermon Preached Before the King … August 28 1614* (Oxford, 1614), pp. 9 (qu.), 34–5, and passim; James VI and I, 'A Remonstrance for the Right of Kings', in *Political Works*, ed. Charles Howard McIlwain (Cambridge, 1918), pp. 213–15.

166 Quoted in Jeanne Shami, 'Kings and Desperate Men: John Donne Preaches at Court', *John Donne Journal*, 6 (1987), pp. 9–23, at p. 14.

167 Shami, 'Donne Preaches', p. 14; James VI and I, 'Remonstrance', p. 212.

168 George Carleton, *Ivrisdiction Regall, Episcopall, Papall* (1610), sig. ¶ 3v.

169 Carleton, *Ivrisdiction*, pp. 5–9, 42–3; the threefold distinction is akin to Horne's.

English kings from repeating Uzziah's error. Moses had consecrated Aaron, but only by an extraordinary divine commission. Strikingly, such comments did not preclude Carleton from calling his monarch *mixta persona*, whereas in the Restoration the same sentiments would lead to a rejection of the epithet.[170] For the Jacobean bishop, kings kept both Tables of the Law, and from them flowed 'a fountain of Iurisdiction, derived as it were into two inferior rivers', spiritual and temporal – a silent reassertion of the Act of Appeals.[171]

Carleton turned to episcopal jurisdiction in chapter 4 of his book, mounting a strong case for bishops as 'placed by the Apostles, to stand and continue till the end of the world'. Christ himself had established equality amongst the apostles (no Petrine supremacy), but also raised them above the Seventy Disciples (*pace* Presbyterians).[172] Carleton unashamedly asserted bishops' duty to critique erring monarchs, as Ambrose had Theodosius, an act 'worthily commended by all posterity'. Bishops might excommunicate, but could not depose, kings.[173] When they met in councils they – not emperors – judged questions of faith. But they undoubtedly established a partnership with temporal rulers so that 'Kings receiue the knowledge of faith and Religion from the Church, and not the Church from Kings: so coactive Iurisdiction the Church receiueth from Kings, and not Kings from the Church'.[174] Chapters 5 to 7 narrated the rise of papal jurisdiction, in three stages: 300 to 500, 600 to 1066, and its peak from 1066 to 1300. This followed earlier accounts in emphasising Phocas giving away imperial rights, the subsequent decline of kings, and popes forging canons to claim superiority over bishops.[175] Carleton also reflected specifically Jacobean interests in his inclusion of a lengthy account of the rise of the deposing power.[176] His final chapter outlined medieval opposition to popes from within the church, with a hint of conciliar preferences. This insisted that the Reformation was a separation from the Court not Church of Rome or, rather, that it was the Roman Church's separation from the true faith.[177] This would be developed in the 1650s.

Carleton sought to reconcile royal supremacy with the spiritual authority of bishops. 'The spirituall Iurisdiction of the Church aboue Princes … we never denied … the coactive Iurisdiction of Princes in matters Ecclesiasticall … we hold.'[178] Such a reconciliation was widely

170 Carleton, *Ivrisdiction*, pp. 4, 60, 63, 27, 17, 15, 35. See below, p. 158.
171 Carleton, *Ivrisdiction*, pp. 33, 22.
172 Carleton, *Ivrisdiction*, pp. 41 (qu.), 47.
173 Carleton, *Ivrisdiction*, pp. 44–5 (qu.), 52.
174 Carleton, *Ivrisdiction*, pp. 61–2.
175 Carleton, *Ivrisdiction*, pp. 81, 84ff, 100–14.
176 Carleton, *Ivrisdiction*, pp. 188–241.
177 Carleton, *Ivrisdiction*, pp. 258.
178 Carleton, *Ivrisdiction*, Admonition to the Reader.

shared. Bishop John King of London wrote that monarchs were nursing fathers *and* servants of the church, and Bishop George Downame of Derry of the spiritual supremacy of bishops. Francis Bacon insisted that churchmen did not threaten sovereignty unless they derived their power from a foreign authority or popular election.[179] But increasingly clericalist sentiment opened a loophole to claims that the rising generation of churchmen disdained their king's authority. The reported words of John Cosin, bishop of Durham, '[the king] is not supreme heade of the Church of England next under Christ, nor haith he anie more poore [power] of excommunication than my man that rubs my horse['s] heeles', were technically true (the king was supreme governor, and he did not hold sacerdotal powers). But they were so blunt that they caused Cosin to be cited before parliament by a prebendary, Peter Smart, who saw an opportunity to score a point against the ritualism which he disliked, and which Cosin promoted.[180] The idea that bishops had come to undermine supremacy was not new, as shown above, but it did acquire new force with the advent of Laudian churchmanship under Charles I, a sentiment which continued after 1660.

Laud believed in the dignity of the clerical estate, and he had a programme for increasing respect for it. All churches until the latter age had bishops, he argued, and their order was established when Christ called the Twelve Apostles and 'made them bishops'. 'He chose them out with a special ordination to a higher function.'[181] Thus the core power of bishops and their jurisdiction integral to this (*in foro conscientiae*) was *iure divino*, albeit the extra powers they were given (*in foro contentioso*) and the exercise of their function, was *iure humano*.[182] Laud's clericalist attitude was far from being papalist. Attacking the Jesuit Fisher, he insisted that church Fathers like Cyprian honoured Rome but did not submit to papal supremacy, for the African church separated itself from Rome, as did Britain under her own patriarch. Since the early church was aristocratic, not monarchical, Rome's extra authority derived from emperors such as Phocas, not from Petrine succession.[183] Laud professed allegiance to the catholic church, of which Rome was only a particular member. 'The Church of Christ is neither Rome, nor a conventicle.'[184] This church

179 Prior, *Jacobean Church*, pp. 129, 141–2; Francis Bacon, 'Of Empire', in *The Essayes or Counsels, Civill and Morall*, ed. Michael Kiernan (Oxford, 1985), p. 62.

180 Anthony Milton, 'John Cosin', *ODNB*.

181 William Laud, *Works* (7 vols., Oxford, 1847–60), VI.172 (qu.), 169, I.82, III.262.

182 Laud, *Works*, III.406–7, IV.196.

183 Laud, *Works*, II.7–8, 190–3, 222, 186, 198–9.

184 Laud, *Works*, II.346, xvii (qu.).

was visible, but it was not infallible; not only the pope, but also general councils, might err.[185] Laud conceived of the Reformation as the cleansing of the particular English church, legitimately done at a national level when universal reform was impossible. At his trial he spoke of the 'power which a National Church hath with leave and approbation of the supreme power, to alter and change any alterable thing pertaining to doctrine or discipline in the church'.[186] Like many Caroline theologians, he saw the origins of the Church of England not in medieval separatists but in the institutional Catholic Church.[187] 'We live in a Church reformed, not in one made new.' As a consequence, he argued that his Church separated only from the errors of Rome, not from her true credal fundamentals; or rather that Rome had separated from her original true faith and thrust out reformers. Rome, not England, was therefore causally guilty of schism, a theme which Laud's colleagues refined in Interregnum polemic against Catholics.[188]

A fundamental difficulty for historians is unpicking whether Laud or Charles initiated the reform programme of the 1630s. The great irony of that decade was that it witnessed the perfect symbiosis of episcopacy and supremacy, even as it was so destructive in other ways. The church which had reformed itself with the approbation of the supreme power was, in Laud's eyes, a partner of the polity. In his sermons to James and Charles he spoke of the 'one Jerusalem' in Hookerian terms:

> Both so near allied, that the one, the Church, can never subsist but in the other, the Commonwealth; nay, so near, that the same men, which in a temporal respect make the Commonwealth, do in a spiritual make the Church; so one name of the mother City serves both.[189]

They flourished together and declined together. Their complementary roles were shown by (for example) convocation deciding what constituted heresy, and parliament enacting a law against it.[190] Laud's belief that clergy should serve the polity and that state councils should heed clerical advice was reiterated in 1641 when parliament sought to exclude clergy from civil offices. Bishops and the state, the archbishop said, gained much from each other; only papal bishops were a danger.[191] Laud's defence of

185 Laud, *Works*, visibility: II.3–23, 181, 210, 292ff; councils: II.32, 214–16, 252–91.

186 Laud, *Works*, II.167, III.322 (qu.).

187 Milton, *Catholic and Reformed*.

188 Laud, *Works*, II.152, 150, 159; III.376, 341 (qu.).

189 Laud, *Works*, I.6; see also pp. 23–4, 64. Hooker's constitutionalist version would not have been shared by Laud.

190 Laud, *Works*, I.112, 121, IV.352.

191 Laud, *Works*, VI.216 and pp. 147–233 passim.

episcopacy and monarchy permitted his paradoxical impeachment both for upholding royal authority *and* for subverting it.

Laud was reticent on the royal supremacy. He attacked Bellarmine on religious points, but only briefly denied the papal deposing power.[192] Although he said little about royal powers over the church, his sermons called James 'God's vicegerent' and Charles 'another Hezekiah'. His refutation of Fisher spoke of the king's duty to keep both Tables, on the models of Hezekiah, Josiah, Theodosius, and Charlemagne. He defended his opposition to common law restrictions on ecclesiastical jurisdiction by saying the king was the source of both civil and ecclesiastical jurisdiction, echoing the Act of Appeals.[193] During the 1630s Laud sought royal authorisation of altar policy and it was Charles who ordered that convocation continue sitting after the Short Parliament had been dissolved.[194] For Laud, a clericalist outlook and obedience to his monarch were compatible.

In the 1630s, there was little polemical need for Laud to enunciate any ways in which divine right episcopacy might restrain royal meddling in the church. In the 1640s, pressure of circumstances forced him to say more. Thus he told Saye and Sele, who advocated banning bishops from civil offices, that he doubted 'whether a company of laymen, without any order or ordinance from Christ ... may, without the Church, take upon them to prune and order this vine [of episcopacy]'.[195] Speaking at his trial on Joseph Hall's defence of episcopacy, Laud explained that 'all the primitive Church all along, gives Bishops to be the Apostles' successors; and then it would be well thought on, what right any Christian state hath (be their absolute power what it will) to turn Bishops out of that right in the Church which Christ hath given them'. A few days later, he admitted that the king and parliament had the legal power to change Christianity to another religion, but argued that they lacked the moral legitimacy to do so. Nothing could have been further from St German's trust in parliament than Laud's denial that it was to be thought morally infallible.[196] For Laud, the state supported rather than determined religious policy. Because he and Charles agreed on the content of religious change in the 1630s, the likelihood of a clash between episcopacy and supremacy was low; only the events of the 1640s would provoke this. Laud's comments at his trial showed the latent potential for *iure divino* episcopacy to restrict

[192] Laud, *Works*, II.376–7. [193] Laud, *Works*, I.116; II.228–9; IV.137.
[194] Davies, *Caroline Captivity*, pp. 253–4. [195] Laud, *Works*, VI.171.
[196] Laud, *Works*, IV.312 (qu.), 353, 361; VI.233.

supremacy, but that was only actualised and enunciated under specific political pressures. By 1640, religious and political tensions had reached a tipping point. The canons made that year only added to the anger of those who had long perceived supremacy ought to lie in other hands and should be used for other purposes.

The canons of 1640 reflected Laudian principles in their contentious defence of divine right monarchy and clerical authority. They reiterated that kings were to care for the church, that they could 'call and dissolve councils', and that it was treason to uphold 'any independent coactive power, either papal or popular'. These were the principles of royal supremacy, although the phrase went unmentioned. The canons encapsulated themes that annoyed a number of different groups. Some disliked the second canon's declaration that 'the most high and sacred order of kings is of divine right', not to be resisted, and which subjects had a duty to supply; claims contentious both for their content and for being propounded by clergy, who were not in charge of property. The oath contained in the sixth canon, possibly drafted by Charles himself, was poorly worded as well as provocative. The *double entendre* of a promise not 'to bring in any Popish doctrine, contrary to that which is so established' riled puritans who saw quite enough popery already. The vow not 'to alter the government of this Church by archbishops, bishops, deans, and archdeacons, etc.' infuriated puritan-Presbyterians and laity resentful of clericalism. The implication of unchangeable church-polity also detracted from the royal supremacy, which went unmentioned or was demoted to 'etc.' – no good word for an oath anyway. When Charles failed to recall the proclamation ordering swearing of the oath, a decree which left out 'popish', he (characteristically) worsened an inflamed situation.[197]

If the content of the canons was unpopular, their legality was dangerously questionable because they had been made in a convocation of dubious legitimacy, for it had continued to sit after the Short Parliament had been dissolved. In 1682, the lawyer John Brydall found the paper office held copies of parliament's resolutions on the power of convocation to make canons and on those made in 1640. He also located a judge's notes arguing convocation should continue until the king dissolved it, even if parliament were dissolved.[198] This was unprecedented for a post-Reformation convocation, as even Laud noted. The Submission of the

[197] 1640/1, 1640/6 (text in Gerald Bray, ed., *The Anglican Canons, 1529–1947* (Woodbridge, 1998), pp. 558–9, 568–9). See Davies, *Caroline Captivity*, ch. 7 and pp. 275–7; and John Wilde, *The Impeachment Against the Bishops* (1641), pp. 2–3; Nathaniel Fiennes, *A Second Speech … Touching the Subject's Liberty* (1641).

[198] Bodl., Tanner MS 271, fo. 62r–v.

Clergy had laid down the need for *royal* summons and dissolution of convocation, and *royal* ratification of its canons, and these the meeting of 1640 had. But the Submission was enacted in statute, and parliament might claim it too ought to ratify canons if they were to become laws binding laity as well as clergy. In 1610, parliament had debated a bill that 'no canon, constitution, or ordinance ecclesiastical heretofore made, constituted, or ordained within the space of ten years last past or hereafter to be made, constituted, or ordained, shall be of any force or effect by any means whatsoever to impeach or hurt any person in his or their life, liberty, lands, or goods, until the same be first confirmed by act of parliament'. Some urged the revival of the defunct *reformatio legum ecclesiasticarum*, and one member even insisted that parliament, not the bishops and convocation, should determine heresy (echoing the Elizabethan Act of Supremacy).[199] Tensions between lay and ecclesiastical law were already high in 1610 owing to anger over High Commission. Another draft bill would have banned the use of *ex officio* process on pain of *praemunire*.[200] Many common lawyers detested this procedure as contrary to English law and forcing self-accusation, and they hated the High Commission for trespassing on their professional turf. In the early seventeenth century they used prohibitions increasingly aggressively to disrupt High Commission's proceedings, and they may have collusively encouraged one of their number, Nicholas Fuller, to deliberately force a test case on High Commission.[201] Not every lawyer thought thus: Thomas Egerton, Baron Ellesmere, wrote that to question High Commission was to question the prerogative – but he had a personal interest in defending jurisdiction outside common law in his capacity as chancellor, presiding over equity.[202] But the most prominent Jacobean common lawyer, Edward Coke, supported Fuller.

In the 1590s Coke had defended the legality of the Commission in imperialist language in the famous Caudrey's Case. Even if the 1559 Act of Supremacy had never been made, Coke declared, the queen might use her ecclesiastical prerogative to create High Commission; and he cited medieval history to prove the antiquity (immemoriality) of royal supremacy.[203] But under James he questioned the Commission's right to fine and jail,

199 Elizabeth Read Foster, ed., *Proceedings in Parliament, 1610* (2 vols., New Haven, 1966), 1.85, 124 and n., 125, 233, 127. The bill lapsed when Bancroft, who held it, died.

200 HMC, *House of Lords, vol. XI (addenda)*, pp. 125–6.

201 See Brooks, *Law, Politics and Society*, pp. 97–118 and Roland G. Ussher, *The Rise and Fall of the High Commission* (Oxford, 1913), chs. 7–10.

202 Foster, ed., *Proceedings in Parliament, 1610*, 1.279–80.

203 Cf. Brooks, *Law, Politics and Society*, p. 120, which has a less imperialist interpretation than Guy, 'Elizabethan Establishment', pp. 132–3.

arguing that the clergy had no such power before the Elizabethan Act of Supremacy, and that the statute of 1559 did not empower the monarch to grant it to them. Statute governed royal letters patent; parliament limited royal supremacy. Coke's *Institutes* also listed examples of prohibitions to High Commission even in purely ecclesiastical causes; common lawyers limited delegated royal supremacy. He insisted that parliament constrained the powers of bishops to define heresy and that common lawyers interpreted parliament's laws on this.[204] And, discussing *praemunire*, he translated the medieval laws which banned use of Rome or 'autre court', *curia Romana et alibi*, as 'other Courts within this Realm', *per aliam legem* or *ad aliud examen*. Pressing his point, Coke noted that some denied this because post-Reformation ecclesiastical jurisdiction derived from the crown (in the Act of Appeals). But Coke thought *praemunire* still applied, for it was mentioned in 24 Henry VIII, *after* supremacy was admitted in convocation, and it was clear in Marian legislation. 'Ecclesiastical Courts within the Realm are within this word [alibi].'[205] Alibi applied even to Admiralty and chancery, and Coke fought a protracted battle with Ellesmere over chancery's jurisdiction using *praemunire*.[206] Coke was not above defending royal supremacy, for example justifying royal commissions of review of ecclesiastical judgements, for the king had 'such authority as the Pope had'. He defended the Act of Appeals, the title *defensor fidei*, and the concept that English kings held imperial not feudatory jurisdiction.[207] But Coke's pride in English common law led him not only to delineate royal supremacy by the boundaries of statutes, but also to measure those boundaries by common law. This slippage from king to parliament to common law sounded like St German, and citations of *Doctor and Student* bespattered Coke's discussions.

Coke was the most famous proponent of such rhetoric, but a less well-known lawyer, Edward Bagshaw, takes the theme forward into the 1630s and 1640s.[208] Bagshaw's war against clerical jurisdiction was waged in his legal practice, in speeches in the Long Parliament, and (until Laud stopped it) his reading of 1640 – an apt example of the variety of sources in which early Stuart political thinking can be found. Bagshaw had intended his Middle Temple reading to be on prohibitions, but thought

204 Coke, *Fourth Institutes*, pp. 324–35; Edward Coke, *The Third Part of the Institutes of the Lawes of England*, 4th edn (1669), p. 43.

205 Coke, *Third Institutes*, pp. 119–23.

206 Coke, *Third Institutes*, pp. 122–6; J. H. Baker, 'The Common Lawyers and the Chancery: 1616', *The Irish Jurist*, n.s. 4 (1969), pp. 368–92.

207 Coke, *Fourth Institutes*, pp. 341–5.

208 Brooks, *Law, Politics and Society*, pp. 218–20.

that too contentious, so instead chose the statute *pro clero* (25 Edw. III c. 7). The result hardly favoured the clergy, as Bagshaw made clear when he opened his reading by announcing his resolution to 'choose some statute that should advance *th*e com*m*on Law of this Land above *th*e Civill and Canon Lawes'.[209] Edward III was a hero for Bagshaw because his legislation was the most antipapal before the Reformation. All clerical rights came from royal grants, Bagshaw insisted, but this monarchist moment soon gave way to a declaration that after Henry VIII, 'all' ecclesiastical rights and laws 'are wholly subject to *th*e Com*m*on Law from whence they were first derived and are ruled and overruled by it'.[210] Four points were crucial. Firstly, Bagshaw insisted that an act of parliament might pass without any bishops being present. This was necessary to justify 'that most excellent statute of 1° Eliz. c. 1 et 2' (and, as Bagshaw would discover two years later, would become vital to defending the Long Parliament's legislation).[211] He later claimed that this was accepted by Lord Keeper Finch, when Bagshaw said that the equivalent applied to temporal lords – and in Littleton's copy of notes on Bagshaw's reading is written '*th*e like if *th*e lay Lords absent or disassenting'.[212] Secondly, Bagshaw denied that clergy could be JPs or exercise civil jurisdiction.[213] Thirdly, he restricted episcopal jurisdiction over heresy.[214] And fourthly, he attacked High Commission. Had he not been silenced at his point, he would have limited the Commission's jurisdiction to the worst offences, as defined by the judges; and denied their authority as a 'meer Eccl*esiasti*call Court' to fine and jail.[215] This became more imperative as he himself was threatened with a citation before it.[216] Bagshaw cited St German and Fortescue and followed Edward Coke's account and examples when saying that ecclesiastical courts could be sued for *praemunire*, albeit denying the application to chancery.[217] Bagshaw also

209 BL, Stowe MS 424, fos. 3r–38r, at fo. 3r; Edward Bagshaw, *A Just Vindication of the Questioned Part of the Reading* (1660), p. 15. Unless otherwise specified, quotations are taken from Stowe MS 424.

210 BL, Stowe MS 424, fos. 4r–5r.

211 BL, Stowe MS 424, fo. 12v; Sir William Thomas, *A Speech … Concerning the Right of Bishops Sitting and Voting* (1641), p. 5; Bagshaw, *Vindication*, pp. 9, 17–22.

212 CUL, MS Mm 6.62, fos. 29r–30r; Bagshaw, *Vindication*, p. 11; 'good law, but not seasonably delivered', according to Finch: *CSPD, 1639–40*, p. 523.

213 BL, Stowe MS 424, fos. 15v–16r; Bagshaw, *Vindication*, pp. 10, 22–5; Maija Jansson, ed., *Two Diaries of the Long Parliament* (Gloucester, 1984), p. 106.

214 BL, Stowe MS 424, fos. 17v–20r; Bagshaw, *Vindication*, pp. 10, 26–32.

215 BL, Stowe MS 424, fos. 23r–26r (qu. 24v), Bagshaw, *Vindication*, pp. 33–42.

216 *CSPD, 1639–40*, pp. 213, 286; TNA, SP 16/437/58, fos. 86v–89r (an apt example of the Commission claiming to rectify Bagshaw's conscience, and thus stepping outside common law).

217 BL, Stowe MS 424, fos. 25v, 28r–29r.

knew his Reformation statutes. He urged Henrician ones to purge corrupt canon laws, as drafted under Edward VI. He praised Edwardian laws which allowed appointment of bishops by royal letters patent, seeing consecration as fairly insignificant.[218] And he urged that laity might excommunicate, though he admitted that no extant law permitted it. Where others applied papal powers to kings, Bagshaw transferred them to parliament: 'a Parli*ame*n*t* may excom*m*unicate'. 'What was said heretofore … Papa potest o*mn*ia is now turned by those Parliam*en*ts w*hi*ch took away his Power Parliamentum potest o*mn*ia. And it is a Rule in *th*e Canon Law that Papa potest Laico potestatem excomunicandi committere ergo a Parliament much more.'[219]

With his curtailed reading 'common discourse' in London,[220] Bagshaw was elected to parliament in 1640. There he continued his campaign as a member of committees on elections, on the state of the kingdom, on Laudian bishops, and on Leighton (the last expanded to consider Lilburne), and defending Peter Smart for his comments on Cosin's sneering at the supremacy. In speeches, some printed, some not, Bagshaw complained of *ex officio* process and High Commission, of episcopal courts kept in bishops' own names contrary to Edwardian law, and of Hall's defence of divine right prelacy.[221] Most significant of all was his attack on the canons of 1640, 'made out of Parliament and so consequently out of Convocation'.[222] The canons' content was *ipso facto* void, for they meddled in property and imposed oaths. The canons were 'a Covenant against the King's supremacy', by denying the king could alter church government 'by his Parliament', either omitting supremacy or hiding it in 'etc.': 'a most unworthy place for so great a Majesty'. By passing them, the clergy were guilty of *praemunire*. Indeed, the common law 'should not in our case be just … if they of the Convocation should not incurre a Premunire'.[223] Bagshaw exploited a rhetoric of royal supremacy against the clergy but he mixed monarchy with parliament. The Act of Submission said canons needed the king's assent, 'which may be interpreted his assent in Parliament, as well his assent and confirmation by his letters Pattents …

218 BL, Stowe MS 424, fo. 29v.

219 BL, Stowe MS 424, fo. 26v.

220 *CSPD, 1639–40*, pp. 522–4; Brooks, *Law, Politics and Society*, p. 221. Archbishop Ussher's library contained a copy: Bodl., Tanner MS 271.

221 Edward Bagshaw, *Mr Bagshaw's Speech in Parliament February the Ninth, 1640* (1641), pp. 2, 6–7. Bagshaw opposed Presbyterianism. See Maija Jansson, ed., *Proceedings in the Opening Session of the Long Parliament, House of Commons*, vol. 1 (Rochester, NY, 2000), pp. 36, 40–1, 43, 47, 60, 64, 76–7, 79, 81, 87–9.

222 Edward Bagshaw, *Two Arguments in Parliament* (1641), p. 13.

223 Bagshaw, *Two Arguments*, pp. 17, 37.

this seems to be the meaning of that Act, that the Parliament should have a Power in establishing the Canons of the Clergie'.[224]

Bagshaw believed in the supremacy of king-in-parliament. He gave money to the Parliamentarian side in the First Civil War, but he did so 'for the preservation of the kinge and parliament ... conjunctively and not divided, and in noe other manner'.[225] 1642 was the last time in a generation that both sides of mixed monarchy could be kept in the balance or treated ambiguously in the way in which lawyers from St German to Bagshaw had done. In 1644, Bagshaw was jailed by parliament; in 1660, he published a defence of royal rights established by law. Hard as moderate Parliamentarians and constitutional royalists sought a compromise in the 1640s, they failed to prevent ultimate choices between mixed and coordinate monarchy, and royal or parliamentary sovereignty. In the 1640s, parliament was forced to govern without the crown, and as part of that process it seized ecclesiastical supremacy for itself.

REVOLUTION? 1642–1660

Ecclesiastical supremacy was a peculiarly English addition to Bodin's marks of sovereignty. As such, it was natural that its location before the 1640s was difficult to decipher and that during the Civil War it was appropriated by parliament. In that disruptive decade, parliament authorised a new liturgy to replace Common Prayer, set down who could preach, and sought to govern excommunication. Parliament vetted Laud's candidates for benefices and it deprived him *ab officio et beneficio* in June 1643.[226] It nominated a vicar-general for Canterbury and in November 1644 appointed Nathaniel Brent a judge of the prerogative court of Canterbury. Ironically, Brent replaced a royalist but was to hold the court in the king's name and use the royal arms on his seal, recalling Edwardian legislation.[227]

Parliament's desire to check any form of clericalism was shown in its relationship with the Westminster Assembly called to advise 'a further and more perfect Reformation'. Advise was the salient word: the Ordinance of 12 June 1643 stated that the Assembly should discuss questions which

[224] Bagshaw, *Two Arguments*, p. 10; Jansson, ed., *Long Parliament Proceedings*, p. 81.

[225] F. Kyffin Lenthall, 'A List of the Names of the Members of the House of Commons that advanced Horse, Money, and Plate for Defence of the Parliament, June 10, 11, and 13, 1642', *Notes and Queries*, 1st ser., 12 (1855), pp. 358–60, at p. 359.

[226] C. H. Firth and R. S. Rait, eds., *Acts and Ordinances of the Interregnum* (3 vols., 1911), 1.157–8, 176; on preaching: 1.677.

[227] Firth and Rait, eds., *Acts and Ordinances*, 1.564–6.

either or both Houses of parliament suggested 'and no other', and it barred the divines from any jurisdiction. In August 1645 parliament ordered that the proposed national synod would 'meet when they shall be summoned by Parliament ... sit and continue as the Parliament shall order, and not otherwise'. These orders echoed limitations on convocation – and the Assembly sat in the Jerusalem Chamber, where convocation had previously gathered.[228] In spring 1646, the Commons complained that the Assembly sought to control rather than give advice on a settlement, and voted the Assembly's resolutions of 23 March 1645 a breach of privilege. Parliament insisted it had 'jurisdiction in all causes, spiritual and temporal'. 'The Parliament doth not pretend to an infallibility of judgement and the Parliament suppose[s] this Assembly will not do so either' snapped one MP. Another ominously mentioned *praemunire*.[229] The sense of a subordinate synod is corroborated in the correspondence of one of the Scottish commissioners in attendance, Robert Baillie, who was astonished that the Assembly needed parliament's permission to write to Scottish Presbyterians. 'This is no proper Assemblie', Baillie moaned, 'but a meeting called by the Parliament to advyse them in what things they are asked.'[230] The desire to hear clerical counsel but not to be ruled by it perpetuated rhetorics originally about royal supremacy and bishops by adapting them into ones about parliaments and Presbyterians.

Relations between the Assembly and parliament were truly derailed in late 1645 and early 1646 by the question of excommunication. In October 1645 an ordinance listed the offences for which laity could be excluded from receiving the sacrament. The appeals system which this set down ended not with a national synod but with parliament. A committee of MPs would also judge suspension for sins unspecified in the ordinance, all MPs could try cases in their own parish, and all were exempted from suspension.[231] This system might have reflected ante-bellum ideas, such as the inexcommunicability of sovereigns, and royal commissions of review of ecclesiastical courts. But it was far from a true Presbyterian system which would give ministers freedom to judge what behaviour warranted suspension. In March 1646 another ordinance admitted that there was 'some difficulty' over excommunication, as parliament wanted to avoid

[228] Firth and Rait, eds., *Acts and Ordinances*, I.180–4, 754; Robert Baillie, *Letters and Journals, 1637–62*, ed. D. Laing (3 vols., Edinburgh, 1841–2), II.107 (Baillie to William Spang, 7 Dec. 1643).

[229] Alex F. Mitchell and John Struthers, eds., *Minutes of the Sessions of the Westminster Assembly of Divines* (Edinburgh, 1874), pp. 456 n. 1, 451, 454.

[230] Baillie, *Letters*, II.89, 107, 186 (qu.) (to Spang, 22 Sept., 7 Dec. 1643, 31 May 1644).

[231] Firth and Rait, eds., *Acts and Ordinances*, I.789–97.

arbitrary clerical power. Any offences not specified would be judged by provincial commissioners nominated by parliament, who would then instruct elders to suspend sinners (this implied the commissioners would be laity). If an offence was committed on the day of the sacrament, the minister could exclude the offender, but had to certify the decision to parliament for an *ex post facto* judgement. In June, an ordinance decreed that a committee of commissioners would report to parliament on whether such cases warranted expanding the list of specified sins. And in August 1648 these ideas were renewed in an ordinance which set down cases in which suspension was justified, retaining the committee to consider new sins to be specified, and certification to parliament (the final court of appeal) of emergency suspensions.[232] Although this proved the last gasp of Presbyterian-Parliamentarianism, and was never fully implemented, *ad hoc* civil supervision of excommunication continued until Cromwell's days.[233]

The desire to limit clericalism as manifested in aggressive excommunication was not new to 1640s England. It had been the stimulus for an attack on Theodore Beza by the Heidelberg physician Thomas Erastus in the later sixteenth century. Historians often use 'Erastian' in a loose sense of civil dominance of the church, a move which is warranted less by Erastus's own works than by developments in 1640s England.[234] In this decade, fears about excommunication were renewed, but the English context in which the supremacy (now wielded by parliament) gave the state large powers over the church widened the sphere in which civil authority could meddle. It was in this decade that Presbyterians began to denounce their opponents as 'Erastians' and to urge the need for a new refutation of Erastus's work (although it was translated into English only in 1659). In 1645–6 debate spilled over from the Westminster Assembly into a series of tracts pitting the 'Erastian' Thomas Coleman against the Scottish Commissioner, George Gillespie, and the Assembly's scribe, Adoniram Byfield.[235] Considering this debate reveals the continuity of arguments and assumptions which had previously been used to delineate supremacy.

[232] Firth and Rait, eds., *Acts and Ordinances*, I.833–8, 852–5, 1188–1215.

[233] John Morrill, 'The Church in England, 1642–9', in John Morrill, ed., *Reactions to the English Civil War 1642–1649* (1982), p. 97.

[234] J. Neville Figgis, 'Erastus and Erastianism', *Journal of Theological Studies*, 2 (1901), pp. 66–101; see also below, Chapter 5.

[235] The order was: Thomas Coleman, *Hopes Deferred and Dashed* (1645); George Gillespie, *A Sermon Preached Before ... the House of Lords ... 27 August 1645* (1645); Adoniram Byfield, *A Brief View of Mr Coleman* (1645); Thomas Coleman, *A Brotherly Examination Re-Examined* (1645); George Gillespie, *Nihil Respondes* (1645); William Hussey, *A Plea for Christian Magistracie* (1645); Thomas Coleman, *Male dicis maledicis* (1646); George Gillespie, *Male audis* (1646).

Quarrels over whether church government was *iure divino* formed part of a discourse of settlement as the First Civil War drew to a close. Some thought minimising divine right claims was best, others thought arguing from them was the solution.[236] If the Bible was reticent about the form of church government, this implied excommunication could be governed by the magistrate, for obedience to civil authority was prescribed in Romans 13. The debate on excommunication turned on a handful of key texts and on the example of the Israelite commonwealth. Was excommunication among God's chosen people a civil censure? The Hebraist John Lightfoot insisted that 'in the Jewish authors excommunication was of a civil import', for Israelite civil and ecclesiastical governance were 'in one hand'. Coleman agreed.[237] In the New Testament, an obstinate sinner was to be treated 'as a heathen and a publican'; had these been excluded from the temple? No, Lightfoot argued; they had still attended. Christians were ordered to tell the church (*dic ecclesiae*) of the sin of a brother; did that warrant judicature? 'There is nothing said that the Church did – not any one act', Colman insisted, and he later cited Erastus at the Assembly.[238] He and his defender, William Hussey, insisted on a binary distinction between jurisdictional coercion and declaration of doctrine, not between civil and ecclesiastical – terms which Hussey thought 'non-sense, and fraud'. Ministers declared and persuaded, only government coerced. 'Give us Doctrine, take you the Government.'[239] Fearing *imperium in imperio* if ecclesiastical government was distinct from the civil, these men insisted that Christ *qua* mediator gave the magistrate authority, and thus that that authority was ecclesiastical. Gillespie differed from them by arguing that Christ authorised civil government, but not in his capacity as mediator. For him, two governments were perfectly possible, for in earthly things churchmen obeyed the magistrate.[240] Nathaniel Fiennes, the man who had denied the Assembly's infallibility when carrying parliament's rebuke to it in spring 1646, argued that if the magistrate could judge excommunication after the fact by appeal, he might direct it beforehand as well.[241]

[236] Minimal: Coleman, *Hopes Deferred*, p. 24; Coleman, *Examination Re-examined*, p. 5; maximum: Byfield, *Brief View*, p. 4; Gillespie, *Sermon*, p. 32.

[237] Mitchell and Struthers, eds., *Minutes of the Sessions*, pp. 439–40; Coleman, *Examination Re-examined*, p. 16; Coleman, *Male dicis*, p. 11; cf. Byfield, *Brief View*, p. 11. On the role of the Old Testament in Erastianism, see Jeffrey R. Collins, *The Allegiance of Thomas Hobbes* (Oxford, 2005), p. 100; and pp. 98–100 on Selden.

[238] Mitchell and Struthers, eds., *Minutes of the Sessions*, pp. 193–203, at pp. 195, 197. Texts from Matt. 18:17.

[239] Hussey, *Plea*, p. 9; Coleman, *Hopes Deferred*, p. 26.

[240] Gillespie, *Nihil respondes*, pp. 12–13; Gillespie, *Sermon*, p. 42; Coleman, *Male dicis*, pp. 15–16.

[241] Nathaniel Fiennes, *Vindiciae veritatis* (1654 (written 1646–8)), p. 13 and appx, p. 21.

This debate was Erastian in both senses of the word. Gillespie criticised notions of civil excommunication as wrongheaded and denounced the 'Erastian way' of the magistrate appropriating all.[242] But the argument also bore traces of discourse about supremacy. Both sides gave the civil magistrate a religious role. But where Gillespie and Byfield continued Cartwright's notion that this was oversight rather than exercise of church government, and urged the Lords to prosecute heresy and profanity, their opponents were willing to say the magistrate was ecclesiastical and played a quotidian role in church government. Both sides cited Constantine, Byfield noting how the emperor did not exercise ecclesiastical government, and Coleman replying that just because he *would* not did not mean that he *could* not.[243] But this imperial example was applied to a discussion of parliament's supremacy. Hussey called parliament 'the great Sanhedrim of the Kingdome'; Coleman said that when parliament discussed religion 'it is an ecclesiasticall Court', although he also spoke more vaguely of 'intrinsecall Church-power in the Civill Magistrate'. The pamphlet debate had been launched with a sermon by Coleman to the Commons, refuted in one preached by Gillespie to the Lords.[244] The Presbyterian Gillespie criticised Coleman in terms reminiscent of sixteenth-century Catholic critiques of supremacy: 'if he make the Magistrate a Church-Officer, he must also give him Ordination'. But Coleman had already denied this: 'I never had it in my thoughts that the Parliament had power of dispensing the Word and Sacraments', applying old limitations of supremacy to a new holder of it.[245] Even the Assembly's resolution that the civil magistrate 'may not challenge authority and power of ministry of divine offices' exactly repeated the Injunctions of 1559.[246] Thus the gradual slide of authority from king to king-in-parliament to parliamentary sovereignty caused 1640s writers to speak vaguely of the Christian magistrate, or inconsistently of kings or parliaments. But questions about the meaning and limits of civil governance of religion were well established through previous arguments over supremacy. The unrealised division in the 1640s was between Congregationalists who believed in a godly magistrate and men whose main aim was to crush clerical power in whatever form it took, the latter exemplified by the puritan lawyer William Prynne.

242 Gillespie, *Male audis*, pp. 11, 19.

243 Byfield, *Brief View*, pp. 25–6; Coleman, *Male dicis*, p. 35.

244 Hussey, *Plea*, sig. A3v; Coleman, *Male dicis*, pp. 23–4.

245 Gillespie, *Nihil respondes*, p. 18; Coleman, *Examination Re-examined*, p. 14. Coleman thought ordination was doctrinal; Gillespie thought it part of government.

246 Mitchell and Struthers, eds., *Minutes of the Sessions*, p. 224.

In late 1644 and early 1645, Prynne perpetuated imprecision about the location of ecclesiastical sovereignty. He constantly attributed supremacy to the civil magistrate, but he was consistently ambiguous as to whom this meant, in a way which unconsciously echoed St German and Bagshaw and which would be repeated in Prynne's Restoration works. Prynne denied all claims of divine right church-polity as made 'with more confidence than evidence of Scripture'.[247] He quoted Selden on the 'civill excommunication' that the Sanhedrim carried out, and said Erastus's questioning of divine right excommunication was 'seconded by many learned men'.[248] Prynne wanted to limit, not abolish, excommunication, but he disliked the practice of suspending someone not excommunicated from the sacrament.[249] In arguing that suspension for a notorious sin before formal excommunication might be claimed 'by no *divine Right*, but only by Parliamentary authority and humane institution', Prynne slipped from Erastus's concern about excommunication to an Erastian attribution of church government to the state.[250]

That civil authority prevented clerical aggrandisement was, for Prynne, more important than the form civil government took. *Truth Triumphing*, dated 2 January 1645 and dedicated to parliament, was subtitled as a vindication of 'the undoubted *Ecclesiasticall Iurisdiction, Right, Legislative, Coercive Power* of *Christian Emperours, Kings, Magistrates, Parliaments* in all matters of *Religion, Church-Government*' and of the laity's right to sit in councils, 'here proved to be anciently, and in truth none other but *Parliaments*'. Prynne argued a threefold case: that the magistrate could summon councils, control their debates, and ratify their canons. He quoted the twenty-first of the Thirty-Nine Articles, which stated that general councils were to be summoned by *princes*, and glossed this as meaning 'Princes *and other supreme temporall magistrates*'. These synods could not debate without licence 'from the King or Parliament', and their decrees might only be enforced with 'speciall Letters Patents under the greate Seale, and by Act of Parliament too'. His logic was occasionally oxymoronic, for he argued both that councils were subordinate to

[247] William Prynne, *Trvth Trivmphing over Falshood* (1645), p. 124; William Prynne, *An Exact Chronological Vindication and Historical Demonstration of our British, Roman, Saxon, Danish, Norman, English Kings Supreme Ecclesiastical Jurisdiction* (3 vols., 1665–6). On Prynne, see William M. Lamont, *Marginal Prynne, 1600–1669* (1963).

[248] William Prynne, *Independency Examined, Vnmasked, Refuted* (1644), p. 10; William Prynne, *A Vindication of Foure Serious Questions … touching Excommunication and Suspention [sic] from the Sacrament of the Lords Supper* (1645), sig. [A4]r.

[249] Prynne, *Vindication*, pp. 1, 3. [250] Prynne, *Vindication*, p. 51.

parliaments and that they were just parliaments.[251] At his most accurate when asserting the control of *past kings* over convocation and the *present parliament* over the Westminster Assembly, Prynne read backwards from this to assert an immemorial joint supremacy. King Lucius had been ordered to rule the church with his council, William I resolved to be 'chiefe *Governour of the Church*' in parliament, and Tudor Reformations demonstrated royal and parliamentary ecclesiastical authority.[252] For Prynne, the legislation of the 1640s was new *proof* of parliamentary governance of religion, but not novel power.

Joint supremacy of crown-in-parliament or sole parliamentary supremacy? It was a question which Prynne never definitively answered, although he did speak of the superiority of collective over individual wisdom.[253] He was probably relieved at the failure to establish Presbyterianism in the 1640s but horrified at the fragmentation of ecclesiastical authority into Independency. He preferred the idea of a national church embodied in parliament. Like Selden, who according to Baillie thought 'that the Jewish State and Church was all one, and that so in England it must be, that the Parliament is the Church', Prynne spoke of 'Churches, Synodically assembled, [subordinate] to the supreame Councell of Parliament (the representative Church and State of England)'.[254] His fears contributed to England's Erastian moment of 1644–6, although those worries would be expressed again in the 1650s.[255] Erastians and Congregationalists could ally to defeat Presbyterian plans in the 1640s because for a short period the notions of civil supremacy and of godly rule came together.[256] But, contrary to Prynne's claims, many Congregationalists desired a godly magistrate, and it was they more than the exiled episcopal church who continued the tradition of magisterial supremacy.

Congregationalists took advantage of the ecclesiastical vacuum of the late 1640s to construct a network of autonomous churches. These

[251] Prynne, *Trvth Trivmphing*, t.p., pp. 11–12 (my emphasis), 24–8, 30 (qu.), 54, 18–19, 33, 38, 49.

[252] Prynne, *Trvth Trivmphing*, pp. 55, 63, 84–9.

[253] Prynne, *Trvth Trivmphing*, pp. 146, 151.

[254] Prynne, *Trvth Trivmphing*, p. 143; Baillie, *Letters*, II.265–6 (to Spang, 25 Apr. 1645).

[255] Theophilus Brabourne, *The Second Part of the Change of Church-Discipline* (1654); Theophilus Brabourne, *The Second Vindication of my First Book of the Change of Discipline* (1654). He too seemed to feel any form of government which kept any form of clericalism in check was acceptable: see Chapter 5, p. 205.

[256] Collins, *Allegiance*, p. 109, rightly notes the alliance but distinctiveness of the two positions. He notes (p. 171) Erastian was applied to an increasingly wide variety of groups in the 1650s, but perhaps tends to follow this too much himself by emphasising the similarities between Cromwellians, magisterial Congregationalists, Erastians, republicans, and Hobbes.

associations worked on quasi-voluntarist lines, insofar as would-be members could seek to join whichever congregation they pleased, although they had to undergo a rigorous process of testifying their faith, and were subject to discipline once they had joined. Congregations each regulated their internal organisation independently of others, but maintained fraternal links for mutual counsel. Fellow-churches could warn, rebuke, and withdraw communion amongst themselves, but could not exercise superior jurisdiction over each other. The manifesto of the Congregational way, the *Apologeticall Narration* of 1643, described this as churches having 'ful [*sic*] and entire' but not 'independent' power.[257] Congregationalists may thus be a more sympathetic term than 'Independents' for this group, although historians frequently use the two interchangeably. The five Dissenting brethren men who signed the *Narration* (William Bridge, Jeremiah Burroughes, Thomas Goodwin, Philip Nye, and Sidrach Simpson) shared a background of exile in Holland in the 1630s, links to New England churches, and – along with the theologian John Owen – would become the leaders of Oliver Cromwell's church in the 1650s.

Two evils were abhorred by this group of Congregationalists.[258] One was intolerance and the other was sectarianism. The Dissenting brethren decried separatism and Brownism and in the 1650s congregations expelled Quakers.[259] In the Interregnum they sought a framework of fundamentals which could tolerate all Reformed orthodoxy, but one which would exclude papacy, prelacy, and Socinianism. Cromwell's regime was the most tolerant and religiously pluralist ever seen in England, but historians have recently emphasised the *limits* of toleration even in the 1650s.[260] Thus John Owen's discussion of toleration in 1649 insisted that 'every particular minute difference' was not to be specified and made compulsory and attacked persecution as originating in papal, and ultimately pagan, Rome.[261] But he also delineated the limits of toleration, which should not

[257] William Bridge, Jeremiah Burroughes, Thomas Goodwin, Philip Nye, and Sidrach Simpson, *An Apologeticall Narration* (1643), p. 14.

[258] I speak here of magisterial Independency, not that of John Milton and John Goodwin, which separated church and state. The *Apologeticall Narration*, p. 23, disowned the epithet 'independent'.

[259] *Apologeticall Narration*, pp. 5, 7, 23–4; D. Nobbs, 'Philip Nye on Church and State', *Cambridge Historical Journal*, 5 (1935), pp. 41–59; Joel Halcomb, 'Congregational Church Practice and Culture in East Anglia, 1642–1660' (MPhil. thesis, University of Cambridge, 2006).

[260] A. B. Worden, 'Toleration and the Cromwellian Protectorate', in William J. Sheils, ed., *Persecution and Toleration* (Oxford, 1984); John Coffey, *Politics, Religion and the British Revolutions: The Mind of Samuel Rutherford* (Cambridge, 1997).

[261] John Owen, *Works*, ed. William H. Goold (16 vols., 1965–8), VIII.193 (qu.), 204, 175–87. Note he uses 'toleration', not 'liberty of conscience'.

countenance popery, idolatry, and blasphemy.[262] Almost precisely halfway through, his account turned from advocating religious liberty to exploring the magistrate's religious duties. Similarly, in 1652 he preached that rulers were not to 'set up forms of government to compel men to come under the line of them', or poke their swords into minor differences – but they were to see the true faith 'protected, preserved, propagated'.[263] The need to police the limits of orthodoxy, and the providential duty to promote truth, echoed in the writings of the magisterial Congregationalists who, as Jeffrey Collins notes, were 'fundamentally statist'.[264]

The culmination of such sentiments was the Savoy Declaration of 1658. This proclaimed that the magistrate had a 'latitude in conscience to tolerate and permit' several forms of worship with 'an indulgency and forbearance'. For 'in such differences about the doctrines of the Gospel, or ways of the worship of God, as may befall men' who do not disturb others 'there is no warrant for the magistrate under the Gospel to abridge them of their liberty'. But 'the magistrate is *bound* to encourage, promote, and protect the professors and profession of the Gospel'. When magisterial Congregationalists emphasised the ruler's role in religion, they spoke the language of duty rather than of empowerment.[265] Owen was aghast at the notion that church and magistrate had nothing to do with one another, which in his eyes invited divine wrath.[266] The magistrate should promote true religion and be a nursing parent to it. Although the ritual law of the Old Testament was abrogated by the Gospel, the moral duty to keep both Tables continued.[267] Like Josiah and Hezekiah, the magistrate was to dispatch preachers of divine revelation. He could support these professors with money and places for worship, and he 'may with the sword lawfully defend the truth'. He punished the sins 'with whose cognizance he is intrusted … [with] condign retribution'.[268] 'You that are in God's way, do God's work', Owen told the Commons in 1649, just as the Dissenting brethren had appealed to parliament in 1643.[269] The magistrate could not meddle with doctrine and for Owen he was not a 'church officer'. But when churches agreed words of communion, the magistrate could add his authority to them (although not force subscription). This was the model

262 Owen, *Works*, VIII.165–7, 195–7.
263 Owen, *Works*, VIII.386.
264 Collins, *Allegiance of Thomas Hobbes*, pp. 102–3 (qu.), 212. He uses 'magisterial Independency'.
265 The Savoy Declaration (1658), in Bray, ed., *Documents*, pp. 533, 537–8; Owen, *Works*, VIII.188, 386.
266 Owen, *Works*, VIII.385, 374.
267 Owen, *Works*, VIII.388, 394. This was distinct from the philosemitism of the Erastians.
268 Owen, *Works*, VIII.188–91; John Owen, *Unto the Questions Sent Me Last Night* (1659).
269 Owen, *Works*, VIII.155.

for Cromwell's church, wherein those agreeing to doctrinal fundamentals could gain public funds; those not subscribing, if orthodox, were permitted but not funded.[270]

Because Congregationalists did not have synods, canon law, or an ecclesiastical hierarchy exercising judicature, some of the classic points at which magisterial supremacy was asserted did not arise in their works. Nevertheless, there were hints. Excommunication of one church by another was impossible without the ruler, but the magistrate might impose 'a power of another nature' to which the Dissenting brethren professed readiness not only to 'submit' but also 'to be most willing to have recourse to'.[271] One of their Interregnum allies, Louis du Moulin, used language more reminiscent of supremacy, writing that magistrates had authority over canons and synods, that the ruler's permission was needed to exercise ecclesiastical authority, and that claiming excommunication *iure divino* was *imperium in imperio*.[272] Du Moulin insisted on magisterial supremacy in ecclesiastical causes on Old Testament models, although he echoed episcopal churchmen in arguing that ecclesiastical advice ought to be heard by sovereigns. Although churchmen offered 'friendly counsell' this could be 'uttered in a commanding way', and wise rulers would hear it.[273] Du Moulin also reiterated a more Erastian language in his call for 'ecclesiastical' and 'civil' to be abolished, for the commonwealth was a 'Christian Visible Church' and in the Old Testament 'we doe read that the Church and Kingdome of the Iewes were the same thing'.[274] Indeed, he went even further by insisting that the magistrate may 'exauctorate, or degrade' clergy, that the Seventy Prophets of Numbers 'prophesied by the spirit of *Moses*, communicated to them', and that the Book of the Law (for which read the scriptural canon) was judged worthy of receipt by kings. He denigrated ordination and noted the sovereign had much 'Sacerdotall' power.[275] These comments made du Moulin's argument qualitatively different from that of magisterial Congregationalists, and rather nearer that of Hobbes.

[270] Owen, *Works*, VIII.200–4; Owen, *Questions*, pp. 6–7. For these men's ecclesiology and its impact on Cromwell's church, see Hunter Powell, 'The Last Confession: A Background Study of the Savoy Declaration of Faith and Order' (MPhil. thesis, University of Cambridge, 2008). I am grateful to Hunter Powell for access to this, and for discussions on the magisterial Congregationalists.

[271] *Apologeticall Narration*, p. 17.

[272] Louis du Moulin, *The Power of the Christian Magistrate in Sacred Things* (1650), pp. 9, 90, 136–7, 11, 61; p. 81 esp. recalls the *Narration*'s argument.

[273] Du Moulin, *Power of the Christian Magistrate*, pp. 66 (qu.), 99–101, 107.

[274] Du Moulin, *Power of the Christian Magistrate*, pp. 5–10, 112–18; pp. 86–7 offer an Erastian interpretation of texts on excommunication.

[275] Du Moulin, *Power of the Christian Magistrate*, pp. 47, 142–4, 146–7.

Du Moulin shared with magisterial Congregationalists a lack of interest in precise forms of civil government, writing a long digression on defactoism in 1650.[276] Owen, Nye, and their associates cared that true religion was promoted and heterodoxy and intolerance restrained, and were less concerned about the relationship between a single person and a parliament. In Cromwell they found their ideal sovereign, for Cromwell shared their perspective sufficiently for Baillie to complain of his 'Erastiane Caesaro-papisme'.[277] Magisterial Congregationalists were not wedded and glued to forms of government, a flexibility which allowed Philip Nye to continue his campaign by an appeal to the royal supremacy after 1660. He was one of a number of Restoration Dissenters who found possibilities in the supremacy to exploit, but his view of the godly magistrate was founded in the 1650s. It was Cromwellians and Congregationalists who perpetuated ideas of supremacy under the guise of godly rule in the 1650s, at the point at which Anglicans were distancing themselves from it, associations proleptic of Restoration paradoxes.

The Puritan Revolution outlawed the English episcopate, and the regicidal coup of 1649 officially abolished the bishops' supreme head. In the 1650s, the Church of England was perpetuated unestablished, in exile both foreign in Paris and domestic in illicit Prayer Book worship. The intellectual challenge to which her defenders responded, however, came from Catholics more than Presbyterians or Independents. The three premier theorists of Interregnum Anglicanism – Henry Hammond, John Bramhall, and Henry Ferne – all wrote with an eye more on Rome than Geneva. Their justifications of the break from Rome, of episcopacy, and of the Reformation and royal supremacy employed familiar arguments. But their accounts occasionally downplayed supremacy and their claim that their Church was still in existence implied that royal patronage was more a useful adjunct than an essential part of it.

Central to these writers' case was insisting that England's departure from Rome was a regrettably necessary separation rather than sinful schism. Schism had occurred, but on Rome's side, in her Donatist-like insistence on being the exclusively Catholic church, by her departure from the ancient Petrine faith, by her unwillingness to reform, and by her treatment of Protestants.[278] Writers of 1650s continued the Caroline turn

[276] Du Moulin, *Power of the Christian Magistrate*, pp. 23ff.

[277] Collins, *Allegiance*, pp. 170 (qu.), 131.

[278] Henry Hammond, *Of Schisme* (1653); Henry Ferne, *Of the Division Between the English and Romish Church Upon the Reformation* (1652), pp. 16, 29, 106; John Bramhall, *Schisme Garded and Beaten Back* (Gravenhagh, 1658), section 9; John Bramhall, *An Answer to M. de la Milletiere*

towards a more charitable view of Rome by insisting they separated only from Rome's errors, not from the credal fundamentals whose retention meant she remained a church. Bramhall repeatedly depicted this as the difference between a garden weeded and unweeded.[279] Anglicans thought their purified version of the church upheld primitive Christianity much better than Rome did, rejecting unwritten verities in favour of true universal tradition.[280] Their church was all the more catholic for being the less Catholic: 'by how much we should turn more Roman … by so much we should render ourselves less Catholic, and plunge ourselves deeper into schism whilst we seek to avoid it'.[281]

Having bishops was ecclesiologically catholic without being papistically Catholic. Hammond, in particular, sought to defend episcopacy (although there was little explicit discussion by these writers of the abolition of bishops). His treatise *Of Schism* neatly refuted both papal and Presbyterian opponents by arguing that unjust separation from a bishop, metropolitan, or patriarch was schism, but denying that papal supremacy existed in the primitive church. Here and elsewhere he defended episcopacy as at minimum apostolic, established with Christ's approbation, and evidenced in the works of the most ancient Fathers, especially the first-century Ignatian epistles, a favoured source-text after 1660 for episcopalians.[282] Both he and Bramhall argued that the pope enjoyed only a primacy of order, not supremacy, noting that arguing for *iure divino* episcopacy was far distant from endorsing papalism.[283] In the mid 1650s Bramhall emphasised a general council as the 'supreme ecclesiastical power', the 'sovereign Ecclesiasticall Tribunal'.[284] But in 1658 he appeared to propose a more collegial than conciliar church, quoting Cyprian's dictum that episcopacy was one power which each bishop possessed in its

(1653), in *Works* (5 vols., Oxford, 1842–5), I.1–81, at p. 61; John Bramhall, *A Just Vindication of the Church of England* (1654), in *Works*, I.83–279, at pp. 100, 127–8, ch. 8; John Bramhall, *A Replication to the Bishop of Chalcedon* (1656), p. 16.

279 Bramhall, *Replication*, pp. 57–8; Bramhall, *Schisme Garded*, p. 415; Bramhall, *Answer*, p. 43; Bramhall, *Vindication*, pp. 113, 199.

280 Bramhall, *Answer*, pp. 53, 65; Bramhall, *Schisme Garded*, p. 179; Ferne, *Division*, pp. 96, 231, 117, 152–3, 204.

281 Bramhall, *Vindication*, pp. 96 (qu.), 109; Bramhall, *Replication*, p. 86; John Bramhall, *A Replie to S.W.'s Refutation* (appended to his *Replication*), p. 31; Henry Ferne, *A Compendious Discourse* (1655), p. 32.

282 Hammond, *Schisme*, pp. 37–59, 163–183; Henry Hammond, *Of the Power of the Keys* (1647), pp. 39, 20–2, 31; Henry Hammond, *A Vindication of the Dissertations Concerning Episcopacie* (1654); Ferne, *Discourse*, pp. 14, 67; Bramhall, *Vindication*, p. 271; Bramhall, *Replication*, p. 71.

283 Bramhall, *Vindication*, pp. 129–30, 189; Bramhall, *Replie*, pp. 33, 54; Bramhall, *Schisme Garded*, p. 52; Bramhall, *Answer*, p. 32; Bramhall, *Replication*, p. 172.

284 Bramhall, *Vindication*, p. 261; Bramhall, *Replication*, p. 32.

entirety, another frequent Restoration strategy. He added that bishops had maintained the church's unity for three centuries without a council.[285] The independence of particular churches was shown in the ancient British church, which even if Rome had founded it (a moot point) did not mean papal supremacy over it.[286] Ancient British ecclesiastical independence was yet another prominent Restoration case.

It was as a self-governing entity that the English church had reformed herself in the sixteenth century, Ferne argued: 'every Nationall Church, having within it self, the whole subordination of Ecclesiasticall Power or Government (the Permission and Authority of the Supreme Civill Power concurring) may reform it self, *i.e.* make a publick nationall Reformation'. Bramhall agreed that a provincial reformation could be carried out in the absence or recalcitrance of a general council.[287] In defending the Reformation, these men showed knowledge of sixteenth-century literature such as *De vera obedientia*.[288] Hammond argued that the clergy's Submission to Henry VIII was made under threat of *praemunire*, but was legitimate because it was correct. The same royal ecclesiastical authority was wielded by the Catholic Mary, the child Edward, and the female Elizabeth.[289] Bramhall parroted the well-established argument that Henrician legislation was declaratory, not introductory.[290] He proudly announced that the Reformation was a joint enterprise established 'by sovereign authority, according to the direction of the Convocation, with the Confirmation of the Parliament'. In the 1650s, Bramhall at least was unconcerned with precisely delineating the respective authority of monarch and parliament in ecclesiastical affairs – or was happy to give parliament a role, speaking of kings and their councils or parliaments governing the church.[291]

On one level the Interregnum witnessed no more than renewed defences of the royal supremacy, although Bramhall was noticeably more forthcoming about it than Hammond and Ferne.[292] He argued that

[285] Bramhall, *Schisme Garded*, pp. 25, 436; Hammond, *Schisme*, pp. 62, 89–90. Bramhall, *Replication*, sig. F4r, claimed episcopal letters communicatory maintained unity, not communion. See Chapter 3 and Chapter 6, p. 248.

[286] Hammond, *Schisme*, ch. 6; Bramhall, *Vindication*, pp. 132, 259–60, 266–9, ch. 5; Bramhall, *Replication*, ch. 5; Bramhall, *Replie*, p. 36; Bramhall, *Schisme Garded*, pp. 5, 15–16, section 4.

[287] Ferne, *Discourse*, p. 26 (qu.); Ferne, *Division*, pp. 22, 25; Bramhall, *Vindication*, pp. 106, 262.

[288] Bramhall, *Replication*, p. 246; Bramhall, *Vindication*, pp. 121–2; Hammond, *Schisme*, p. 135.

[289] Hammond, *Schisme*, pp. 136–7, 143–6, 148.

[290] Bramhall, *Schisme Garded*, pp. 271–2, see also 67–9, sect. 3; Bramhall, *Replie*, p. 17.

[291] Bramhall, *Replication*, pp. 108 (qu.), 119; Bramhall, *Vindication*, pp. 95–6.

[292] John Spurr, 'Schism and the Restoration Church', *Journal of Ecclesiastical History*, 41 (1990), pp. 408–24, at pp. 413–14.

Christ was spiritual head of the church, that general councils were ecclesiastical heads, and kings political heads. He moaned that his opponents muddled 'politicall Supremacy with ecclesiasticall'.[293] He offered a familiar account of how supremacy was a political headship which ensured clergy fulfilled their duties and which did not include any sacerdotal authority, and he cited well-worn texts as authorities. 'Our Laws … never invested the King with any Spirituall power or Iurisdiction, witnesse the Injunctions of Queen *Elizabeth*.' English kings were no Uzziahs.[294] This could on occasion sound rather critical of royal power. Bramhall certainly disliked royal *headship* as a title, thinking supreme governorship sounded more palatable.[295] And he echoed Grindal's rebuke to Elizabeth – that she should not pronounce *quasi ex auctoritate* in spiritual matters – when he said kings held power over the church 'as truly and as justly, but not as fully, nor as absolutely' as they did temporal authority.[296] Both he and Hammond insisted that bishops held jurisdictional powers. But the threefold division of episcopal authority between order (the sacraments), interior jurisdiction (in the court of conscience), and exterior jurisdiction (with coercive force), the first and second inherent in bishops and the third from royal gift, merely reiterated what Horne and Carleton had argued. Furthermore, although consecration invested bishops with the 'habit' of jurisdiction, their exercise of such authority required royal permission.[297] Hammond added that the magistrate was not to excommunicate, although neither was he to be excommunicated.[298] Bramhall's work on schism outlined four areas of royal sovereignty over the church: patronal, legislative, appellate, and dispensatory. Constantine judged bishops. Emperors authorised canons and councils.[299] All sovereigns held such authority, and all had the right to defend such liberties against popes.[300] If Hammond hinted that *rex in regno suo est imperator*, Bramhall made the analogy explicit by stating

293 Bramhall, *Replication*, p. 144 (qu.); Bramhall, *Schisme Garded*, p. 349.

294 Bramhall, *Schisme Garded*, pp. 170 (qu.), 63, 70, 89; Bramhall, *Answer*, p. 29; Bramhall, *Vindication*, pp. 115 (parsing the Act of Appeals), 272; Bramhall, *Replication*, pp. 143–4, 290, 177.

295 Bramhall, *Vindication*, p. 115; Bramhall, *Replication*, p. 294.

296 Bramhall, *Replication*, p. 293.

297 Bramhall, *Schisme Garded*, pp. 161, 166; Bramhall, *Vindication*, p. 152; Bramhall, *Replication*, pp. 160–1, 292; Hammond, *Keys*, p. 55.

298 Hammond, *Keys*, pp. 87, 124; see Bramhall, *Replication*, p. 175, distinguishing excommunication from refusing communion.

299 Bramhall, *Replication*, pp. 299–300; Bramhall, *Schisme Garded*, p. 119; Hammond, *Schisme*, p. 121.

300 Bramhall, *Vindication*, ch. 7; Bramhall, *Schisme Garded*, p. 322; Bramhall, *Replication*, p. 284.

that Henry VIII had the same authority as Justinian.[301] And Bramhall repeated earlier assertions of the importance of clerical counsel to kings' church-governance. 'Though we give to Sovereign Princes within their own Dominions a Legislative Power in Ecclesiasticall causes, yet not without good advise, especially ... in high points of Faith ... and who are more fit Counselors for Princes in such cases then Synods, and Bishops?' When monarchs 'have a learned Councel of Ecclesiasticall persons to direct them', they could not be thought of as 'ignorant Laymen'. Purely spiritual causes should be referred to bishops; questions of external government pertained to kings.[302]

Interregnum churchmen occasionally assumed the continuity of supremacy; Hammond, for example, presumed the ecclesiastical hierarchy which his work described existed under the king, and that the British church had been founded on national lines to match the state.[303] Despite the increasingly urgent need to renew the episcopate in the late 1650s, churchmen would not act without Charles II's nomination of bishops elect. But the very existence – and assertion of the existence – of the Church unestablished was contrary to the precedent of a century. When Ferne spoke of a national church, limited by national borders, ancient provincial boundaries, or civil authority, he described 'the whole subordination of Church governments' as deacons under priests under bishops under a primate – but no supreme governor was mentioned. He said 'every nationall Church' had power to determine questions of faith by scripture and to decide *adiaphora*; whether this included a role for the king was left unspecified (but the ability to judge doctrine implies it did not).[304] Like his fellow writers, Ferne insisted that his church was persecuted but not extinguished, as Christianity had been in its first three centuries.[305] Hammond stated the Church was '*preserved* in *Bishops* and *Presbyters rightly ordained*, and *multitudes rightly baptised*', and was silent on Charles II as supreme governor of these people. Discussing the origins of the British church, Bramhall was sceptical about King Lucius and Hammond thought him superfluous. And Bramhall placed his insistence that supremacy was not sacerdotal amongst the minor questions of his *Vindication*.[306]

301 Hammond, *Schisme*, p. 59; Bramhall, *Vindication*, p. 178.
302 Bramhall, *Replication*, pp. 305, 308; Bramhall, *Schisme Garded*, pp. 342, 120.
303 Hammond, *Schisme*, p. 32; Hammond, *Vindication*, p. [68] (mispag. 60).
304 Ferne, *Discourse*, pp. 16, 48–9.
305 Ferne, *Division*, sigs. [A6]r–[A8]r; Bramhall, *Answer*, p. 64; Bramhall, *Replication*, p. 110.
306 Hammond, *Schisme*, pp. 179–80 (qu.), 109; Bramhall, *Schisme Garded*, p. 300.

These men did not reject the royal supremacy. When they felt the need to they defended it, but that need was felt less often than before. They found complementary roles for bishops and kings but rarely pronounced on what happened if the two clashed – for after Worcester Charles remained supportive (in a passive way) of the Church. The threat of apostasy to a Catholic or Presbyterian alliance was not realised after 1651, and the Restoration came just in time to prevent the need to consecrate bishops independently of the king. Yet the Interregnum proved that legal establishment was perhaps the *bene esse* rather than the *esse* of the Church of England, which could be justified as catholic, ancient, and episcopal. It was, therefore, the intellectual resources forged in the experience of survival, and that experience itself, *combined* with an actively oppositional royal governor which was required to pit supremacy against episcopacy. Such a situation arose not in the 1650s, but with the Restoration, and the rest of this book shows how parliaments, clergy, Dissenters, anticlerical writers, and Catholics responded to it. All these disparate groups could exploit the supremacy because, as this chapter has shown, the many versions of supremacy which had been canvassed between 1530 and 1660 legitimated a wide variety of interpretations of it.

CHAPTER 2

The crown and the cavalier Anglicans: prerogative, parliament, and ecclesiastical law

The Civil Wars and Interregnum did not change the English polity into a constitutional monarchy. The Restoration Settlement restored both the powers and the problems which had existed in 1641. Only the memory of 'the world turned upside down' and Charles II's politicking prevented renewed breakdown for some years. It was not surprising that religion played a major role in these events, for it was a historic flashpoint between crown and parliament. As the previous chapter has shown, many Tudor and early Stuart MPs and common lawyers asserted that statute and common law as well as royal prerogative governed the church, canons, and convocation. Such claims often derived from men who sought further reformation and in the 1640s they had their way.

Yet there was a great change in the parliamentary politics of religion after 1660, as the Commons shifted from being a forum for further reformation to one which offered entrenched support for an unreformed church. Simultaneously monarchs sought to relax uniformity rather than enforce it. Nonconformists seeking indulgence were, therefore, dependent on the royal prerogative in unprecedented ways and some (as Chapter 4 will show) both took and sought opportunities to use it. Discourse about Christian toleration, persecution, and schism existed alongside a 'constitutional' argument over prerogative dispensation with statute. This chapter considers the latter type of clashes, which arose over dispensing, in particular regarding the Declarations of Indulgence of 1662 and 1672. It explores how MPs, the Lords, and lawyers tried to uphold a just royal supremacy whilst rejecting prerogative indulgence, for many MPs (particularly the less vocal ones) remained wary about invading royal authority.[1] Only crises provoked clear claims of parliamentary supremacy. Thus, in

[1] On MPs' conservatism, see John Miller, 'Charles II and his Parliaments', *Transactions of the Royal Historical Society*, 5th ser., 32 (1982), pp. 1–23, at pp. 20, 23, although his assertion of no constitutional debate and English mixed monarchy is more dubious. John Morrill states that two thirds of Cavalier Parliament MPs are silent in our records ('Between Conventions: The Members

the aftermath of the Revolution of 1688, when parliament considered the state oaths, claims of a long tradition of supremacy resting in crown-in-parliament were renewed.

Dispensing was not a new question in the Restoration, but it was problematic on a wholly novel scale. The question of dispensing provoked many of the discussions about supremacy, parliament, and ecclesiastical law. Yet this did not stop older issues echoing on. The final section of this chapter recovers a set of debates about convocation and ecclesiastical jurisdiction, long neglected by previous historians, which highlight the role that contemporaries saw convocation as having. The lack of actual activity by convocation between 1662 and 1689 thus did not preclude discussion of it. Since these discussions, like those on dispensing, had technical legal as well as constitutional dimensions, this survey considers legal theorists and common law as well as MPs and statute.[2] All these discussions shared common themes about legal, statutory, and historical precedents for a supremacy which was not purely royal. But, as will be seen, even those in the same parliament or the same profession, using the same authorities, fundamentally disagreed about the nature of supremacy.

The king's power to dispense individuals from the effects of statutes, or to suspend statutes universally, was his main means to exempt nonconformists from the obligation of religious uniformity. This power had both ecclesiastical and juridical aspects. Legal as well as constitutional discourse was invoked for and against Charles and James, along with claims about toleration and schism. Whilst this study concentrates on the debates around dispensing with religious statutes, it is necessary to remember that these were only one aspect of legal argument: key case law derived from economic questions, while the implications for temporal laws if ecclesiastical ones could be circumvented was an important concern.[3]

of Restoration Parliaments', *Parliamentary History*, 5 (1986), pp. 125–32, at p. 131); although cf. Annabel Patterson, *The Long Parliament of Charles II* (New Haven, 2008), p. 152, on debates on religion including even the normally silent. This study largely adheres to the model of paraphrasing not quoting parliamentary diarists; where direct quotation is used, I endeavour to identify the diarist as the potential author of the words.

2 Two books (Michael Landon, *The Triumph of the Lawyers: Their Role in English Politics, 1678–1689* (Alabama, 1970) and Howard Nenner, *By Colour of Law: Legal Culture and Constitutional Politics in England, 1660–1689* (Chicago, 1977)) have discussed the political importance of lawyers, and Alan Cromartie, *Sir Matthew Hale, 1609–1676: Law, Religion and Natural Philosophy* (Cambridge, 1995), offers a detailed case study, but of Restoration legal history proper there is a dearth.

3 For literature on dispensing, see E. F. Churchill, 'The Dispensing Power of the Crown in Ecclesiastical Affairs', *Law Quarterly Review*, 38 (1922), pp. 297–316, 420–34; E. F. Churchill, 'The Dispensing Power and the Defence of the Realm', *Law Quarterly Review*, 37 (1921), pp. 412–41; E. F. Churchill, 'Dispensations under the Tudors and Stuarts', *English Historical Review*, 34 (1919), pp. 409–15; Paul Birdsall, '"Non Obstante": A Study of the Dispensing Power of English Kings',

It was clear in law that kings enjoyed the prerogative of mercy: the ability to pardon an offender from the penalties of their crime, whatsoever it be. Equally clearly, monarchs could not jettison statutes wholesale; they could only be repealed by crown-in-parliament. But 'dispensation' of particular individuals from certain statutes had long been practised – regarding religion, the example of kings dispensing foreign 'stranger' churches from the Acts of Uniformity was often cited – and this was considered an equitable necessity, given parliament might not be sitting, have time, or need to repeal the entirety of a law, which could never account for every circumstance. Royal ability to 'suspend' laws universally was a larger power, but one little questioned before the Restoration since monarchs used it with care. From the 1670s, however, the distinction between dispensing and suspending became blurred, and in 1689 the Bill of Rights declared any use of the suspending power 'illegal'. But even then many were chary of outlawing the dispensing power wholesale. The Bill of Rights left to judicial construction a statutory ban on the use of the dispensing power 'as it hath been exercised of late', although in practice the crown never again attempted to use that power.[4]

Judicial pronouncements preceding and during the Restoration placed several limitations on royal dispensing.[5] *Mala in se*, matters against divine law, could not be permitted, although they might be pardoned. But *mala prohibita*, things outlawed only by human law (in practice, statute) could be allowed under letters patent, *non obstante* the statute. In 1487 the judges ruled that without a *non obstante* clause a dispensation was invalid.[6] This key distinction was in practice of limited use regarding dispensing with uniformity. Dissent was banned by statute (*malum prohibitum*), but was it also the sin of schism (*malum in se*)?[7] In the landmark Restoration case of *Thomas* v. *Sorrell* (1674), Chief Justice Sir John

in Carl Wittke, ed., *Essays in History and Political Theory in Honour of Charles Howard McIlwain* (Cambridge, MA, 1936); Carolyn A. Edie, 'The Irish Cattle Bills: A Study in Restoration Politics', *Transactions of the American Philosophical Society*, n.s., 60 (1970), number 2; Carolyn A. Edie, 'Revolution and the Rule of Law: The End of the Dispensing Power, 1689', *Eighteenth-Century Studies*, 10 (1977), pp. 434–50; Carolyn A. Edie, 'Tactics and Strategies: Parliament's Attack upon the Royal Dispensing Power, 1597–1689', *American Journal of Legal History*, 29 (1985), pp. 197–234; Dennis Dixon, '*Godden* v. *Hales* Revisited – James II and the Dispensing Power', *Journal of Legal History*, 27 (2006), pp. 129–52.

4 Edie, 'Revolution and the Rule of Law', esp. pp. 448, 440–4; Edie, 'Tactics and Strategies', pp. 230–3; Birdsall, 'Non Obstante', pp. 75–6.

5 Birdsall, 'Non Obstante', pp. 55–7; Edie, 'Tactics and Strategies', p. 199; Edie, 'Revolution and the Rule of Law', p. 435.

6 Birdsall, 'Non Obstante', pp. 44, 50.

7 Sir Edward Herbert, *A Short Account of the Authorities in Law … in Sir Edward Hales his Case* (1688), p. 31.

Vaughan argued that *malum in se* and *malum prohibitum* had 'more confounded … than rectified' understanding of dispensing. He deemed whether a particular (individual) subject could bring an action more important, for such a right precluded a royal dispensation.[8] Dispensation was permitted only where there was a discernible common good (*pro bono publico*), not where kings acted out of self-interest (*pro bono suo*). This came to hinge on whether the king's action permitted a 'nuisance' inherently opposed to public welfare, for example dispensing with payments to repair a broken bridge. Nevertheless, Vaughan in 1674 sought to prevent statutes labelling anything a nuisance (as parliament had famously labelled Irish cattle), declaring kings could dispense with 'nominal' nuisances.[9] Dispensing was also illegitimate if it tampered with property law, damaged a third party, or if the suit was brought purely in the king's name on behalf of a private person. Some thought that, if a statute rewarded an informer, kings might only dispense before an action was brought, a not insignificant question since so many statutes against Dissent rewarded informers.

Thomas v. *Sorrell* was not only a landmark case, but was also being heard in 1673, when parliament was debating Charles's Declaration of Indulgence. MPs expressed wariness about dispensation rendering statutes useless, but their reaction against the Declaration included the First Test Act. Later, James II orchestrated the case of *Godden* v. *Hales* in order to prove his power to dispense Catholics from the Test, winning only after he had purged the (already strongly royalist) judiciary.[10] The case involved many of the questions surrounding dispensation mentioned above.[11] Not the least of the reasons for James's victory was the claim that the Test interfered with the duty of subjects to serve the crown, and therefore

[8] Edward Vaughan, ed., *The Reports and Arguments of that Learned Judge Sir John Vaughan* (1677), pp. 330–59 (124 Eng. Rep. 1098), at pp. 332 (qu.), 341; 89 Eng. Rep. 63, Freeman KB 85; cited by Herbert, *Short Account*, pp. 20–1; see Dixon, '*Godden* v. *Hales* Revisited', p. 146. On *Thomas* v. *Sorrell*, see Edie, 'Irish Cattle Bills', p. 57, n. 15; Edie, 'Revolution and the Rule of Law', pp. 438–9; Edie, 'Tactics and Strategies', pp. 220, 224–6, 224, n. 57 on reports of the case. This indeed fuelled *Godden* v. *Hales*, for Godden sued for his reward as an informer.

[9] Edie, 'Irish Cattle Bills', pp. 24, 28, 30–3, 57, and 57, n. 15.

[10] For the trial, see: *State Trials*, XI.1165–1316; 89 Eng. Rep. 1050, 2 Shower KB 475; 90 Eng. Rep. 318, Comberbach 21 (miscited as *Godwin* v. *Hales*); Anon., *The Case of Sir Edward Hales* (1689); Herbert, *Short Account*; William Atwood, *The Lord Chief Justice Herbert's Account Examin'd* (1689); Sir Robert Atkyns, *An Enquiry into the Power of Dispensing with Penal Statutes*, 2nd edn (1689); Birdsall, 'Non Obstante', pp. 68–75; Dixon, '*Godden* v. *Hales* Revisited'. Modern historians have tended to uphold the decision: Churchill, 'Dispensing Power in Ecclesiastical Affairs', p. 434; Birdsall, 'Non Obstante', pp. 74–5; but cf. Dixon, '*Godden* v. *Hales* Revisited', passim, esp. p. 152.

[11] E.g. *State Trials*, XI.1193–5; Herbert, *Short Account*, pp. 8, 31, on *malum prohibitum* versus *malum in se*.

might be dispensed with, according to the *Case of Sheriffs* of 1487.[12] In 1689, whig lawyers rejoined that employing Catholics contravened the public welfare of a Protestant kingdom.[13] James's opponents, including those advising Archbishop Sancroft, were further irked by the 'odious' origins of dispensing in 'the sulphureous Fountain of *Rome*'.[14] The politicisation of dispensing was intensified when Chief Justice Herbert argued that the king, as sovereign, could dispense with his own laws; Sir Robert Atkyns and William Atwood tried to refute this by arguing that England was a mixed polity.[15] Thus, while legal language infiltrated the religious question of indulging Dissent and Catholicism, comment on the courts' judgment on the legality of dispensing was coloured by constitutional and religious attitudes.

There are, therefore, three sources of discussion of the dispensing power, the use of which shaped debate during the first half of Charles II's reign and most of his brother's. First, there was parliament, which contested the legality of bypassing statutes. Secondly, there were lawyers, who commented on the relationship between the supremacy, statute, and canon law. Thirdly, there was printed debate over the benefits of toleration and threat of schism. Although these groups naturally overlapped, this chapter considers the first two, and Chapter 4 the third.

PREROGATIVE VERSUS PARLIAMENT: THE 1660S

Between 1660 and 1662 the situation of a lenient king and an intolerant parliament was established. Charles's Declaration of Breda had offered liberty to tender consciences but hoped for an act for the 'full granting' of indulgence. In the autumn of 1660 there was an attempt to convert the Worcester House Declaration into statute – a motion defeated by Court speakers, whether or not with Charles's permission.[16] Uniformity

[12] *State Trials*, XI.1194; Herbert, *Short Account*, pp. 17–19; Atkyns, *Enquiry*, pp. 37, 55; Atwood, *Herbert's Account Examined*, pp. 23, 27; Birdsall, 'Non Obstante', p. 51; Dixon, '*Godden* v. *Hales* Revisited', pp. 138–42.

[13] Atwood, *Herbert's Account Examined*, pp. 44, 46; Atkyns, *Enquiry*, p. 28.

[14] Atwood, *Herbert's Account Examined*, p. 6 (qu.); 'The Original of Non-Obstantes, & *the* Opinion of *the* Wise conc[erning] *them*': Bodl., Tanner MS 460, fo. 79r; Atkyns, *Enquiry*, pp. 14–16, 19, 21, 51. 'Sulphureous Fountain' is from John Speed, *The History of Great Britaine* (1614), p. 530, who cites Matthew Paris: see 'A short view of the Dispensing Power in relation to Acts of Parlament': Bodl., Tanner MS 460, fo. 61r. Edie, 'Revolution and the Rule of Law', p. 435, similarly identifies papal origins.

[15] *State Trials*, XI.1196, 1199; Atkyns, *Enquiry*, pp. 18, 23, 39–40, see also p. 12; Atwood, *Herbert's Account Examined*, pp. 5, 25, see also p. 72.

[16] J. R. Jones, 'Political Groups and Tactics in the Convention of 1660', *Historical Journal*, 6 (1963), pp. 159–77.

itself crawled through parliament in autumn 1661 and spring 1662. As late as 17 March 1662 Clarendon introduced a proviso which, invoking the Declaration of Breda ('the intenc'on whereof must bee best knowne to his Ma*jes*tie'), allowed Charles to dispense any minister from wearing the surplice or making the sign of the cross in baptism. By insisting that the king hoped for eventual conformity, the clause implied that such dispensations would be temporary. The Commons not only rejected this on 22 April, but also fixed pensions to deprived ministers at a fifth of their incomes, instead of leaving the amount to royal discretion.[17]

Having failed to insert a loophole into the Act of Uniformity, Charles next sought to bypass it. In the summer of 1662, as Presbyterian ministers agonised over whether to conform or be deprived, the king urged that the implementation of the Act be delayed. He was strongly opposed by Sheldon, who reportedly defeated any such delay in council on 28 August.[18] But many lay councillors supported indulgence for either principled or prudential reasons. As George Abernathy has shown, Clarendon as well as Bennet favoured the Declaration of Indulgence of 26 December 1662. This asserted Charles's desire to uphold his promise made at Breda, but wavered over his power to do this, pleading for 'some such Act ... as may enable Us to exercise with a more universal satisfaction, that Power of Dispensing, which We conceive to be inherent in Us'.[19]

When parliament reconvened in February 1663, it did so in the midst of rumours that nonconformists had seized with glee on the Declaration, citing it against magistrates who came to arrest conventiclers.[20] Particularly pernicious was a rumour that Edmund Calamy (the elder) had challenged his arrest beacuse of a defect in the Act of Uniformity: MPs felt it needed strengthening, not relaxing.[21] In fact, although Congregationalists welcomed the Declaration, Baxterian Presbyterians rejected it. So too did the Commons. Both the king's defence of his proclamation, and the

[17] HMC, *Seventh Report*, pt I, appx, pp. 162–3 (10 Mar. 1662); *LJ*, XI.409 (17 Mar. 1662); *CJ*, VIII.413, 414 (22, 26 Apr. 1662). On the proviso, see Paul Seaward, *The Cavalier Parliament and the Reconstruction of the Old Regime, 1661–1667* (Cambridge, 1989), pp. 14, 175–8; Andrew Swatland, *The House of Lords in the Reign of Charles II* (Cambridge, 1996), pp. 99, 157–8, 167–70; on the passage of the Act, see Seaward, *Cavalier Parliament*, pp. 166–7, 174–5; Swatland, *House of Lords*, pp. 165–7; George R. Abernathy, jr, 'The English Presbyterians and the Stuart Restoration, 1648–1663', *Transactions of the American Philosophical Society*, n.s., 55 (1965), number 2, at pp. 84–6.

[18] Seaward, *Cavalier Parliament*, p. 180.

[19] *His Majesties Declaration ... December 26 1662* (1662), p. 8; George R. Abernathy, jr, 'Clarendon and the Declaration of Indulgence', *Journal of Ecclesiastical History*, 11 (1960), pp. 55–73.

[20] TNA, SP 29/72/12, 29/70/13, 29/67/36.

[21] Calamy might not have linked his challenge to the Declaration but Lady Anglesey did: see TNA, SP 29/67/31.

Commons' reasons against it, provided foundations for later opposition to prerogative indulgence.

The royal speech of 18 February asserted a principled opposition to religious persecution. As in the Declaration, Charles stated he 'wish[ed] I had such a Power of Indulgence' to comfort peaceable Dissenters. He also claimed that Catholics might 'fairly hope' for some indulgence – but denied any desire to tolerate them or grant them offices, as 'some Mistake' the Declaration to say. Asserting he had been sadly misunderstood would become a favoured royal tactic. Charles's insistence that he 'will not yield to any therein, not to the Bishops themselves' in his zeal for Protestantism offers historians some dramatic irony.[22]

On 25 February the Commons thanked the king for declaring his intent to uphold the Act of Indemnity, avoid military rule, legislate against popery and impiety, and support religious uniformity. These were, indeed, parts of the Declaration. Yet its crux, indulgence, was rejected. The committee nominated to draw up reasons for this included Heneage Finch, John Vaughan, Thomas Meres, and John Birkenhead, all of whom would oppose the Declaration of 1672. The reasons reported by Finch to the House on 27 February insisted that indulgence was 'in no sort adviseable'. Firstly, Breda was no promise to indulge, but only to be advised by parliament; 'no such Advice [to indulge] was ever given, or thought fit to be offered'. To the committee's draft, the House added that 'there were Laws of Uniformity then in being, which could not be dispensed with, but by Act of Parliament'.[23] Secondly, parliament represented Dissenters, who had thereby consented to the statute. To claim a right to the Declaration of Breda against the statute, to say proclamation overrode crown-in-parliament, was 'to dissolve the very Bonds of Government'.

After these legal-constitutional arguments against the manner of giving indulgence, the House rejected its content. Indulgence ridiculed church government and ecclesiastical censures: 'Schism by a Law'. To legislate uniformity and then undo it rendered derisory parliament's dignity. It made the king a target for all Dissenting pleas. Indeed, the likely outburst of sectarianism would end in sedition, or a new church government, or popery. One addition made by the Commons on 27 February neatly united the religious and legal-constitutional cases: the Declaration was 'a thing altogether without Precedent; and will take

[22] *LJ*, XI.487–8; Patterson, *Long Parliament*, p. 81; *His Majesties Declaration*, pp. 9–12.
[23] Perhaps a sign of the rejection of Interregnum repeal of the 1559 Act of Uniformity.

away all Means of convicting Recusants, and be inconsistent with the Method and Proceedings of the Laws of England'. The king's answer of the following day neither surrendered nor argued; unlike 1673, Charles did not fight on.[24]

Perhaps Charles procrastinated because the Lords had not yet finished with the Declaration. On 23 February a bill establishing the Declaration had been offered by James, Duke of York. This asserted that no fixed law could regulate Dissent as well as the royal prerogative could. Unlike the Declaration, it insisted that no Catholic worship or officeholding was permissible.[25] But it ran aground over the clause allowing dispensing with not only the 1662 Act, but also other statutes on uniformity or oaths about the church. The Committee of the Whole House of 28 February ordered the Attorney-General to specify which acts would be affected. When a list of thirty-seven acts was returned on 5 March, the House struck out the king's power to dispense with anything except the 1662 statute. The seriousness of the issue is highlighted by the order for all to attend to debate it on 12 March; but the 'long Debate' recorded in the *Journal* appears to have been inconclusive.[26] The Lords' changes highlight the argument, not articulated by the Commons in 1662 but prevalent in later episodes, that dispensing with ecclesiastical statutes dangerously facilitated bypassing temporal ones.

Charles was at a disadvantage regarding the Act of Uniformity because it contained no clear protection for his powers. By contrast, the Restoration Act restoring ecclesiastical jurisdiction included a proviso saving the rights of the supremacy, which would prove helpful to James II's defence of his ecclesiastical commission.[27] In the late 1660s, Charles moved towards protecting his supremacy in such provisos, as seen in the Second Conventicles Act of 1670. This rapidly followed the Scottish Act Asserting the King's Supremacy (November 1669), which fulsomely advocated the 'inherent Right of the Crown' to the ordering of the external government of the church, notwithstanding any civil or ecclesiastical laws or customs to the contrary, a claim dubbed by Andrew Marvell 'absolute Power to dispose of all things in religious Matters'.[28] The English bill was sponsored by staunch Anglicans in the Commons, but given 'mighty

[24] *CJ*, VIII.440, 442–3, 444 (25, 27, 28 Feb. 1663).

[25] HMC, *Seventh Report*, appx, pt I, pp. 167–8; *LJ*, XI.482 (25 Feb. 1663); Abernathy, 'Clarendon', p. 69.

[26] *LJ*, XI.486, 487–8, 491 (28 Feb., 5, 12 Mar. 1663).

[27] 13 Chas. II c. 12. See Chapter 6, pp. 255, 266.

[28] *Act Asserting His Majesties Supremacy* (Edinburgh, 1669); *The Poems and Letters of Andrew Marvell*, ed. H. M. Margoliouth, 3rd edn (2 vols., Oxford, 1971), II.313 (Andrew Marvell to William Popple, 21 Mar. 1670).

Alterations' by the Lords. Some of these concerned peers' privilege, but the '*Scotch* Clause of the King's Power in Externals'[29] was accepted on 28 March only in an amended form:

> Provided always ... that neither this Act, nor any thing therein contained, shall extend to invalidate or avoid his Majesty's Supremacy in ecclesiastical affairs, ~~or to destroy any of his Majesty's Rights, Powers, or Prerogatives, belonging to the imperial Crown of this realm, or at any time exercised or enjoyed by himself, or any of his Majesty's royal predecessors, Kings or Queens of~~ England; but that his Majesty, his heirs and successors, may, from time to time, and at all times hereafter, exercise and enjoy all such powers, and authorities aforesaid, as full and as amply as himself, or any of his predecessors, have or might have done the same; any thing in this Act, ~~or any other Law, Statute, or Usage to the contrary~~ notwithstanding.[30]

As in 1663, it was Finch who brought in reasons against the original proviso. As in the Lords in 1663, fear of extending ecclesiastical supremacy too far into the temporal realm might have been significant; it certainly was for Sir Thomas Lee, who quoted Henrician statutes showing the equivalence of temporal and ecclesiastical supremacy to warn the proviso gave (in Grey's words) 'an immense power'. Yet MPs worried that opposing the proviso broke their oaths of allegiance and supremacy: what if the Lords accused them of denying the supremacy?[31]

Marvell's cynical suggestion that 'some' opposed a proviso which permitted the king to dispense with the bill entirely was probably true; the poet himself spoke of the 'reserving clause for his Majestyes ancient prerogative in all Ecclesiasticall things'.[32] But others were genuinely keen to maintain royal prerogative so long as it remained within what they saw as its due boundaries. What those were was, of course, unclear. It was little surprise that MPs' natural recourse was to Tudor legislative precedent – and no wonder that this did not solve the issue. As Finch reported, 'the King has, by Law, a Supremacy; that of 21 *Henry* VIII was but a restoration of what the King had before', but 'we hope that no obscure

[29] Marvell, *Poems and Letters*, II.314–15 (Marvell to Popple, 21 Mar. 1670). I am grateful to John Spurr for directing me to Marvell. Patterson, *Long Parliament*, pp. 156–7, and Swatland, *House of Lords*, p. 182, focus on privilege not the supremacy.

[30] Anchitell Grey, *Debates of the Honourable House of Commons* (10 vols., 1763), I.246 (28 Mar. 1670). The copy of the proviso in the state papers, dated 26 March, has the deleted clause enclosed in square brackets, and – a change which Grey's *Debates* omit – the deletion of 'afores[ai]d' after 'authorityes' and the substitution of 'Ecclesiasticall', as in the final act, consolidating specifically ecclesiastical supremacy: TNA, SP 29/274 pt 1/31.

[31] Grey, *Debates*, I.249 (28 Mar. 1670).

[32] Marvell, *Poems and Letters*, II.104 (Marvell to Hull, 26 Mar. 1670). It was cited in later arguments for indulgence.

thing may be revived by this Proviso'.[33] Charles could, therefore, get his prerogative protected in bills that MPs liked the content of. When he twisted that prerogative to his own desires, he failed; and he failed most spectacularly in 1673.

PREROGATIVE VERSUS PARLIAMENT: THE 1670S

The 1662 Declaration provided important precedents for later arguments, but it had little time to take effect locally. By contrast, that of 1672 was in place for nearly a year before parliament reconvened. When it did meet, it was at first treated firmly by the king. Charles's speech of 5 February admitted that the Declaration had been misconstrued as giving Catholics more freedom than nonconformists, but warned he was committed to it.[34] On 7 February the 'dedicated Anglican'[35] Thomas Meres expressed uncertainty over the Declaration's legal status and asked what royal ecclesiastical power entailed. The next day's discussion mutated into one on the advantages and disadvantages of naturalising foreign Protestants,[36] but from 10 February to 8 March the Declaration dominated debates. On 19 February the Commons addressed the king as 'bound in duty to inform your Majesty, that penal Statutes, in matters ecclesiastical, cannot be suspended but by Act of Parliament'. Pleading that laws remain in force until an act provided otherwise, they asked Charles to remove any 'apprehensions or jealousies' caused by his proclamation.[37] On the twenty-first and twenty-second the House pressed Charles for his answer, which came two days later. The king expressed sorrow at 'the questioning of his power in Ecclesiasticks; which he finds not done in the reigns of any of his ancestors'. He disclaimed any innovatory intent to unilaterally alter properties, rights, liberties, doctrine, or discipline; and looked forward to parliament offering him a bill to remove penalties on nonconformists.[38] After an agony of indecision, the Commons replied on 26 February that this was 'not sufficient' to dispel the worries which 'justly remain' over the king's suspending power – not least since he still seemed to be claiming it.

[33] Grey, *Debates*, I.254 (30 Mar. 1670). 21 Hen. VIII: a slip for either the Act in Restraint of Appeals or the Submission of the Clergy.

[34] Grey, *Debates*, II.2 (5 Feb. 1673). In fact they had less: permitted private but not public worship.

[35] Basil Duke Henning, *The House of Commons, 1660–1690* (3 vols., 1983), III.49.

[36] Basil Duke Henning, ed., *The Parliamentary Diary of Sir Edward Dering, 1670–1673* (New Haven, 1940), p. 111, pp. 113–14 records it being too late to begin the reading; Grey, *Debates*, II.9, 12–13 (7 Feb. 1673).

[37] Grey, *Debates*, II.42 (19 Feb. 1673); text at II.26 (14 Feb. 1673). The delay was caused by the change of Speaker.

[38] Grey, *Debates*, II.48, 54–5 (qu. 54) (21, 22, 24 Feb. 1673).

We humbly conceive, your Majesty hath been very much misinformed; since no such power was ever claimed, or exercised, by any of your Majesty's Predecessors; and, if it should be admitted, might tend to the interrupting of the free course of the Laws, and altering the Legislative Power, which hath always been acknowledged to reside in your Majesty, and your two Houses of Parliament.[39]

Finally, on 8 March, Charles reported that he had cancelled the Declaration, and that it would not in future 'be drawn into consequence or example'. Thanks were exchanged.[40] Although questions of schism and toleration were raised in these debates, the argument over prerogative versus statute was prevalent in parliament. But historians must treat it carefully. Not a few individual members genuinely feared entrenching on proper royal prerogatives; the House sought a way out of the impasse rather than open confrontation.

Not the least cause of members' tentativeness was their uncertainty over what they were dealing with. When debate was initiated on 10 February it was at first punctuated by long silences.[41] 'What we complained of', the diarist Dering wrote, 'was rather what we feared than what we felt', a sentiment evidenced in the oppositional Henry Powle's long speech, which focused on the risk that *any* law might be dispensed with, though professing willingness to indulge Dissenters legally. Although supremacy was an ancient royal right, toleration was a decision for parliament. The appalling implication of the Declaration was religion determined by royal whim.[42] Charles's first answer to the House gave insufficient security for Meres, who pointed out that promising that dispensing *would* not be done again implied it *could* legitimately be done.[43]

Past precedents loomed large in the minds of members, who invoked examples of earlier failed attempts at toleration. The first response to the Declaration was to read the votes of 1663 against its forebear. When searching for words in which to put their case to the king, Sir William Coventry suggested the House use those of Breda, which denied religious laws could be dispensed with except by statute. When Archbishop Abbot denied that toleration by prerogative was legitimate, James I heeded his advice.[44] But precedents had a nasty habit of pointing in contrary directions. The tolerationist Edmund Waller listed the powers kings had always had to dispense, invoking Coke's authority. Were not traitors pardoned?

[39] Grey, *Debates*, II.62 (26 Feb. 1673). [40] Grey, *Debates*, II.91–2 (8 Mar. 1673).
[41] Grey, *Debates*, II.13; Henning, ed., *Parliamentary Diary of Dering*, pp. 114–15 (10 Feb. 1673).
[42] Henning, ed., *Parliamentary Diary of Dering*, p. 117 (qu.); Grey, *Debates*, II.15–16 (10 Feb. 1673).
[43] Grey, *Debates*, II.56 (24 Feb. 1673); see also II.53 (Strangways, 22 Feb. 1673).
[44] Henning, ed., *Parliamentary Diary of Dering*, p. 115; Grey, *Debates*, II.13, 22, 16 (10 Feb. 1673).

Had not kings always issued dispensations to stranger churches? Waller reminded MPs of their consent to the proviso protecting the supremacy in 1670.[45]

Nobody was quite certain where to locate the dispensing and suspending powers on the constitutional spectrum. Meres wanted to ask the judges for their advice. Dering questioned the difference between repeal and a universal timeless suspension. Powle invoked *Thomas* v. *Sorrell*, which suggested that suspension and abrogation (which only parliament could do) were the same.[46] Attorney-General Heneage Finch argued that Charles's ecclesiastical headship meant that changes to religion and canons needed statutory authority, but insisted kings could dispense particular individuals. Dispensing the whole population did not constitute repeal: better that Charles retained flexibility than bound himself to indulge by statute.[47] When, on 24 February, a member invoked 'necessity' as the reason for Charles's use of the prerogative (a word which suggested extra-legal royal power, but which the king's answer did not use), Vaughan, whose father was sitting in judgement on the Exchequer case, replied that a wartime prerogative did not amount to ability to repeal statutes, to which suspension amounted.[48] The House's sympathy appeared to be with Vaughan. When another member sneered at Vaughan's conflation of particular (individual) and general (universal) dispensation, he was called to order and forced to apologise.[49] The staunch defender of the Church Giles Strangways argued on 10 February that pardoning (dispensing with penalties) was possible, but dispensing popery or Dissent was not. Against the previous speaker (and soon to be Speaker) Edward Seymour, who thought that an act limiting the king's power could not be had, Strangways insisted that parliament should defend its rights. Every kingdom needed a legislative power, and in England that power included the consent of Lords and Commons.[50]

Firm expressions of the illegality of a Declaration which apparently violated the mixed monarchy of the kingdom were offered by Meres and Vaughan in particular. Meres declared lawyers told him universal suspension was illegal. Vaughan attacked the Declaration on 10 February in, according to Grey, unequivocal language:

[45] Grey, *Debates*, II.14–15; Henning, ed., *Parliamentary Diary of Dering*, p. 115 (10 Feb. 1673).

[46] Grey, *Debates*, II.51 (22 Feb. 1673); Dering agreed: Henning, ed., *Parliamentary Diary of Dering*, pp. 116–17; Grey, *Debates*, II.15 (10 Feb. 1673).

[47] Grey, *Debates*, II.20; Henning, ed., *Parliamentary Diary of Dering*, pp. 115–16 (10 Feb. 1673).

[48] Grey, *Debates*, II.58–9 (see pp. 54–5 for the king's answer) (24 Feb. 1673), II.63 (26 Feb. 1673).

[49] Grey, *Debates*, II.66 (26 Feb. 1673).

[50] Grey, *Debates*, II.16–17 (10 Feb. 1673). Milward (Grey, *Debates*, II.67, 26 Feb. 1673) pointed out that the king could pardon simony but not dispense with the law against it.

if this Declaration signifies any thing, the Church of *England* signifies nothing ... This Declaration is a repeal of forty Acts of Parliament, no way repealable but by the same authority that made them – This Declaration does repeal fourteen Statutes of this King ... It is point-blank opposite to his Laws; they and this cannot consist ... This Prerogative is illegal.[51]

Meres's scornful rejection of worries about the novelty of demanding that the king speedily reply to the Commons' Address bluntly blamed Charles for provoking them with an unprecedented Declaration.[52] The insistence in the answer of 26 February that 'the Legislative Power ... hath always been acknowledged to reside in your Majesty, and your two Houses of Parliament' hinted that mixed monarchy was palatable.[53]

A preliminary reading of the debates might suggest a united body of offended members angrily pursuing the king, an impression fuelled because the most irate were often the most outspoken. But further perusal of the evidence suggests an extraordinary care *not* to offend Charles, to protect due royal authority, and to avoid open rupture with the Court. To address the king rather than immediately vote the Declaration illegal was suggested by several members (for differing reasons) on 10 February: Henry Coventry, Charles's secretary of state, who noted some ability to dispense was vital in case of emergencies; Robert Howard, a royalist, though one concerned with parliament's rights; and the Dissenter Francis St John, who endorsed Coventry's idea of citing the Declaration of Breda in order to avoid offending the king.[54] The king's answer of 24 February, perhaps intentionally, split the House between those (such as Finch) who would offer thanks for security graciously offered and those (such as Meres and Powle) who still felt it too precarious.[55]

One means to respectful opposition was to invoke the concept of counsel. The rhetoric of a monarch misled by his counsellors explained away the Declaration as an error more than an evil. Coventry suggested that Charles would never violate the laws, but he might be 'mistaken', Strangways that the king could not hurt his subjects but his advisors might. On 26 February MPs bemoaned Charles being 'very much

[51] Grey, *Debates*, II.13–14, 21 (qu.); see also Harbord: 'Laws must be altered by the same authority they were ordained by' (Grey, *Debates*, II.25, 10 Feb. 1673).

[52] Grey, *Debates*, II.51 (22 Feb. 1673).

[53] Grey, *Debates*, II.62 (qu.), 67–8 (26 Feb. 1673). Finch was, with Coventry, one of the two courtiers whom the House would hear in 1673: Henning, *Commons, 1660–1690*, II.321.

[54] Grey, *Debates*, II.18, 22, 24; Dering endorsed an address: Henning, ed., *Parliamentary Diary of Dering*, pp. 116–18 (10 Feb. 1673).

[55] Grey, *Debates*, II.56–60 (24 Feb. 1673). Lee (p. 58) wanted to offer thanks but desired more security.

misinformed'.[56] The sincerity of such language is hard to assess, but sometimes dubious. Thomas Lee, tolerant towards Dissenters but intolerant of the ecclesiastical prerogative, wished the king would hear parliament's advice, since he had been misled before. Powle invoked a tradition of counsellors erring over supremacy: on canons, on High Commission.[57] William Garway, an advocate of comprehension but an opponent of the suspending power, and part of the government insofar as he was a customs commissioner, ominously stated that those who advised the Declaration needed a general pardon.[58] When one member argued that the king had issued the Declaration on the advice of his council, another desired Charles might hear his Great Council – parliament. When addressing the king on 14 February, the Commons invoked their conciliar 'duty to inform' him about the limitations of his prerogative.[59]

An alternative suggestion was for parliament to appropriate the king's policy by replacing the Declaration with a bill. The Commons' address to the king asked that the penal laws stand in force 'untill it shall be otherwise provided for by Act of Parliament', and John Birch (who had opposed the Declaration because it relieved Catholics) wanted a vote on a bill of indulgence before addressing the king.[60] Dering reported advocacy of this as showing Charles 'that we did not dislike the matter of his declaration but the manner, and did not doubt the prudence but only the legality of it'. However sincere such sentiments may have been, one cannot help feeling that Finch was nearer the mark when he argued that focusing on the illegality of the Declaration would not charm Charles.[61]

In response to the Commons, the king turned to the Lords, who set up a committee on 5 March, chaired by Shaftesbury, to prepare a bill of advice to the king. Although the Lords refused to vote that the Commons had breached their privileges in addressing alone, they endorsed Charles's answer as 'good and gracious'.[62] Lord Treasurer Clifford suggested drafting a bill which would allow the king 'power (if it be not in him already) to suspend penal statutes in matters ecclesiastical out of time of

[56] Grey, *Debates*, II.13, 53, 62 (8, 22, 26 Feb. 1663). On 10 Feb. Strangways argued that the best counsel was to maintain the laws (Grey, *Debates*, II.17).

[57] Grey, *Debates*, II.19 (10 Feb. 1673), 61 (25 Feb. 1673).

[58] Grey, *Debates*, II.110 (15 Mar. 1673). [59] Grey, *Debates*, II.24, 26 (10, 14 Feb. 1673).

[60] Grey, *Debates*, II.15, 27, 26 (qu.), 29 (10, 14 Feb. 1673).

[61] Henning, ed., *Parliamentary Diary of Dering*, p. 119 (qu.); Grey, *Debates*, II.34 (14 Feb. 1673). On 19 Feb. the Speaker was ordered to present the address but not to mention the bill: Hening, ed., *Parliamentary Diary of Dering*, p. 124.

[62] *LJ*, XII.543 (4 Mar. 1673); HMC, *Ninth Report*, appx, pt II, p. 25 (1 Mar. 1673).

Parliament'. The parenthetical caveat carefully bypassed defining precisely where power to dispense lay, making the bill ambiguously either declaratory of an ancient prerogative or introductory of a new one. Setting down the manner by which dispensing would take place, the bill promised that any future declarations would specify the exact laws they affected except in great emergencies. Another bill, drafted by Anglesey, opened by insisting that the king had never sought to dispense with laws establishing the religion or discipline of the established Church, or with the liberties and property of the subject; and 'so for the future he shall not nor may not suspend or dispense with penal laws in matters ecclesiastical'. Insisting, dubiously, that the king 'hath always delighted to be assisted by' parliament's counsel, which 'is in a way unquestionable', the bill specified which laws would be suspended for five years.[63]

Efforts to provide for royal discretion in the subsequent indulgence bill were thwarted by the shadow of the Declaration. Parliament reasserted control over national worship by adding a preamble to their own bill of indulgence to reiterate that only parliament could suspend statutes.[64] Whilst one MP advocated using the Declaration as a model, another took fright that using the Declaration's mode of JPs licensing nonconforming ministers implied MPs had liked it.[65] On 28 March the Commons baulked at the Lords' amendment of the bill for easing Protestant Dissenters, which provided that the king could remove liberty of conscience from any Dissenter who abused it.[66] Meres and Vaughan vociferously complained that such a proviso retarded the bill to the same status as the Declaration, although others thought parliament retained ultimate authority by empowering the king.[67] The next day the Lords defended their amendment as necessarily granting the king less power than that contained in the bill as a whole. But MPs' fears of the implications of such a grant surfaced again in Powle's comment that Charles doubtless meant well, but was being given a power to end parliaments. Vaughan characteristically expressed the more militant line, dismissing the proviso as a law to break law. The king might pardon, and this was right and proper; but

[63] HMC, *Ninth Report*, appx, pt II, p. 25 (7 Mar. 1673) (35 Eliz. c. 1 and the Conventicles Act). On these bills, see Douglas R. Lacey, *Dissent and Parliamentary Politics in England, 1661–1689* (New Brunswick, NJ, 1969), p. 67; Swatland, *House of Lords*, p. 192.

[64] Grey, *Debates*, II.100 (13 Mar. 1673).

[65] Grey, *Debates*, II.94 (Hale, 10 Mar. 1673), 70 (Swynfin, 27 Feb. 1673).

[66] *CJ*, IX.279–80 (28 Mar. 1673), agreed by the Lords the previous day. The Lords usually offered more ease of Dissenters than the Commons allowed: Swatland, *House of Lords*, p. 186; D. T. Witcombe, *Charles II and the Cavalier House of Commons, 1663–1674* (Manchester, 1966), p. 138.

[67] Grey, *Debates*, II.163–4, 167, 165–6 (28 Mar. 1673).

MPs could not grant the power to indulge. Charles, his patience by now exhausted, prorogued parliament.[68]

The spectre of the Declaration could not be exorcised. When the Commons questioned Buckingham and Arlington in January 1674, they bitterly recollected a Declaration which undermined civil and religious laws for the sake of popery.[69] The illegality of the Declaration was presented as an uncontested legal opinion by Meres when he mentioned it in October 1675 in debates over the bill for episcopal custody and education of the royal children.[70] Little stimulus was needed to excite memories. In a debate on supply in 1676, Meres recalled the Declaration.[71] And, naturally, it would be cited as a precedent by both supporters and opponents of James II's policies of indulgence. When parliament met in November 1685, concern was immediately expressed at royal dispensations with the Test to allow Catholics military offices, described by Seymour as 'dispenseing with all the Lawes at once … we must remember tis Treason for any man to be reconciled to the Church of Rome'. Thomas Clarges similarly thought the breaking of the Test a 'breach on our Liberties … this struck at here is our all'.[72] Members wavered over how to protest successfully to the king, eventually agreeing an address thanking him for the defeat of Monmouth's Rebellion: a threat to 'our Religion by Law Establisht which is most dear unto us', reminding James of his promises to defend it. His Catholic officers, they insisted, had legal incapacities which could be removed 'no wayes' but by statute. Although MPs were preparing a bill of indemnity, they asked the king to remove any apprehensions about dispensing.[73] James's reply expressed amazement at 'such an Address' and declared he ought to be trusted – at which (echoing 1673) there was 'a profound Silence some Space'. Later that day, the puritan whig Thomas Wharton moved a debate to consider the speech, seconded by the Member for Derby, John Coke, who said, 'I hope we are all Englishmen and are not to be frighted out of our duty by a few high words.' Though Coke was sent to the Tower, the infuriated James prorogued parliament two days later.[74]

68 Grey, *Debates*, II.178, 179 (29 Mar. 1673).

69 Grey, *Debates*, II.226–7 (Monson, 12 Jan. 1674), 239 (Powle, 13 Jan. 1674).

70 Grey, *Debates*, III.311 (20 Oct. 1675). On these, see below, p. 233.

71 Grey, *Debates*, IV.114 (21 Feb. 1677).

72 The Queen's College Oxford, MS 280, fos., 148v, 147r, Grey, *Debates*, VIII.358, 356 (12 Nov. 1685). The latter is not Grey's own record, though he may have used the former (from which I quote).

73 The Queen's College, Oxford, MS 280, fos. 150v–151r; Grey, *Debates*, VIII.362 (16 Nov. 1685).

74 The Queen's College, Oxford, MS 280, fos. 157v–159v; Grey, *Debates*, VIII.369–70 (18 Nov. 1685).

PREROGATIVE VERSUS PARLIAMENT: 1689

Since James II repeatedly delayed parliament's meeting from 1686 to 1688, debate on dispensing took place outside it. Dispensing was clearly going to be an issue in the Revolution Settlement, although, as previously stated, simple abolition was deemed too blunt a solution. The Revolution Church, and William's powers over it, were hotly debated in the changes to the coronation oath and state oaths in spring 1689; parliament's role in church government was also considered by tory and whig lawyers. The promise in the newly formulated third section of the coronation oath to maintain 'the Protestant Reformed Religion Established by Law' split whigs[75] from tories, not least because both comprehension and toleration were under discussion.[76] Whigs argued that the new oath sent a negative message of intransigence and, perhaps, made it impossible for the king to assent to future liberalisation, they and their allies seeking to insert 'as it is, or shall be, Established by Law'. Tories, well aware of William's sympathy for Dissent, opposed any such clause, arguing (perhaps disingenuously) that 'Established by Law' incorporated future changes.[77] The puritan diarist Roger Morrice recorded the difficulties of the debate – not changing the words would offend foreign churches, altering them impugned the Church of England – but gloomily noted the final decision (by 188 to 149 votes) not to rephrase the oath as a key tory victory.[78] Later the moderate whig Thomas Pelham attempted that age-old strategy, a proviso, for nothing in the Act to preclude royal assent to changing 'any Form or Ceremony', if church doctrine, 'a' public liturgy, and episcopacy were preserved. This provoked the whig lawyer George Treby into asserting that parliament had 'always' retained authority to change *adiaphora*; no new authorisation was needed. But a disparate group argued the proviso implied similar authorisation would be needed to allow royal assent to changing temporal laws, successfully forcing its withdrawal.[79] As in

[75] As describing positions in the spring of 1689, although individuals varied between strongly Williamite, and future Junto or Country whig positions.

[76] *CJ*, x.35, 61, 64–5 (25 Feb., 22, 25 Mar. 1689); the first not mentioned in Grey, the second omitted; 1 Gul. & Mar. c. 6.

[77] Grey, *Debates*, IX.191 (qu.), 192–8 (25 Mar. 1689).

[78] *EB*, Q514, Q516; Grey, *Debates*, IX.198 (25 Mar. 1689).

[79] *CJ*, x.69; Grey, *Debates*, IX.200–4 (28 Mar. 1689). Of the last group, Sir Robert Sawyer had acted as counsel for the Seven Bishops and originally supported Mary's sole claim before accepting William. Thomas Lee was a Williamite, but showed caution in arguing that the Declaration of Rights should contain only ancient rights, not new ones. Joseph Tredenham was a tory, but favoured comprehension. Sir Robert Cotton opposed declaring the throne vacant and wished

1663 and 1673, the civil implications of ecclesiastical supremacy assisted the triumph of unreformed Anglicanism.

Part of the significance of the Revolution of 1688–9 for the English church-state lay in the 'Act of Toleration' and 'the failure of comprehension'.[80] But whilst the implications of the new state oaths are traced in the well-documented 'Allegiance Controversy',[81] that the Supremacy Oath changed is not always highlighted. Henry Horwitz speaks of legislation changing the 'oath of allegiance', 'to revise the Jacobean oath'; Caroline Robbins of replacing the Jacobean oaths of fealty and allegiance.[82] But complex parliamentary debates included tussles over the Oath of Supremacy as well. The chronology of changes is rendered opaque by the lack of source material: several diaries end with the Convention, Grey's account omits the most crucial debates, and – as ever – Lords' documentation is limited.[83] The following examination of changes to the oaths shows how apparently minor questions about conditions and dates of enforcement were controversial because they provoked conflicts between monarchical and parliamentary supremacy.

The two Houses agreed on 8 February to replace the Elizabethan and Jacobean oaths with two new ones, to 'be Faithfull and beare true Allegiance' to William and Mary, and to 'Abhorr Detest and Abjure as Impious and Hereticall' the overthrow or murder of princes excommunicated or deposed by the pope, declaring that 'noe Forreigne Prince, Person, Prelate State or Potentate hath or ought to have any Power Jurisdiction Superiority Preeminence or Authoritie Ecclesiasticall or Spirituall within this Realme'.[84] The initial stimulus to considering the oaths was their

to exempt the clergy from the new oaths. The new oath was not questioned in the Lords: *LJ*, XIV.165, 168, 169 (3, 5, 6 Apr. 1689) and received royal assent on 9 Apr. (*LJ*, XIV.172; *EB*, Q530).

80 Gordon J. Schochet, 'The Act of Toleration and the Failure of Comprehension: Persecution, Nonconformity, and Religious Indifference', in Dale Hoak and Mordechai Feingold, eds., *The World of William and Mary: Anglo-Dutch Perspectives on the Revolution of 1688–89* (Stanford, CA, 1996).

81 Charles F. Mullet, 'Religion, Politics, and Oaths in the Glorious Revolution', *Review of Politics*, 10 (1948), pp. 462–74; Caroline Robbins, 'Selden's Pills: State Oaths in England, 1558–1714', *Huntington Library Quarterly*, 35 (1971–72), pp. 303–21; David Martin Jones, *Conscience and Allegiance in Seventeenth Century England: The Political Significance of Oaths and Engagements* (Rochester, NY, 1999), pp. 201–22; Mark Goldie, 'The Revolution of 1689 and the Structure of Political Argument', *Bulletin of Research in the Humanities*, 83 (1980), pp. 473–564.

82 Henry Horwitz, *Parliament, Policy and Politics in the Reign of William III* (Manchester, 1977), pp. 21, 22; Robbins, 'Selden's Pills', p. 319. Jones, *Conscience and Allegiance*, p. 203, mentions supremacy in passing.

83 On the complexities of debate, see Horwitz, *Parliament, Policy and Politics*, p. 23.

84 *LJ*, XIV.121 (8 Feb. 1689); 1 Gul. & Mar. c. 1 (qu.); Andrew Browning, ed., *Memoirs of Sir John Reresby* (Glasgow, 1936), p. 555 (12 Feb. 1689). On Nottingham's involvement see Henry Horwitz, *Revolution Politicks: The Career of Daniel Finch, Second Earl of Nottingham, 1647–1730* (Cambridge, 1968), p. 82. The rumour (Horwitz, *Nottingham*, p. 82, n. 4) that Bishop White of Peterborough – a nonjuror – drafted the new oaths seems far-fetched: see Michael Mullett, 'Thomas White', *ODNB*.

hindrance to converting the Convention into a parliament: some members felt bound by their oaths to James, and the omission of the oaths at the opening of the Convention impugned its legality.[85] But further legislation, provoked by reports of recalcitrant clergy, was encouraged by the king.[86] The various reasons behind the alterations were revealed in what amounted to three bills: one in the Commons and two in the Lords.[87]

The Commons bill, which would be discarded by the Lords in favour of their own, began by invoking the Declaration of Right of 12 February, proceeding to replace the Jacobean Oath of Allegiance with the promise to 'be faithful and bear true allegiance'. It continued by substituting for the Elizabethan Oath of Supremacy the abjuration of papal excommunication or ecclesiastical supremacy of any but the prince in the realm. Finally, it abolished the penalties for refusing the Militia Oath or the declaration against resistance from the 1662 Act of Uniformity.[88] The Lords' first draft simply recited the two old and two new oaths, citing as justification for changing them the need for 'the better discovery of Popish recusants and repressing all usurped and foreign power, and preserving the King and Queen's Majesties in their persons, and the more assured support of their government'.[89] Such claims, which implicitly reiterated the necessity of securing the church so as to protect the state, were dropped in the amended preamble, which simply cited the statutes of 1559 and 1606. The sections of these dealing with oaths were 'Repealed utterly Abrogated and made Void'.[90]

Three issues proved particularly contentious as the bill was amended and re-amended in the two Houses and their committees: the sacramental Test, royal commissions to tender the oaths, and their imposition on the episcopate. Some whigs made repeated attempts to incorporate the repeal of the Test into the Oaths Bill: William Sacheverell and Henry Capel in the Commons on 25 February and 18 March;[91] and there were

85 *CJ*, X.31 (19, 20 Feb. 1689); Grey, *Debates*, IX.97–100, 102, 103 (20 Feb. 1689); *EB*, Q475; see Lois G. Schwoerer, 'The Transformation of the 1689 Convention into a Parliament', *Parliamentary History*, 3 (1984), pp. 57–76, esp. pp. 63–4, 71.

86 For such reports, see *EB*, Q487, Q503, Q519; see Reresby, *Memoirs*, p. 562 (4 Mar. 1689), on most bishops swearing 'a locall and temporary oath'.

87 The Lords bill was so much redrafted that it was in effect new.

88 HMC, *Twelfth Report*, appx, pt VI, pp. 63–6. On its passage: *CJ*, X.43, 48, 52 (7, 14, 18 Mar. 1689); *EB*, Q496, Q499, Q507; omitted by Grey; *LJ*, XIV.152, 153 (18, 19 Mar. 1689).

89 HMC, *Twelfth Report*, appx, pt VI, pp. 52–3 (qu. 52). I.e. the Lords acted as if both new oaths replaced both old ones; the Commons were more specific. The Lords later incorporated the repeal of the Militia and non-resistance oaths.

90 1 Gul. & Mar. c. 8, clauses i–ii.

91 *CJ*, X.35; Grey, *Debates*, IX.110–11 (25 Feb. 1689); *EB*, Q482, Q507; Horwitz, *Parliament, Policy and Politics*, p. 22, on the tory opposition. Lacey, *Dissent and Parliamentary Politics*, p. 233, describes Hampden encouraging the king to push for the repeal of the Test. *EB*, Q488, Q496, later reported that Sacheverell was ordered to bring in a bill to repeal the Corporation Act.

similar moves in the Lords on 21 and 23 March. Eight Lords dissented from the decision to retain the Test, six from the rejection of the proposal to allow qualification for office by communion 'in any Protestant congregation'. The formal dissents of these whig and Williamite Lords recall the debates over the coronation oath. The Test damaged Protestant unity at home and abroad, and it was illogical: either everyone (not just office-holders) ought to be punished for not taking Anglican communion, or it was not a crime to omit it.[92] But the government's supporters were too divided to force the issue: the Williamite Howard wanted the abolition of the Test, but as a separate issue, and the tory Nottingham disliked the Lords committee's clause on the sacrament.[93]

The second and third issues, over the king's ability to tender the oath in ways and at times other than those laid down in the bill, and its enforcement on the episcopate, were interwoven. As the Houses gradually specified the details of the mode of swearing and penalties for refusal,[94] defenders of the clergy complained increasingly vociferously about the bill's provisions. When the Commons insisted that bishops, peers, and barons of parliament take the oath in public court, not privately at home, Finch and Christopher Musgrave argued that this was indecorous.[95] Whilst the tory Anglicans managed to defeat a motion for corporal punishment of nonjuring bishops, they could not prevent a clause suspending such bishops from 1 August, with a six-month deadline to conform on pain of deprivation. What the clerical faction meant by asking 'what the B*isho*ps of tender Consciences in this point might be Exempted from takeing this oath' is obscure, but royal grants of a third of nonjurors' bishoprics and no fines or jailing were mooted.[96]

[92] *LJ*, XIV.156–7, 159 (21, 23 Mar. 1689); Reresby, *Memoirs*, p. 567 (23 Mar. 1689), mentions the debates. The six dissenters were John Lovelace, 3rd Baron Lovelace (Williamite activist and radical whig), Philip Wharton, 4th Baron Wharton (Presbyterian and Williamite Privy Councillor), Aubrey de Vere, 20th Earl of Oxford (Williamite whig), Charles Mordaunt (Williamite Privy Councillor), Ralph Montagu (Williamite Privy Councillor), and William Paget, 7th Baron Paget (puritan whig). Lovelace and Wharton were the only two to dissent both times; on the first occasion they had been joined by Henry Booth, 2nd Baron Delamer (whig, Williamite activist, and Privy Councillor), North (identity uncertain), Thomas Grey, 2nd Earl of Stamford (whig), Philip Stanhope, 2nd Earl of Chesterfield (tory), Ford, Lord Grey (whig), and John Vaughan, 3rd Earl of Carbery (whig). *EB*, Q511, expected that removal of the sacramental Test would fail; Q521–2 listed the dissenting Lords.

[93] Grey, *Debates*, IX.111 (25 Feb. 1689); HMC, *Twelfth Report*, appx, pt VI, p. 53; *EB*, Q507; see Horwitz, *Parliament, Policy and Politics*, p. 22, on Nottingham and on Anglican relief at keeping the Test.

[94] HMC, *Twelfth Report*, appx, pt VI, pp. 54–7; 1 Gul. & Mar. c. 8, clauses iii–ix; *CJ*, x.87 (13 Apr. 1689); *LJ*, XIV.157 (22 Mar. 1689).

[95] *EB*, Q525–6 (also qu. in Horwitz, *Parliament, Policy and Politics*, pp. 24–5). All days omitted by Grey; *CJ*, x.81, 82, 85 (5, 6, 9, 12 Apr. 1689).

[96] *EB*, Q526, Q531 (qu.); see clause vii of the Act.

MPs were wary of allowing the king to alter their provisions. The Lords tried to strike out the requirement of clergy swearing by 1 August and substitute when 'they shall be required thereunto by Order from His Majesty in Council' before royal commissioners. This in effect reduced to the clergy alone the proviso in the draft bill, already rejected by the Lords, allowing *ad hoc* royal commissions to tender the oaths.[97] Although such commissions were not unprecedented in the history of supremacy (1559 being the obvious example), they were hotly opposed in the Commons. Whigs such as Sacheverell, Lee, and Hugh Boscawen detected a ploy to let the bishops off, however much the Speaker (and, later, Nottingham) insisted they only intended to facilitate *early* tendering of the oaths for royal security. Both political worries about episcopal Jacobitism and anticlerical resentment about the greater favour shown by the Lords to the clergy were expressed by the Commons.[98] The conference between the Houses on 22 April exposed differing views of the supremacy. Although the Lords' statement that 'the King should be empowered' to tender the oaths immediately implied such authority was not inherent in him, they insisted that royal commissions had good historical precedent. But Williamite whig MPs such as Williams and Goodrick rejected such ideas as akin to the dispensing power. Goodrick even argued that refusal to swear should constitute *praemunire*.[99] Their argument would be reinforced when Lord Chief Justice Pollexfen later pronounced that the king could not tender the oaths early, not finding 'any law that will warrant such a Commission'. In exchange for accepting the Commons' amendments, the Lords insisted on a proviso – the last clause of the act – that the king could allow a maximum of twelve nonjurors up to a third of their benefices.[100]

From several perspectives the deprivations of the nonjurors do not appear novel: Sancroft was the fifth of eleven archbishops since the Reformation to die disgraced,[101] while both the Marians in 1559 and the Bartolomeans in 1662 had lost their positions for refusing to obey parliamentary legislation on the church. However, the changes of 1689 appeared more purely

[97] HMC, *Twelfth Report*, appx, pt VI, pp. 54–5; 1 Gul. & Mar. c. 8, clause vi; *CJ*, x.93 (19 Apr. 1689); *LJ*, xiv.154 (20 Mar. 1689); Horwitz, *Parliament, Policy and Politics*, p. 26, suggests that Compton and Burnet were acting directly against the king.

[98] Grey, *Debates*, ix.211–17, 221 (19–20, 22 Apr. 1689); *CJ*, x.96 (20 Apr. 1689); *LJ*, xiv.184 (20 Apr. 1689).

[99] *LJ*, xiv.186 (qu.); *CJ*, x.98; Grey, *Debates*, ix.218, 222, 224 (22 Apr. 1689).

[100] HMC, *Twelfth Report*, appx, pt VI, p. 55; *LJ*, xiv.188 (23 Apr. 1689). Even this concession was minimal: the Commons rejected allowing twelve clergy total exemption from swearing as the Act prescribed, or all nonjuring clergy up to a third of their benefices.

[101] Cranmer, Grindal, Abbot, Laud, and Sancroft; cf. Pole, Parker, Whitgift, Bancroft, Juxon, and Sheldon.

politically motivated: neither doctrinal 'error' nor schism could be levelled against the deprived bishops. Nonjuring authors expressed especial resentment at *parliamentary* condemnation of bishops.[102] Furthermore, it was not only the nonjurors who saw a shift from royal to parliamentary supremacy. 'A Resolution of 3 Important Questions By * * A Civilian' can be roughly dated by the response to the third question: on whether bishops who had been uncanonically deprived could protest to their chapters when 'their places are about to be filled by a Conge d'estire'. This was the situation in April 1691, when William III finally moved to replace the nonjurors.[103] The author (probably Roger North, who advised Sancroft) could see no bar to such protests, if peaceful, in civil or canon law, thinking it a rather good idea to publicly proclaim new bishops intruders. Common law was more problematic, for a Henrician statute forbad interference with the process of episcopal elections laid down in the statute, on pain of *praemunire*.[104] Various laws also differed on the legality of the deprivations. Arguing from canon law and the glossators, the author insisted that even a deprivation *ipso facto* required a declaratory sentence from a 'proper' (ecclesiastical) judge. Bishops are 'not to be deprived sine Causas Cognitione, or a fair tryall at law'. But the Civilian warned of his divergence from ideas of lay judicial governance of religion:

I am Not Ignorant *tha*t our Municipall lawyers, (who take upon them to be judges, & Interpreters of every statute, *tha*t hath *th*[e] least Reference to Ecc*lesiastica*ll persons or causes) Require No Conviction in *the* Case of an Ipso facto deprivation. but say voidance p*er* act de parl*amen*t ne besoigne d'aver ascun sentence declaratoir.[105]

[102] On nonjuring preference for royal over parliamentary supremacy, see Henry Dodwell, *A Defence of the Vindication of the Deprived Bishops* ('1695' [1697]), p. 107; Henry Dodwell, *The Doctrine of the Church of England, Concerning the Independency of the Clergy on the Lay-Power* ('1697' [1696]), pp. 50–1; and for a juring defence of parliament, see Edward Welchman, *A Second Defence of the Church of England* (1698), p. 17. The nonjurors dealt fulsomely with why they saw 1689 as different from Tudor deprivations, esp. those of 1559: Thomas Browne, *Some Reflections on a Late Pamphlet, Entituled A Vindication of their Majesties Authority to Fill the Sees of the Deprived Bishops* (1691), p. 20; John Kettlewell, *Of Christian Communion, to be Kept on in the Unity of Christ's Church* (1693), pt II, pp. 33–4; Dodwell, *Doctrine*, pp. 60ff; Nathaniel Bisbie, *Unity of Priesthood Necessary to the Unity of Communion in a Church* (1692), pp. 41–9.

[103] BL, Add. MS 32523 (endorsed 'A Resolution of Questions about B*isho*ps Depriuation by a Civilian'), fo. 81r. According to Halifax's notes, the king wanted to keep bishoprics 'vacant for some time' on 22 May 1689, to dispose of those 'naturally' coming into his hands on 3 July, to delay appointing a new archbishop (especially if it had to be Compton) on 18 August, and not to change the archbishop at all on 21 August: H. C. Foxcroft, *The Life and Letters of Sir George Savile, Bart, First Marquis of Halifax* (2 vols., 1898), II.218, 223, 230, 232.

[104] BL, Add. MS 32523, fo. 81r–v, citing 25 Hen. VIII c. 20. For North's advice, see below, p. 238, n. 33.

[105] BL, Add. MS 32523, fo. 79v, 'proper': fo. 78r.

The second question was whether canon and civil laws allowed deprivation of bishops 'without a sentence of a sinod [*sic*] of Bishops'. Ancient canons insisted on an exclusively papal right to deprive, but were 'not of force with us, as being Contrary to o*ur* laws, & Customes of *th*e Realme, & to *th*e prerogative Royall'. Canonically, bishops were deposed by a synod, if not patriarchal then at least provincial, or at minimum by the sentence of twelve bishops. English kings 'never claimed to themselves *th*e power of deposing any clergyman', for this would have broken medieval canons. Henry II had asked his episcopate to depose the bishop of Chichester, 'Implying … it were not in his power to depriue him himself'. Princes only expelled bishops 'a civitatibus, uel sedibus … when they Greevosly offended ag*ains*t *th*e Canons'.[106]

Had this altered in the Reformation? Pleading ignorance of Tudor records, the author nevertheless noted deprivations 'by comission from those princes to certain Delegates, ~~very~~ many of them very often meer lay men'. But this had recently been revolutionised, for

> this was by vertue of *th*e Supremacy of those princes in Ecc*lesiastica*ll Causes, w*hi*ch seems to be disowned & anulled by *th*e late act w*hi*ch abrogates *th*e oath of supremacy … Especially if we Consider, there is no proviso in *th*at act for sauing *th*e Kings supremacy, w*hi*ch was Wont to be in act's seeming to Entrench[107] upon his pr*e*rogative in those affairs. p*articular*lie in st. 13 Car. 2 12 in fine.[108]

Could parliament really remove royal supremacy at whim? According to this author, by 1689 such claims were not unthinkable. For the supremacy

> Must be Necessarily abrogated by *th*at act [1º Gul. & Mar. c. 8] If *th*e doctrine of some Great men in these Days be true, *th*at *th*e supremacy was first Given to o*ur* princes by statute. And *th*at those statutes were not declaratory, but Introductory laws. For what was first onely given by law when *th*at law is abrogated, *th*e thing given by it is abrogated.[109]

Here is a significant admission (if not endorsement) of the idea that Henrician legislation was introductory not declaratory, and hence had in effect established parliamentary not royal supremacy. The only remaining task was to rewrite Tudor history as if that had always been the intention. In 1689, the whig lawyer Robert Washington did exactly that.

Some Observations upon the Ecclesiastical Jurisdiction of the Kings of England is far from a canonical piece of political thinking, yet it deserves attention here as a post-Revolution discourse on sovereignty, which

[106] BL, Add. MS 32523, fo. 80r–v. [107] Or possibly 'Encroach'.
[108] BL, Add. MS 32523, fo. 80v; the statute was that restoring ecclesiastical jurisdiction.
[109] BL, Add. MS 32523, fo. 81r.

pondered the pre- and post-Reformation powers of kings and parliaments. Its author is obscure: he appears to have taken no part in the great legal cases of James's reign. Washington's whiggish nostalgia for Anglo-Saxon limited monarchy infused his history with inaccuracy; yet he distinguished in a sophisticated way between ancient immemorial powers shared by crown and parliament and additional ones granted by Reformation parliaments: sometimes to all future kings, sometimes to Henry VIII alone. His prefatory epistle explained that his opponents[110] all wrongly ascribed to the king the power which 'the very Original Constitution of our Government' placed in 'the Legislative body of the Kingdom; and which the King is intrusted onely with the Administration of'. Although the supremacy had been vindicated against foreign usurpations, its domestic legal standing needed clarifying, especially regarding ecclesiastical commissions (half of Washington's tract attacked James II's ecclesiastical commission).[111] The distinction between internal and external *imperium* was crucial: none, Washington wrote, would deny the Holy Roman Emperor to be imperial, but he had less power within the empire than other monarchs in their countries.[112]

Washington continuously contrasted 'modern conceptions' with ancient supremacy, legally unchanged but frequently misunderstood as 'a *Personal unbounded Supremacy*' whereas, in reality, 'the *Ancient Ecclesiastical Supremacy* of the Kings of this Realm, was no *personal Prerogative*'.[113] True notions of the supremacy were under attack from *iure divino* clericalism on the one side, and common law arguments for royal prerogative on the other. Hence Washington appealed to history, pre-eminently Anglo-Saxon, early medieval, and Henrician times, which he felt showed an ancient uncorrupted supremacy. Any remnants of this had been retained in parliament, which interpreted it far more strictly and properly than the 'modern Opinions' of the judges.[114] Judicial error held, for example, that the ecclesiastical prerogative exceeded the temporal,[115] whereas pre-Reformation kings enjoyed more temporal authority, 'and therefore they cannot have greater [ecclesiastical] *now*, unless some *Act of Parliament* give it them'. Never in all the centuries of pre-Reformation

[110] Henry Care, Bulstrode Whitelocke, and Nathaniel Johnston: see Chapter 6, pp. 260–7.
[111] Robert Washington, *Some Observations upon the Ecclesiastical Jurisdiction of the Kings of England* (1689), sig. A2r–v.
[112] Washington, *Observations*, p. 133.
[113] Washington, *Observations*, pp. 7 (qu.), 34, 5 (qu.), 8 (qu.).
[114] Washington, *Observations*, pp. 38–9, 44, 72 (qu.).
[115] The *Letter from a Person of Quality to his Friend in the Country* (1675) (sometimes attributed to Anthony Ashley Cooper, Earl of Shaftsbury) also complained of this (p. 4).

supremacy, Washington inaccurately but sincerely insisted, was personal royal *imperium* evidenced. No statutes, not even 1 Eliz. c. 1, had given kings a personal supremacy, and if they declared old powers, they did not transfer papal powers to monarchs.[116] Records stating laws were made by a particular king employed shorthand for legislation by king and the community or estates of the realm.[117] 'The whole Fabrick of the *English Saxon Church* was built upon Acts of Parliament.'[118] Parliament, embodying the consent of the realm, legislated on ecclesiastical matters. Whilst kings had invested bishops, it was parliament which conferred bishoprics. Statutes bound kings to resist papal legates.[119] Anselm appealed to parliament as his monarch's supremacy 'was so far from being *Personal*, that an Archbishop did as it were, *appeal* from himself in *Person* to himself in *Parliament*, and ... the *King* submitted, and owned the Jurisdiction'.[120]

The absolute unity of church and state before 1066 was preferable to the Norman division of spiritual and civil courts. Furthermore, from the thirteenth century popes gained power by dispensing, a trick which they taught kings.[121] But Washington denied that papal actions justified kings dispensing with *statutes*, a power Rome never claimed. How strange, Washington bitterly mused, that after so many complaints about *non obstantes* they should be

> screwed up to such a transcendent Soveraignty, as to frustrate *Laws*, *Statutes*, and *Acts of Parliament*; and that by vertue of an *Ecclesiastical Supremacy* by which the King is pretended to have whatever power the *Pope* had, when the *Pope himself* was never allowed *this*.[122]

For all the 'little Distinctions' invented by judges between private and public interest statutes, *mala prohibita* and *mala in se*, kings could not override laws. The solemnity with which statutes were passed militated against kings blithely suspending them, a power never asserted until Charles II, under whom it was 'twice damned in Parliament'.[123]

The sophistication of Washington's account lay in his willingness to admit that the Reformation, whilst claiming to restore ancient powers, had in fact introduced new ones as well. Since supremacy had been 'so long overshadowed, as to be almost forgot', men 'did not upon the

[116] Washington, *Observations*, pp. 77 (qu.), 56; p. 288 hinted that Washington might write further on 1 Elizabeth, but this does not seem to have happened.
[117] Washington, *Observations*, p. 24. [118] Washington, *Observations*, p. 20.
[119] Washington, *Observations*, pp. 10, 43; bishops: pp. 10–12, 33; legates: pp. 30–2.
[120] Washington, *Observations*, pp. 25, 28–9, qu. pp. 37–8.
[121] Washington, *Observations*, pp. 26–7, 49, 51–3, 84.
[122] Washington, *Observations*, pp. 78–9.
[123] Washington, *Observations*, pp. 68–9, 84–6 (qu. 68, 84).

Restitution of it, return all things to their former Estate'. Washington quoted the preamble to Henry's Act of Appeals, but then pointed out that 'sundry old authentic histories and chronicles' authorised no ecclesiastical commission, nor indeed any ecclesiastical prerogative independent of what parliament allowed.[124] Appeals to the king in person or in chancery were wholly new, and only refined late in Elizabeth's reign when the lawyers introduced commissions of review 'to make these *Acts* consistent with their imaginary *personal* Supreme Headship'.[125] Perhaps surprisingly, Washington refused to commit himself to specifying that canons were only legal if ratified by king-in-parliament. But he insisted that the king and clergy could not unite to tyrannise parliament. 'As soon as ever the foreign Yoke was cast off, [parliament] put in for their share of the *Supremacy* … they joyn'd with [Henry] in tying up the hands of the *Clergy*.'[126] Many powers were granted to kings (powers to appoint bishops and suffragans, archiepiscopal power to dispense when the king needed it), but these derived from parliamentary authority; they were not inherent royal rights.[127] The capstone of Henrician supremacy, the royal power to decide doctrine, was a parliamentary grant of 32 Hen. VIII c. 26; but this 'personal' power 'died with him, and was never pretended to by any of his Successors'. Since parliament gave it, parliament must have held it, for 'it is greater to give than to receive'.[128]

Henry's supremacy surpassed any other monarch's, blazing 'like a Meteor', yet its extra powers still *derived from parliament*. The doctrine, discipline, rites, rights, and jurisdiction of the Church of England were erected by parliament, not king or clergy. 'No one Pin was fastned in this Tabernacle, but according to what the *Legislative Body* of the *Kingdom* prescribed … unquestionably … there is a greater and more Soveraign *Supremacy* in Matters *Spiritual* and *Ecclesiastical*, in the *King* and both *Houses* of *Parliament*, than is lodged in the *King* himself, or in the *King* and *Convocation*.'[129] For Washington, the Act of Supremacy did not translate papal power to the king, and only the clergy, not the laity, submitted to royal supremacy. Henry became no absolute '*Dominus fac-totum in Spiritualibus*'. Every exercise of the supremacy proceeded according to particular and positive laws, not vague absolute royal authority. 'The

[124] Washington, *Observations*, pp. 41, 97–101.
[125] Washington, *Observations*, pp. 103–5 (qu. 105), 113–14.
[126] Washington, *Observations*, pp. 117, 122 (qu.).
[127] Washington, *Observations*, pp. 119–20, 138–9, 123–4; p. 142 asserts that bishops were deprived by parliament, a crucial claim in 1689.
[128] Washington, *Observations*, pp. 143–4. [129] Washington, *Observations*, pp. 145, 157–8.

King's *Supremacy* was not accounted any such unbounded Power, as some fancy ... *Parliament* retain'd its share in the Jurisdiction over *Ecclesiastical* Persons and Things, notwithstanding the restitution, recognition (or call it what you will) of the *Supremacy*.'[130]

That it was lawyers who analysed the legitimacy of 1689 in the light of Tudor statutes, and that they reinterpreted that legislation in the context of the Revolution, should not surprise us. Some were more sympathetic to royal, some to parliamentary supremacy. Turning in more detail to Restoration legal thought will further reveal the role which common law, as distinct from kings and parliaments, was seen as having over the church.

LAWYERS AND THE SUPREMACY

Whether or not there was a seventeenth-century common law mind,[131] legal training primed men to consider the relationship between royal prerogative, statute, and common law. It is important to remember that not every common lawyer was a secret parliamentarian, or proto-whig: Chief Justices John Vaughan and Francis North were not averse to the prerogative. Nor were all lawyers common lawyers. The bibliophilic Civilian John Godolphin included a disquisition on the supremacy in his *Repertorium canonicum*, a work given its imprimatur by North and Bishop Compton of London.[132] Godolphin's book was a classic example of the type of argument which worried Washington. Parliament was barely mentioned, whilst the king's supremacy was paralleled with the pope's – a not uncommon legal comment.[133] Early Christian emperors, Anglo-Saxon kings, and Tudor monarchs governed the church, bishops, and convocations.[134] Godolphin did cite a variety of laws – statutory, common, Civil, and canon – and he did state that canon law is received by custom. He even allowed the king to be 'Supream Ordinary by the Ancient Common

[130] Washington, *Observations*, pp. 109, 127–8, 132 (qu.), 142–3 (qu.).

[131] J. G. A. Pocock, *The Ancient Constitution and the Feudal Law* (Cambridge, 1957; reissued, 1987).

[132] John Baker suggests that this might have been penance for Godolphin's Civil War Admiralty judgeship: *Monuments of Endlesse Labours: English Canonists and Their Work, 1300–1900* (1998), p. 79. His library catalogue is included in *Catalogus variorum & insignium librorum instructissimarum bibliothecarum ...* (1678).

[133] John Godolphin, *Repertorium canonicum; Or, An Abridgement of the Ecclesiastical Laws of this Realm, Consistent with the Temporal* (1678), pp. 4, 5. For lawyers' use of papal supremacy as a model see 75 Eng. Rep. 734, 2 Plowden 493 (*Grendon* v. *Bishop of Lincoln*, 1573), 82 Eng. Rep. 84, Jones W. 158 (*Evans and Kiffins* v. *Askwith*, 1625), 78 Eng. Rep. 750, Cro. Eliz. 500 (*Austen* v. *Twynne*, 1595).

[134] Godolphin, *Repertorium canonicum*, intro. p. 3, pp. 97, 99.

Law of *England*', but this was combined with an absolutist account of the king as 'the Law it self, and the only chief Interpreter thereof'. This power could be lent, but not abdicated, to judges.[135] The chapter on convocations explained that they were 'subordinate to the establish'd Laws of the Land', as canons were subject to royal authority. But this made church law legally binding, even without parliament's assent, and it left royal prerogative intact.[136]

Common law could prove the antiquity of *royal* supremacy for a man like Godolphin; for other legal theorists it governed the royal prerogative. But even less zealously royalist lawyers did not always transfer the ecclesiastical prerogative, as Washington did, simply from crown to parliament. For them, the ingredients of a proper mixed monarchy included a strong dose of unwritten law, and this affected the ecclesiastical as well as temporal prerogative.

The most intellectual lawyer of the early Restoration was Sir Matthew Hale, a prolific writer, although a reluctant publisher; several of his key tracts were printed only posthumously. Versed in pre-Civil War legal education, Hale's career spanned the Interregnum before coming to rest in the highest echelons of Charles II's legal establishment: Chief Justice of Kings Bench from 1671 to 1676. One of his manuscripts focused specifically on royal ecclesiastical supremacy,[137] but the ideas in it echoed his other juridical and devotional writings.[138] Hale's erenicism encompassed royalists during the Interregnum, but manifested itself after 1660 in familiarity with moderate Anglicans such as Barrow, Tillotson, Stillingfleet, Wilkins, and the Calvinist Bishop Barlow. He knew Ussher, advised Laud, and was a joint executor with Sir John Vaughan (the second most intellectual Restoration lawyer) of John Selden's will; Cromartie identifies Seldenian proclivities in Hale.[139]

135 Godolphin, *Repertorium canonicum*, pp. 131, 9, 6.

136 Godolphin, *Repertorium canonicum*, pp. 587–9.

137 Sir Matthew Hale, *The Royal Supremacy* (n.d.); a nineteenth-century printing.

138 Sir Matthew Hale, *Pleas of the Crown* (1678), Wing H254 is the authorised version, see sig. A2r on its unauthorised predecessor; Sir Matthew Hale, *Historia placitorum coronae* (2 vols., 1736, but with a reference at I.307 to 'this day, viz. 13 Car. 2'); Sir Matthew Hale, *The Judgment of the Late Lord Chief Justice Sir Matthew Hale, Of the Nature of True Religion, the Causes of its Corruption, and the Churches Calamity by Mens Additions and Violences, with the Desired Cure* (1684); Sir Matthew Hale, 'Reflections by the Lrd Cheife Justice Hale on Mr Hobbes his Dialogue of the Lawe', printed in W. S. Holdsworth, *A History of English Law*, vol. V (1924), pp. 499–513. On this piece, see D. E. C. Yale, 'Hobbes and Hale on Law, Legislation and the Sovereign', *Cambridge Law Journal*, 31 (1972), pp. 121–56; Cromartie, *Hale*, ch. 7.

139 W. S. Holdsworth, 'Sir Matthew Hale', *Law Quarterly Review*, 39 (1923), pp. 402–26, at pp. 406, 403, and 403, n. 4; Cromartie, *Hale*, pp. 178, 106.

Hale considered royal ecclesiastical power in detail in his uncompleted treatise on royal prerogative, first published in the context of nineteenth-century debates over ecclesiastical courts.[140] Wary of clerical aggrandisement, he subjugated the clergy to crown and parliament. Hale began with the standard distinction between the power of order and that of jurisdiction, the latter itself divided into internal and external. The power of order (priesthood, consecration, and chrism) originated, 'so much as is not superstitious', from Christ, although the time, place, person, and manner of use thereof was 'originally inherent in the Crown'. The monarch was the source of external jurisdiction, 'either formally to exercise, or at least virtually to derive', although the court of conscience had a 'higher commission'.[141] Clerical power derived from legitimate custom and illicit fraud. Churchmen, correctly fearing that civil authority could remove the powers it granted them, 'subrogated and interwove into men's minds a pretence and opinion of a higher right', 'pretended and imposed divine authority'. Hale repeated an anticlerical or antiprelatical narrative of royal folly in allowing such claims ('connived at or ignorantly entertained') to blossom because the clergy's socio-cultural power seemed politically useful.[142] Elsewhere he characterised the medieval period as dominated by the resulting problem of 'a double supreme power, or two kingdoms in every kingdom'.[143]

The true authorisation and extent of clerical power could, Hale argued, be discerned by a historical investigation into the English reception of ecclesiastics' authority. This Seldenian idea stressed the supremacy of civil powers (common law, custom, parliament, and monarchy) as those which determined and controlled ecclesiastical laws and courts. Ecclesiastical laws bound Englishmen 'not as laws of the Church, but as laws admitted by the kingdom'. Nonetheless this account could *defend* properly warranted ecclesiastical jurisdiction. Although Hale's *History of the Pleas of the Crown* declined to 'meddle' with ecclesiastical courts, he noted in passing their derivation from the crown, all their proceedings in criminal cases 'in some kind *Placita coronae*' which the king might discharge or pardon as he pleased.[144] Religion and politics were so intertwined that denying Christianity could be tried in King's Bench, for 'Christian religion is a part of the law it self'.[145] Yet, adjudicating a case in 1663, where

[140] Hale, *Royal Supremacy*, p. 3. [141] Hale, *Royal Supremacy*, pp. 9–10.
[142] Hale, *Royal Supremacy*, pp. 11–12. [143] Hale, *Historia placitorum coronae*, II.324.
[144] Hale, *Royal Supremacy*, p. 13; Hale, *Historia placitorum coronae*, I, sig. bv.
[145] 84 Eng. Rep. 906, 3 Keb. 607 (*R.* v. *Tayler*, 1675).

the creditors of a wife *de facto* separated from her husband sued him for the debts she had incurred, Hale deferentially acknowledged the role of church courts in regulating marriage. All eventualities were provided for by law, but that provision might derive from church courts. Although 'not the common law', their jurisdiction is 'appointed by the common law' which permits 'their coercion and proceedings' despite those being 'after another law'.[146] Hale's justification of church courts differed little from that of the more royalist judge Sir Robert Hyde, who pronounced that 'although the proceedings and process in the Ecclesiastical Courts are in the names of the bishops, yet these Courts are the King's Courts, and the law by which they proceed is the King's law'.[147] A vision of cooperative magistracy and ministry was never far from Hale's eyes, but he shifted between king, parliament, and judiciary determining what ecclesiastical jurisdiction was totally rejected and what controlled by prohibitions. 'The judge of the common law was the judge of the extent of [clerical] jurisdiction', the 'rule, extent, or subject [of ecclesiastical law] was alterable by Parliament'.[148]

Dividing his treatise on supremacy into pre- and post-Reformation periods, Hale occasionally spoke of the monarch wielding ecclesiastical supremacy. Pre-Christian kings had such authority; Christian monarchs issued dispensations for pluralism, granted sanctuaries, and heard appeals from visitations.[149] Changes to ecclesiastical courts and the creation of free chapels further demonstrated royal control of religion.[150] Even before the 1530s the foundation of 'most if not all' ecclesiastical power was in the civil magistrate, whatever clerical and papal *iure divino* rhetoric existed. Admitting that temporal power assisted ecclesiastical prosecution of heresy and excommunication, Hale yet spoke of the 'subordination and subservience' of ecclesiastical authority.[151] Clerical usurpation of powers did not necessarily mean, Hale hastened to add, that their pre-Reformation jurisdiction was void. Even an illicit power could 'grow into a settled right' by custom, adverse possession founding a prescriptive right to power less than supreme. But 'though usage could acquire a subordinate right from the Crown, it cannot an independent', so even erroneous *iure divino* claims did not and could not 'introduce an independent

[146] *Manby* v. *Scott*: Hale's judgment is given in Matthew Bacon, *A New Abridgement of the Law*, 7th edn (8 vols., 1832), I.714–19, qu. at p. 718.

[147] 86 Eng. Rep. 781, 1 Mod 124 (*Manby* v. *Scott*, 1663), qu. at 86 Eng. Rep. 786, 1 Mod. 133.

[148] Hale, *Royal Supremacy*, p. 13.

[149] Hale, *Royal Supremacy*, pp. 11, 15, 18; p. 19 ponders whether this is royal prerogative rather than purely ecclesiastical authority.

[150] Hale, *Royal Supremacy*, pp. 20–1, 16–17.

[151] Hale, *Royal Supremacy*, p. 23.

right unsubordinate to the supreme power of the Crown of England'. Henrician parliaments could therefore re-annex ecclesiastical powers to the crown.[152]

Hale's monarchist language slipped seamlessly into an argument for royal supremacy exercised by or in conjunction with parliament. To Hale, pre-Reformation history made it clear that

> the King *with those concurrences requisite* for the making of a temporal law, might likewise make an ecclesiastical, viz., *with the consent of Parliament* ... though ... the courteous usage of this kingdom did in former times indulge a kind of power legislative to the convocation of the clergy, as before, yet the same was without exclusion of the King's power *by assent of Parliament* to make laws in matters ecclesiastical.[153]

Ratification of canons was not a mere monarchical action, it being 'illusory and vain' for convocation to legislate without parliament.[154] Canons were 'subject to the lay power of the King (necessary requisites concurring)'; they might be admitted 'yet by the King by consent of Parliament to be altered'.[155] But even parliamentary supremacy metamorphosed into lawyerly supremacy: 'the courteous usage of this kingdom'. Canons and clerical privileges 'were not binding here, nor so taken farther than either by acts of parliament or the common acceptation of the kingdom they were received'. For Hale (as for St German and Bagshaw), it was lawyers who manned the ramparts of the common law against canonist invasions, who decreed how much of a canon was received. Prohibitions were as significant as statutes in setting boundaries to ecclesiastical courts. Thus clerical privileges 'received divers alterations and corrections and restrictions by the temporal judges, as the occasion required'.[156]

The final third of Hale's tract on the supremacy sought to establish ecclesiastical power on a firm but properly humble footing. The 1530s expelled papal authority but left ordinary (English episcopal) ecclesiastical power intact; no royal commissions newly authorising episcopal jurisdiction were needed.[157] Hale praised the new royal ability to dispense with a statute which contradicted a good canon (e.g. against pluralism). No excessive powers were given to Henry VIII, for though 'not altogether

[152] Hale, *Royal Supremacy*, pp. 24–5.

[153] Hale, *Royal Supremacy*, p. 14 (my emphasis); another example is in his attack on Hobbes, which begins with the Oath of *royal* Supremacy, and then limits royal dispensation: Hale, 'Reflections', pp. 508, 509–12.

[154] Quoted in Cromartie, *Hale*, p. 179. [155] Hale, *Royal Supremacy*, pp. 14–15.

[156] Hale, *Historia placitorum coronae*, II.329–30.

[157] Hale, *Royal Supremacy*, pp. 25–7. He was certain that the Edwardian statute on bishops and church courts was repealed.

declarative, but in respect of some points of civil interest enacting', no statute 'did or could' grant monarchy 'any other authority, but what was fundamentally in it, or what upon reasonable Custom admitted and received into the kingdom was established'.[158] Here again custom and reason seem to govern even mixed monarchical supremacy. The Act of Appeals meant the monarch held both civil and ecclesiastical power, but it 'did unite' and 'did not confound' the two. Hence the use of prohibitions, even *praemunire*, was still licit if one sphere of royal power threatened another.[159] The final pages of Hale's considerations on the supremacy described Henry VIII as 'the vicary-general of God on earth as well in causes spiritual as before in temporal'. Yet his tract ended abruptly, and on an ambiguous – even impenetrable – note. 'Now whether the settling by custom of a jurisdiction ecclesiastical in the Pope, and after an annexation of that Power to the Crown, hath not enabled the Crown in some things which if it had continued ever together could not be done without Act of Parliament.'[160]

Whether this constituted a concluding question, or one preliminary to a more profound exploration of the supremacy, is not clear. But Hale's musings show that debate on ecclesiastical jurisdiction and canons continued outside parliament. In fact, further probing reveals more discussion of convocation inside parliament than initially appears.

PARLIAMENT, CONVOCATION, AND ECCLESIASTICAL JURISDICTION

The natural point of contact between parliament and the church was convocation. The clergy's legislative body met in two houses, the upper (bishops) and lower (elected representatives of the parochial clergy). This not only mirrored parliamentary organisation, it was in a way part of parliament and normally met simultaneously. The Reformation left convocation able to vote taxes on the clergy and draft canons, although canons had to be ratified by the crown in order to be legally binding. The most heated pre-Civil War debates over whether parliament, as well as the monarch, should ratify canons apparently lapsed after 1662. Convocation met during the Restoration, but the agreement between Sheldon and Clarendon that clerical taxation would be decided in parliament drastically reduced its prominence. This, along with limited surviving evidence, has led

[158] Hale, *Royal Supremacy*, pp. 30, 26 (qu.), 28 (qu.).
[159] Hale, *Royal Supremacy*, p. 28. [160] Hale, *Royal Supremacy*, p. 30.

historians to assume that the *de facto* abeyance of convocation means that there is no story to be told about it between the revision of the Prayer Book in 1662 and the furore over comprehension in 1689. Lathbury's study of convocation under Charles II focused exclusively on its revision of the Prayer Book; the more recent study of *Parliament and the Church* omits the Restoration entirely.[161] However, whilst convocation did not engage in prolonged activity, this did not mean that it went unmentioned.[162]

If the ghost of convocation did not exactly haunt the Restoration, its shadowy presence can nevertheless be glimpsed. During debates over nonconformity in 1666 and 1668, several MPs referred to convocation as both sitting and active. Milward recorded a debate on whether to pass the bill to suppress atheism and blasphemy, to consult 'the Convocation now sitting', or call 'some divines' to a committee.[163] MPs divided over whether comprehension was their business or that of the clergy: some thought convocation should be consulted, whilst others thought it useless. The former press licenser John Birkenhead thought members should not 'trouble' the king with the question, but rather ask convocation to draft reconciliatory measures – perhaps a strategy to avoid change.[164] Yet another group felt that only parliament could legislate to loosen uniformity: Coventry told Birkenhead that the king had referred the question to parliament, and a committee of religion ought to consider it. Another member argued that the Declaration of Breda could not override a statute; the only option was to repeal the Act of Uniformity.[165] Edmund Waller opposed reference to convocation, as only parliament could make civil laws. Convocation, he argued, dealt with purely spiritual questions, but parliament decreed which questions were purely spiritual.[166] Sir Charles Wheler, shortly

[161] Thomas Lathbury, *A History of the Convocation of the Church of England*, 2nd edn (1853), ch. 10; J. P. Parry and Stephen Taylor, eds., *Parliament and the Church, 1529–1960* (Edinburgh, 2000; *Parliamentary History*, 19). The skeletal records are in *Concilia magnae Britanniae et Hiberniae*, ed. David Wilkins (4 vols., 1737), IV.556–619. On the cession of clerical self-taxation, often seen as the reason for convocation's decline, see Norman Ravitch, *Sword and Mitre: Government and Episcopate in France and England in the Age of Aristocracy* (The Hague, 1966), pp. 202–5.

[162] A parallel exists here to parliaments between 1681 and 1685: not called, but nevertheless frequently spoken of and so possible to study; see Grant Tapsell, 'Parliament and Political Division in the Last Years of Charles II, 1681–5', *Parliamentary History*, 22 (2003), pp. 243–62, esp. pp. 245, 262.

[163] Caroline Robbins, ed., *The Diary of John Milward, Esq., Member of Parliament for Derbyshire, September, 1666 to May, 1668* (Cambridge, 1938), pp. 18, 25 (qu.) (9, 16 Oct. 1666); Grey, *Debates*, I.106, 126 (qu.) (4 Mar., 8 Apr. 1668).

[164] Milward, *Diary*, p. 220 (qu.); see also Goodrick (p. 214) and Grey, *Debates*, I.114, 110 (11 Mar. 1668).

[165] Grey, *Debates*, I.114; Milward, *Diary*, pp. 220, 214 (11 Mar. 1668).

[166] Milward, *Diary*, p. 249; Grey, *Debates*, I.128 (8 Apr. 1668).

before arguing for reform of ecclesiastical abuses, suggested a joint committee consult with convocation, noting that the Commons had denied convocation power to alter the Book of Common Prayer in 1662.[167] But although parliament could claim governance of matters which traversed the spiritual/political divide, members might invite clerical involvement for amending or drafting the details of bills.[168] Did such episodes evidence deference to the wisdom of the clergy in religious matters, or a doctrine of parliamentary control over ecclesiastical affairs: parliament – like monarchs – inviting clerical counsel which it could accept or reject at pleasure?

The Lords endeavoured to protect clerical rights. Their petitions to summon convocation in the 1670s show both a sense of that body as sliding into obsolescence and a feeling that it was the king's right to call it. On 19 November 1675, after debating Henrician and Elizabethan statutes and canons, the Lords petitioned the king 'that the Convocation of the Clergy may meet frequently', that deceased members be replaced, and that 'they do make unto the King's Majesty such Representations, as may be for the Safety of the Religion established'.[169] The final plea is noteworthy, for both this episode and another in February 1677 took place during discussion of bills to secure the Protestant religion. The 1677 petition was identical, and the king replied that he would 'give Command that the Places vacant in the Convocation be filled up; and that they meet frequently, and go upon the Work which is proper for them to do'.[170] This, considered worthy of report by a newsletter writer, was perhaps a sentiment held more strongly by the Lords than the Commons; no evidence of any attempt at a joint petition is extant.[171] But nor can any challenge be found to the inclusion of members of convocation in parliamentary privilege, a privilege established in 1429 and invoked on several occasions during the Restoration. Henry Brunsell, prebend and proctor for Ely, when arrested in Nottingham in 1666 by Thomas Ash, cited the 1429 statute. In December 1667 the Lords summoned Ash, but discharged him as Brunsell did not appear to make his case.[172] In February 1670 Ash was summoned

[167] Grey, *Debates*, I.112 (11 Mar. 1668).
[168] HMC, *Ninth Report*, pt II, appx, p. 83 (1 Mar. 1677); Grey, *Debates*, III.180 (21 May 1675).
[169] *LJ*, XIII.30 (19 Nov. 1675); HMC, *Ninth Report*, pt II, appx, p. 43 (13 Nov. 1675) (25 Hen. VIII c. 19: the Act of Submission of the Clergy; 13 Eliz. c. 12: the Act confirming thirty-six of the Thirty-Nine Articles).
[170] *LJ*, XIII.50, 52, 54 (22, 23, 26 Feb. 1677).
[171] Folger Shakespeare Library, x.d.529, fo. 7. I am grateful to Stephen Taylor for this reference.
[172] *LJ*, XII.43 (10 Dec. 1666), 136 (14 Nov. 1667), 173 (17 Dec. 1667); HMC, *Eighth Report*, appx, p. 104 (10 Dec. 1666). 1429: 8 Hen. VI c. 1.

again, and he claimed he had thought an arrest permissible after parliament was prorogued. He was discharged with a warning 'as well to take Notice of the Privilege belonging to the Members of the Convocation, as to the Members of Parliament'.[173] In spring 1668 Sir William Juxon brought a writ of *quare impedit* against Robert Pory, who had claimed the mastership of a hospital against Juxon's nominee; as a member of convocation, Pory was protected from lawsuits by parliamentary privilege. The Lords threw out Juxon's petition against their judgment for Pory.[174] And in February 1674 the Lords heard a complaint against two Dorsetshire bailiffs who, having arrested William Zouch during convocation's sitting, refused to discharge him 'notwithstanding that the Statute of Privilege of Members of the Convocation was read to them'.[175] Whilst the decisions in favour of the clergy might be interpreted as a defence of *parliament*'s rights, it is significant that they nonetheless suggest that convocation was seen as an integral part of parliament. Citations for breach of privilege are not extant after the middle of the 1670s – perhaps a sign of convocation's accelerated decline.

Assertions of parliamentary control of the church and convocation can also be found, particularly expressed in the Commons. 'In' is the salient word, for some *members* of the Commons spoke out like this, but it is hard to discern the Lower House moving as a single body against the clergy. Indeed, an individual's perception of convocation's role could vary according to the particular proposal. In January 1674 the Yorkist William Coventry rejected a motion to ban Catholics and nonconformists from voting on the grounds that convocation would determine the franchise. But in spring 1675 he claimed that a bill on popery was a question for convocation, not the Commons.[176] In March 1662 the Lords thanked convocation for their help with the Uniformity Bill, but it was the Commons who prompted the Lords to ask convocation to prepare a canon for royal approval on reverend gestures to be used in church, since they saw this matter as properly governed by canons from convocation not provisos to statutes.[177] Whilst in April the Commons voted by a narrow margin (96–90) to reject debate on the amendments made by convocation to the Prayer Book, they next voted to affirm that convocation's

173 *LJ*, XII.294 (26 Feb. 1670), 295 (qu., 28 Feb. 1670). On 21 Feb. the Lords ordered Brunsell be released: *LJ*, XII.292.

174 *LJ*, XII.195 (2 Mar. 1668), 230–1 (23 Apr. 1668); HMC, *Eighth Report*, appx, p. 117 (2 Mar. 1668). *Quare impedit*: a writ to override clerical opposition to lay patronage.

175 *LJ*, XII.631 (qu.); HMC, *Ninth Report*, pt II, appx, p. 42 (9 Feb. 1674).

176 Grey, *Debates*, II.225 (7 Jan. 1674), III.16 (21 Apr. 1675).

177 *CJ*, VIII.415 (28 Apr. 1662); *LJ*, XI.408, 449, 451 (15 Mar., 7, 8 May 1662).

changes 'might, by the Order of this House, have been debated'.[178] Moderation in *exercising* supremacy over convocation did not translate into restraint in *asserting* it.

Another potential stimulus for claims of parliamentary or judicial power over the church was discussion of the relative authority of ecclesiastical and civil courts. Jurisdiction over two causes in particular, intestacy and marriage, was divided between temporal and spiritual authority in ways liable to fuel disagreement.[179] Questions about marital jurisdiction repeatedly arose in the 1660s and 1670s. In September 1666 the antiprelatical doyenne William Prynne offered a bill against episcopal power to grant marriage licences.[180] In a debate on a Lords bill in February 1678 the anti-papist William Sacheverell, an early advocate of Exclusion, argued for common law jurisdiction over clandestine and incestuous marriages.[181] On 30 and 31 March 1670 the Commons worried about whether convocation ought to be consulted over the Roos divorce bill. Would consulting the clergy oblige MPs to follow their decision? Or was the issue beyond parliament's competence? John Ernle, Robert Atkyns, and Sir Charles Harbord – all usually court supporters – argued that divorce was an ecclesiastical question for convocation, as parliament could not enact matters divine.[182] Again the Commons appear divided and uncertain, as wary of overstepping their own authority as they were tetchy about surrendering any of it, muddled about the role of convocation.

Were the Lords any clearer? In June 1678 they were confronted with the issue of their ecclesiastical jurisdiction when Charles Cottington petitioned them about his potentially bigamous marriage. Having married in Turin, Cottington abandoned his wife, Gallina, upon discovery that her earlier divorce was collusory.[183] She, following him to England, won her case in the Courts of Arches and Delegates; he appealed to the Lords. The House initially referred the case to their committee of privileges, but

[178] *CJ*, VIII.408 (16 Apr. 1662).

[179] On intestacy see HMC, *Eighth Report*, appx, p. 118 (4 Mar. 1668, although this may not have intended a change in jurisdiction); Milward, *Diary*, pp. 271–2 (23 Apr. 1668), 244 (3 Apr. 1668). Another Lords bill is reported in HMC, *Ninth Report*, pt II, appx, p. 115 (25 May 1678); Grey, *Debates*, I.121–2 (27 Mar. 1668); Hening, ed., *Parliamentary Diary*, pp. 72–3 (7 Feb. 1671).

[180] Milward, *Diary*, p. 8 (27 Sept. 1666). The bill was rejected.

[181] Grey, *Debates*, V.59, 202 (4, 23 Feb. 1678). The Commons lost the bill.

[182] Grey, *Debates*, I.251–63, at 252, 256, 259, 260 (30, 31 Mar. 1670). On the divorce, and Charles's potential favouring of it as a model for his own succession problems, see Lawrence Stone, *Road to Divorce: England, 1530–1987* (Oxford, 1990), pp. 309–12.

[183] Thomas Barlow's discussion of the case suggested that Gallina claimed she was forced into marriage with her first husband, although she had lived with him for two years and had a daughter. Barlow focused on showing the Cottington–Gallina cohabitation was illicit in ecclesiastical law: The Queen's College, Oxford, MS 289, fos. 153r–158r.

Cottington soon renewed his petition, claiming he feared excommunication, whereupon the Lords sought legal advice.[184] Invoking Henrician statutes and Caudrey's Case, Attorney-General William Jones argued 'that the King had two jurisdictions, ecclesiastical and temporal', marriage falling under the first. But 'the Lords had no jurisdiction', for they lacked the 'mixed qualification' which meant 'anointed kings are capable of Spiritual causes'. Although bishops sat in the House, they did so by reason of their temporal baronies alone, meaning the Lords were 'not competent judges of Spiritual causes'. Henrician statutes which laid down the course of ecclesiastical appeals did not allow the Lords a role, nor was one given by Elizabeth in 1559. Supremacy was royal: 'the King does grant a review from the Delegates, but yet exclusive of this House, and only by his supremacy'; Henrician and Elizabethan statutes were 'for the King's Supremacy; the case was not altered as to this House'. Other lawyers challenged this by claiming either that marriage and divorce were secular types of spiritual causes, or that the canon law which governed them was 'part of [i.e. subordinate to] the law of England'. But the Attorney-General begged to disagree. Although, he explained, the House could judge ecclesiastical persons and the king could ask their advice, this did not constitute jurisdiction over spiritual causes. Prohibitions issued from the law courts, not the Lords. Furthermore, while spiritual questions which touched on temporal cases could be judged by lay courts, when 'wholly spiritual', as Cottington's, they were untouchable.[185]

In his own record of the case, which the king apparently asked him to attend, Nottingham advised that it was correct not to challenge a decision given in a foreign court. Ever hostile to the Lords' appellate jurisdiction, he agreed a commission of review was a matter of royal grace, citing a case from 1628 in which the Lords told a petitioner (claiming an interest in a will opposed by the Delegates) to ask the king for a commission of review.[186] Accepting Cottington's petition 'invaded' the king's ecclesiastical supremacy.[187] Nottingham also dismissed as spurious the roll-call of sources offered in support of parliamentary supremacy: medieval statutes, Prynne's *Plea for the Lords*, Selden's *De synedriis*, and Selden's historical works on pre-Norman civil and ecclesiastical courts sitting together.[188] On 12 June the committee

[184] *LJ*, XIII.217, 226, 231, 241, 243 (10, 23, 28 May and 6, 8 June 1678).

[185] HMC, *Ninth Report*, pt II, appx, p. 113 (10 May 1678). Barlow stated that English canons were as lawful as statutes: The Queen's College, Oxford, MS 289, fo. 156r.

[186] D. E. C. Yale, ed., *Lord Nottingham's Chancery Cases* (2 vols., 1957 and 1961), II.661–3.

[187] Yale, ed., *Nottingham's Chancery Cases*, II.661.

[188] Yale, ed., *Nottingham's Chancery Cases*, II.663; see also I.cix–cx.

for privileges reported their decision that the Lords had no jurisdiction in the case, a decision which the House endorsed five days later, perhaps flattered by Essex's suggestion that their consent to the Henrician statute on appeals meant a voluntary cession of power, not an inherent defect in it.[189] Cottington's case was cited in 1679 by Nottingham when judging another complaint about the Delegates. 'There can be no resort to Parliament by way of appeal for any injustice done in the spiritual courts.'[190]

Other lawyers, however, were less reticent in asserting the primacy of lay judicial supremacy over marital causes. Thomas Hunt, who had defended the right of bishops to judge capital cases in the Lords in 1679, was by 1682 heatedly challenging ecclesiastical jurisdiction. In *Mr Emmerton's Marriage with Mrs Bridget Hyde Considered*, he proclaimed the supremacy of statute and common law over ecclesiastical jurisdiction. The case was politically charged. Bridget Hyde was the stepdaughter of the London banker-goldsmith Sir Robert Viner and an heiress on her mother's side too. Her maternal aunts plotted her clandestine marriage to her cousin, John Emerton, in 1674 (when she was twelve). When Viner arranged her (willing) marriage to Viscount Dumblane, Danby's son, Emerton sued, and the case became mired in the ecclesiastical courts for eight years – not least, ironically, because key witnesses could not be called since they had been excommunicated for participating in a clandestine marriage! The Court of Delegates upheld the Emerton marriage in 1680, in 1682 Danby forced a review of their judgment, and he was finally forced to pay off Emerton in 1683 since Hyde had by then married Dumblane (whereupon the Delegates quashed the Emerton marriage).[191] Hunt mischievously suggested that the slowness of church courts in giving judgment had only worsened the situation.[192] In the midst of a historical disquisition on prohibited marriages, he asserted that marriage existed long before government, and certainly before priesthood; *pace* Dryden's famous couplet, 'marriage was no invention of Priest craft', and should thus be decided by civil not clerical authorities: 'alwayes and every-where judged by the ordinary Courts of Judicature ... not dictated by the Priests'.[193] Control

[189] *LJ*, XIII.246, 251 (12, 17 June 1678); Yale, ed., *Nottingham's Chancery Cases*, II.663–4.

[190] Yale, ed., *Nottingham's Chancery Cases*, II.735; see also I.cxii. Judicial authority might be, of course, increased by commissions of review rather than appeals to the Lords.

[191] See Andrew Browning, *Thomas Osborne, Earl of Danby* (3 vols., Glasgow, 1951), I.138–41, 245, 351, II.104–8. Dering recorded a debate on the case: Maurice F. Bond, ed., *The Diaries and Papers of Sir Edward Dering Second Baronet, 1644 to 1684* (1976), pp. 75–6 (30 Apr. 1675).

[192] Thomas Hunt, *Mr Emmerton's Marriage with Mrs Bridget Hyde Considered* (1682), pp. 21–2.

[193] Hunt, *Emmerton's Marriage*, pp. 26, 28; see pp. 26–7 on Dryden as 'a prophane immoral man' whose 'Leud Rhime' (*Absalom and Achitophel*) calls marriage priestcraft and who 'owes all his esteem to the Debaucherys of the Age'.

of wedlock by the church was a relic of papal usurpation, evidence of an incomplete Reformation. Leaving common law to judge fact and church courts to decide right erects 'two thwarting Judicatures that are not subordinat'.[194] But to think that this must be the case was an error. Hunt derided his target, Chief Justice Vaughan, for wrongly interpreting Henrician statutes. Henrician legislation initially excluded only the pope from determining prohibited degrees of marriage; Vaughan was wrong to argue that the power these acts gave to English church courts meant that marriage was under lay control. If English ecclesiastical courts could add extra prohibitions, canons could forbid more than common law did. Hunt scorned Vaughan's assumption that 'a Lawful *Canon* is the Law of the Kingdom, as well as an Act of Parliament':

> This is a great Paradox indeed, that *Canons* are Laws, that they can controul Laws. That a *Parliament* can give away the Legislative Authority, and impower any Synod or Convocation, to Abrogate their Laws.[195]

Only 32 Hen. VIII c. 34 finally gave 'full and compleat remedy ... against the unreasonable assumings of the Canon Law' and 'restor'd' marriage to civil courts.[196]

Hunt's case was at times predicated on a parliamentary supremacy demonstrated by the power of statute to incorporate and make binding other laws. Henrician statutes decreed that marriages were incestuous if so defined by divine law: in scripture, which Hunt insisted meant only the degrees prohibited in Leviticus (with none of the exemptions). Although Leviticus was not in fact obligatory divine law, the statute said it was, and so it must therefore be taken to be.[197] Yet other parts of his pamphlet seemed to attribute supremacy more to common law judges than to parliament. Common-law courts are 'competent to understand and Interpret a Chapter of *Leveticus* [*sic*] and a Law of *Moses* as well as any other Writing, or as our own Statute Laws', and 'consequently the Authority of the Church [is] precluded'. Churchmen can 'gloss' scripture, but it is judges who give 'a Legal and binding interpretation'.[198] If churchmen seek to interfere, they will be subject to prohibitions, for an 'Ecclesiastical Court cannot allow of what the temporal Law hath declared to be contrary to the Law of God', it has no cognizance of statute.[199] For Hunt, the

194 Hunt, *Emmerton's Marriage*, pp. 31, 21 (qu.).
195 Hunt, *Emmerton's Marriage*, pp. 42 (qu.), 31–5.
196 Hunt, *Emmerton's Marriage*, pp. 35, 38.
197 Hunt, *Emmerton's Marriage*, pp. 3, 38.
198 Hunt, *Emmerton's Marriage*, pp. 4, 36.
199 Hunt, *Emmerton's Marriage*, pp. 40–1 (qu. 40). He did allow church courts some role over conjugal rights, incest, and incontinence: pp. 24–5.

church could exhort and persuade but it could not legislate other than on the two sacraments of communion and baptism. His citations of Selden and Grotius betrayed an unsurprising intellectual genealogy.[200]

Ecclesiastical power could be contained by prohibitions, clerical defiance threatened with *praemunire*. Ideally monarchs, parliaments, convocations, and courts would work in harmony to support true religion and uphold the Church of England. As this chapter has shown, Restoration monarchs' pursuit of indulgence disrupted this relationship. But that was not the only changing factor in the later seventeenth century. The increasingly strident clericalism of many leading figures in the Church, as the following chapter demonstrates, also destabilised the royal supremacy and rendered dubious not only the king's status as defender of the English Protestant faith, but also churchmen's willingness to accept it.

[200] Hunt, *Emmerton's Marriage*, pp. 28–9, 43.

CHAPTER 3

Spiritual authority and royal jurisdiction: the question of bishops

In 1660, amidst heated debates over the nature of the church settlement, the Huguenot divine Jean Gailhard published a tract on *The Controversie Between Episcopacy and Presbytery*. In favour of the latter, he attacked the notion, 'most uncharitable' to European Reformed Protestantism, that episcopal ordination was necessary for legitimate ministry. Gailhard highlighted the dangers of exalted claims for episcopacy. 'To prove, their Prelacy to be of a divine Right', he wrote of English churchmen, 'is to disown the Kings Supremacy from whom they acknowledge to receive that preferment'.[1] Gailhard was not the only Restoration writer to express such worries, for many Dissenters and their sympathisers insisted that *iure divino* episcopacy and supremacy were incompatible.

This chapter considers how far such claims were justified and the extent to which a churchman's view of episcopacy altered their understanding of supremacy. After surveying the mentality of the Restoration Church, it considers two churchmen who offered detailed accounts of supremacy: the defender of liturgical conformity William Falkner and the dean of Salisbury, Thomas Pierce. It then discusses the attitudes to supremacy held by Edward Stillingfleet and John Tillotson, two preachers who offered limited support for episcopacy, who were open to comprehension of Dissenters, and who were only promoted in the novel circumstances of the post-Revolution Williamite Church. The final two sections of the chapter dissect the prevailing clerical and clericalist rhetoric of *iure divino* episcopacy and restraints on supremacy. They consider the theologian Herbert Thorndike, who helped produce both the Polyglot Bible and the 1662 Book of Common Prayer, and the high-church[2] pastor Simon Lowth, along with a supporting cast of authors: the Master of the

[1] Jean Gailhard, *The Controversie Between Episcopacy and Presbytery* (1660), pp. 8, 38.

[2] The term was not used until the late 1670s, but is preferable to the more obscure 'Canterburian' and to 'Laudian', which seems fraught with difficulties even if detached from Charles I's archbishop.

Temple William Sherlock, Bishop Benjamin Laney of Ely, and the patristic scholar William Cave. The language of these men contained latent potential for conflict between bishops and kings. This was, however, actualised only when royal policies contradicted churchmen's aims. If the experience of Interregnum independence from supremacy focused clerical minds on their church as a holy catholic society rather than a body by law established, the policies of their restored supreme governors did much to encourage this shift of emphasis. It was the contingent choices of kings as to whether to support the Church or to patronise Dissent or Catholicism which determined how far a writer would endorse supremacy at any given time. The events of 1660 to 1689 proved that spiritual and sovereign authority were separable and, in this atmosphere, *iure divino* claims proved a useful counterweight to royal preferences.

IURE DIVINO OR *IURE HUMANO*? THE RESTORATION CHURCH AND EPISCOPACY

Historians have sometimes asserted that the authority of the post-1660 episcopate was waning. Whilst recognising the vehemence of campaigns to prosecute Dissent, they have seen these as reliant on civil support because ecclesiastical power was emasculated, and thus as patchy and occasional, dependent on the cooperation of local magistrates and tory gentlemen.[3] It was indeed true that cooperation with lay judicial powers was needed for prosecution to be effective, and that without High Commission independent action by the church was inhibited. Local laity were more likely to turn against their recusant neighbours, whether of the 'popish' or 'fanatic' variety, in the aftermath of scares about rebellion or rumours of plots: persecution had a political chronology and its intensity a political stimulus. In part the constant complaints of churchmen that they were not receiving sufficient aid in their war against irreligion and nonconformity demonstrated their dependence on external assistance. But such dependence was accepted and justified by the idea of coercive powers as appurtenances of spiritual authority, whilst jeremiads about backsliding justices were a constant feature of the early modern

[3] John Spurr, *England in the 1670s* (Oxford, 2000), pp. 231, 234–5; John Spurr, 'Religion in Restoration England', in Lionel K. J. Glassey, ed., *The Reigns of Charles II and James VII & II* (Houndmills, Basingstoke, 1997); Claire Cross, *Church and People: England, 1450–1660*, 2nd edn (Oxford, 1999), ch. 10; Robert E. Rodes, jr, *Lay Authority and Reformation in the English Church: Edward I to the Civil War* (Notre Dame, IN, 1982), pp. 242–3; Robert E. Rodes, jr, *Law and Modernisation in the Church of England: Charles II to the Welfare State* (Notre Dame, IN, 1991), pp. 2–10.

lay-clerical landscape. Instead one might emphasise the unabashed clamour for intolerance, its explicit justification on theoretical grounds, and the willingness of Anglican royalists to seize the ecclesiastical initiative. While they might have to implement their desires via the royal person, this merely meant that they 'told the king what his will should be'.[4]

The assertiveness of the Church's polemic was furthermore complemented by concrete demands: the narrowness of the Act of Uniformity and its new requirement of episcopal ordination, debates in 1661 to 1663 as to the status of bishops as peers, and the action for *scandalum magnatum* brought by Bishop Compton of London against the maverick pastor Edmund Hickeringill in 1682.[5] The power of the Restoration episcopate was both institutionally and intellectually entrenched. Walter Simon notes the authority of bishops in the Lords, but wrongly suggests that churchmen did not seek self-government.[6] Jeffrey Collins's view of the rise of ecclesiological dualism causing a new level of conflict between crown and episcopate is more accurate, and this chapter pursues his account of the 1660s across the Restoration period.[7] Although the intellectual justifications of *iure divino* episcopacy had implications for supremacy, high churchmanship and supremacy came into conflict because of royal policies of toleration, indulgence, and Catholicisation. It was not supremacy *per se* but its use (or abuse) by Charles II and James II which irked churchmen.[8]

Restoration churchmen did not share an ecclesiology, although their claims about episcopacy tended to be extremely forceful. The idea of *iure divino* episcopacy was not hegemonic, especially during the reconstruction of the national church between 1660 and 1662. The harsh cadences of high-church rhetoric were softened by the circulation of Archbishop Ussher's arguments for moderated episcopacy, and the willingness of

[4] Mark Goldie, 'Danby, the Bishops and the Whigs', in Tim Harris, Paul Seaward, and Mark Goldie, eds., *The Politics of Religion in Restoration England* (Oxford, 1990), p. 77; Mark Goldie, 'The Theory of Religious Intolerance in Restoration England', in Ole Peter Grell, Jonathan I. Israel, and Nicholas Tyacke, eds., *From Persecution to Toleration: The Glorious Revolution and Religion in England* (Oxford, 1991).

[5] See *LJ*, XI.338, 480–1 (26 Nov. 1661, 19–21 Feb. 1663); *EB*, P329. For Hickeringill, see pp. 194–7 below.

[6] Walter G. Simon, *The Restoration Episcopate* (New York, 1965), pp. 7, 71–2, 67, 107. However, the bishops did not always vote the same way, and rarely joined the inner 'cabinet' council: Simon, *Restoration Episcopate*, pp. 68, 89, ch. 5; Andrew Swatland, *The House of Lords in the Reign of Charles II* (Cambridge, 1996), pp. 32–3.

[7] Jeffrey R. Collins, 'The Restoration Bishops and the Royal Supremacy', *Church History*, 68 (1999), pp. 549–80.

[8] This follows Collins's sense that both an intellectual shift and Restoration politics were necessary to the change in the Church's mentality ('Restoration Bishops', passim).

men such as John Lloyd (later Vice-Chancellor of Oxford and bishop of St Davids) to find a role for presbyters arguably give the period before 1662 a different flavour from that of the post-Uniformity age.[9] After 1662, arguments for episcopacy by human law or custom or convenience fell away, perhaps becoming inexpressible. As Collins notes, the Restoration ecclesiastical establishment 'swept aside moderate justifications of episcopacy'.[10]

Thus, if any trend made the Restoration Church distinct, it was the prevalence of high churchmanship, founded both in the tangible experience of Civil War existence without establishment and in the intellectual discovery of clerical identity in patristic sources. The church of the 1640s and 1650s, no longer by law established, discovered a new and firmer basis than government favour. During the Interregnum, with royal leadership in abeyance, clergy (primarily Gilbert Sheldon and Henry Hammond, neither of whom were then bishops) kept Anglicanism alive.[11] In a mentality of exile, whether experienced abroad or in England, clerical eminence no longer derived simply from institutional position, but from the extent of Civil War suffering. Charles I had signed the Clerical Disabilities Act and seemed willing to abandon prelacy in the late 1640s, a policy his son's Scottish alliance put into effect. If the church–state alliance had been a necessary coalition rather than a natural and perfect partnership, then the regicide paradoxically emancipated the Anglican Church.[12] Without a nursing parent, there was no need to remain a child. The restored Church viewed Charles II with wary eyes, its distrust of him (perhaps begun with his failure to renew the Interregnum episcopate) repeatedly reinforced when Anglican restoration was interrupted by royal indulgences which disrupted the prosecution of nonconformity and interfered with the building of Jerusalem.

[9] James Ussher, *The Reduction of Episcopacie* (1660); Ephraim Udall, *The Bishop of Armaghes Direction, Concerning the Lyturgy, and Episcopall Government* (repr. 1660). John Lloyd, *A Treatise of the Episcopacy, Liturgies, and Ecclesiastical Ceremonies of the Primitive Times* (1660), is ambiguous (e.g. p. 72), advocating presbyters (p. 63), presbyters and bishops (pp. 12–13, 25, 58–9), and supporting episcopacy as apostolic (pp. 19–21, 74).

[10] Collins, 'Restoration Bishops', p. 561. Anon., *Episcopal Government and the Honour of the Present Bishops Proved Necessary to be Maintained* (Dublin (but addressed to the 'Citizens of London'), 1679), p. 5, defending episcopacy on the grounds that it was best suited to the temper of Englishmen, stands out as unusual.

[11] John W. Packer, *The Transformation of Anglicanism, 1643–1660, with Special Reference to Henry Hammond* (Manchester, 1969), p. 45 and passim; Victor D. Sutch, *Gilbert Sheldon: Architect of Anglican Survival, 1640–1675* (The Hague, 1973), p. 47 and ch. 3. On Sutch, see Robert Beddard's review article, 'Sheldon and Anglican Recovery', *Historical Journal*, 19 (1976), pp. 1005–17.

[12] Simon, *Restoration Episcopate*, pp. 20, 22; Collins, 'Restoration Bishops', pp. 558 (emphasising suffering for prelacy not just royalism), 567.

When Restoration writers looked back on their Civil War experience of deprivation and suffering, they saw in it a reflection of the pre-Constantinian persecuted church. Crucial to Restoration clerical mentality was intensified patristic study, both a symptom of an increasingly independent church identity and a stimulus to the confidence of the clergy. As Jean-Louis Quantin has shown, over the early modern period English churchmen shifted emphasis ever backwards to earlier Fathers, increasingly emphasising the pre-Nicene and Greek Fathers, although never surrendering to a Catholic notion of tradition.[13] Patristic scholarship both upheld episcopacy and marked the coming of age of churchmen whose polemical aims coincided with precise scholarly research. The importance of Cyprian and Ignatius hints how it may also have been a reaction to notions of 'primitive' being conflated with 'moderate' episcopacy. The writings of Ignatius, martyred in the early second century under Trajan, argued clearly for the importance and power of the bishop in the first generation succeeding the Apostles. Until the 1640s English scholars had had to rely on the 'Long Recension' of Ignatius's epistles, which contained both spurious letters and interpolated texts. Although European Protestants expressed doubts over the textual tradition, it was the Irish archbishop James Ussher who identified six genuine epistles in his *Polycarpii et Ignatii epistolae* of 1644; a seventh was shown to be genuine by the Restoration scholar John Pearson in 1672.[14] This scholarship pitted Anglicans against Huguenots, who were worried that Ignatius outlawed non-episcopal churches. His letters' unambiguous nature indeed overturned any Hieronymian case for episcopacy *iure ecclesiastico*,[15] proving

[13] Jean-Louis Quantin, *The Church of England and Christian Antiquity* (Oxford, 2009). Quantin's is the first study which devotes serious attention to Restoration patristics. On post-Revolution patristic study, see Leslie W. Barnard, 'The Use of the Patristic Tradition in the Late Seventeenth and Early Eighteenth Centuries', in Richard Bauckham and Benjamin Drewery, eds., *Scripture, Tradition and Reason* (Edinburgh, 1988); Robert D. Cornwall, 'The Search for the Primitive Church: The Use of Early Church Fathers in the High Church Anglican Tradition, 1680–1745', *Anglican and Episcopal History*, 59 (1990), pp. 303–29. On the pre-Civil War period, see H. R. McAdoo, *The Spirit of Anglicanism* (1965), chs. 9–10. Gareth Vaughan Bennett, 'Patristic Tradition in Anglican Thought, 1660–1900', *Oecumenica* (1971–2), pp. 63–85, says a little on the Restoration; see the citations of de Quehen and Packer in n. 15 below. On sixteenth-century English patristics, see Stanley L. Greenslade, *The English Reformers and the Fathers of the Church* (Oxford, 1960); Stanley L. Greenslade, 'The Authority of the Tradition of the Early Church in Early Anglican Thought', *Oecumenica* (1971–2), pp. 9–31.

[14] John Pearson, *Vindiciae epistolarum S. Ignatii* (Cambridge, 1672). Ussher had followed Jerome in thinking the epistle to Polycarp a mere reprise of another.

[15] Jerome had argued that episcopacy arose by church custom and consent. On seventeenth-century textual scholarship, see Hugh de Quehen, 'Politics and Scholarship in the Ignatian Controversy', *The Seventeenth Century*, 13 (1998), pp. 69–84; J. B. Lightfoot, *The Apostolic Fathers, Part II: St Ignatius, St Polycarp* (3 vols., 1889), vol. 1; Packer, *Transformation of Anglicanism*, pp. 17, 58, 106–11.

that *episcopus* was not just a name in the early church, but involved power over presbyters. 'We ought to regard the bishop', Ignatius explained, 'as the Lord Himself', a dictum cited by the Anglican royalist Laurence Womock in 1662.[16]

Cyprian, like Ignatius, spoke to Restoration clerical minds by insisting on the importance of order and unity against the threat of internal decay and schism. Cyprian's *De unitate ecclesiae* (251), translated by Dean John Fell of Christ Church in 1681, supported bishops 'who preside in the Church'. Cyprian's text was potentially dangerous because it existed in two versions. The 'primary' or 'primacy' text could be read as emphasising papal supremacy ('a primacy is given to Peter'); the revised one stressed Peter symbolised unity. But both contained plenty of emphasis on individual bishops' authority and the crucial statement that in Christ's church there is 'but one Episcopacy', held by many individual bishops who 'each possesseth the authority entire'.[17] Fell's 'Advertisement' printed at the end of the text explained that this case for apostolic equality implied that old manuscripts and editions which omitted papalist claims were genuine, demolishing the 'primary text'.[18] Evidence exists that such scholarship, arcane though it may now seem, had an impact. Despite having been ordained by presbyters, Simon Patrick, later bishop of Ely, sought out a bishop after reading 'Dr Hammond on Ignatius' Epistles and Mr Thorndike's Primitive Government of the Church; whereby I was fully convinced of the necessity of episcopal ordination'.[19] As will be shown, an important element of Restoration churchmanship insisted on the unity and catholicity of the church without surrendering anything to the Roman version of Catholicism, and patristic scholarship exactly suited this milieu.

'Milieu' is an appropriate epithet for another characteristic of the Restoration Church: its dense network of scholarly cooperation,

[16] St Ignatius, bishop of Antioch, epistle to the Ephesians, in Lightfoot, *Apostolic Fathers*, II.545. The Epistles are printed in translation at II.543–74; see esp. pp. 544–5, 551–2, 554, 555, 569–70, 573. Laurence Womock, *Anti-Boreale* (1662), p. 94; Simon Lowth, *Of the Subject of Church-Power* (1685), pp. 41, 82–3, uses Ignatius.

[17] St Cyprian, bishop of Carthage, *Of the Unity of the Church*, trans. John Fell (Oxford, 1681), p. 7. For the primacy text, see St Cyprian, *The Lapsed; The Unity of the Catholic Church*, ed. Maurice Bévenot (1957), pp. 46–7. Fell had once asked Hammond to produce a complete edition of the Fathers: Packer, *Transformation of Anglicanism*, p. 70. On the use of Cyprian's dictum see Chapter 6, pp. 247–9.

[18] John Fell, 'An Advertisement', in St Cyprian, *Unity of the Church*, pp. 38–9. See Bennett, 'Patristic Tradition', p. 74. Cyprian's modern editor thinks both genuine, but that reading papal supremacy into the primary text was a later development: Cyprian, *Unity of the Catholic Church*, ed. Bévenot, pp. 6–8, 74–5, 106–8.

[19] Quoted in Packer, *Transformation of Anglicanism*, p. 61.

correspondence, citations, and not least, friendships. Archbishop Sheldon had cooperated with Fell in the late 1660s to organise Oxford's printing licence; he was instrumental in Fell becoming bishop of Oxford in 1676. Fell published the patristic scholarship of George Bull, brought to his attention by his protégé William Jane, regius professor of divinity at Oxford.[20] To assert the 'typicality' of high- or low-church ideologists would be misleading, since the establishment, spiritual and temporal, was riven with disputes. Lord Chancellor Hyde thought Thorndike's writings 'greatest scandal'; Falkner felt the need to rebut some of their implications.[21] More salient is assessing the sentiments of the most powerful churchmen. Since most bishops were too busy to publish after their elevation, this is hard to judge; endorsement is often only indirectly discoverable by the tacit encouragement of promotion or implicit punishment of obscurity.[22] Some harder evidence exists. Sheldon mobilised the bishops in parliament and organised the control of their proxies if absent; he also wrote to MPs to encourage them to pass laws against Dissent, drafting some legislation himself.[23] Falkner's works were consistently dedicated to archbishops: Sheldon in 1674, Sancroft in 1678. The bishop of London later recommended Falkner for a deanery, though he knew him 'no otherwise then by his booke'. Sancroft's satisfaction was apparent enough for the posthumous edition of Falkner's tracts and sermons to be dedicated to him by its editor, William Sherlock.[24]

The *iure divino* thesis could serve as a weapon against both Catholic and Presbyterian claims, but two other targets existed. One was 'Erastians', men thought to cede all church power to the state, typified by Hobbes and Selden. From the time he read *De cive* Thorndike spent a career pursuing '*Erastus* his Doctrine, which dissolveth all Ecclesiasticall Power into the Secular, in States that are Christian'.[25] There might be something in Erastus's attacks on the strongly Calvinist Theodore Beza, Lowth conceded, but his works had been distorted by Selden, and in

20 McAdoo, *Spirit of Anglicanism*, p. 400; Barnard, 'Use of the Patristic Tradition', p. 175; Vivienne Larminie, 'John Fell', *ODNB*.

21 Hyde: quoted in Collins, 'Restoration Bishops', p. 576 (see pp. 574–7 on Clarendon's ecclesiology); William Falkner, *Christian Loyalty*, 2nd edn (1684), pp. 66, 70; see below, p. 137.

22 Simon, *Restoration Episcopate*, p. 32, notes the dearth of publications (even of sermons: p. 32, n. 46).

23 Sutch, *Gilbert Sheldon*, pp. 136, 146.

24 William Falkner, *Libertas ecclesiastica*, 2nd edn (1674); Bodl., Tanner MS 36, fo. 35 (Compton to Sancroft, 6 June 1681); Falkner, *Christian Loyalty*; William Falkner, *Two Treatises … to Which are Annexed, Three Sermons* (1684), ep. ded.

25 Herbert Thorndike, *A Discourse of the Right of the Church in a Christian State* (1649), sig. A2r; Thorndike, 'Review', in *Right of the Church*, p. cxv.

part by Grotius, who claimed that power could only ever be external and corporal.[26] Lowth criticised Hobbes less than Selden, who 'contemptuously treads upon whatever is like a Church Power in any instance of it'.[27] Such comments suggest that historiographical attention to the reception of Selden and Grotius rather than Hobbes alone would be revealing. But appalling though Erastus, Hobbes, and Selden seemed, they were not the only threat the Church of England faced. The doctrine of a state-run church, Thorndike wrote, was one which 'only the Leviathan maintains outright', but which 'others' had 'insinuated' 'with more art and malice'.[28] Basing the church on the will of the state seemed most dangerous when advocated by divines who favoured *iure humano* episcopacy and permitted Nicodemist denial of one's faith in the face of hostile powers. This was no academic debating point, for it had been a key question for men during the Civil Wars, and it might arise in the future under a Catholic king. Maximum bitterness was expended on lax latitudinarians whose sloppy concessions to nonconformists were held to sully the purity of the Anglican Zion. Bishop Herbert Croft's *Naked Truth*, the opening salvo in a campaign to relax conformist rigour, was soundly refuted by high churchmen. Philip Fell complained of 'Latitudinarian Arians, and Theists' led by 'our Divinity-Common-Wealths-man' who would 'set on foot a Christian *Oceana*'.[29] Laurence Womock thought appeasement of Dissent scandalous, the church 'betray'd by a *Latitudinarian Neutrality*'. Sherlock complained of men 'prepared to accommodate and comprehend away' the Church.[30] The danger point to the supremacy came when the king was perceived to be assisting such men in pursuit of comprehension, indulgence, or toleration. What Collins calls an 'ecclesiastically powerful, but theologically hostile, secular power' did not crush episcopal authority

[26] Lowth, *Church-Power*, pp. 193, 197–201 on Grotius, pp. 185–6, 188, 192, 211, 235, and ch. 4.

[27] Lowth, *Church-Power*, p. 190 (qu.), also pp. 151–2.

[28] Herbert Thorndike, 'The Plea of Weakness and Tender Consciences Discussed and Answered: In a Discourse upon Romans xv:1' [*c.*1667–8], in *Theological Works* (6 vols., Oxford, 1844–56), v.364–5.

[29] Philip Fell, *Lex talionis: Or, the Author of Naked Truth Stript Naked* (1676), pp. 6, 40. See Simon, *Restoration Episcopate*, pp. 172–3, 104. Herbert Croft: converted to Catholicism in youth; recanted; deprived in Civil Wars; bishop of Hereford, 1662; sympathetic to diocesan puritans; allowed the reading of James II's Declaration of Indulgence by distinguishing 'reading' from 'assent'; took the oaths to William and Mary (William Marshall, 'Herbert Croft', *ODNB*). *Oceana*: the *magnum opus* of the idiosyncratic republican James Harrington, published in 1656; Fell refers to the anticlerical tone of a work which barred clergy from standing for election due to their anti-civic spirit.

[30] Laurence Womock, *The Associators Cashier'd* (1683), p. 28 (qu.); Laurence Womock, *Suffragium Protestantium* (1683), p. 32; William Sherlock, *A Vindication of a Passage in Dr Sherlock's Sermon Preached Before the Honourable House of Commons, May 29. 1685* (1685), p. 25.

but provoked defiance. Bishop Wren, jailed during the Civil War, told Charles II 'I know my way to the Tower'.[31] Womock sharply pointed out the royal duty to aid bishops *against* indulging Dissent. Benjamin Laney more daringly preached to the king in April 1663, in the aftermath of a failed royal project to loosen uniformity, that more time and less 'Indulgence' would bring nonconformists to their senses.[32] The reigns of Charles II and James II are in no small part stories of clerical endeavours to bring monarchs to their Anglican senses.

ADVOCATING SUPREMACY: WILLIAM FALKNER AND THOMAS PIERCE

It would be erroneous to think that Restoration churchmen simply jettisoned the supremacy. Tudor and early Stuart arguments for it echoed after 1660, partly to distinguish the Church of England from 'popish' and 'fanatic' antimonarchism, partly from principled belief in the reciprocal benefits of establishment, partly from the advantages that this could offer an individual. In the aftermath of Charles II's Declaration of Indulgence of 1672 to 1673, Womock indignantly asked how anyone could question the Church's loyalty to her prince. The English Church, unlike the Roman, exercised passive obedience and suffered under unjust monarchs. She was dependent on her king; caught between two millstones (popery and presbytery), without royal aid she would be ground to powder. Womock reminded his readers that the canons of 1604 ordered quarterly sermons on the supremacy, excommunicating opponents thereof.[33] He was not the only cleric to reiterate an earlier language of supremacy.

William Falkner's *Christian Loyalty*, penned in the rising tide of animus towards the bishops in the late 1670s, contained the fullest explication of the positive rights of supreme governors. Concerned to defend the supremacy against both Catholic and Calvinist attacks, Falkner had to correct his fellow Anglicans as well. The supremacy's 'lawfulness, fitness, and reasonableness' was all the more necessary to uphold since 'a very learned man' (Thorndike) had hastily condemned certain clauses of the Oath of Supremacy.[34] The status of the king as supreme governor of the

[31] Collins, 'Restoration Bishops', pp. 558, 579.

[32] Womock, *Suffragium Protestantium*, pp. 182, 275; Benjamin Laney, *Five Sermons, Preached before His Majesty at Whitehall* (1669, citing Wing L342), p. 29.

[33] Laurence Womock, *The Religion of the Church of England the Surest Establishment of the Royal Throne* (1673), pp. 5, 36, 12–13; Womock, *Anti-Boreale*, p. 69.

[34] Falkner, *Christian Loyalty*, p. 7. Falkner cites ch. 20 of Thorndike's *Just Weights and Measures* (1662); see below, p. 158.

Church was manifest in his 'actual, constant, visible *exercise*' of a power so 'ample' as to encompass all persons, '*acknowledged* and *confirmed*' by the laws. As the words 'acknowledged' and 'confirmed' suggest, Falkner saw statutes which delineated supremacy (those of *praemunire* (1393), appeals (1533), and supremacy (1559)) as declaratory, not introductory. He also outlined how the Articles and canons of the Church of England declared supremacy.[35] Like his Tudor and early Stuart forebears, Falkner insisted that supremacy was jurisdictional, not spiritual, bewailing the vanity of men 'who will understand nothing else by the Kings Supremacy … but this, that he may assume to himself the *performance* of all proper *Ecclesiastical actions*'. The supreme governor does not personally exercise the powers held by his subjects.[36] The king cannot usurp church property or alienate church lands, and he cannot change what is good or evil by divine or natural law, so he cannot alter faith or worship.[37] It is crucial to note that this vehement defence of supremacy came from a man who thought episcopacy divinely instituted, not to be abolished. 'The exercise of the Keys is not to be guided by the pleasure of a Prince as its rule.' But the Reformation had committed no such sacrilegious sins. Elizabeth's Injunctions, the Thirty-Seventh of the Thirty-Nine Articles, and 'divers good writers' had refuted notions of spiritual power. Under Henry and Edward the '*spiritual authority* of the Clergy, was … owned to be really distinct from the *secular* authority, and was not swallowed up into it'.[38]

In a succession of chapters Falkner outlined the patterns and sources for royal supremacy, reiterating pre-Restoration arguments. His first chapter discussed the English Reformation, the second and third the Old Testament, the fourth Christian doctrine and sovereignty, and the fifth the primitive church. Perhaps with Thorndike's rejection of Old Testament models in mind, Falkner stressed the importance of Davidic precedent to the Church of England.[39] Godly Israelite kings had given orders for moving the Ark and repairing the Temple, purged idolatry, and exercised a 'manifest Soveraignty' over priests and prophets. Allegations that the sanhedrin was the real sovereign in Israel were false, subverting both royal and ecclesiastical government.[40] Solomon had ordered the dedication of the Temple, although of course he had not consecrated it himself.[41] Nor

[35] Falkner, *Christian Loyalty*, pp. 5–8. [36] Falkner, *Christian Loyalty*, pp. 13–15 (qu. 15).

[37] Falkner, *Christian Loyalty*, pp. 15–17 (p. 17 includes Christ's officers as unchangeable); see also Falkner, *Libertas ecclesiastica*, p. 355.

[38] Falkner, *Christian Loyalty*, pp. 173 (qu.), 17–19, 26 (qu.); Falkner, *Libertas ecclesiastica*, pp. 72, 403.

[39] Falkner, *Christian Loyalty*, p. 50, although cf. p. 76.

[40] Falkner, *Christian Loyalty*, pp. 52–7 (qu. 54).

[41] Falkner, *Christian Loyalty*, pp. 70–2.

were such rights peculiar to Old Testament kings. Every king had a duty to care for worship as part of the public good, although Christian monarchs were especially enjoined to be nursing parents to their churches.[42] It was particularly difficult, Falkner admitted, to see how princes not of the church could exercise such powers. But he concluded that in such a 'sad and heavy calamity' royal rights stood intact. Any sovereign can by their secular authority enforce scriptural truths 'plain and *manifest*', Christian doctrine, and church councils. But none, even Christian, can erect heresy.[43] The care Falkner took to show that Constantine had been baptised late in life, so that many of his acts protecting the church had taken place before this event, demonstrated the safety of the church under a pagan, but protective, emperor. The early church was a model of beneficent imperial oversight of power really exercised by synods.[44] Here was the Anglican model for the Catholic heir presumptive, James II.

Falkner suggested a complementary relationship of supremacy and episcopacy and his work came closest to repeating the Tudor ideal, language, and examples of supremacy. He had an agenda: to prove bishops were an advantageous part of the polity, and to negotiate the prospect of a Catholic supremacy.[45] Other men were less subtle in manipulating supremacy for their own purposes. In 1683, Thomas Pierce made large claims for royal authority over bishops. Every good subject, Pierce began by saying, must maximise royal authority as much as possible, especially royal powers of ecclesiastical patronage evidenced in Henrician and Edwardian statutes and described by Edward Coke.[46] Although Pierce claimed that without royal supremacy the Church was prey to those who would vote episcopacy down, his intent was not to protect ecclesiastical authority. He abruptly dismissed the importance of the divine derivation of church power, since any practice of it must depend on royal authority. Imperial monarchy meant the king exercised a 'Despotical' power over bishops, and it was 'as *endless*, as it is *easy*, to Muster up Instances of the *Regale* over *Churches* and *Church-men*'.[47] This was no disinterested account of English ecclesiology, but continued an old battle between Pierce and his bishop, Seth Ward. Pierce, who had befriended Hammond in the Interregnum, resented Ward's having been an Oxford professor in the 1650s, even though Ward

[42] Falkner, *Christian Loyalty*, pp. 51, 114–17, 122–3.

[43] Falkner, *Christian Loyalty*, pp. 130–1, 43–4, 523; also Falkner, *Libertas ecclesiastica*, p. 56. He argues orders to commit heresy or sin can be disobeyed without allowing a right of resistance.

[44] Falkner, *Christian Loyalty*, pp. 134–49, 154–72.

[45] For the context see Goldie, 'Danby'.

[46] Thomas Pierce, *A Vindication of the King's Sovereign Rights* ('printed for private use', 1683, citing Wing P2208), pp. 2–6.

[47] Pierce, *Vindication*, pp. 28, 29, 8–9, qu. pp. 45, 14.

had avoided swearing the Covenant and resigned his college headship at the Restoration. Ward trampled on the dean's jurisdictional rights over local peculiars; Pierce counter-claimed that Salisbury itself was directly under royal authority. As Robert Beddard has shown, the battle between bishop and dean continued under James II, who, perhaps surprisingly, chose to support the bishop.[48]

The first chapter of Pierce's book thus explained how monarchs might depose prelates. The king was patron paramount, and none appointed better than he and his Commission for Ecclesiastical Promotions.[49] He could erect and dissolve bishoprics (witness the fleeting bishopric of Westminster of 1540 to 1550), dissolve and restore dioceses (the see of Durham had been dissolved by John Dudley, duke of Northumberland, and restored by Mary I). He could place livings *in commendam*, alter secular and regular canons, grant his patronal rights to his subjects. He could even, *de facto* (although not *de jure*) appoint laymen to church posts: Thomas Cromwell became dean of Wells.[50] No bishop should think himself secure once appointed. Pierce dubiously stated that 'all' agreed that English kings 'have power to *Suspend*, or *Deprive* a Bishop (as Ours has done an *Arch-bishop* [Alexander Burnet of Glasgow] …) as Q. *Mary and Elizabeth did*: and of our Kings not a few'.[51] For the king was more than supreme ordinary or patron. 'But he is himself in Person, the Supreme and Sovereign Bishop of every Diocess in *England*.' 'In Person' sounded rather sacerdotally overblown, but Pierce did more than retain it in the second edition of the tract, inserting after the word 'person' '*Persona Sacra & mixta cum Sacerdote*, (as his *Vestis Dalmatica* does import in his Coronation)'. Even the title page of the second edition tellingly quoted the Oath of Supremacy. One owner added a note that the canons of 1604 excommunicated anyone denying the supremacy.[52]

[48] Robert Beddard, 'The Church of Salisbury and the Accession of James II', *Wiltshire Archaeological and Natural History Magazine*, 67 (1972), pp. 132–48. For details, see E. A. O. Whiteman, 'The Episcopate of Seth Ward, Bishop of Exeter (1662 to 1667) and Salisbury (1667 to 1688/9), with Special Reference to the Ecclesiastical Problems of his Time' (D.Phil. thesis, University of Oxford, 1951), ch. 10.

[49] Pierce, *Vindication*, pp. 13, 20. [50] Pierce, *Vindication*, pp. 25–6.

[51] Pierce, *Vindication*, p. 19. Alexander Burnet: archbishop of Glasgow, 1664; his repression of Scottish nonconformists and politicking against Lauderdale led the king to force his resignation in 1669; he was reappointed in 1674 (David George Mullan, 'Alexander Burnet', *ODNB*). See Julia Buckroyd, 'The Dismissal of Archbishop Alexander Burnet, 1669', *Records of the Scottish Church History Society*, 18 (1973), pp. 149–55; John A. Lamb, 'Archbishop Alexander Burnet, 1614–1684', *Records of the Scottish Church History Society*, 11 (1952), pp. 133–48, at pp. 139–41.

[52] Pierce, *Vindication*, p. 32; 2nd edn, 'Things of Consequence to be Added', p. 5; annotation on University of Illinois copy, reproduced on Early English Books Online. Dalmatic tunic: vestment worn by deacons and by kings at their coronations.

Falkner carefully sought a subtle balance between episcopacy and supremacy, and whatever potential threats loomed in the future, in the late 1670s Danby's regime provided a moment in which the two seemed compatible. Pierce's excessive focus on royal powers would have been anathema to many of his clerical colleagues, but again seemed feasible in the Anglican royalist glory days of the Tory Reaction. But many Restoration churchmen thought a monarchical–episcopal alliance not always congenial, and sought to refute suggestions of civil control of religion. As two churchmen discovered, such suggestions were dangerously easy to slip into.

IURE HUMANO EPISCOPACY AND SUPREMACY: EDWARD STILLINGFLEET AND JOHN TILLOTSON

One of the most prominent men who sought to justify the Reformation whilst negotiating the defence of conformity against Dissent was Edward Stillingfleet. A popular London preacher, occasionally labelled 'latitudinarian', Stillingfleet's works spanned the Restoration to the Revolution, after which he became bishop of Worcester. His treatises and sermons provide not only a route to explore how notions of supremacy fitted with a *iure humano* account of episcopacy, but also a demonstration of how even low-church divines increasingly emphasised episcopacy over the course of the Restoration. They furthermore show how difficult it was to stabilise an account which denied the claims of Dissenting and Catholic opponents of the Church and defended Reformation supremacy without sliding into civil domination of religion.

Stillingfleet began boldly, with a tract that would haunt the rest of his career. His *Irenicum*, published before the church was re-established, contributed to debates about ecclesiastical restoration by showing the legitimacy of obeying decisions on rites and worship left undetermined in the Bible (*adiaphora*), but nevertheless urging governors to restrain their impositions. True adherence to pure apostolic Christianity, Stillingfleet urged, meant limiting conditions for communion to soteriological necessities; a 'unity of love ... not a bare uniformity of practice'.[53] Whilst Stillingfleet's account of the lawful imposition of *adiaphora* concurred with that of many of his immediate contemporaries, he made two crucial claims.[54] The first was that episcopacy was not obligatory; the second

53 Edward Stillingfleet, *Irenicum* ('1661' [1660]), pp. viii, 121, sig. a2v. For the potential debt to Jean Daillé, see Quantin, *Christian Antiquity*, pp. 286–7.

54 For the context, see Jacqueline Rose, 'John Locke, "Matters Indifferent", and the Restoration of the Church of England', *Historical Journal*, 48 (2005), pp. 601–21.

was the role of the civil magistrate in determining church affairs. It was these claims which loomed large in the reception of his work, in which the role he granted the church was overlooked. The youthful Stillingfleet rejected the biblical case for divine right episcopacy, the Twelve Apostles and Seventy Disciples. He did not, moreoever, seem to think bishops apostolic. He was sceptical of claims to know what the primitive government of the church was, given 'the *Defectiveness*, *Ambiguity*, *Partiality*, and *Repugnancy* of the records'. But he did not see this as especially problematic, because what suited early Christians might not best befit seventeenth-century England. Providentially, since Christians lived under many different forms of civil government, they were able (and ought) 'to contemperate the Government of the Church to that of the State'.[55] As long as there was *a* government which maintained order in the society of the church (needed by *juris divini naturalis*), its form was insignificant (*juris divini permissivi*). 'Which particular way or form it must be, is wholly left to the prudence of those in whose power and trust it is to see the peace of the Church.'[56]

Whose task it was to decide the form of church government, and to determine *adiaphora*, was frequently left ambiguous by Stillingfleet, whose language of 'lawful authority' was often vague. He spoke of 'the lawfull Governours of the Church', 'the supream authority in the Church of God', 'the power of lawfull authority in the Church of God'.[57] But occasionally he was more forthcoming about how the question 'must be removed from the Court of Common Law of Nature, to the Kings Bench'.[58] It is civil authority which decides in favour of a particular form of church government and worship, and imposes these on a nation. 'For when the Church is incorporated into the Commonwealth, the chief authority in a Commonwealth as Christian, belongs to the same to which it doth as a Commonwealth.'[59] For Stillingfleet, the key aspect of a law was its power to *oblige* obedience. Since God's Word left episcopacy indifferent, obligation to obey it 'must arise from our subjection and relation to the Magistrate', for 'he only hath power to oblige who hath power to punish'. This did not exclude a role for churchmen in deciding the best content of ecclesiastical resolutions. The church advises, and the magistrate

[55] Stillingfleet, *Irenicum*, pp. 218, [294] (mispag. 286), 180–1. Contemperate: synchronise.

[56] Stillingfleet, *Irenicum*, pp. 10, 3 (qu.).

[57] Stillingfleet, *Irenicum*, pp. 416, 124, 27, 53.

[58] Stillingfleet, *Irenicum*, p. 88. He was probably speaking of civil power in general rather than a specifically monarchical version of it, given his view that the form of civil government was not *iure divino*: ibid., p. 11.

[59] Stillingfleet, *Irenicum*, p. 127.

legislates; the church declares, but the government enacts. Nevertheless, the decisions and deciders may be 'ecclesiastical' but 'the force and ground of the obligation of them is wholly civil'. What the church has ordered, the magistrate may abolish.[60]

These passages seemed to grant the church a role in advising on the content of laws, but very little actual governing power or ability to enforce its decisions. At other points Stillingfleet did begin to circumscribe civil authority, writing that the magistrate kept both Tables but defended only 'the publike and professed religion of a Nation', and did not have authority over religion *per se*. His power was objective and external (jurisdictional), not internal and formal ('elicitive' ministerial actions).[61] Stillingfleet not only refrained from totally conflating the membership of church and state, but also noted that 'the officers of one are clearly distinct from the other'. And he mentioned that churchmen might excommunicate, for despite the royal supremacy, the church was distinct from civil society.[62] Nevertheless, the overwhelming emphasis on the civil origins of obligation, the disdain for episcopacy, and the suggestion that the best settlement was Newport monarchy and Ussherian primitive episcopacy[63] were radically out of line with the sentiments of the restored Church of 1662. Stillingfleet undermined his case by arguing that the magistrate could defend 'the religion he owns as true', by implication even if it was false. If any reader discovered the comments about the priesthood of fathers of families, of Moses, and of civil authorities, they might have detected a whiff of Hobbism.[64] When some readers did discover the recognition that Archbishop Cranmer had attributed sacerdotal power to Henry VIII, Stillingfleet was excoriated, years after his work had been printed.[65] Tellingly, despite being by one of the most popular Restoration preachers, it was reprinted only once after 1662, in 1681.

Either criticism or the realisation of the dissonance of his text compared to the new establishment caused Stillingfleet to append a defence of church authority to the 1662 edition of *Irenicum*. That this discussed the power of excommunication was telling, for it was an attack on aggressive excommunication which had led Erastus and his Civil War followers to seek civil limitations on ecclesiastical authority until, as Stillingfleet put

60 Stillingfleet, *Irenicum*, pp. 44–8, 13 (qu.).

61 Stillingfleet, *Irenicum*, pp. 39–41.

62 Stillingfleet, *Irenicum*, pp. 192–3, 143.

63 Stillingfleet, *Irenicum*, p. [415] (mispag. 417).

64 As they did with Samuel Parker: Jacqueline Rose, 'The Ecclesiastical Polity of Samuel Parker', *The Seventeenth Century*, 25 (2010), pp. 350–75.

65 Stillingfleet, *Irenicum*, pp. 39–40, 89–92, 391–3. For the subsequent debate, see Chapter 5, pp. 221–8.

it, they '*melted down* all *Spiritual power* into the *Civil State*, and *dissolved* the *Church* into the *Common-wealth*'.[66] He shifted his emphasis from the obligative force of civil authority to outline the nature of the society of the church as distinct from civil society, with its own governors established by Christ. Christ 'not only *appointed a society*, but *officers* to rule it' – although Stillingfleet remained reticent about who these actually were, not taking the chance to emphasise bishops specifically. These governors could do more than declare doctrine; they might also exercise the Keys of discipline, admitting and removing members of the church – and Christians would submit to them, voluntarily. If this was no coactive power, it was visible government.[67] Incorporation into a Christian state changed the church, for then 'the *right* of supream *management* of this *power* in an *external* way doth *fall* into the *Magistrates* hands', who could then add civil penalties, or remove them when hearing cases on appeal. These temporal censures were '*cumulative*, and not *privative*' and did not obviate the obligation to profess Christianity, *pace* Leviathan. 'I know no incongruity', declared Stillingfleet desperately, 'in admitting *imperium in imperio*'.[68]

The insistence on the need to profess Christianity in the face of sovereign opposition separated Stillingfleet from the Nicodemism of Hobbes and, as John Marshall has argued, of his fellow London preacher John Tillotson.[69] Preaching before a somnambulant sovereign in 1680, Tillotson's vindication of Protestantism 'from the charge of singularity and novelty' offered a brief criticism of Dissenters, a lot of refutation of Catholics, and a Hobbesian interlude sandwiched inbetween. This middle section began in standard Protestant mode, urging the magistrate to support the true religion in the tradition of Old Testament kings and Christian emperors, but denying kings power to reject true religion, alter the scriptural canon, or 'to make a false Religion so currant by the stamp of his Authority, as to oblige his Subjects to the profession of it'. Should a monarch so err, his subjects were bound to passive resistance.[70] But then Tillotson announced:

I cannot think … that any pretence of Conscience warrants any man, that is not extraordinarily commission'd as the Apostles and first Publishers of the Gospel

[66] Edward Stillingfleet, *A Discourse Concerning the Power of Excommunication in a Christian Church, by Way of Appendix to the Irenicum* (1662), p. 2.
[67] Stillingfleet, *Power of Excommunication*, pp. 6, 16–17, 29.
[68] Stillingfleet, *Power of Excommunication*, pp. 30, 31, 9–13.
[69] John Marshall, 'The Ecclesiology of the Latitude-Men, 1660–1689: Stillingfleet, Tillotson, and "Hobbism"', *Journal of Ecclesiastical History*, 36 (1985), pp. 407–27, at pp. 413, 422–3.
[70] John Tillotson, *The Protestant Religion Vindicated from the Charge of Singularity and Novelty* (1680), pp. 9–11.

were, and cannot justify that Commission by Miracles as they did, to affront the establish'd Religion of a Nation (though it be false) and openly to draw men off from the profession of it in contempt of the Magistrate and Law.

He justified this by sarcastically pointing out that no Protestant felt an obligation to court martyrdom by proselytising in Catholic countries, and the danger of death did not alter their conscientious duties.[71] This concurred with Hobbes's account of no lay Christian being required to die for their faith. It seemed to many that, if Tillotson's sermon were *The Protestant Religion Vindicated*, such a vindication was possible only because Protestantism chanced to be the established religion rather than for its intrinsic merits. In a church in which, as we shall see, focus was moving from national legal establishment towards catholic universality and apostolic tradition, this was deeply problematic. Tillotson seems not to have seen the potential problems of his account, for when the sermon was reprinted in a collection in 1686, under the Catholic James II, he merely added that every Christian had the *right*, but not the *duty*, to denounce a false religion, and left the rest of the offending passage intact.[72] This did not stop him in practice joining the criticism of a Catholicising regime, along with Stillingfleet, who by 1685 was well established as an anti-Catholic writer.

Defending England's Reformation became the focus of most of Stillingfleet's Restoration polemical career, and he was willing to undertake the battle against both Catholic and Dissenting opponents. During the 1670s and 1680s he honed his account of the royal supremacy, noting the need to defend ecclesiastical rights, and offering an increasingly strong account of episcopacy as apostolic. Stillingfleet never went as far as some of his contemporaries in justifying episcopacy and church authority, perhaps proleptic of his future as a Williamite bishop rather than a nonjuror. Indeed, his emphasis on submission to one's bishop reached its apogee in the middle of the 1680s – reflecting the Tory Reaction's crackdown on Dissent – before necessarily succumbing to the politics of Anglican schism a decade later.

Against Rome, Stillingfleet constantly defended the Reformation as just and legitimate. He, like many others, denied that the catholic church was synonymous with Rome, or that Rome had a monopoly on arguments from antiquity and tradition. Where the Stillingfleet of *Irenicum* had scorned deference to tradition, in the 1670s he laid claim to true

[71] Tillotson, *Protestant Religion Vindicated*, pp. 11–13. [72] Marshall, 'Latitude-Men', p. 424.

catholic tradition via the Vincentian Rule.[73] In a sermon of 1673 he implicitly likened the Anglican appeal to the Bible and pure antiquity to Paul's defence of Christianity to Caesar; in 1686 he insisted that the Church of England 'owns the Doctrine of the Primitive Church more frankly and ingenuously, than any Church in the World'.[74] Against Dissenters, this growing bent towards tradition manifested itself in a defence of episcopal government. In two works which dismayed the Dissenters who once thought him a champion of their cause, his sermon on *The Mischief of Separation*, and its printed defence, *The Unreasonableness of Separation*, Stillingfleet defended obedience to episcopal government. He never discarded a sense of the Church of England as a national church, governed by national laws and articles, and he criticised nonconformists for thinking themselves better able to judge worship than kings and parliaments. Indeed, in the sermon, he condemned Dissenters for breaking national laws ordering uniformity, rather than for ecclesiological flaws of not having bishops. But he also incorporated wider claims for episcopacy as apostolic, and spoke the Cyprianic language of 'one altar, one bishop', suggesting that separation from one's bishop was schism.[75] Part Three of his *Unreasonableness* descanted on Cyprian's account of 'the ancient and regular *Discipline* and *Order* of the *Church*' by which 'there ought to be but *one Bishop* in a *City*'. Separation from the bishop was schism, for 'non secundus, sed nullus', a comment which ought to have embarrassed its author after 1689. This lengthy account of the 'best and purest *Antiquity*' was foreign to the perceived impossibility and irrelevance of early church government in *Irenicum*. Then the records were too weak a foundation for an ecclesiological argument; now it was 'unreasonable to question the *succession* of *Bishops* from the *Apostles*, when the matter of fact is attested by the most early, knowing, honest, and impartial *Witnesses*'.[76] Although there was a new wealth of patristic scholarship on which Stillingfleet might have drawn, his change of sentiments was driven by more than disinterested textual scholarship. In a sermon of 1685, he noted that although the Bible included 'no plain Text' for episcopacy, the 'Universal Consent

[73] Stillingfleet, *Irenicum*, pp. 320, 317 (tradition in the loose sense of respect for long-established customs); Edward Stillingfleet, *An Answer to Several Late Treatises* (1673), p. 180; Edward Stillingfleet, *The Council of Trent Examin'd and Disprov'd* (1688), pp. 21–2. For this argument, see below, pp. 150–1.

[74] Edward Stillingfleet, *The Reformation Justify'd*, 2nd edn (1674), pp. 19–20; Edward Stillingfleet, *An Answer to Some Papers Lately Printed* (repr. Dublin, 1686), p. 6.

[75] Edward Stillingfleet, *The Mischief of Separation*, 3rd edn (1680), pp. 17–18, 27; Edward Stillingfleet, *The Unreasonableness of Separation* (1681), pp. 114–15; Marshall, 'Latitude-Men', pp. 416–17.

[76] Stillingfleet, *Unreasonableness*, qu. pp. 247, 246, 237, 290.

of the Church' gave 'great Reason to believe, the *Apostolical Succession* to be of *Divine Institution*', and to 'continue to the World's End'. Similarly, in a tract against Catholicism of 1686, he called episcopal succession 'as certain as *Rome* it self'.[77]

This was a change of opinion about episcopacy, but one which co-existed with consistent (if brief) treatments of the royal supremacy after 1662. Stillingfleet's change of tone seems to be associated with polemical needs more to do with Dissenters than with kings. Or, to put it another way, his new argument was already in place by the time a king professing a false religion, James II, came to the throne. Although Stillingfleet saw the church as incorporated with the state, he insisted that it was 'a Society in its Nature, Design, Duties, Offices, Censures, really distinct from any mere Humane Institution', with 'peculiar Officers', 'a Society distinct from the Commonwealth'.[78] If this was stated under a Catholic king, the problem was James's Catholicism, not his lay kingship, for we find a similar account in a repudiation of Catholic notions of papal infallibility in the 1670s. Here Stillingfleet noted that when a church was incorporated 'in some respects' with the polity, nevertheless 'its Fundamental Rights remain distinct'. James's Catholic supremacy merely required this to be reiterated with more urgency:

> Altho' we attribute the *Supream Jurisdiction* to the King; yet we do not question but there are *inviolable Rights of the Church*, which ought to be preserved against the *Fancies* of some, and the *Usurpations* of others.[79]

Stillingfleet believed that the church could be defended against kings, even before he shifted his views of episcopacy in response to Dissenting threats. He does not make clear, however, whether episcopacy is one of the 'inviolable rights' that cannot be removed, although he did insist that individual Christians *ought* to profess their belief, in contrast to Tillotson's lacklustre addition of a single comment on the *right* to do this. Stillingfleet told the House of Commons in 1678 that true religion was not decided by the government and he warned Dissenters in 1681 not to think themselves persecuted for the true faith.[80] Anglicans did not believe their faith because it was enstated, but followed the true religion, which happily happened to be established.

77 Edward Stillingfleet, *A Sermon Preached at a Publick Ordination at St Peter's Cornhill, March 15th 1684/5*, in *Ten Sermons* (1697), pp. 570–1; Stillingfleet, *Answer to Some Papers*, p. 13.

78 Stillingfleet, *Sermon Preached at a Publick Ordination*, p. 545.

79 Stillingfleet, *Answer to Several Late Treatises*; Stillingfleet, *Answer to Some Papers*, p. 17.

80 Edward Stillingfleet, *A Sermon Preached on the Fast-Day at St Margaret's Westminster, Novemb. 13 1678*, in *Ten Sermons* (1697), pp. 209–10; Stillingfleet, *Unreasonableness*, p. 148.

Stillingfleet protested his desire to protect the rights of the church, increasingly emphasised the importance of apostolic episcopacy, and criticised Dissenters' separation from a church which they confessed was true in fundamentals. But his works were vague on many of the details of what rights the church held and how they should be defended, and what bishops' authority should be. Episcopacy was undoubtedly legitimate, perhaps even the best church polity, but he never suggested that its omission unchurched the Dissenters. Nonconformity was irrational because its followers admitted that the Church of England did not err in fundamentals and thus practised partial or occasional communion. Unlike those who urged the government to resist comprehension, Stillingfleet continued to encourage the establishment to relax its ceremonial demands in order to comprehend Dissenters.[81] His insistence on the distinction between church and polity was counterbalanced by his clear preference for incorporation and establishment, revealed after the Revolution. In 1691, he crossly told the nonjurors that a church not incorporated into a Christian state was either popish or fanatical, and contrary to Anglican practice and the royal supremacy. 'The *Church* is and must be Incorporated into the State.'[82] The strand of churchmanship which he represented may have come to the fore in the Williamite Church, but before 1689 it was present rather than prevalent. Picking their way between sacerdotalism and Erastianism, many Restoration churchmen leaned towards the former – perhaps because the latter was baited with Hobbism. The newly prominent dualist account of church and state focused churchmen's minds on the duties more than the rights of their supreme governor,[83] and helped them subordinate supremacy to clerisy.

CATHOLICITY AND *IURE DIVINO* EPISCOPACY

England's bifurcated Reformation, endorsing Calvinist doctrine but retaining medieval ecclesiastical structures and a hybrid liturgy, could be glossed as primarily Reformed or catholic. Later Stuart churchmen frequently stressed the latter: less antagonistic towards Rome but wary of foreign Protestant churches, and encouraging sacramental and liturgical

81 Stillingfleet, *Unreasonableness*, passim (irrationality), preface, pp. 92–3.

82 Edward Stillingfleet, *A Vindication of their Majesties Authority to Fill the Sees of the Deprived Bishops* (1691), pp. 18–20 (1st pag.), qu. p. 17 (2nd pag.).

83 As Collins states ('Restoration Bishops', p. 563), the implications of *iure divino* episcopacy were newly admitted.

more than sermon-based worship.[84] The sixteenth-century rhetoric of a national church as a branch of the catholic faith was subtly shifted towards universality rather than particularity. Thorndike in particular argued that the catholic church (a credal fundamental) could not exist if national borders demarcated churches.[85] Both he and Benjamin Laney, bishop of Ely, stressed the continuity not caesura of the Reformation. Catholicity was fundamentally historical. Whilst self-reformation by a national church was possible, its legitimacy was determined by the standard of the primitive church. Without this measure the vital distinction between reformation and innovation could not be made.[86]

Related to this were descriptions of the church as an independent, self-governing, visible society, although one which 'pretendeth not to bee a Commonwealth' and so did not challenge sovereignty.[87] While the visible church held authority as the body (*corpus*) of Christ, ideas about civil corporations were applied to religious institutions. In 1659 Thorndike compared tithes to the stock of a public corporation, albeit thinking the church 'a society, body, or corporation of men' by divine not monarchical charter, 'before and without dependence upon any state or commonwealth'.[88] Lowth's metaphor of the church as 'a City within it self' showed it as self-regulating, and he spoke of both the Church 'of' England and 'the *Church of God* here in *England*', implicitly stressing its catholicity. This society was independent of 'outward advantages, or … *Votes of the People*, whether in *Parliament*, or out of it', 'antecedent' to parliaments, and not built upon the sandy soil of the 'Wills and Passions of Princes'.[89] Royal temporal and priestly spiritual authority were separate, and holding one

[84] It was, for example, during this period that the European, especially Swiss, influences on the sixteenth-century English reformation were written out of church history (see Diarmaid MacCulloch, 'The Myth of the English Reformation', *Journal of British Studies*, 30 (1991), pp. 1–19). For examples, see Laurence Womock, *Pulpit-Conceptions, Popular-Deceptions* (1662), pp. 8, 24–5; Thorndike, *Right of the Church*, pp. 116–17, 326–30; Herbert Thorndike, *Just Weights and Measures* (1662), pp. 96, 111, 154.

[85] Thorndike, *Just Weights*, pp. 229, 232.

[86] Herbert Thorndike, *A Discourse of the Forbearance or the Penalties which a Due Reformation Requires* (1670), pp. 15–18; Thorndike, *Just Weights*, pp. 1–2, 45; Laney, *Five Sermons*, p. 17.

[87] Thorndike, *Just Weights*, p. 33 (qu.); Thorndike, 'Review of the Discourse of the Primitive Government of Churches', in *Two Discourses* (Cambridge, 1650), p. 27.

[88] Herbert Thorndike, 'The Church's Right to Tithes, as Found in Scripture' [*c.*1659], in *Theological Works*, VI.3. See also Henry Jones, *A Sermon Preached at the Consecration of … Ambrose Lord Bishop of Kildare … June 29 1667* (Dublin, 1667), pp. 6–7; William Cave, *A Discourse Concerning the Unity of the Catholick Church Maintained in the Church of England* (1684), p. 4. Corpus was used in the sense both of Christ's body and a legal incorporation.

[89] Lowth, *Church-Power*, pp. 244–5, 265, 168–9 (qu. 169), 224–6, 394 (qu.); Simon Lowth, *A Letter to Edw. Stillingfleet* (1687 (licensed 1686)), pp. 82–3 (qu.).

was no entitlement to the other.[90] Of course Lowth recognised there had been Christian emperors, but saw alongside them church councils with a 'real, Autoritative [*sic*] Power'. The Council of Nicea, so often in previous polemic the symbol of Constantinian oversight of the church, exemplified for Lowth the 'self-existing, eminent, independent, underivable Power that is in the Church of Christ, wholly in her self, and in none else beside'.[91]

On the surface this rhetoric was a confident, steady, and self-assured balance of church and state. Yet minimal probing reveals uncertainty, insecurity, and a sense of desperate assertiveness about the inviolability of the church. Thorndike's 'Review' of his *Right of the Church* argued that Christ must have explicitly given the Keys to a particular set of ministers, or else they would default to the state, which was, he implied, unthinkable.[92] The brash brutality of Anglican polemic is an undeniable feature of the Restoration, but vigorous defences of the Church were symptomatic of insecurity (justified or otherwise), not complacency. And those defences were necessary against a variety of opponents: Roman Catholic, Dissenting, and sometimes monarchical. The idea of *iure divino* episcopacy perhaps became hegemonic because it so usefully buttressed the Church against all these opponents at once.

It is vital to recognise that Restoration assertions of catholicity helped *refute* notions of Rome's authority over the English Church. Appealing to patristic authority was far from surrendering to Catholic tradition. Against Counter-Reformation assertions of the authority of the *present* church, Anglicans championed the early church, citing Lancelot Andrewes's motto: 'one canon … two testaments, three creeds, four general Councils, five centuries, and the series of Fathers in that period'. They reiterated the rule of Vincent of Lérins: tradition is 'what has been believed everywhere, always, and by all'.[93] *Iure divino* episcopacy was a mainstay of the patristic model of a pre-papal episcopate, with every bishop sovereign in his diocese and all bishops equally so in the universal church. Divine right episcopacy most obviously seems to challenge Presbyterianism and lay elders;

90 Lowth, *Church-Power*, pp. 122–3, 65–71.

91 Lowth, *Church-Power*, pp. 108–110.

92 Thorndike, 'Review', in *Right of the Church*, p. xlvii.

93 Andrewes: quoted in Barnard, 'Use of Patristic Tradition', p. 186; but cf. Quantin, *Christian Antiquity*, pp. 155–6 on this as a shared Reformed Protestant statement. See Cornwall, 'Search for the Primitive Church', pp. 308–9, 314; Greenslade, 'Tradition of the Early Church', pp. 21–2. Womock, *Religion of the Church of England the Surest Establishment*, p. 6, says the oldest Fathers are best. The four councils were those of 325, 381, 431, and 451. Cf. Quantin, *Christian Antiquity*, pp. 53–4, on Vincent aiding Catholics more than Protestants.

and indeed it did. But it also raised the status of *every* bishop by deriving their authority independently of the pope. It is salient to remember that popes during the Council of Trent had vehemently warded off notions of *iure divino* episcopacy in order to shore up their own position.[94]

Arguing that episcopal authority derived from a power shared equally between the apostles neatly refuted Petrine supremacy. Although this case was not new, authors such as Falkner professed willingness to accept the especial significance of the bishop of Rome, but offered him respect, not jurisdiction. Citing Cyprian, the patristic touchstone for episcopal independence, Falkner claimed that Petrine 'priority' did not preclude apostolic parity, for all were given the same Keys and charged with the same duties.[95] Marking an increasing Restoration tendency, he condemned popes for usurping episcopal as well as sovereign rights.[96] The break from Rome was not a post-Reformation innovation, but glossed as a return to ancient liberty and purity. Womock and Lloyd asserted the independence and equality of bishops in general and the British episcopate in particular.[97] In 1687 the royal chaplain George Hickes defiantly stated both the equality of bishops and, explicitly, the anti-papal connotations of such claims.[98]

Refuting Rome, writers kept more than a wary eye on Geneva. Earlier arguments against Presbyterianism were reiterated. No church had been without bishops until Calvin's time; only Aerius had questioned their powers.[99] The wide application of the word *episcopos* in scripture did not preclude a distinction of offices and early superiority over presbyters.[100] Jerome's exaltation of presbytery was to uphold this office against hubristic deacons; he had, crucially, still denied presbyters the power of sole

[94] For Catholic episcopal resistance to papal interference, see Robert Trisco, 'Carlo Borromeo and the Council of Trent: The Question of Reform', and John M. Headley, 'Borromean Reform in the Empire? *La Strada Rigorosa* of Giovanni Francesco Bonomi'; both in John M. Headley and John B. Tomaro, eds., *San Carlo Borromeo: Catholic Reform and Ecclesiastical Politics in the Second Half of the Sixteenth Century* (Cranbury, NJ, 1988), pp. 52, 234–5.

[95] Falkner, *Christian Loyalty*, pp. 222–4, 231–2, 242, and ch. 7, pt i; Falkner, *Two Treatises*, pp. 155–6, 540–1; Lowth, *Church-Power*, pp. 280–98 (citing Cyprian on p. 300).

[96] Falkner, *Christian Loyalty*, p. 3, on papal usurpation of episcopacy.

[97] Laurence Womock, *The Religion of the Church of England More Sound, More Safe, More Primitive and Catholick than that of Rome* (1648, repr. 1679), p. 25; William Lloyd, *An Historical Account of Church-Government* (1684), pp. 66, 81; William Lloyd, *Considerations Touching the True Way to Suppress Popery* (1677), pp. 84–5.

[98] George Hickes, *An Apologetical Vindication of the Church of England* (1687), pp. 57–8, 50. See below, Chapter 6, pp. 245–51.

[99] William Cave, *A Serious Exhortation* (1683), pp. 13–14; Jones, *Sermon*, sigs. A3v, [C4]v–Dr, Fr–F2r; Laurence Womock, *Sober Sadnes* (Oxford, 1643), p. 30. Aerius was not to be confused with the heretic Arius: Quantin, *Christian Antiquity*, p. 102.

[100] Fell, *Lex talionis*, p. 26; Jones, *Sermon*, pp. 19–23.

ordination.[101] For episcopacy was dominical or apostolic, practised by Timothy, Titus, and James, bishop of Jerusalem. After the collapse of clerical authority during the Civil Wars, especial care was taken to emphasise the importance of due apostolic succession. 'Due' meant episcopal ordination, not 'a mere nullity of ordination by presbyters against the consent of their bishops'.[102] This sentiment was not confined to printed polemic but was enshrined in law in the Act of Uniformity's requirement of episcopal ordination. The statute was symptomatic of waning sympathy with foreign churches: the lack of excuses and caveats for non-episcopal churches by many authors suggests either dislike of or lack of interest in their European Reformed brethren.[103] William Cave pointedly remarked that church-polity was a mark of a church's perfection. Sherlock grudgingly admitted stranger churches on royal sufferance, but demonstrated what might be called a Laudian concern to ensure that nonconformity could not hide itself in stranger churches, saying that if these communicated with English Dissenters, even the foreign churches became schismatic. Lowth snidely commented that Christians in non-episcopal churches might achieve salvation, but could not think themselves members of a real church.[104]

As shown above, the episcopalianism of the Church even infected Stillingfleet. But the zealous pursuit of episcopacy was truly exemplified in Thorndike's writings. In the early 1640s he was willing to grant at least an advisory role to presbyters, since presbyteries would make the Church of England properly primitive. But he did not deny the lawfulness of episcopacy, nor support the 'undue opinion' that the form of church government was *adiaphorous*.[105] He later stressed that presbyters' role was *merely* advisory; they could not act without bishops. Episcopal ordination could be bypassed only in necessity, and even then validity rested merely on a reasonable presumption of divine pardon.[106] Both the Twelve Apostles and Seventy Disciples were directly chosen by Christ and called his

[101] Cave, *Serious Exhortation*, p. 14; Fell, *Lex talionis*, p. 28; Jones, *Sermon*, p. 18. This was a typical strategy: Quantin, *Christian Antiquity*, pp. 100–1.

[102] Thorndike, 'Plea of Weakness', v.358 (qu.); Womock, *Anti-Boreale*, p. 42.

[103] Two exceptions are Sir Edmund Peirce, *The English Episcopacy and Liturgy Asserted* (1660) and Richard Hooke, *The Bishop's Appeale* (Newcastle, 1661); both notably pre-1662.

[104] Cave, *Unity of the Catholick Church*, p. 11; William Sherlock, *A Letter to Anonymus* (1683; 'anonymus' is William Atwood), p. 13; see also p. 14 for his reluctance to allow such churches; on Laud, see Anthony Milton's *ODNB* entry. Lowth, *Church-Power*, p. 417.

[105] Thorndike, 'The Primitive Government of Churches', in *Two Discourses*, p. 70, ch. 7, pp. 128, 134 (qu.).

[106] Thorndike, *Right of the Church*, pp. 132–3, 293–9. For him, the Civil War abolition of bishops does not seem to have constituted necessity.

'Apostles', but the Seventy were 'Governours of another Rank', evangelists and assistants to the patriarchal Twelve.[107] Thorndike's stress on unity and catholicity emphasised bishops as providing the networks which upheld the unity vital for the survival of Christianity. Some permanent locus of authority is needed for the church to legislate for herself: 'the Lawes of it will necessarily change ... but the authority whence they proceed must needs continue the same'. Unlike Stillingfleet, Thorndike explicitly depicted this authority as episcopal. Both the form of church government and the interpretation of faith were left by the apostles to their successors, the bishops, mainstays of a visible and united church. The Keys, crucial in Thorndike's conception of church power, were given by Christ in person to every bishop equally but not equally to presbyters.[108] 'Episcopacy [is] inviolable in all opinions; And the Church a standing synod.' Thorndike pointedly removed church legislation from the sphere of the civil magistrate. 'The Unity of the Church is not derived from *Constantine*, but from our Lord and his Apostles.'[109]

Iure divino episcopacy denied claims to church government made by lay elders as well as popes and presbyters. Allowing the people to choose their minister savoured of Dissent, of conventicles, and the anarchical dissolution of the lay/clerical distinction during the Interregnum. In a church so wedded to patristic models it was vital to refute notions that early Christians had chosen their clergy. Lowth glossed popular attendance at elections as due to worshippers' knowledge of the characters of candidates; their absence would not have invalidated the process. Priests and laity were distinguished by God Himself in the Old Testament and priesthood given by Christ to the apostles and their successors, 'who alone have the Power of its conveyance'. 'There is something peculiar in the Clergy ... which the People have not, and consequently cannot give.'[110] Thorndike thought it good to satisfy the people of the rectitude of the clergy, but gave them no greater role.[111] Part of his animus against Presbyterianism was the way in which the clergy ended up being subjected

[107] Thorndike, *Right of the Church*, pp. 72–3 (qu. 72); see also Thorndike, 'Review', in *Right of the Church*, pp. lxvii–lxxvi; Thorndike, 'Review of the Discourse of the Primitive Government', in *Two Discourses*, p. 4.

[108] Thorndike, *Just Weights*, pp. 45–6 (qu.), 40; Thorndike, *Right of the Church*, pp. 183, 72; Thorndike, 'Review of the Discourse of the Primitive Government', in *Two Discourses*, pp. 9, 39–40; Thorndike, 'Review', in *Right of the Church*, ch. 1 and p. lxvii.

[109] Thorndike, *Just Weights*, p. 40, sig. A2v (the latter also quoted in Collins, 'Restoration Bishops', p. 568).

[110] Lowth, *Church-Power*, ch. 1 (qu. at pp. 6, 21).

[111] Thorndike, 'The Primitive Government of Churches', in *Two Discourses*, pp. 111–12; Thorndike, *Right of the Church*, pp. 82–4, 160–2.

to lay elders. Allowing consistories to excommunicate ended by 'investing a Civile Court with the Power of the Keys'.[112]

Yet opposition to lay meddling in ecclesiastical affairs slid towards outlawing lay monarchical supremacy. Lowth's description of 'the People choosing, the Bishop consecrating, the Emperor assenting' did not locate the right of investiture in the crown.[113] The first chapter of his *magnum opus* refuted popular holding of church power; the second denied royal possession of it. As clergy, the polemicists discussed in this chapter had sworn the Oath of Supremacy, and we should not assume that they swore it lightly, or without careful consideration of its meaning. But they could be strikingly reticent about outlining how the king was empowered by the supremacy, often expending energy on denying him any spiritual authority or barring him from the power to change church government. Supremacy was a tool to be exploited against popery, presbytery, and one's opponents within the Church. It was also a danger and a worry, a threat which had to be neutralised either by subordinating a willing monarch to clerical counsel, or by rebuking a recalcitrant one for invading God's sphere.

RESTRAINING SUPREMACY

Several hints of restraints on supremacy by those who advocated *iure divino* episcopacy can be found. The Bible, for example, offered instances of ungodly as well as godly monarchy which could be employed to elucidate the limits as well as powers of supremacy. II Chronicles 26 told the story of Uzziah, a pious king upheld by God, but one who grew complacent and hubristic, provoking divine wrath by attempting to burn incense in the Temple himself. Ignoring warnings from the priests to stop, he was smitten with leprosy, and never regained God's favour. In the 1560s, Uzziah was deployed by Catholic opponents of the supremacy; John Bridges asked whether there was 'any one Popishe writer on this question of Supremacie, but he alleageth this exa*m*ple'.[114] A century later Uzziah featured in Anglican texts, signalling authorial intent to warn monarchs of their limitations. Simon Lowth cited Uzziah in delineating royal from clerical power in investing priests, Henry Jones mentioned him, and Womock drove home the point that Uzziah had

[112] Thorndike, *Right of the Church*, pp. 68, 319–20 (qu. 320).

[113] Lowth, *Church-Power*, p. 21. Compare John Gauden, *A Pillar of Gratitude* (1661), p. 61, on the clergy choosing, the church approving, and the king confirming.

[114] John Bridges, *The Supremacie of Christian Princes* (1573), p. 1094.

been punished *despite* his holding public regal authority.[115] Falkner cited Uzziah along with Corah, who had attempted to usurp the priesthood. Corah's troop of sacrilegious men, often mapped on to nonconformists, had been swallowed up by the earth (Numbers 16). John Lloyd was far from endorsing a sacerdotal supremacy when he commented that the Christian magistrate might preach and administer the sacraments 'as lawfully as the 250 persons spoken of in the sixteenth chap. of *Numbers*, took censers and offered incense, and as lawfully as King *Uzziah* did the like'.[116]

The inviolability of the sacerdotal was sometimes invoked to deny royal power to abolish bishops. Thorndike's *Right of the Church* became increasingly confident in protecting episcopacy, from saying its abolition 'might' be beyond any earthly power (p. 129), to that it certainly could not be changed if it has always been present (p. 154), to arguing that even episcopacy erected by church custom alone was beyond 'the compasse of any Secular Power upon Earth' (p. 314). Even a parliament with an assembly of divines, exercising the greatest possible power in any Christian state, could not erect Presbyterianism, since its institution would not be 'by the Constitution of the Church' (p. 322). By the time he came to write his 'Review' Thorndike thought that the abolition of episcopacy meant the dissolution of the church.[117] He was clear that when obligations to spiritual and civil authorities conflicted, one must, *pace* Hobbes and his followers, openly profess Christian truths in defiance of sovereign dislike. Those entrusted with church power had a duty to 'provide for the subsistence thereof, without the assistance of Secular Powers'. Furthermore, *every* Christian, not just the clergy, should obey the church before the state. This was the basis of Thorndike's pastoral advice to avoid conforming to Cromwell's church – totally contrary to the practice of men like Tillotson. '[It is] requisite for Christians, in a doubtfull case, at their utmost perils, to adhere to the Guides of the Church, against their lawfull Soveraigns, though to no further effect, then to suffer for the exercise of Christianity, and the maintenance of the Society of the Church in

[115] Jones, *Sermon*, p. 10; Lowth, *Church-Power*, pp. 62–3 (see also p. 493); Womock, *Pulpit-Conceptions*, p. 18. See also Womock, *Anti-Boreale*, pp. 80–2, on Uzzah, commissioned by David to help move the Ark of the Covenant, and who had reached out to steady it on a rocky path. Uzzah's pious intent gained him nothing; his hand shrivelled and he died on the spot (II Samuel 6:6–7).

[116] Falkner, *Two Treatises*, p. 313; see also Falkner, *Christian Loyalty*, pp. 31–2; Lloyd, *Treatise*, p. 78, who says the magistrate may in fact only 'oversee, facilitate and corroborate' clerical actions.

[117] Thorndike, 'Review', in *Right of the Church*, p. xc.

Unity.'[118] Restoration Dissenters did not have a monopoly on noisy shows of martyrish suffering.

Another arena in which supremacy's limitations as well as powers were admitted was with regard to episcopal appointments. That the supreme governor held the primary right of patronage in the Church of England was an inescapable institutional fact. Priests and bishops held divine authority, but individual exercise thereof in a particular office was enabled by the king alone. Refuting jibes that Anglican bishops were 'parliament-bishops', John Bramhall patiently explained that 'we hold our Benefices by human right, our offices of Priests and Bishops both by divine right and human right'.[119] God makes the bishop, the king gives the bishopric, said John Brydall; that was why *sede vacante* the spiritualities went to the cathedral chapter and the temporalities to the king. The 'Office' of a bishop was distinct from the 'Place, Station and Power wherein that Office is exercised'. No sovereign claimed the authority to consecrate bishops, albeit none other created and allocated dioceses.[120] Thus no one denied royal rights of appointment to dioceses. But all decreed that rites of consecration were not in monarchical hands. Philip Fell told Herbert Croft that priestly power was divine 'as to its Nature and Original', although limited by secular authority 'in its Exercise and Application'.[121] Bramhall justified the canonical validity of Archbishop Parker's consecration, admitting that 'the essentialls of Ordination' did not derive from statutes or royal commissions. Between royal 'Confirmation of the Election, which is a politicall Act' and consecration, 'a purely spirituall Act', bishops are only bishops *elect*; and they cannot do homage, receive their temporalities, or sit in parliament (i.e. their parliamentary seats are not mere baronies). Even *iure humano* bishops could not be removed by the king.[122] Ecclesiastical jurisdiction also constituted a combination of spiritual censures, derived from a cleric's ordination; and coercive power, stemming from the king. Even Lowth allowed all the temporal appurtenances of the church (deaneries, temporalities, and power to *coerce* payment of tithes)

118 Thorndike, *Just Weights*, pp. 27, 228; Thorndike, *Discourse of the Forbearance*, pp. 29, 90–1, 112, and ch. 22; Thorndike, *Right of the Church*, qu. pp. 234–5; see Herbert Thorndike, *A Letter Concerning the Present State of Religion Amongst Us* (1656).

119 John Bramhall, *The Consecration and Succession of Protestant Bishops Justified* (Gravenhagh, 1658; repr. London, 1664), p. 238. A parallel exists with certain arguments for kingly and husbandly authority: the future subjects or wife choose the individual, God delegates the power.

120 John Brydall, *The Clergy Vindicated* (1679), pp. 6–7.

121 Fell, *Lex talionis*, p. 24.

122 Bramhall, *Consecration and Succession*, pp. 41–2 (qu. 41), 100 (qu.), 119, 210–11, 238–9. Pages 96 and 174 distinguish legality from validity. Catholics claimed Parker had been consecrated in a tavern.

to derive from princes. 'Laws and Judicatures' are run by bishops 'in their own Names, but by an antecedent Power derived from, and by the Prince devolved unto them'.[123]

If these sentiments about appointments and jurisdiction followed earlier ones, the emphasis on the limits of supremacy became more fulsome, integral to descriptions of church-polity, rather than an appended afterthought *a la Irenicum*. Amidst the common language which denied supremacy was sacerdotal, each theorist had their own explanation of why monarchs did not personally perform ecclesiastical actions. Lowth depicted supremacy as an earthly power which replaced papal jurisdiction not spiritual orders. God was supreme ruler of all, Christ of the church, pastors on earth, and the prince only of earthly government. Optatus, writing during an era of persecution, had argued that Christians believed the emperor to be second only to God, 'but Church-Power is still supposed a quite differing thing' Lowth hastily added. Church authority did not escheat to emperors on their conversion.[124] Falkner distinguished ecclesiastical power in a limited sense, exercised only by churchmen, from it in a large sense, cared for by monarchs. Thorndike called these ecclesiastical power and power in ecclesiastical matters respectively.[125] Sometimes he distinguished them by their origins (only the church *iure divino*), at others by qualities, faculties, and habits.[126] Lowth argued that a lack of sacerdotal powers did not impair princely functioning; princes were nurses and protectors, not parents, of the church, having no 'Generative, Procreative Power', neither bishops themselves nor able to delegate such powers to others. '*Constantine*'s Episcopacy consisted only in his outward care of the Church … it reacheth not to the inward Power … the Sacred Function or Office it self.'[127] Solomon was held to have appointed Zadok, but it was questionable 'whether *Solomon*'s placing him in the *High-Priest's Chair*, did by virtue of his *Kingly Power* alone, create him *High Priest*'.[128] Lowth cited Andrewes on priestly and princely power being 'united, but not confused'. Laney told Charles II that God had not left temporal and

[123] Lowth, *Church-Power*, pp. 161, 89, 351, 361 (qu.). On the significance of 'in their own names', see Chapter 4, pp. 194–202.

[124] Lowth, *Church-Power*, pp. 203–4, 103 (qu.), 90. St Optatus: late-fourth-century Bishop of Milevis in North Africa; his attack on the Donatists based on their lack of catholicity provided a basis for Augustine's refutation of Donatism.

[125] Falkner, *Christian Loyalty*, pp. 179–80; Thorndike, *Right of the Church*, pp. 164–5.

[126] Thorndike, 'Review', in *Right of the Church*, pp. cxv–cxx. He seems too little interested in the state to formulate a theory of the origins of political power.

[127] Lowth, *Church-Power*, pp. 86, 64, 67.

[128] Lowth, *Letter to Stillingfleet*, p. 81; i.e. Solomon could not have created Zadok's right to the high priesthood, had it not existed beforehand.

spiritual officers 'in common'. Sherlock thought the two 'very distinct' although 'very consistent'.[129] Laney claimed that he could not think the king 'an Ecclesiastical Person', since he had never been ordained. 'When some Learned in our Laws affirm, that the *KING* is Supreme Ordinary, and *mixta persona*, it must be understood in some other sense.'[130]

Nothing was harder, Thorndike complained, than explicating the right of the state in church affairs. There had been no national church in the New Testament. There were no Christian princes until Constantine. And he doubted how far Old Testament models could be mapped on to Gospel states (despite employing such examples).[131] Thorndike did not seek total exclusion of temporal authorities from matters ecclesiastical, for he saw the state as vital to the reformation and reinvigoration of the church. It may – at times must – purge the church of impurities, establish a reformation, reinvigorate church discipline.[132] It may do so even against clerical opponents, changing them (as in the Old Testament) if necessary, although it must not make superfluous alterations to ecclesiastical persons. The state does not err if it prevents churchmen from abusing their powers, yet it must not remove them arbitrarily. 'The State is indowed with no Ecclesiasticall Right, though it hath great Right in Ecclesiasticall matters.' Perhaps prudently, Thorndike refused to decree how in practice the state might satisfy itself that ecclesiastical power was not abused.[133]

If Thorndike found a role for *a* royal supremacy, he remained only ambiguously committed to contemporary forms of it. Henry VIII had had 'just occasion' to declare himself supreme head, but his Reformation produced 'a Sect of Erastians, very dangerous to Christianity'. The Oath of Supremacy, later hedged about with caveats about not claiming spiritual power, nevertheless might be interpreted more widely, and needed rewriting.[134] Falkner, whilst holding that the Oath was sufficiently clear, thought that the change of title from headship was prudent, it being 'much misunderstood by divers Foreigners' and disliked by Jewel. It was meant only, as Elizabethan and early Stuart writers had explained, in the sense of supreme governance and enforcement of clerical duties, the

[129] Lowth, *Church-Power*, p. 492; Laney, *Five Sermons*, p. 123; Sherlock, *Letter to Anonymus*, p. 24.

[130] Laney, *Five Sermons*, pp. 137–8 (also qu. in Collins, 'Restoration Bishops', pp. 563–4).

[131] Herbert Thorndike, 'The Right of the Christian State in Church-Matters, According to the Scriptures' [*c*.1659], in *Theological Works*, VI.69–71.

[132] Thorndike, *Right of the Church*, p. 274, sig. A2v; Thorndike, 'Review', in *Right of the Church*, pp. xvii–xviii. See, similarly, Thorndike, *Discourse of the Forbearance*, pp. 44–5.

[133] Thorndike, *Right of the Church*, pp. 274-[275] (mispag. 575), 41 (qu.).

[134] Thorndike, *Just Weights*, ch. 20 (qu. p. 131); see also Thorndike, *Discourse of the Forbearance*, pp. 158–9 (pp. 156–7 stated that the Oath unfairly targeted papists, whereas it should also incorporate a denial of nonconformist sedition).

ways in which Henry VIII and Edward VI had employed it, as explicated in the *Institvtion of a Christen Man* and Edwardian Ordinal.[135] Thorndike, while disowning Henry VIII's actions, protested that he did not dislike the supremacy as 'unjust, but as *indefinite*, and unlimited'.[136] Excommunication must not slip from clerical hands in a Christian state, for 'no Excommunication … no Church'.[137]

Despite criticising Thorndike's views of the supremacy, Falkner still cited him approvingly on the polity's right to maintain, but not meddle with, ecclesiastical authority.[138] Dicta that the state must take clerical advice when reforming the church soon turned into arguments that it had no choice but to follow churchmen: counsel became command. Supremacy, rightly defined, supported the dual edifice of magistracy and ministry. But everything hinged on that caveat, 'rightly defined'. Too many men, both inside and outside the Church of England, seemed to grant too much under the rubric of supremacy; these had to be corrected. And Charles and James seemed to mistakenly think that they could use their ecclesiastical powers to implement their own, rather than the Anglican Church's policies; they had to be restrained, pre-emptively by advice, and *ex post facto* by admonition.

The claim to clerical counsel rested on the congruity of church and commonwealth, and it both reflected and departed from humanist-classical and Aristotelian-scholastic arguments about proper kingship as counselled.[139] Even in temporals, clerical counsel might be useful. As John Gauden – moderate enough to retain a living in the 1650s – explained in 1661, a Christian state without religious counsel was a compass without a needle.[140] Although the debate in 1679 on bishops' votes in parliament became mired in medieval history, Thomas Hunt's early salvo discussed Israelite and Christian kings hearing advice from bishops who, over the

135 Falkner, *Christian Loyalty*, pp. 21–6 (qu. 21).

136 Thorndike, *Discourse of the Forbearance*, p. 103.

137 Thorndike, *Right of the Church*, pp. 40–1; Thorndike, *Just Weights*, pp. 25 (qu.), 122; pp. 181, 254 link this to reviving penance.

138 Falkner, *Christian Loyalty*, p. 17, citing Thorndike, *Right of the Church*, p. 168.

139 On the first, see John Guy, 'The Rhetoric of Counsel in Early Modern England', in Dale Hoak, ed., *Tudor Political Culture* (Cambridge, 1995); on the latter, see Mark Goldie, 'The Reception of Hobbes', in J. H. Burns and Mark Goldie, eds., *The Cambridge History of Political Thought, 1450–1700* (Cambridge, 1991), esp. pp. 597–600. See further Jacqueline Rose, 'Kingship and Counsel in Early Modern England', *Historical Journal*, 54 (2011), pp. 47–71. David Colclough, *Freedom of Speech in Early Stuart England* (Cambridge, 2005).

140 Gauden, *Pillar of Gratitude*, pp. 27–8, 3; see also Jeremiah Stephens, *An Apology for the Ancient Right and Power of the Bishops to Sit and Vote in Parliaments* (1660), pp. 42–3, 54 (copying Gerald Langbaine, *Episcopall Inheritance* (Oxford, 1641), pp. 19–21, 32). Collins, 'Restoration Bishops', p. 560.

centuries, had been ambassadors and privy councillors: 'no Persons more fit', 'none better qualified for Counsel'. Womock argued that the king deserved his bishops' counsel and the country their service.[141]

In religious matters, clergy could claim greater rights than lay advisors. If supremacy was as much a responsibility of nursing parenthood as a juridical right of power, a consequential duty of hearing those wise in matters divine was integral to exercising supremacy – or at least a supremacy that was morally integral. Supreme governors 'may' rule their church alone, but would 'best' govern with episcopal advice.[142] Thorndike wrote that his sovereign protector of the church might 'Judge for it self' about religion, 'yet the Church, and the Law of the Church, is the Rule by which it is to judge'. Parliament merely enforces what the 'consent and Authority' of synods decrees: statutes 'cannot bee the Measure of Religion, though they should bee the Fense and the Bulwark of it'.[143] The key word in Thorndike's definition of sovereign power in ecclesiastical matters was 'cumulative'. Royal supremacy is 'not destructive, but cumulative': monarchs can enforce church power; they cannot take it away.[144] The concept was widely shared. Falkner in 1678, Brydall in 1679, and Womock in 1681 all wrote that sovereigns held power 'cumulative' 'not privative'.[145] This linked to the idea that princes confirmed (never suppressed or created) Christian truths.[146]

Religious questions pointed up a paradox of early modern theories of counsel. Kings ought to hear godly and reject ungodly advice, but how did they judge which was which? Arianism had infiltrated imperial courts by flattery;[147] Dissent and Romanism might now be doing the same. Thus, whilst hearing counsel was a moral, not legal, obligation, institutionalising it in the privy council, convocation, and parliament might enable churchmen to strike down indulgence and toleration when their advice went unheard. Nevertheless, Anglicans preferred to use informal, verbal, and fluid counsel, given privately or in the quasi-public space of the

141 Thomas Hunt, *The Honours of the Lords Spiritual Asserted* (1679), esp. pp. 4–8, 10 (qu.), 17–21; Laurence Womock, *An Answer to the Gentleman's Letter to his Friend* (1680), p. 18. Goldie, 'Danby', passes over the role of counsel in this debate.

142 Lloyd, *Treatise*, p. 26.

143 Thorndike, *Just Weights*, qu. pp. 51–2, 226, 24; Thorndike, *Discourse of the Forbearance*, pp. 40–1; Thorndike, *Right of the Church*, pp. 223, 230.

144 Thorndike, *Right of the Church*, pp. 168, 221; Thorndike, *Just Weights*, p. 135 (accumulative).

145 Falkner, *Christian Loyalty*, p. 38; Brydall, *Clergy Vindicated*, p. 25; Laurence Womock, *The Verdict upon the Dissenters Plea* (1681), p. 25.

146 Falkner, *Christian Loyalty*, pp. 177, 40–2; Thorndike, 'Plea of Weakness', v.367.

147 Fell, *Lex talionis*, pp. 12–13; see also Samuel Parker, *Religion and Loyalty* (2 vols., 1684–5), 1.422, 462–3, see also 1.389, 403, 441.

court pulpit. Furthermore, if wisdom justified giving advice, any minister could assert this – for it was freely admitted that all Anglican priests were spiritually superior to lay monarchs. No doctrine of *iure divino* episcopacy was needed to assert clerical counsel, although the two ideas were often expressed by the same writers. Lowth explained that ministers' status as teachers 'immediately implies Superiority and Prelation'.[148] Although kings could not be excommunicated, and must be admonished with 'reverent respect', they were 'to be urg'd and taught publickly, as are others, and particularly in private, and where due opportunity to be severely warned'.[149] These men had none of Tillotson's reticence to stand up and profess their faith to hostile rulers. Every minister must 'speak before Kings' and criticise a false religion, albeit an established one.[150] Opportunities for so doing came in court sermons and services, and they were not passed by. Laney told Charles II he had to listen to his preachers, for 'the *Priest's lips* could not *preserve knowledge* unless it were received from his mouth by hearing'. Gilbert Sheldon reportedly put precept into practice when he refused to serve his sovereign communion. And the Seven Bishops in 1688 claimed their petition to James was no libel, but an example of their duty to counsel the monarch about the church – as well as his obligation to listen.[151]

The association rather than indelible causal link between counsel and *iure divino* episcopacy reflects the wider pattern of relationships between views of episcopacy and of supremacy. Their confluence was not coincidental, but nor was it inevitable. As this chapter has shown, the Restoration witnessed both a more widespread rhetoric of *iure divino* episcopacy and plenty of restrictions on supremacy. The two sentiments were rooted in a shared polemical need: to prevent kings who were only semi-committed to the established Church from using their supremacy against it. Churchmen agreed that kings could not meddle with the fundamentals of faith, but they disagreed about whether church-polity was included in those necessities and about what response was required if kings overstepped their authority. However, as Chapter 6 shows, even those who

[148] Lowth, *Church-Power*, pp. 34–5. See, similarly, Falkner, *Christian Loyalty*, pp. 176, 178.

[149] Lowth, *Church-Power*, qu. p. 360; see pp. 97–9, 104–5 on Ambrose and Theodosius; Falkner, *Christian Loyalty*, pp. 316–19 (qu. 318), 321, 225, 466.

[150] Lowth, *Church-Power*, pp. 157–60, 165, 383–5, 410. Cf. Thomas Barlow's caution: the king has a soul to be saved, but is still a great man: *The Original of Kingly and Ecclesiastical Government* (1681), p. 11.

[151] Laney, *Five Sermons*, pp. 56 (qu.), 66–7, 113; Sheldon: Simon, *Restoration Episcopate*, p. 92; on the Seven Bishops, see Chapter 6, pp. 267–74.

claimed Nicodemism was not wrong stood up to James II's Catholic supremacy in the later 1680s.

Dissenters and their supporters were wrong to claim that divine right episcopacy necessarily destroyed supremacy. They were on firmer ground when noting how churchmen wavered between exalting and undermining kings.[152] The Restoration Church proclaimed *iure divino* kingship as a bulwark against relapse into another civil war. It promoted *iure divino* episcopacy as a form of defence of its own existence should kingship be removed again or – *monstrum horrendum* – surrender to the Church's opponents. Churchmen could not afford to forget the lure of popery and Dissent, temptations to which Restoration kings seemed all too prone to succumb. In those situations, supremacy would soon change from benefiting the establishment to undermining it. How Dissenting and anticlerical writers and a Catholic king recognised and exploited this is the story of the second half of this book.

[152] Collins, 'Restoration Bishops', p. 573, emphasises divine right as the key shift from earlier churchmen; in fact, the rest of his article suggests that it was the use to which this was put rather than the theory itself which caused new tensions.

CHAPTER 4

Dissenters and the supremacy: the question of toleration

The Restoration Settlement endeavoured to erase the events of the Civil Wars, but seemed unable to eradicate the religious pluralism which had flourished in the Interregnum. Politicians and divines treated denominational diversity in a variety of ways. The most fundamental division lay between those upholding a national church coextensive with the polity and those accepting that the established church would become one of several means of worship. Significantly, this fissure did not neatly coincide with that between conformity and Dissent (itself a blurred boundary). Not only was total separation of church and polity rarely advocated, there was also no inexorable rise of toleration.[1] This was partly because prosecution (or persecution, depending on one's point of view) rose and fell over time, and its impact differed in different areas and on different religious groupings. Informal tolerance or stigmatism also diverged from official dicta.[2] But the prevalence of the idea of a national church made attractive the alternative to toleration: comprehension. This would broaden the church to incorporate those who dissented only on matters 'indifferent'; not fundamentals of belief, but rites and ceremonies that the Bible did not prescribe; or who objected only to the fact of imposition rather than the items imposed.[3] Those abandoning comprehension in favour of recognising sects outside the Church of England could rarely hope for sympathy from the strongly Anglican parliaments of the Restoration, even when

[1] Cf. A. A. Seaton, *The Theory of Toleration under the Later Stuarts* (Cambridge, 1911).

[2] John Miller, 'James II and Toleration', in Eveline Cruickshanks, ed., *By Force or by Default? The Revolution of 1688–1689* (Edinburgh, 1989), p. 12; Frank Bate, *The Declaration of Indulgence, 1672: A Study in the Rise of Organised Dissent* (1908), pp. 41, 43; Alexandra Walsham, *Charitable Hatred: Tolerance and Intolerance in England, 1500–1700* (Manchester, 2006).

[3] The importance of comprehension is stressed by Roger Thomas, 'Comprehension and Indulgence', in Geoffrey F. Nuttall and Owen Chadwick, eds., *From Uniformity to Unity, 1662–1962* (1962); Mark Goldie, *Roger Morrice and the Puritan Whigs* (Woodbridge, 2007), pp. 234–46. But cf. Gordon J. Schochet, 'From Persecution to "Toleration"', in J. R. Jones, ed., *Liberty Secured? Britain Before and After 1688* (Stanford, CA, 1992), pp. 132–6; R. A. Beddard, 'Vincent Alsop and the Emancipation of Restoration Dissent', *Journal of Ecclesiastical History*, 24 (1973), pp. 161–84.

proposing liberty for only Protestant not Catholic recusants. Instead they turned to royal prerogative 'indulgences', which unilaterally proclaimed liberty to tender consciences. In a sharp change from previous reigns, after 1660 Protestants dissatisfied with the Church looked to Whitehall, not Westminster. Comprehension was mooted in 1660, 1661, 1667, 1668, 1674, 1675, 1680, and 1689. Indulgences were promulgated in 1662, 1672, 1687, and 1688. Only in 1689 did parliament pass an act of limited toleration.[4]

Despite widespread historiographical recognition that 'toleration' did not become current in the Restoration, many studies detect a shift towards emphasising political considerations in debates on religious liberty. Mark Knights, Gordon Schochet, and John Miller emphasise the pragmatic question of whether toleration was expedient, perhaps natural in the circumstance of an established national church.[5] But whilst these historians draw a distinction between theologico-religious and political discourse, and place the question of toleration in the latter arena, a third *ecclesiological* dimension goes unheralded. Naturally, discussion of toleration did have reference to political order, but the ecclesiological aspect of debate was vital, since it focused on the relationship between church and polity. It is also true that there was a 'constitutionalist' strain within Dissent, especially of the Presbyterian variety, which sought a limited monarchy in line with the conditions offered to Charles I in the 1640s, valued and participated vigorously in parliamentary politics, and whose significance has

[4] Miller, 'James II and Toleration', pp. 23–4. Schochet, 'Persecution to "Toleration"', p. 156, characterises it as simply the next attempt to deal with nonconformity. On the substance of these events, see John Spurr, 'The Church of England, Comprehension and the Toleration Act of 1689', *English Historical Review*, 104 (1989), pp. 927–46. On 1662, see George R. Abernathy, jr, 'Clarendon and the Declaration of Indulgence', *Journal of Ecclesiastical History*, 11 (1960), pp. 55–73. On the 1672 Indulgence, see Jacqueline Rose, 'Royal Ecclesiastical Supremacy and the Restoration Church', *Historical Research*, 80 (2007), pp. 324–45; Mark Goldie, 'Toleration and the Godly Prince in Restoration England', in John Morrow and Jonathan Scott, eds., *Liberty, Authority, Formality: Political Ideas and Culture, 1600–1900* (Exeter, 2008); Richard Ashcraft, *Revolutionary Politics and Locke's Two Treatises of Government* (Princeton, 1986), ch. 2; and Bate, *Declaration of Indulgence*. On the 1674 bill, see Thomas, 'Comprehension and Indulgence', pp. 215–16. On the Exclusion proposals, see H. Horwitz, 'Protestant Reconciliation in the Exclusion Crisis', *Journal of Ecclesiastical History*, 15 (1964), pp. 201–17; Gary De Krey, 'Reformation in the Restoration Crisis, 1679–1682', in Donna B. Hamilton and Richard Strier, eds., *Religion, Literature, and Politics in Post-Reformation England, 1540–1688* (Cambridge, 1996), pp. 238–9. On James's Declarations, see Richard E. Boyer, *English Declarations of Indulgence 1687 and 1688* (The Hague, 1968); Mark Knights, '"Mere Religion" and the "Church State" of Restoration England: The Impact and Ideology of James II's Declarations of Indulgence', in Alan Houston and Steve Pincus, eds., *A Nation Transformed: England After the Restoration* (Cambridge, 2001).

[5] Knights, 'James II's Declarations', pp. 43, 45; Gordon Schochet, 'John Locke and Religious Toleration', in Lois G. Schwoerer, ed., *The Revolution of 1688–1689: Changing Perspectives* (Cambridge, 1992), pp. 148, 160; Miller, 'James II and Toleration', p. 10; Schochet, 'Persecution to Toleration', pp. 125–6.

only recently been emphasised.[6] But religious and political liberty did not always develop in tandem. This chapter develops themes noted by Gary de Krey and Mark Goldie about how Dissenters allied with kings against bishops. This Foxean exercise in further reformation saw the magistrate as a means to subdue clerisy.[7] As a mode of argument, it emphasised a tradition of godly monarchy, or at least of monarchical suppression of ungodly prelacy. It nostalgically looked back to the Anglo-Saxon polity, not for witans and parliaments, but for a totally unified church and state.[8] It longed for the pre-papal era of Constantinian supremacy over a deferential church. And it spoke with much pride, although with limited accuracy, of Tudor monarchs who had connived at further reformation, celebrating their royal supremacy over a bench of subdued bishops. Charles II and James II sometimes willingly played their roles in this ideology, when brave enough to challenge the combined opposition of prelates and parliaments who told them that toleration was sinful and declarations of indulgence were illegal.

To seek royal patronage for reforming the established church was, furthermore, far from new. The English Reformation itself might be characterised as a revolt of the monarch and a minority of enlightened clergy leading the recalcitrant majority out of the corrupt captivity of the papal church. Tudor sovereigns had been appealed to by those seeking further reformation, whether they responded (like Edward VI) or not (as Elizabeth I). Puritan–Dissenting endorsement of the supremacy was two-pronged. Partly it was a destructive critique of episcopal authority as undermining royal supremacy. The increasing case for *iure divino* episcopacy fuelled nonconformists' sense of a popish prelacy inhibiting supremacy and therefore (crucially) thwarting reform (which – of course! – monarchs would endorse if not blinded by evil counsellors). The second part of this case was, however, a positive endorsement of godly magistracy. A partnership of king and minister ensured moral reformation – although it is easy to detect this to be an unequal partnership, for the puritan sense of supremacy slipped easily into making the crown a mere tool to enforce the ministry's demands. Those who sought to attack bishops therefore tended to be most enthusiastic about the supremacy.

6 Goldie, *Puritan Whigs*; to an extent reviving Douglas R. Lacey, *Dissent and Parliamentary Politics in England, 1661–1689* (New Brunswick, NJ, 1969).

7 De Krey, 'Reformation in the Restoration Crisis', pp. 242–5; Mark Goldie, 'Priestcraft and the Birth of Whiggism', in Nicholas Phillipson and Quentin Skinner, eds., *Political Discourse in Early Modern Britain* (Cambridge, 1993), passim, esp. pp. 214–15.

8 See Goldie, *Puritan Whigs*, pp. 183–4.

For over a century the nonconformist argument met with no positive royal response. Elizabethan and early Stuart reformation would be had through parliament, not the crown. What changed after 1660 was not that bishops and nonconformists appealed to the monarch, but that the former's counsel was rejected in favour of conciliating the latter. This chapter considers Dissenting 'supremacism' in response to the three key Declarations of Indulgence (1662, 1672, and 1687), turning finally to the intermittent attacks mounted on ecclesiastical jurisdiction which used the supremacy to neutralise episcopal power. Not every Dissenter was willing to engage in such strategies; conversely, men who conformed to the legal requirements of Anglican worship might endorse the idea of using supremacy to relieve tender consciences. But the power and prevalence of Dissenting use of supremacy throughout the Restoration is newly demonstrated here. Remaining loyal to the principle of godly monarchy, but being offered toleration rather than a national church through supremacy, puritanism mutated into Dissent.

The Dissenting case for supremacy thus had deep Reformation roots, but it flourished unprecedentedly during the Restoration. Although after 1673 Charles did not attempt another declaration of indulgence, his subjects (Dissenting and Anglican) were not to know that. Nonconformists not only responded to indulgence offered, but also lobbied for it, their confidence renewed by James II's Declarations. Nonconformist exaltation of monarchical supremacy over the Church might look paradoxical, but it made sense as a strategy to bypass episcopal intolerance. One pamphleteer in 1688 scorned Anglican promises of liberty of conscience: 'as often as it hath been granted by Royal Dispensations, you have been angry at it; as oft as it has been propos'd in Parliament, you have Oppos'd it'.[9] To where else could Dissenters turn but the throne?

THE ESTABLISHMENT OF UNIFORMITY AND RESTORATION DISSENT

Even before the Act of Uniformity was passed, the case for prerogative indulgence was in the air. Considering three writers who argued for tolerance early in the Restoration demonstrates the diverse range of ways in which liberty for nonconformists could be defended. Peter Pett was a conformist protégé of the Earl of Anglesey who endorsed comprehension. Philip Nye was one of the leading Interregnum Congregationalists,

[9] Anon., *The Countrey-Minister's Reflections on the City-Minister's Letter to his Friend* (1688), p. 8.

who proposed an alliance between the supreme governor and Congregationalism. Bulstrode Whitelocke was a lawyer who had opposed the regicide but participated in Interregnum politics, favoured liberty of conscience, and who now offered a legal and historical case justifying royal prerogative indulgence. Whilst the speed of the promulgation and withdrawal of Charles's Declaration of Indulgence of December 1662 – really only proposed, never fully issued – limited public debate, those who wrote in defence of toleration in this period would do so again in 1672 and 1687. There is thus a parallel with the phenomenon described in Chapter 3: the foundations of responses (parliamentary or polemical) to later Declarations were laid at the start of the Restoration.

In 1661 Peter Pett, who later defended James II's Declarations, condemned ecclesiastical rigour for damaging peace, unity, and trade, illogical given the popularity of nonconformists and the unpopularity of the bishops. Pett also surveyed European examples of toleration.[10] He added a more unusual case: the argument from lay anticlericalism. Modern gentry were no longer willing to swallow cases for *iure divino* church government, denial of which might more 'gratifie the power of Princes, then the Maxim, *No Bishop no King* can do'. Pett did not wish to remove episcopacy, but he thought tempering high-church rhetoric would decrease provocations of the laity, who might otherwise be

> tempted to cry up the Divine Right of *Erastianisme*, and say *No Erastian no King*; which opinion doth as much exceed the Episcopal in giving power to the King, as the Episcopal doth the Presbyterian, or that the Independent perswasion.[11]

Pett's sceptical tory perspective was not the only case made for indulgence.[12] In 1662 the Congregationalist Philip Nye embarked on a long investigation into the Oath of Supremacy and power of the civil magistrate over the church, a tract anonymously reprinted under a different title in 1670 and 1686.[13] In the Middle Ages, Nye explained, popes had held the 'whole Nation' under 'a devotional slavery', ended by Henry VIII's Reformation.[14] Nye drew five distinctions between clerical and

[10] Peter Pett, *A Discourse Concerning Liberty of Conscience* (1661), pp. 21–37, 61–6, 68–9, 87ff.

[11] Pett, *Discourse*, pp. 50–3, qu. 52, 71. The maxim was James I's famous (and famously opaque) *bon mot* at the Hampton Court Conference of 1604.

[12] On this perspective, see Mark Goldie, 'Sir Peter Pett, Sceptical Toryism and the Science of Toleration in the 1680s', in W. J. Sheils, ed., *Persecution and Toleration* (Oxford, 1984).

[13] Philip Nye, *The Lawfulness of the Oath of Supremacy and Power of the Civil Magistrate in Ecclesiastical Affairs and Subordination of Churches thereunto* (1662); repr. 1670 and 1686 as *The Best Fence against Popery: Or, a Vindication of the Power of the King in Ecclesiastical Affairs.*

[14] Nye, *Lawfulness*, pp. 7 (qu.), 8.

magisterial authority. Spiritual authority referred primarily to the First Table not the Second, it worked directly on the soul, it was ministerial not dominative, limited to one congregation, and it could not vary from place to place.[15] All churchmen were subject to the supremacy, for none could claim exemption from political subjection simply beacuse of their clerical status.[16] But Nye insisted that the supremacy created a godly prince, not a secular pope (as he complained the conservative Henrician Stephen Gardiner and the authoritarian late Elizabethan bishop Richard Bancroft had done). 'Although a power in spiritual causes be given to a secular Prince, yet it's not a *spiritual power*, and such a jurisdiction as the Pope claims, but such a power only and in such a way as is put forth and exercised in ordinary Civil affairs.'[17] Supremacy extended the sphere of monarchical action; it did not change the nature of such authority.

The purpose of a godly prince was to make a godly people. Government being for 'the *moral* good of men's souls', Nye envisaged prince and clergy working together, the first using temporal and the latter ecclesiastical means to advance national holiness. When kept within their proper spheres, these 'sweetly comply and agree': like Moses and Aaron, Zerubbabel and Joshua. '"*Jungamus Gladios* [we hold the sword]" said an Emperor to his Bishop.'[18] Supreme governance is the duty to further spiritual welfare: to uphold the ministry, encourage churchgoing, and remove corrupt teachers, theatres, and brothels.[19] (Nye clearly felt Charles II might be tempted to inspect a few of these institutions.) Even the Apostle Paul 'could not do so much as the meanest Civil Magistrate in such a Coercive way', a power which 'cannot well be wanted' in a godly commonwealth.[20] Here Nye echoed earlier descriptions of magisterial oversight and enforcement of clerical duties and scriptural praise of royal fatherly care for the '*Nurse-Child*, or Infant' of the church.[21]

But whilst half of Nye's book described the nature and history of the royal supremacy, the rest sought to prove its compatibility with Independent congregations. For Nye, church power was held by every congregation, a 'particular' branch of the universal church being more like a family than a country. Magna Carta's statement that the church in England 'shall be free' and the coronation oath to protect the church meant churches in the plural sense: individual congregations.[22] *Iure divino* episcopacy, ran the puritan complaint, was tantamount to denying the

[15] Nye, *Lawfulness*, ch. 3, pp. 55–65. [16] Nye, *Lawfulness*, pp. 46–7.
[17] Nye, *Lawfulness*, pp. 28–9. [18] Nye, *Lawfulness*, pp. 49, 54.
[19] Nye, *Lawfulness*, pp. 69, 72. [20] Nye, *Lawfulness*, pp. 73–4.
[21] Nye, *Lawfulness*, p. 81. [22] Nye, *Lawfulness*, pp. 58, 98–101, 110–11.

royal supremacy; small local churches, Nye said, were 'much more *consistent*' with royal supremacy than powerful bishops.[23] The counterpart of nonconformist loyalty was an aggressive attack on episcopal authority through ratcheting up royal supremacy. The sixth and final chapter of Nye's book firmly subordinated synods and ecclesiastical courts to royal will. Nothing that a synod (which draws its authority only from particular churches) can do is impossible for the magistrate to carry out instead.[24] If the king so wishes, he may 'suspend for what time he shall please, yea wholly deprive' a bishop. Since final appellate jurisdiction rested with the king and the ecclesiastical laws were his, he might dispense with any of them and 'indulge the omission of what is enjoyned by them ... make void the crime and remove the penalty ... give faculty to do or practise otherwise' if divine law is respected.[25]

Publicly Charles acquiesced in the rejection of his Declaration. Privately, he took steps to assert his rights. He turned to the legal expert Bulstrode Whitelocke, whose diary records the king's request on 13 March 1663 for his opinion on royal ecclesiastical prerogative, since Charles had heard 'that Wh*itelocke's* judgem*ent* was high for his Ma*ies*tyes power in matters Ecclesiasticall'. On 25 March Whitelocke sent his study of 'The Kings Right to graunt Indulgence in matters of Religion Asserted by B. W. Kt' to Charles, a 'great buisnes, w*hi*ch he had studyed before & now collected and putt into method his former notes'.[26] 'Politie' suggested the value of indulgence in preserving public peace and fostering trade and population, particularly after the ravages of civil war. Invoking the language of interest, Whitelocke noted that indulgence would bring nonconformists to an 'intire' or 'perfect' dependence on the crown, before turning to a less political argument focusing on the nature of Christianity (to persuade, not coerce).[27] He thereafter offered an ecclesiological case drawn from the 'constant and general practice' of Christian and pagan kings supreme in spiritual matters: first the patriarchs, then Hebrew, Chaldean, Greek, Persian, and Roman kings. 'Most Nations of the

[23] Nye, *Lawfulness*, pp. 127–8, 122 (qu.), 131, 137.

[24] Nye, *Lawfulness*, pp. 166–7. [25] Nye, *Lawfulness*, pp. 162, 164.

[26] Ruth Spalding, ed., *The Diary of Bulstrode Whitelocke, 1605–1675* (Oxford, 1990), pp. 663–4; see Ruth Spalding, *The Improbable Puritan: A Life of Bulstrode Whitelocke, 1605–1675* (1975), pp. 237–8; p. 279 states the notes were from the 1630s. The MS is BL, Add. MS 21099; prefaced by Henry Care and printed as Bulstrode Whitelocke, *The King's Right of Indulgence in Spiritual Matters, with the Equity thereof, Asserted* (1688 (preface dated 26 Oct. 1687)); attributed to Anglesey. The following citations are from the manuscript, with the printed pagination in parentheses. I have noted deviations where significant.

[27] BL, Add. MS 21099, fos. 33r–34v (p. 9, omitting 'perfect'), chs. 2–3 (chs. 2–3). On trade, fos. 13r–16r, 29v–33r (pp. 4, 7–8).

World, after the President of the Hebrews, placed the Supream Spiritual Jurisdiction in their Kings and Supream Rulers, and it were improbable to conclude that the right of Indulgence was excepted out of that Jurisdiction.'[28] The clergy had claimed no superiority over emperors for 850 years, they had to supplicate rulers to summon councils, the French clergy supported their monarch against the pope, even elective Polish kings enjoyed supremacy.[29] Turning specifically to England, Whitelocke invoked King Lucius before surveying ecclesiastical legislation by Anglo-Saxon kings and royal investiture of bishops long after the Conquest. He praised the 'stout and wise' Edward I for recovering many royal rights, noted monarchs exempted clergy from ordinaries' jurisdiction ('no slender argument of the kings right to graunt Indulgence in those matters'), and argued the dissolution of the monasteries showed 'as much supremacy in the king, in matters of the church, as may be imagined'.[30] Ending his historical excursus with Charles I's reign, Whitelocke proposed the 'present occasion' required delving more deeply into the relationship of crown and parliament.[31]

Chapter 6 was the crux of Whitelocke's argument, locating the authority to indulge firmly in the king. His case was atypical in focusing on the king as *mixta persona*, 'a person united with the priests of the holy church'. All princes sought to prevent papal aggrandisement. But English kings alone (Whitelocke said) were elevated by being anointed, an act creating a 'reall relation' which 'doth more peculiar [*sic*] and appropriate the State Ecclesiastique to our King, so it makes him not only the supream Head and Governor, but also the chiefe guide and guardian'. (This was, however, not historically unique: Israelite kings were mixed persons; King Lucius preached to his soldiers.)[32] If the king bore a spiritual character, then claiming that only spiritual persons could grant indulgence in religious matters did not exclude him. Popes had granted indulgences, but kings were more certainly supreme heads of the church than popes were, and could therefore grant indulgence.[33] Both supreme headship and dispensations for nonconformity ('not *malum in se*, but only, perhaps,

[28] BL, Add. MS 21099, fos. 60v–64r (pp. 18–21, qu. 18, 21). Ch. 4 is entitled 'That Supream ecclesiastical jurisdiction ~~in England~~ is in ~~the~~ kings and princes' (fo. 58r; cf. p. 17: 'Of *Supreme Spiritual Jurisdiction*, and consequently a Right of *Indulgence* in *KINGS*').

[29] BL, Add. MS 21099, fos. 65v, 68r and ff, 70v–72v, 76r (pp. 21–2, 24).

[30] BL, Add. MS 21099, fos. 78r–108r (pp. 25–32), passim: esp. 78r (p. 25), 93r (qu.) (p. 28), 101r (qu.) (cf. p. 30: 'which manifests his own Supream Spiritual Jurisdiction'), 118v–119r (qu.) (p. 33).

[31] BL, Add. MS 21099, fo. 133r–v (omitted on p. 35).

[32] BL, Add. MS 21099, fos. 134r–140v, qu. 134v (p. 35), 137r–138r (p. 36: 'this real Relation doth more peculiar and appropriate the *State Spiritual* to our King').

[33] BL, Add. MS 21099, fos. 141r–145r (p. 38).

Bonum prohibitum') were warranted by common law.[34] To prevent persecution for opinions was reasonable power, not so different from exemptions from episcopal jurisdiction and prohibitions ('a great Indulgence to the people').[35] If Charles II could dispense stranger churches from the Act of Uniformity, surely he might extend such relief to his own subjects – a power which could not be removed 'without expresse words in an Act of Parliament', and which had not been taken away in 1662.[36]

In 1663 Whitelocke judiciously refrained from commenting on the extent of indulgence, particularly where the Commons had already pronounced on it. But when his manuscript was printed in 1687 with a preface by James II's propagandist, Henry Care, two more chapters appeared: one showing examples of persecution and another with examples of indulgence. 'Generally Indulgence hath been given in Spiritual Matters, and the right of giving it, exercised by Monarchs' the printed text stated.[37] Both scribal and printed texts concluded by insisting that ecclesiastical supremacy was a manifest power of the king, 'one of the highest cleerest rights, and most beautifull flowers of his Crown'.[38] In 1663, no immediate royal response seems to have been predicated on the basis of Whitelocke's advice, but Charles was willing to be patient. In 1672, he tried again.

COMPREHENSION AND INDULGENCE, 1667–1673

Even if Clarendon was not responsible for the oppressive penal legislation which bore his name, his fall in 1667 inaugurated a new era in Restoration government. The Cabal was not united in its religious views, but Clarendon's disgrace (in effect from the Dutch attack on the Medway in June) opened up new ecclesiological possibilities pursued in late 1667 and early 1668 by an alliance of government advisors such as Matthew Hale and Orlando Bridgeman, the 'latitudinarian' bishop John Wilkins, and moderate Presbyterians such as Thomas Manton and William Bates. John Corbet's *Discourse of the Religion of England* of November 1667 has

[34] BL, Add. MS 21099, fo. 145r–v (qu. p. 41).

[35] BL, Add. MS 21099, fos. 151r–152r, 153r (1st foliation) (p. 43), qu. 153r (2nd foliation; not in printed version).

[36] BL, Add. MS 21099, fo. 196r–v (p. 54).

[37] BL, Add. MS 21099, fo. 199r–v; cf. pp. 56–74, qu. p. 65. Goldie suggests the changes are Whitelocke's: 'Toleration and the Godly Prince', p. 47. Whitelocke did write a history of persecution from Abel to the seventeenth century, beginning it in 1670 and resuming it during the 1672 Indulgence (see Spalding, ed., *Diary of Whitelocke*, pp. 762, 797 (21 Nov. 1670, 16 July 1672)). The printed text also begins with Abel, but confines itself to Biblical examples. The printed additions might therefore be Whitelocke's, Care's, or a combination of the two.

[38] BL, Add. MS 21099, fo. 200v (p. 75).

sometimes been taken to herald the beginning of the campaign for comprehension; in fact the opening sally, an anonymous pamphlet by the Presbyterian John Humfrey, came in June. Archbishop Sheldon's chaplain, Thomas Tomkins, refuted Humfrey; Richard Perrinchief was ordered by Sheldon to rebut Corbet (Herbert Thorndike's draft replies were not printed at the time).[39] Both Corbet and Humfrey replied in 1668.[40] The debate was inflamed by the series of pamphlets, inaptly entitled *A Friendly Debate*, by the future bishop of Ely, Simon Patrick, defended by the soon-to-be-infamous Samuel Parker in his *Discourse of Ecclesiastical Politie*.[41] John Owen, the leader of the Independents, attacked Parker, whose later reply came under fire from Andrew Marvell.[42] By the time that Marvell was writing, the debate had moved from comprehension to the period of the 1672 Indulgence, and it was in the context of royal apostasy from the Church that authors replied to Marvell. Since several pamphlet wars were running in parallel, differences can be discerned both within the establishment and amongst its opponents, as well as between them. Presbyterians blamed Owen for the collapse of comprehension in 1668;[43] Independents were not interested in widening the establishment if they could secure liberty of conscience outside it. Andrew Marvell, John Locke, and Henry Stubbe were not nonconformist ministers, but they agreed with Dissenters' claims. Nor is it possible to talk in monolithic terms of 'the government'; each member of the 'Cabal' regime had distinct purposes and reacted in different ways when the royal Declaration

[39] John Corbet, *A Discourse of the Religion of England* (1667); John Humfrey, *A Proposition for the Safety and Happiness of the King and Kingdom Both in Church and State* (1667); Thomas Tomkins, *The Inconveniences of Toleration* (1667); Richard Perrinchief, *A Discourse of Toleration* (1668); Herbert Thorndike, 'The True Principle of Comprehension' and 'The Plea of Weakness and Tender Consciences Answered', in *Theological Works* (6 vols., Oxford, 1844–56), v.299–380. Derek Hirst, 'Making all Religion Ridiculous: Of Culture High and Low: The Polemics of Toleration, 1667–1673', *Renaissance Forum*, 1 (1996), para. 7, stresses Corbet and Owen, not Humfrey (www.hull.ac.uk/renforum).

[40] [John Humfrey], *A Defence of the Proposition* (1668; p. 5 refers to 'my' proposition, the title page to the 'same' author); John Corbet, *A Second Discourse of the Religion of England* (1668).

[41] Simon Patrick, *A Friendly Debate Between a Conformist and a Non-Conformist*, 5th edn (1669); Simon Patrick, *A Continuation of the Friendly Debate* (1669); Simon Patrick, *A Further Continuation and Defence, or, A Third Part of the Friendly Debate* (1670); Simon Patrick, *An Appendix to the Third Part of the Friendly Debate* (1670); Samuel Rolle, *A Sober Answer to the Friendly Debate* (1669); Samuel Parker, *A Discourse of Ecclesiastical Politie* (1670 [1669]).

[42] John Owen, *Truth and Innocence Vindicated* (1669); Samuel Parker, *A Defence and Continuation of the Ecclesiastical Politie* (1671); Samuel Parker, *A Discourse in Vindication of Bp Bramhall and the Clergy of the Church of England from the Fanatick Charge of Popery* (1673); Andrew Marvell, *The Rehearsal Transpros'd and the Rehearsal Transpros'd the Second Part*, ed. D. I. B. Smith (Oxford, 1971).

[43] N. H. Keeble and Geoffrey F. Nuttall, eds., *Calendar of the Correspondence of Richard Baxter* (2 vols., Oxford, 1991), no. 760 (from Thomas Manton, 26 Sept. 1668).

was challenged.[44] The uses to which royal supremacy was being put exposed those divisions.

'Supremacist' arguments were not the only ones for indulgence. Three other key justifications were conscience, economic advantage, and political prudence. Many claimed that conscience, under God's direct governance, *could* not be coerced by man, and *should* not be by Christians. Elevating the private individual conscience over the public conscience of the Church reinterpreted Dissent not as wilful recalcitrance but as an insuperable inability to conform.[45] John Humfrey refuted in detail Parker's argument that human laws invariably bound the conscience. 'The Supremacy of the King, I hope, is over the Subject, as to their Persons and their Causes, not over their Consciences.'[46] Another case for indulgence was that it was thought to encourage industrious, but often Dissenting, merchants and artisans, both English and immigrant. Securing their loyalty was especially important given Anglo-Dutch commercial rivalry and war.[47] Conversely, failed coercion had dangerously alienated many groups. Safety stemmed from bringing conventicles into the open – quite literally: Dissenting meetings were licensed on condition they kept their doors open, to prevent seditious talk. 'Whispering must be less tolerated than preaching', wrote Locke.[48] These justifications were interspersed with examples of the wisdom and success of toleration.[49]

[44] Maurice Lee, jr, *The Cabal* (Urbana, IL, 1965), p. 195.

[45] John Owen, *A Peace-Offering in an Apology and Humble Plea for Indulgence and Liberty of Conscience* (1667, citing Wing O790), p. 19; John Owen, *Indvlgence and Toleration Considered* (1667), pp. 13, 16–17; Owen, *Truth and Innocence*, pp. 264–6; Marvell, *Rehearsal Transpros'd the Second Part*, p. 326; Humfrey, *Proposition*, p. 77; Sir Charles Wolseley, *Liberty of Conscience upon its True and Proper Grounds Asserted & Vindicated* (1668), pp. 10, 46–7; John Locke, 'An Essay on Toleration' (1667), in *Political Essays*, ed. Mark Goldie (Cambridge, 1997), p. 139; Corbet, *Second Discourse*, pp. 19, 25–6; Anon., *A Few Sober Queries upon the Late Proclamation for Enforcing the Laws against Conventicles* (1668), pp. 6–7; Richard Baxter, *The Difference Between the Power of Magistrates and Church-Pastors* (1671), proposition 55 (p. 37).

[46] John Humfrey, *The Obligation of Human Laws Discussed* (1671); John Humfrey, *A Case of Conscience* (1669), pp. 8 (qu.), 5, 26–7.

[47] Anon., *A Second Letter to a Member of the Present Parliament, against Comprehension* (1668), p. 3; Locke, 'Essay on Toleration', p. 159; Owen, *Truth and Innocence*, pp. 77–81; John Owen, 'The State of the Kingdom with Respect to the Present Bill against Conventicles', in *Works*, ed. William H. Goold, vol. XIII (repr. 1967), pp. 583, 585; W. D. Christie, *A Life of Anthony Ashley Cooper, First Earl of Shaftesbury* (2 vols., 1871), II, appx I and II.72; see also Henry Stubbe, *A Further Iustification of the Present War Against the United Netherlands* (1673), p. 29.

[48] Locke, 'Essay on Toleration', pp. 148 (qu.), 154–6; Nicholas Lockyer, *Some Seasonable and Serious Queries upon the Late Act against Conventicles* (1670), p. 10; Sir Charles Wolseley, *Liberty of Conscience the Magistrates Interest* (1668), pp. 3–4, 17; Humfrey, *Proposition*, p. 57; Stubbe, *Further Iustification*, p. 66.

[49] Anon., *A Speech Touching Toleration in Matters of Religion* (1668); W. K., *An English Answer to the Scotch Speech, Shewing the Intolerableness of Tolleration* (1668).

Stubbe, Baxter, and Charles Wolseley deployed a phalanx of tolerant early Christian emperors, perhaps partly in response to Restoration Anglican veneration for the Fathers and well-established examples of supremacy. John Owen emblazoned across his *Peace-Offering* the edict of Constantine, that model of *imperium*, 'THAT THE LIBERTY OF WORSHIP WAS NOT TO BE DENIED UNTO ANY'.[50]

The rich supremacist seam which this study uncovers should not preclude recognition of the fact that some nonconformists remained chary of advocating indulgence by royal prerogative. The Bartolomean Philip Henry noted those who accepted licences (as he reluctantly did) were criticised for giving Charles 'a power above the lawes' and 'so wee doe above such bad lawes as *tha*t of uniformity'. When the Indulgence was withdrawn he reflected that liberty from God alone was perhaps the best and sweetest sort.[51] Some Dissenters pointed to statutes, primarily those of 1559 and 1670, which upheld monarchical supremacy.[52] But others did still look to parliament. In 1667 and 1668 Humfrey and Owen could profess hope that parliamentary intolerance demonstrated in 1662 might have changed. 'Our confidence in those *Royal Declarations* hath not hitherto been weakened by the interveniency of so many occasions, as have cast us under another condition … we expect *no liberty*, but from his Majesty's favour and authority, with the concurrence of the Parliament.'[53] By 1673, such optimism had surely foundered. The anonymous *Vindiciæ libertatis evangelii* (1672) expressed impatience with those who spurned royal aid because they disliked the prerogative. 'Cannot the King suspend the penalty of an Act of Parliament, but he must be Head of the Church? … is it imaginable that an absolute Supremacy [over Christ] is intended?'[54] The power to dispense was an ancient royal power, frequently exercised, and often admitted by parliament. 'Do we make his Majesty Arbitrary, by accepting his free offer to suspend the Execution of Ecclesiastical Laws, which Himself declareth inherent in himsels [*sic*], and Parliaments have Recognized to belong to his Throne?'[55]

[50] Stubbe, *Further Iustification*, pp. 33–61; Wolseley, *Liberty of Conscience the Magistrate's Interest*, pp. 18–19; Richard Baxter, *Sacrilegious Desertion of the Holy Ministery Rebuked, and Tolerated Preaching of the Gospel Vindicated* (1672), p. 14; Owen, *Peace-Offering*, p. 25.

[51] Matthew Henry Lee, ed., *Diaries and Letters of Philip Henry* (1882), pp. 253 (qu.), 262.

[52] Anon., *Short Reflections on a Pamphlet Entituled, Toleration Not to be Abused* (1672), pp. 8–9.

[53] Humfrey, *Defence of the Proposition*, p. 96; Owen, *Indvlgence and Toleration Considered*, pp. 25–6; Owen, *Peace-Offering*, p. 32 (qu.).

[54] Anon., *Vindiciæ libertatis evangelii: Or, a Justification of our Present Indulgence, and the Acceptance of Licenses* (1672), pp. 7 (qu.), 6, 14.

[55] *Vindiciæ libertatis evangelii*, p. 25.

The monarchical rather than parliamentary nature of the supremacy, crucial to defending Charles's actions in 1672, was the theme of the memoranda submitted by Henry Stubbe to his patron, Henry Bennet, Earl of Arlington, Charles's secretary of state.[56] Stubbe extrapolated from Tudor history, when supremacy was undeniably present.[57] Parliaments, Stubbe insisted, had never exercised authority over the spiritual aspects of the church during the Middle Ages; they had never been usurped by the papacy, having no usual, obligatory, or proper role in ecclesiastical matters. Nor could they claim powers from having confirmed Henrician reforms which replaced two separate jurisdictions, temporal and spiritual, with royal meddling in religious doctrine and church property.[58] Quoting the Act in Restraint of Appeals, Stubbe noted that 'the *jurisdiction*, and *Supremacy* of the *King* [in ecclesiastical affairs], was contradistinct from what ariseth from the *Parlament*, and *Common Lawes* of the Realme: certainely the *measures thereof* are not to bee taken from *thence*'. In a penetrating analysis of how Henry (if not his ministers) saw the role of parliament, Stubbe described how supremacy was 'not from the *Parlament*, except by way of *corroboration*'.[59] In any case, biblical proof of sovereign supremacy denied it to parliament – there being no coordinate power in scripture.[60] The king 'is Mixta persona, the Parlament was never styled so'.[61]

The full panoply of Henrician powers had not decayed over time. Tudor proclamations, Stubbe somewhat dubiously asserted, needed no parliamentary sanction, and liturgy, doctrine, and discipline were all regulated by them.[62] Edward VI had issued injunctions and proclamations before parliament met, while a statute avowed the royal supremacy over the bishops exercised by letters patent.[63] In 1559, however, 'a great *State-intrigue*' was plotted 'whereupon more seems to bee fixed in the Parlamentary power then of due appertained unto it, or was by the Queene intended to bee annexed thereunto'. Forced on to the defensive by the Marian bishops, Elizabeth was

56 Henry Stubbe, 'An Inquiry into the Supremacy Spirituall of the Kings of England: Occasioned by a Proviso in the Late Act of Parlament against Conventicles' (TNA, SP 29/319/220); Henry Stubbe, 'The History of the Spirituall Supremacy as it was Exercised by Qu: Elizabeth' (TNA, SP 29/319/221); Henry Stubbe, 'An Answer unto Certaine Objections formed against the Proceedings of His Majesty to Suspend the Lawes against Conventicles by His Declaration March 15 1672' (TNA, SP 29/319/222). The scribal foliation is referred to throughout. On this phase of Stubbe's career see James R. Jacob, *Henry Stubbe, Radical Protestantism and the Early Enlightenment* (Cambridge, 1983), ch. 6, and p. 129 for Stubbe's link to the Dissenters' patron Anglesey.

57 Stubbe, 'Inquiry', fo. 322.

58 Stubbe, 'Inquiry', fos. 320–1, 324, 326, 330; Stubbe, 'History', fo. 344.

59 Stubbe, 'Inquiry', fo. 325. 60 Stubbe, 'Inquiry', fo. 330.

61 Stubbe, 'History', fo. 344. 62 Stubbe, 'Inquiry', fo. 333.

63 Stubbe, 'Inquiry', fos. 331–2.

'enforced to supply the deficiency of *Ecclesiasticall authority* in *Convocation* by the shewe of *Parlamentary Authority* ... *Shee* did hereby humble the *Clergy*, and subject them to the *Layety*'. Having justified this as a necessary action to avoid Catholic opposition, Stubbe cheerfully dismissed any precedents for parliamentary action, the events of 1559 simply 'an intrigue of State, and not an establishment of Right in *th*e Parlament'.[64]

Stubbe's study of Tudor *imperium* argued that the king could 'authorise' the Church of England to tolerate 'Schismaticall and Hereticall conventicles', and that Elizabeth had exercised a 'mercifull connivence' to 'Papists in Conscience, and not in Faction'.[65] Another memorandum refuted five objections to the 1672 Indulgence. First, the coronation oath to protect the church did not outlaw toleration, since by his extraordinary prerogative the king could mitigate or suspend statutes for the common good, either in an emergency or for equity. Second, the proviso to the Second Conventicles Act showed religious matters were decided by the king alone, not under the 'proper cognisance' of parliament. Even taking parliamentary advice on them was 'but a moderne practise in comparison of the ancient way'. That informers could not be rewarded for reporting a former crime now legalised was but a by-product of suspending the law. Third, both popes and Protestant rulers had issued universal as well as individual dispensations. Fourth, the novelty of a *declaration* of indulgence was insignificant, since all that was held necessary to a law was its promulgation, by whatever means.[66] The Declaration, Stubbe said insouciantly, was no more novel than Thomas Cromwell's vicegerency in spirituals. Finally, he dismissed suggestions that it was rather embarrassing to suspend a statute within a few years of its making – an argument which parliament had made in 1663 against Charles's earlier Declaration. Not weakness but wisdom, Stubbe insisted, led the king to change his mind. Charles had used his ecclesiastical supremacy and 'hath not exceeded it'.[67]

An alternative case for supremacy to Stubbe's historical excursus was that for godly rule. In a work not published until 1687, but written in mid 1672, Nye argued that laws made by crown-in-parliament were 'more fixed and stable' than those made by the monarch alone. But 'these Powers are not equal, the King hath the Supremacy', and thus a peculiar right of 'Mitigating, Exempting, Dispensing, Licensing, Pardoning, *&c.* and all this

64 Stubbe, 'History', fos. 343–4.
65 Stubbe, 'History', fos. 345, 346.
66 Stubbe, 'Answer', fo. 348. Lawyers argued that dispensation could not occur where a third party, in this case the informer, would be damaged.
67 Stubbe, 'Answer', fo. 349; *CJ*, VIII.443 (27 Feb. 1663).

more especially in Ecclesiastical Matters'.[68] From the nature of sovereignty, Nye inferred the necessity of equitable dispensation, often needed more speedily than the time it took for parliament to repeal an act. He appealed to Jacobean legal authority in arguing that the use of the *non obstante* formula allowed dispensation with *mala prohibita*, albeit not *mala in se*.[69] The ecclesiological parallel was that monarchs held sway over external forms and circumstances of worship; here he cited the Jacobean theorist Richard Mocket.[70] It could hardly be held, Nye scorned, that rites were intrinsic necessities for the common good, and he praised Charles for preventing the prosecution of a nonconformist under an Elizabethan statute originally intended against Catholics.[71] Examples of royal lenience were not hard for Nye to find: James I attempting to reduce ceremonies, and being balked by parliament; Tudor and early Stuart monarchs authorising the worship of stranger churches; and Charles II in 1660, 1661, 1662, and, implicitly, in 1670. The proviso to the 1670 Act was, for Nye, a tacit recognition and offer by parliament that if severity proved a failure, the king might abandon it.[72]

Nye was increasingly dismissive of parliament's ecclesiastical powers. Some equivalent of the Tudor commission to reform ecclesiastical law could be set up to review and purge ungodly statutes.[73] Charles might need help with this, but such counsel should come from godly divines, not MPs. Although 'the ablest Statesman' needs the 'advice and direction' of Christ's ministers to make the best ecclesiastical laws, parliament was unqualified to decide religious policy. MPs, chosen 'by Vote of the promiscuous Multitude', could not be relied on to make godly laws, since godliness was 'little or not at all attended [to]' by the electorate.[74] By contrast, the king had sufficient supremacy to tolerate by 'that Power God and the Nation have intrusted him with, though not with concurrence of Parliament, so much and so often desired by him'.[75]

[68] Philip Nye, *The King's Authority in Dispensing with Ecclesiastical Laws, Asserted and Vindicated* (1687), p. 2; see pp. 45, 64 for references to twelve years of uniformity, which dates the work to 1672; Nye died in September of that year.

[69] Nye, *King's Authority*, pp. 3–6; citing Sir Henry Finch's *Nomotexnia* (publ. 1613, written *c*.1585).

[70] Nye, *King's Authority*, pp. 8–9. Richard Mocket: reputed author of *God and the King* (1615), a defence of the Oath of Allegiance; his *Doctrina et politia ecclesiae Anglicanae* (1616), a collection of Anglican texts and defence of ecclesiastical jurisdiction, was for uncertain reasons objected to by James I and burnt: Bertha Porter, 'Richard Mocket', rev. Glenn Burgess, *ODNB*.

[71] Nye, *King's Authority*, p. 17. 'It is Righteousness, and not Ceremonies, that Establish a Nation': Nye, *King's Authority*, p. 45.

[72] Nye, *King's Authority*, pp. 13–14, 23, 28, 50–1, 30. On the 1670 proviso, see above, p. 97.

[73] Nye, *King's Authority*, pp. 14–15.

[74] Nye, *King's Authority*, qu. pp. 36, 13, see also p. 14.

[75] Nye, *King's Authority*, p. 60.

As the prospect of episcopal and parliamentary consent to indulgence waned, Dissenters increasingly looked to the king. When their hopes were fulfilled, they unsurprisingly engaged in fulsome praise of the Christian qualities of a beneficent ruler, exalting the jurisdictional supremacy which offered them relief. The Presbyterian poet Robert Wild professed a fear that celebrations were premature before parliament had confirmed the Indulgence, but decided to enjoy the experience whilst he could, gleefully celebrating the king abandoning the bishops.[76] For Wild, the royal Declaration exceeded half a millennium of Rome's indulgences. In his mocking account, upon seeing the Declaration Wild bowed to the royal arms, celebrating a second Magna Carta and a new feast day when the king 'took possession of his whole *Dominions*, and the *Affections* of all *Israel*'.[77] Wild's rampant rhetoric was echoed in a more sober, but no less telling, poém by 'T. S. of Grayes-Inne':

> The Title of *Supremacy* is now
> Not lessen'd, but increas'd: all *Sects* allow
> *Charles* their Supreme, and from him as *Head* obey;
> Owning themselves *Conformists* from this day.
> Thus hath his Mercy added to his Store:
> He's *Head* of *Churches* now, but *one* before.[78]

The rhetoric of the king as common father of his people was widespread, whether as an encouragement to grant indulgence or as thanks when it was given. John Humfrey asserted that his brethren needed the 'gentle rayes and warm beams' of indulgence, a metaphor also employed by the Bartolomean Samuel Rolle.[79] Fatherly compassion to suffering nonconformists was praised by Corbet in 1667, Wolseley in 1668, Rolle in 1669, and Nye in 1672.[80] Since the Indulgence upheld the value of the Church of England, wrote Stubbe, by it Charles

[76] Robert Wild, *A Letter from Dr Robert Wild to his Friend Mr J.J. upon Occasion of His Majesty's Declaration for Liberty of Conscience* (1709), p. 8. Wild had been arrested at a conventicle in July 1669: *CSPD, Oct. 1668 to Dec. 1669*, p. 430 (28 July 1669). One of the replies to Wild noted the anticlerical foundations of his royalism: 'Our freedom is inlarg'd, and that's a thing, / Will make me *love*, the once *loath'd* Name of *King*': J. J., *Flagellum Poeticum: Or, a Scourge for a Wilde Poet* (1672), p. 13.

[77] Wild, *Letter*, pp. 7, 5–6 (qu. 6).

[78] T. S. [Thomas Sherman?] of Grays Inn, *Upon His Majesties Late Declarations for Toleration and Publication of War Against the Hollander* (1672), p. 1.

[79] Humfrey, *Proposition*, p. 52; Rolle, *Sober Answer*, pp. [220] (mispag. 120), 245. Rolle conformed in 1677.

[80] Corbet, *Discourse*, sig. [A3]r; Wolseley, *Liberty of Conscience the Magistrates Interest*, p. 9; Rolle, *Sober Answer*, p. 231; Nye, *King's Authority*, p. 48; see also Humfrey, *Proposition*, p. 88; Humfrey, *Defence of the Proposition*, pp. 104, 119.

expresseth himself to be the *common Father of His People*, at the same time *He* demonstrateth himself likewise a *zealous* and perfect *Son of the Church*. He revives the *Primitive Policy* of *Constantine*, and acteth like a *Bishop over those that are without*, whilest he defends and owns the *Orthodox Bishops over those that are within*.[81]

This was not the only citation of what may have been no more than a flippant imperial remark.[82] John Owen also invoked the Constantinian topos, while going one step further in saying toleration made the king akin to Christ.[83]

Whether comprehension and/or indulgence came from king or parliament, Dissenters often implied that either or both of these institutions had ultimate authority over the nature and extent of the Church of England, and thus over its bishops. Here supremacy was a gift to anti-prelatical and anticlerical rhetoric: a profession of loyalty to the monarch was a means of subverting the established Church hierarchy. When the bishops were out of favour such claims could be enunciated more explicitly, in the Cabal milieu of rumours about episcopal disgrace and confiscation of church lands.[84] The clergy, nonconformists told Charles, saw him merely as an executor of their intolerant wills, debasing his power and enslaving it to the Church. Baxter reminded magistrates that the pope was not the only clerical threat to their power. 'No Magistrate should be debased, so as to be made the Churches Executioner.'[85] The Anglican, but anticlerical, John Locke complained that *iure divino* claims to episcopal authority mistakenly set the clergy up against their royal masters. Where kings submitted to following clerical dictates, they were rewarded by being dubbed *iure divino* themselves; but woe betide rulers who defied

[81] Stubbe, *Further Iustification*, p. 32, partially quoted in Goldie, 'Priestcraft', p. 230, but without the crucial distinction of within and without the church. See also *Short Reflections*, p. 5; Marvell, *Rehearsal Transpros'd the Second Part*, p. 280.

[82] Eusebius, *Life of Constantine*, bk IV, ch. 24. See the edition by Henry Wace and Philip Schaff (Oxford, 1905), p. 546 and n.; Raymond Van Dam, 'The Many Conversions of the Emperor Constantine', in Kenneth Mills and Anthony Grafton, eds., *Conversion in Late Antiquity and the Early Middle Ages* (Rochester, NY, 2003), pp. 138–9.

[83] Owen, *Truth and Innocence*, pp. 318–19, 299; John Owen, *Correspondence*, ed. Peter Toon (Cambridge, 1970), p. 126.

[84] For such rumours, see *CSPD, Nov. 1667 to Sept. 1668*, pp. 165, 238 (13 Jan., 18 Feb. 1668); *CSPD, Oct. 1668 to Dec. 1669*, p. 320 (10 May 1669); Samuel Pepys, *Diary*, ed. Robert Latham and William Matthews (11 vols., 1970–83), VIII.584, 587, 596 (20, 23, 30 Dec. 1667), IX.1–2, 53, 485 (1 Jan., 6 Feb., 16 Mar. 1669). On church property specifically, see Pepys, *Diary*, IX.45, 347, 473 (31 Jan., 4 Nov. 1668, 7 Mar. 1669); and see *A Few Sober Queries*, p. 11, for an incitement to such confiscation.

[85] Baxter, *Difference Between the Power of Magistrates and Church-Pastors*, sig. A2v, pp. 10–14; qu. proposition 64 (p. 39).

clerical dominion.[86] Humfrey denied that the king had the power of the Keys, but insisted that he had 'some Superintendent inspection', for

> he is not to be a blind Executor onely of the Bishops will, in putting a Sanction on their Canons, and enforcing the observance, without having the *Book of the Law delivered to him* [Deuteronomy 17:18–19], and consequently a Judgement of Discretion, whether they be agreeable to the Rule of Gods Word, and condition of his People.[87]

The king's power is external, and emphatically not spiritual; he is only keeper of the Two Tables, and cannot change their content. But, nevertheless, as God's minister for good (Romans 13:4) he can thwart the plots of ungodly bishops.

Assertions of godly kingship subduing the church can be found across the denominational spectrum. Wolseley advocated a separation of church and state, yet recalled the days of Christian empire, of Constantine's calling himself a bishop, before the Roman episcopate muddled spiritual and temporal matters.[88] Nye admitted that godly bishops had been granted authority by emperors, but complained of the 'wither[ing]' of 'the civil Authority, and Glory of Secular Princes and States' with the rise of ecclesiastical power.[89] And Andrew Marvell wrote in bitter language of the decay of both Christianity and civil power after the conversion of imperial Rome. With the fourth-century incorporation of church into state – the 'unnatural Copulation of Ecclesiastical and Temporal' – 'Ecclesiastical persons … began exceedingly to degenerate':

> They follow'd the Courts of Princes, and intangled themselves in secular affairs, beyond what is lawful or convenient to the Sanctity of their Vocation … well-nigh ever since it has been more then half the business of Princes to regulate the brabbles and quarrels that have been unnecessarily sow'd by some of the Clergy; and they have brought the World to that pass that indeed it cannot longer subsist then Kings shall have and exercise an Ecclesiastical Supremacy as far as it can be stretched.[90]

Believing that the church needed regular purges of corruption, Marvell claimed that the royal supremacy was vital to ensure such cleansing actually took place, as the clergy were seemingly incapable of carrying it out themselves.[91]

[86] Locke, 'Toleration A' (*c.* 1675), in *Political Essays*, ed. Goldie, p. 234; see *A Few Sober Queries*, p. 11.
[87] Humfrey, *Case of Conscience*, p. 21.
[88] Wolseley, *Liberty of Conscience upon its True and Proper Grounds*, pp. 27, 26, 22.
[89] Nye, *Lawfulness*, pp. 42, 127 (qu.).
[90] Marvell, *Rehearsal Transpros'd the Second Part*, pp. 237–8.
[91] Marvell, *Rehearsal Transpros'd the Second Part*, pp. 239–40.

For these men, intolerance was the fault not of the king, but of Anglican ministers who provoked and incited him to enforce penal laws against Dissenters in order to uphold their own power.[92] One poet explained how '*Ghostly Bigots*' summon 'the *Militia* of our SOV'RAIGN's Laws; / *Troop* up to *Arms*, the pœnal Acts, march on', calling on the king to snuff out the lights of the Church so that Englishmen were no longer scared by ecclesiastical lanterns.[93] *Vindiciæ libertatis evangelii* argued for the acceptance of royal licences to worship, even if for no other reason than to staunch the flow of episcopal oppression. 'The Lord hath made his Majesty the Instrument to accomplish an intermission of Hostility against us.'[94] How could Dissenters afford to spurn Charles II, God's agent against Anglican despotism?

Nonconformist 'supremacism' was encouraged by royal indulgences; its expression was provoked by Anglican polemic. Conformists, like their opponents, were sometimes wary of closely examining royal prerogative. Instead they questioned whether prosecution (of unruly individual whims) could be dubbed persecution (suffering for the truth).[95] Erring private consciences must either rectify themselves or be disciplined, supervened by public laws and the 'imperial and superlative' conscience of the king.[96] Conformists challenged the applicability of examples of toleration, such as early Christian emperors.[97] And some reminded Presbyterians of their history of conforming whilst seeking comprehension, always before opposing separation, schism, and toleration.[98] William Assheton's collection of previous writings against

[92] *A Few Sober Queries*, pp. 8, 10; Baxter, *Sacrilegious Desertion*, p. 136.

[93] Anon., *Loyalty and Nonconformity* (1669), pp. 8 (qu.), 6.

[94] *Vindiciæ libertatis evangelii*, pp. 26, 29–30, 20 (qu.).

[95] Richard Perrinchief, *Indulgence Not Justified: Being a Continuation of the Discourse of Toleration* (1668), pp. 9, 5–7; Anon., *The Toleration Intolerable* (1670), p. 18. Francis Fullwood, *Humble Advice to the Conforming and Non-Conforming Ministers and People* (1673), pp. 32–40, argued for obedience in *adiaphora*; B. P., *A Modest and Peaceable Letter Concerning Comprehension* (1668), p. 8, showed the paradox of how Anglicans now claimed their consciences could not countenance royal policies.

[96] *Toleration Intolerable*, p. 15; Tomkins, *Inconveniences of Toleration*, pp. 1–2; Parker, *Ecclesiastical Politie*, p. 304; Samuel Parker, *A Reproof to the Rehearsal Transprosed* (1673), p. 485 (qu.).

[97] Perrinchief, *Indulgence Not Justified*, pp. 19–26; *Toleration Intolerable*, pp. 10–11. The latter disclaimed assertions of Old Testament or apostolic tolerationism: pp. 5–8; Perrinchief, *Discourse of Toleration*, pp. 22–3.

[98] Francis Fullwood, *Toleration Not to be Abused, Or, a Serious Question Soberly Debated, and Resolved upon Presbyterian Principles* (1672), pp. 22, 23; Fullwood, 'A Dialogue betwixt the Independent and Presbyterian', in *Humble Advice*, pp. [89–90]; Tomkins, *Inconveniences of Toleration*, p. 29; Patrick, *Friendly Debate*, p. 158: his nonconformist is a Presbyterian, refuting association with Quakers (p. 41), Independents (p. 51), and ideas of universal toleration (p. 57); Patrick, *Continuation*, p. 26.

toleration included correspondence from London Presbyterians in 1645 and puritan sermons as well as a royal speech which he dated to 1604 and MPs' resolution of 1663. Assheton, chaplain to Ormonde, was cited by Fullwood in 1672; in March 1671 he was reportedly presented to the king by the name of his book, *Toleration Disapprov'd*.[99] John Hacket, bishop of Coventry and Lichfield, was quick to purchase a copy, describing the author as a 'nameless good man' to Sheldon in April 1670.[100] For conformists, unity and uniformity were synonymous, undermined only by rumours of relaxation of the penal laws.[101] Implicitly rebuking temporal magistrates from the sovereign to the parish constable, Anglicans moaned that laws being on the statute book but never enforced made a mockery of the Restoration confessional state.[102]

Open opposition to royal policy was extremely difficult. Francis Fullwood avoided outright censure of the Indulgence, claiming only to prove that the pernicious consequences of toleration were unavoidable. Schism was *malum in se*, not permissible.[103] Citing Presbyterian opposition to religious liberty, Fullwood slyly declared 'your *sence* about *Toleration*, and not *my own*' – a sense which Fullwood, as a former Presbyterian, would have known very well.[104] 'Toleration' was a pejorative term; it did not mean the king *liked* separatism. Forbearing to execute a penalty supposed an offence had been committed, so suspending the punitive part of penal laws left their 'most *proper* and obliging' preceptive part intact.[105] Thorndike was boldest in stating that the change in ecclesiastical laws which comprehension required was impossible for the sovereign to carry out 'without the authority and against the consent of the Church'.[106]

Whether Charles read Fullwood or Thorndike is questionable, but he should have heard the sermon given before him by George Seignior on 17 April 1670 (unless he characteristically took the chance for a nap). Preaching in the aftermath of the Second Conventicles Act, Seignior

99 Anon., *A Letter of the Presbyterian Ministers in the City of London, Presented the First of Jan. 1645* (1668); William Assheton, *Toleration Disapprov'd and Condemn'd* (1670); Fullwood, *Toleration Not to be Abused*, p. 23; *CPSD, Jan. to Nov. 1671*, p. 143 (24 Mar. 1671).

100 Bodl., Tanner MS 44, fo. 196 (Hacket to Sheldon, 23 Apr. 1670). Hacket died in Oct. 1670.

101 Tomkins, *Inconveniences of Toleration*, pp. 4, 6; Perrinchief, *Indulgence Not Justified*, p. 2.

102 E.g. Perrinchief, *Discourse of Toleration*, pp. 31–2.

103 Fullwood, *Toleration Not to be Abused*, pp. 6, 16.

104 Fullwood, *Toleration Not to be Abused*, pp. 11, 22 (qu.).

105 Fullwood, *Toleration Not to be Abused*, pp. 5, 15 (qu.).

106 Thorndike, 'Plea of Weakness', p. 364.

may have sincerely celebrated the unity of 'Moses and Aaron',[107] showing to Dissenters the public face of a united establishment.[108] But under his praise lay a subtext of admonitory advice warning the king not to jettison the Church. Seignior's other sermons leave no doubt that he was opposed to tolerating or comprehending those he deemed schismatics.[109] Punning on the episcopal promoter of such schemes, the universal language theorist John Wilkins, he drily commented that 'you may give [toleration] a new name, and by an *Universal Character* Style it *Comprehension*', but it was still, at heart, a project of Babel.[110] This sermon exemplified Locke's comment that, when pleased with princes, the Anglican Church preached up their divinity: for Seignior said that, although kings were not priests, scripture called them gods and prophets.[111] But he also engaged in the high-church rhetoric which Locke, Marvell, and Dissenters condemned, uncompromisingly asserting clerical authority. The high priest spoke for the prince and simultaneously for his own divine authority, derived from apostolic succession, and he was 'by *no means* to be *excluded Senates*'.[112] Seignior warned Charles that new laws (read, the Conventicles Act) should be enforced, and old ones reinforced.[113] By praising an ideal Anglican supreme head, Seignior warned his real one not to shirk his duties.

1672 was the high tide of Dissenting supremacism under Charles II. Forced to withdraw his Declaration by parliamentary and fiscal pressure in 1673, the king associated himself with an Anglican-royalist policy for the rest of his reign. In the mid 1670s this was impelled by his chief minister, Danby, and was a necessary defence for the monarchy in the crisis of 1678 to 1682. Even thereafter Charles at minimum did not prevent vigorous prosecution of Dissenters, a campaign which took persecution to new heights of viciousness. If the seemingly indolent and once-tolerant monarch whose main concern was to keep his throne allowed such a campaign, Dissenters might have hoped for little in February 1685, when he was succeeded by an authoritarian, absolutist, and dedicated Catholic.

107 The title of his sermon.

108 See, similarly, Perrinchief, *Discourse of Toleration*, p. 55; John Howes, *A Sermon Preached at the Assizes at Northampton, August the 9th 1669* (1670), sig. A2v.

109 George Seignior, *God, the King, and the Church* (1670), pp. 186–8, 172–3, 240, 248.

110 Seignior, *God, the King, and the Church*, p. 70.

111 Seignior, *God, the King, and the Church*, pp. 29, 14–15, 22.

112 Seignior, *God, the King, and the Church*, pp. 6, 9 (qu.); pp. 115–16 assert apostolic equality, p. 142 apostolic succession against 'our *Modern Erastians*'.

113 Seignior, *God, the King, and the Church*, p. 33.

JAMES II AND THE DISSENTERS

The apparent paradox of a Catholic–Dissenting alliance had been hinted at before 1685. As Duke of York, James had forged links with Dissenters in 1675–6.[114] But in the first months of his reign he seemed firmly wedded to Anglican absolutists. It is hard to tell whether this alliance was broken by James's promotion of Catholics or Anglicans' pre-emptive criticism of any such intentions. The 1685 parliament ended in acrimony over appointments of Catholic officers to regiments raised against Monmouth, and in March 1686 James pardoned imprisoned nonconformists. Although his Declaration of Indulgence of 4 April 1687 promised to respect the established Church and not to restore church lands, it asserted James's 'constant sense and opinion… that conscience ought not to be constrained'.[115] Because of his unshakeable conviction that proper understanding of Catholicism would lead to mass conversions, James could pursue the most liberal policy yet seen (no licences were needed for worship) and believe that this was a route to re-Catholicisation.[116] But he wanted to hurry things along by promoting Catholics into offices, bypassing the Test Acts by using the prerogative power of dispensing particular individuals, and then generally suspending the penal laws by his Declarations. The wisdom of the policy was dubious, its legality questioned.[117] Charles II, whatever his true religious beliefs, had at least publicly adhered to the Church of England, but ingrained prejudices about Catholic intolerance meant his brother encountered even greater suspicions. Separation of Catholic belief from political popery was rare.[118]

In suggesting that debate on toleration changed under James, past historiography has underestimated the continuing significance of supremacy.[119] The political nation faced a monarchical policy founded not upon Enlightenment principles of freedom of thought, but one whose supporters invoked Tudor precedents for interference in the universities, subjugating the Church by a semi-lay Ecclesiastical Commission, dispensing and suspending the penal laws and Test Acts by an absolute

[114] John Miller, *James II*, rev. edn (1989), pp. 77–8.

[115] John Coffey, *Persecution and Toleration in Protestant England, 1558–1689* (Harlow, 2000), pp. 187–91 (qu. 188). In May 1687 James expressed pleasure with the success of the Declaration: Boyer, *Declarations of Indulgence*, p. 78.

[116] Miller, 'James II and Toleration', p. 16.

[117] See Chapter 2, p. 104 and Chapter 6, pp. 267–74.

[118] Although managed by Peter Pett: Goldie, 'Pett', pp. 255, 261.

[119] As in Miller, 'James II and Toleration', pp. 19–20; Knights, 'James II's Declarations', pp. 44, 53–4, 69.

ecclesiastical and political supremacy.[120] To deny James's desires provoked discussion of the relative supremacy in ecclesiastical affairs of crown and crown-in-parliament, and an excursus into Tudor history. The past was the solution to ecclesiological dilemmas. The ensuing problem was the diverse types of supremacy which could be found in that past.

The Declarations of 1687 and 1688 stimulated an outburst of publication more than an outpouring of writing. Caution is needed in treating tracts on indulgence and supremacy, since many originated with one of Charles II's Declarations, though published only under James. Henry Care's edition of Whitelocke's manuscript was unusual only in its honest declaration of being written 'divers years ago'.[121] Philip Nye's *Discourse of Ecclesiastical Lawes and Supremacy of the Kings of England in Dispensing with the Penalties thereof* was published by his son in 1687 and dedicated to James, but it had been penned to uphold the Declaration of 1672, like the tract on the dispensing power by the Catholic Richard Langhorne, a Popish Plot martyr, published in 1687. The possibility of royal sponsorship of some of these printings, issued by 'H. H.' (Henry Hills, the royal printer?), is tantalising. The popularity of James's Declarations is easily mistaken; whilst none of the above writers would necessarily have been unwilling to write in favour of James, the number of newly written pieces on indulgence and supremacy was far more limited than bare dates of publication suggest. Nevertheless, dispensing was discussed in detail by two short pamphlets, John Wilson's tract and Peter Pett's lengthy study of *The Obligation Resulting from the Oath of Supremacy to Assist and Defend the Pre-eminence or Prerogative of the Dispensative Power.*

Unusually, Pett based his argument on the implications of the Oath of Supremacy, perhaps appealing to a tory royalist more than whig Dissenting audience. A dialogue about the royal ecclesiastical prerogative between 'A' and 'B' – a Hobbesian echo which may not have been wholly coincidental, given Pett refers to *Behemoth* – it consisted of two parts.[122] The first was dedicated to Melfort, James's secretary of state for Scotland, infamous for constructing a cross to Mary I; the second, continuously paginated, part to the privy councillor Sir Thomas Powys, Pett's ally against Clarendon.[123] At first published separately, it was appended at

[120] See Chapter 6.

[121] Henry Care, preface to 'Anglesey' [Whitelocke], *King's Right of Indulgence*, sig. A2r.

[122] Peter Pett, *The Obligation Resulting from the Oath of Supremacy to Assist and Defend the Pre-eminence or Prerogative of the Dispensative Power* (1687), p. 22; Goldie, 'Pett', p. 259.

[123] George deF. Lord, gen. ed., *Poems on Affairs of State: Augustan Satirical Verse, 1660–1714* (7 vols., New Haven, 1963–75), IV.228n; Goldie, 'Pett', pp. 250, 252.

Sunderland's order to Pett's long-running massive *Happy Future State of England*.[124] Pett tied together the Oath, the dispensing power, and loyalty to Reformation monarchy. No dispensing, no Reformation, for

> it was the *Regal* Power of *Dispensing* with the *Canons* and *Customs* that *disabled* Lay-men from intermedling in *ecclesiastical* Jurisdiction, that laid the *foundation* of the Reformation in *Harry* the *8th*'s time, as it was the same Power of dispensing with the *Canons* and *Customs* that *disabled* Clergy-men from intermedling in *saecular* Employments, that perfected the *superstructure* of it in the reign of *Edward* the *6th* that young *Josias*.[125]

The Supremacy Oath bound takers to defend monarchical rights and actively to oppose any attack on royal powers (Exclusion, for example), for without defending particular prerogatives obedience was 'but a kind of loud *noisy* nothing'.[126] It meant that no subject could be disabled from giving his service to the king, for it was dishonourable to deny him his choice of counsellors; to debar clerical advisors denied the ecclesiastical head its ecclesiastical senses.[127] But benefits were mutual. All Protestants should be thankful for this joint dispensatory-interpretative power, Pett insisted, because it soothed consciences by declaring the exact (jurisdictional not spiritual) connotations of the supremacy. It had upheld the authority of church courts acting in their own names.[128] No one ever questioned royal power to pardon *praemunire*.[129]

Most importantly of all, Pett argued that the Oath implied a *personal* and *monarchical* supremacy, because it was the monarch, not parliament, who interpreted statutes, and Pett thought that dispensing was just a variety of interpretation, showing that an obligation did not apply in a particular case.[130] He demonstrated his awareness of contemporary legal debates in discussing *Thomas* v. *Sorrell*.[131] Moreover, interpretation should not be feared as subverting law: as the Catholic jurist Suárez said, dispensing was 'in' not 'with' the laws.[132] Pett's eclecticism led him to overwhelm his reader with a barrage of disparate authorities for dispensing. Parliament in

[124] Goldie, 'Pett', p. 252.
[125] Pett, *Obligation*, pp. 59 (qu.), 69. See also John Wilson, *Jus regium coronae* (1688), p. 71.
[126] Pett, *Obligation*, pp. 19–21, 23, 26, 41, 144, qu. [34] (mispag. 40).
[127] Pett, *Obligation*, pp. 42–3, 61, 49. The last point cites Bishop Williams as quoted in Jeremiah Stephens, *An Apology for the Ancient Right and Power of the Bishops to Sit and Vote in Parliaments* (1660), p. 101.
[128] Pett, *Obligation*, pp. 114–15, 134–5, 83–4. The positive gloss on confirming ecclesiastical process hints at a non-Dissenting audience.
[129] Pett, *Obligation*, p. 132. [130] Pett, *Obligation*, pp. 39, 120.
[131] Pett, *Obligation*, pp. 28–30, 140, ep. ded. to pt II. See above, p. 92.
[132] Pett, *Obligation*, p. 79.

1660 had not repudiated the Worcester House Declaration but welcomed it. Nor had it complained of dispensations in the Petition of Right of 1628. The Conventicles Acts of 16 and 22 Charles II enhanced ecclesiastical prerogative, albeit not to the extent that it was exalted in Charles's northern kingdom in the Scottish Act of Supremacy (1669). This continued the rise of 'Erastianism' begun by William Prynne and Thomas Coleman during the Civil Wars.[133] Furthermore, great councillors did not oppose dispensing: Shaftesbury's 1675 *Letter* distinguished civil from ecclesiastical prerogative, whilst Anglesey said, when Pett read him a manuscript of his own about the reaction to the 1672 Indulgence, that the Lords never opposed it and the Commons opposed only the suspending power.[134] In 1669, Anglesey had begun a book 'seconding mr prinnes 3 Great volumes concerning the Kings Ecclesiasticall Jurisdiction' and denouncing popery, which he would 'Dedicate to the king'. He bemoaned the decline of clergy from pious users of 'holy rhetorick' to meddlers in government, who 'in ordine ad spiritualia graspe all'.[135]

Pett discussed a range of Anglican and Dissenting divines: the Elizabeth theorist Thomas Bilson and puritan William Stoughton, the 1604 canons, the nonconformist *Protestation* of 1605 upholding the supremacy, even Edward Bagshaw.[136] The Anglican divine Jeremy Taylor had insisted that the king held legislative power over the church, which she 'allow'd our *Princes* in the introducing the *Reformation*' and which could not be withdrawn 'in the Case of a *Prince* of any other Religion coming to the Crown'.[137] Dispensing was imperial, not popish; it exhibited the majestic attribute of mercy, and had been properly understood in the Tudor and Jacobean eras.[138] Royal dispensing, founded in scripture, was more ancient than papal indulgence, and Henrician statutes on supremacy were introductory not declaratory. England's religion was not a parliamentary one; if parliament '*confirm'd*' royal powers, they must have been '*firm*' beforehand.[139] Pett's conclusion tantalisingly delayed the burning question of the repeal of the Tests until the next time A and B met.[140]

133 Pett, *Obligation*, pp. 89–91, 104, 12–15, 9.

134 Pett, *Obligation*, pp. 105, 101. He even bizarrely claimed (p. 101) that parliament asking for no further dispensations in July 1663 was an expression of support for the power – presumably in its recognition that it did exist. On Anglesey, see Goldie, 'Pett', p. 249.

135 Bodl., Clarendon MS 87, fo. 57r.

136 On supremacy and/or dispensing: Pett, *Obligation*, pp. 143 (Bilson), 116 (Stoughton), 41 (canons), 39, 67, 114–15 (Nye), 47 (1605), 138 (Bagshaw).

137 Pett, *Obligation*, p. 122.

138 Pett, *Obligation*, pp. 125–6, 124.

139 Pett, *Obligation*, pp. 56, 63–5, 140.

140 Pett, *Obligation*, p. 141.

Mercifully shorter than Pett's tome were a broadsheet by the government propagandist and Carolean newspaper writer Roger L'Estrange, the anonymous *Dispensing Power Explicated*, and John Wilson's *Jus regium coronae*. These focused on the lawfulness of dispensing more than the religious motivation behind it. Wilson, a client of Ormonde and defender of James's succession, proudly entitling himself 'J[uris]C[onsulte]', sought to justify James's dispensations to military officers.[141] He and L'Estrange insisted that governments needed the power to dispense in order to preserve themselves, and it logically inhered in the king with other attributes of majesty.[142] Could not kings pardon? Was not mercy a royal attribute?[143] Legislation establishing liberty of conscience or declaring persecution *malum in se* would be inviolable, as a law in which subjects as well as monarchs had an interest.[144] Although it was always wrong in common law, Wilson wrote, to deny the royal supremacy, not swearing the oath to uphold it was only *malum prohibitum* (banned by statute). Casuistically distinguishing dispensing from an absolute discharge of the oaths, Wilson thought James could even dispense MPs from taking the Tests, as long as a dispensation was issued before they were incapacitated.[145] All three authors strongly attacked the Tests as meddling with royal rights to service, a form of Exclusion which broke the relationship of subjection and protection. L'Estrange described the disastrous impact of Charles I's mistaken view that he could not dispense with an act denying him the service of certain subjects. Other pamphleteers also claimed it improper, indeed ridiculous, for governments to lose subjects' service.[146]

Such detailed probing into the mysteries of monarchical prerogative was, as before, eschewed by many polemicists, who offered instead consciential, economic, and prudential cases. The inviolability of conscience meant persecution was unchristian, a case propounded by the Quaker William Penn in particular, although not uniquely.[147] 'Whatever

[141] Wilson, *Jus regium coronae*, title p. and pp. 77–9. Jurisconsulte: legal expert (which Wilson was).

[142] Roger L'Estrange, *Two Cases Submitted to Consideration* (Edinburgh, 1687); Wilson, *Jus regium coronae*, pp. 6, 20–3, 59, 39–40.

[143] Wilson, *Jus regium coronae*, pp. 8, 18, 12.

[144] Anon., *The King's Dispensing Power Explicated and Asserted* (1687), pp. 6–8.

[145] Wilson, *Jus regium coronae*, pp. 49–51.

[146] Wilson, *Jus regium coronae*, pp. 42, 33; *King's Dispensing Power Explicated*, pp. 3–4; L'Estrange, *Two Cases*, p. 2; Anon., *The True Interest of the Legal English Protestants* (1687, citing Wing T2714), p. 5; William Penn, *A Perswasive to Moderation to Dissenting Christians* (1685), pp. 23–5.

[147] William Penn, *Considerations Moving to a Toleration and Liberty of Conscience* (1685), p. 1; William Penn, *Good Advice to the Church of England, Roman Catholick, and Protestant Dissenter* (1687), pp. 2–6; William Penn, *The Reasonableness of Toleration and the Unreasonableness of Penal Laws and Tests* (1687), p. 2; George Villiers, Duke of Buckingham, *A Short Discourse upon the Reasonableness of Men's Having a Religion*, 3rd edn (1685), sigs. A3v–[A4]r, p. 19.

the Church of *England* is, 'tis certain Christ is for a Toleration, and his Doctrine is always in Fashion.'[148] If belief was involuntary, coercion might change the will but the will was powerless to alter opinion, so making liberty of conscience a natural right.[149] Mixing religion with politics, the Tests infringed the sanctity of conscience, tempting men to perjury.[150] The argument that indulgence would foster peace and unity[151] might constitute a specific claim that it would encourage trade. The judges instructed in 1688 to encourage support for repealing the penal laws were told to say that trade had already increased.[152] Yet more ink seemed to be spilt over whether English Protestantism was safe from Catholic persecution than whether the economy would benefit, despite the debate taking place in the context of an influx of Huguenot refugees.

Appeals to trust James were difficult since they had to be made to two constituencies: Anglicans and Dissenters, both of whom wanted safeguards against popery but whose other interests were hard to reconcile. James's supporters dubbed the Tests useless but '*Idoliz'd Security*' and offered grand charters of liberty of conscience to which all would swear instead.[153] L'Estrange, the hack writer Henry Care, and the convert poet John Dryden argued that Catholic infallibility and Protestant liberty could coexist.[154] The anonymous *Discourse for Taking Off the Tests* insisted that English Catholics, being a minority, were safer for nonconformists to trust than Anglicans.[155] Penn, James's Quaker friend, seemed especially well placed to argue that toleration *of* Catholics did not endanger

[148] Penn, *Good Advice*, p. 5.

[149] Penn, *Reasonableness*, p. 31; William Popple, *A Letter to Mr Penn with his Answer* (1688, citing Wing P2963), p. 16 (Penn's answer); Anon., *The Judgment and Doctrine of the Clergy of the Church of England Concerning … Dispensing with the Penal Laws* (1687), p. 41.

[150] William Penn, *Som Free Reflections upon Occasion of the Public Discourse about Liberty of Conscience* (1687), pp. 9–10; Penn, *Reasonableness*, p. [35] (mispag. 33).

[151] Roger L'Estrange, *An Answer to a Letter to a Dissenter* (1687, citing Wing L1195), p. 4; Penn, *Free Reflections*, p. 3.

[152] John Gutch, *Collectanea curiosa* (2 vols., Oxford, 1781), I.391–2; Penn, *Perswasive*, p. 33; Penn, *Considerations*, pp. 4–5.

[153] Anon., *A Third Dialogue Between Simeon and Levi* (1688), p. 5 (qu.); Anon., *A Discourse for Taking off the Tests and Penal Laws about Religion* (1687), sigs. A2v–A3r; Giles Shute, *A New Test in Lieu of the Old One* (1688), pp. 15, 5, 9–10; Henry Care, *Animadversions on a Late Paper Entituled A Letter to a Dissenter* (1687), pp. 36–7; Penn, *Free Reflections*, p. 6; Henry Care, *The Legality of the Court held by His Majesties Ecclesiastical Commissioners Defended* (1688), p. 33; Anon., *Advice to Protestant Dissenters Shewing 'tis their Interest to Repeal the Test* (1688), p. 6; William Penn, *The Great and Popular Objection Against the Repeal of the Penal Laws* (1688), p. 10.

[154] L'Estrange, *Answer to a Letter to a Dissenter*, p. 7; Henry Care, *Animadversions on a Late Paper*, pp. 11–13; p. 20 argued that Catholics and nonconformists were united only by interest, and not a seditious alliance. John Dryden, *The Hind and the Panther* (1687), in *Works*, vol. III, ed. H. T. Swedenberg, Earl Miner, and Vinton A. Dearing (Berkeley, 1969), p. 120.

[155] *Discourse for Taking off the Tests*, pp. 38–9.

the state or the Church, and that toleration *offered by* Catholics could be trusted.[156] Yet his willingness to tolerate Catholics led him to be labelled a closet papist and his Dissenting friend William Popple, future translator of Locke's *Letter Concerning Toleration*, wrote urging him to clear his name.[157]

Debate on the supremacy was sometimes unavoidable. Because Halifax's *Letter to a Dissenter* asserted the illegality of the dispensing power,[158] those who replied had perforce to prove James to be within his rights. Care distinguished between repealing a law (which only parliament might do) and dispensing with a penalty (a common-law right of the king, confirmed in 1670).[159] L'Estrange agreed, daring Halifax to overrule 'an *Imperial Prerogative* … by a *Pamphlet*'.[160] Penn rebuked nonconformists who were uneasy about the manner rather than the matter of indulgence. Unexpected Catholic tolerationism bore the mark of divine providence.[161]

The history of failed Restoration declarations of indulgence was increasingly used to assert that monarchical clemency had been foiled only by bishops and parliaments. Penn highlighted the Declarations of October 1660, 1662, and 1672, whilst one of his opponents cited in refutation Parker's *Ecclesiastical Politie* and Assheton's *Toleration Disapprov'd*.[162] Why, Penn wrote, should the established Church claim exclusivity and legal privilege? Why would a true church want to? A *truly* national (popular) church would not constantly need to invoke the magistrate's aid against its own people: 'a National Religion by Law, where it is not so by Number and Inclination, is a *National Nusance*'.[163] And yet when the king diverged from the hierarchy's purposes it turned against him, contrary to

[156] Penn, *Good Advice*, pp. 9, 43, 45; Penn, *Great and Popular Objection*, p. 7; Penn, *Free Reflections*, p. 11.

[157] Popple, *Letter to Mr Penn*, pp. 4–10.

[158] George Savile, Marquess of Halifax, *A Letter to a Dissenter* (1687, citing Wing H313), pp. 9, 14. This went through three printings with over 20,000 copies: Boyer, *Declarations of Indulgence*, p. 75.

[159] Care, *Animadversions on a Late Paper*, pp. 27–9. Contrary to lawyers, Care equated dispensing from a penalty with pardoning.

[160] L'Estrange, *Answer to a Letter to a Dissenter*, p. 34.

[161] Penn, *Free Reflections*, p. 20; Penn, *Great and Popular Objection*, pp. 5–6, 17; see, similarly, *Advice to Protestant Dissenters*, p. 1.

[162] Penn, *Considerations*, pp. 6–7; Anon., *An Answer to a Late Pamphlet, Intituled, The Judgment and Doctrine of the Clergy of the Church of England* (1687), p. 39 (misciting Assheton's work as *Tolleration Discus'd*).

[163] Penn, *Great and Popular Objection*, p. 23 (qu.); Penn, *Good Advice*, pp. 12–13, 18; Anon., *A New Test of the Church of England's Loyalty* (1687), p. 7; Anon., *The Minister's Reasons for his not Reading the Kings Declaration, Friendly Debated* (1688), pp. 4, 16; Care, *Animadversions on a Late Paper*, p. 39. On the legal significance of nuisance, see above, p. 92.

all ecclesiastical dependence on the crown since the Reformation. 'She made him [the king] to be great by him: If She might be the *Church*, He should be the *Head*.' In a rare moment of agreement between God and Caesar, the Church ended by defying both.[164]

Many, like their forebears in 1672, recognised that an appeal to the king might well be the only way to bypass the bishops. L'Estrange and Care warned Dissenters uneasy about relying on royal prerogative that they had few alternatives, since the Church of England's new promises of friendship were equally risky.[165] Writers denounced the ingratitude of spurning James's offer. Care called the king the Dissenters' '*best Friend*'.[166] Dryden pointed out to sects that if James offered indulgence, 'they should both receive it, and receive it thankfully'.[167] L'Estrange told nonconformists to take their physic and not examine it. The sectarian Giles Shute similarly characterised the king as a doctor curing nonconformists of the scars of Anglican intolerance. The penal laws had been fathered on the king, but the fact that he was forbidden to repeal them showed they were really children of the lord bishops.[168] George Care bitterly threw back Anglican claims of Dissenting sedition at bishops themselves:

> The Gentlemen that *Tore* the King's Declaration of *Indulgence* from him, were high *Church-men*; and they opposed his *Political Capacity* to his *Natural* ... by which distinction the late Civil War was made; so that 41 overtook 73, or that return'd to 41.[169]

Penn, whose attitude was coloured by his own positive relationship with the king,[170] complemented his attack on the Church of England's wavering loyalty with claims that Dissenters had been James's most faithful servants. Like Wolseley in 1672, Penn argued that indulgence allowed James to balance different factions within his subjects, all sects hanging their keys on the girdle of the civil magistrate.[171] Although rarely exhibiting the bitter anticlerical animus of some Dissenting supremacists,

164 Penn, *Good Advice*, pp. 38, 40 (qu.), 17.

165 L'Estrange, *Answer to a Letter to a Dissenter*, pp. 6, 11, 26; Care, *Animadversions on a Late Paper*, p. 10.

166 Care, *Animadversions on a Late Paper*, p. 10.

167 Dryden, *Hind and Panther*, p. 120.

168 L'Estrange, *Answer to a Letter to a Dissenter*, p. 3; mocked in Thomas Brown, *Heraclitus ridens redivivus* (1688), p. 2; Shute, *New Test in Lieu of the Old One*, pp. 37, 13.

169 George Care, *A Reply to the Answer of the Man of no Name* (1685), p. 23. See also Penn, *Perswasive*, p. 30. Care may have been an associate of Buckingham, whom the man of no name had attacked.

170 See Vincent Buranelli, *The King & the Quaker: A Study of William Penn and James II* (Philadelphia, 1962), ch. 9, and pp. 99–101.

171 Penn, *Perswasive*, pp. 24–5, 32, 47.

even Penn opened his *Reasonableness of Toleration* (1687) with the criticism that it

> hath been for many hundreds of years the main Scope and Aim of the Clergy in most Opinions, to grasp into their Clutches the exercise of Temporal Jurisdiction; & as in former times, so now of late our Church of *England* Men, have not been the least ambitious of that Authority.

Unable to do this of their own accord, they had climbed up by clinging to civil authority, frightening the magistrate with tales of nonconformist sedition. Yet their arrogant exclusivity in denoting only Anglican episcopalians to be the church was a mere refiguring of papalism, 'to Preach down one Antichrist, and set up six and twenty'.[172] In so doing the clergy had deteriorated from 'the true duty of Bishops to Instruct, Perswade, Exhort' into the 'highest product of degenerate Usurpation', compulsion.[173] Penn, like Marvell (whose *Essay on Councils* was republished in 1687)[174] held that early Christian emperors had opposed such misdeeds, tolerant in the era of Constantine, although later succumbing to ecclesiastical intolerance, trepanned into penal legislation.[175] James's Declaration restored ancient monarchical tolerance, stimulating Penn's sugary praise of a king 'free[ing] from Spiritual Bondage, the Enslav'd Consciences of his Suffering Subjects, Groaning under the Tyranny of Ecclesiastical Jurisdiction'. Resembling God in his Christian compassion, James – in a somewhat disturbing image – spread 'the Cherubim Wings of his Mercy over multitudes so lately tormented with the Unsanctified Vexation'.[176] How could anyone distrust him?

Quite easily, Anglicans might reply. Like Archbishop Sancroft's chaplain, Henry Maurice, few conformists deferred to royal endorsement of indulgence, noisily refuting the consciential and economic cases for liberalisation.[177] Maurice angily denied that toleration was necessary for Presbyterians who practised occasional conformity, or for Independent meetings small enough to escape laws which defined conventicles as more than five people outside the family.[178] Princes may – must – enforce

172 Penn, *Reasonableness*, pp. 1, 5. 173 Penn, *Reasonableness*, pp. 13, 11.

174 *A Seasonable Discourse Shewing the Unreasonableness and Mischeifs of Impositions in Matters of Religion* (1687) is Marvell's 'Essay on Councils' for which see below, p. 199.

175 Penn, *Considerations*, pp. 8–10; Penn, *Perswasive*, pp. 10–11, 50; Penn, *Reasonableness*, pp. 17–18.

176 Penn, *Reasonableness*, p. 37 (qu.); see, similarly, *A Poem Occasioned by His Majesty's Most Gracious Resolution Declared in His Most Honourable Privy Council, March 18 1686/7 for Liberty of Conscience*, repr. in Lord, ed., *Poems on Affairs of State*, IV, lines 1–9 (p. 102).

177 Henry Maurice, *The Antithelemite, Or An Answer to Certain Quæries by the D[uke] of B[uckingham]* (1685), pp. 53–4, 71, 16–19, 39–43.

178 Maurice, *Antithelemite*, pp. 73–4.

doctrine, for Christ's pacifism 'can be no direction to him that is invested with civil power, and sustains a Person quite different from the Character our Saviour bore'.[179]

Anglicans repeatedly told nonconformists that James was not to be trusted, playing on preconceptions that Rome meant repression.[180] But distrust of nonconformists as well as of Rome pervaded Anglican attitudes, despite claims of increasing charity.[181] Halifax's *Letter*, although offering friendship, nevertheless sneered at nonconformist thanks for the Declaration: had such ministers been bribed? Had they had addresses of thanks written for them?[182] He rebuked Dissenters for conniving at dispensing, an act of arbitrary government, thanks for which 'look like Counsel retained by the Prerogative against your old Friend *Magna Charta*'. Could they not have waited until the next parliament? Even Catholics 'do not think, that the single Power of the Crown is in this Case a good Foundation'. If James thought his prerogative stretched to indulgence, would he be interested in parliament?[183] Gilbert Burnet warned that the apparent restraint in the Declaration of Indulgence (nonconformist meetings only to be prosecuted if seditious) was no guarantee for the future, noting the offer of 'benefices' to Scottish Catholics.[184] He complained of the Scottish Declaration's absolutist language, surprised when the English Declaration refrained from employing such terms, but still suspicious.[185]

It is true that many Dissenters refused to support James's policy because of constitutionalist concerns about prerogative indulgence, innate distrust of Catholicism, or both. But while Presbyterians in particular shunned collaboration, the tradition of Dissenting exploitation of supremacy against bishops and Anglican-royalists in parliament continued. As Chapter 6 will show, battles between Catholics and Anglicans also focused on issues arising from James's use of the powers that the supremacy gave him. If 'modern' ideas of toleration were forged partly

179 Maurice, *Antithelemite*, p. 11.

180 Halifax, *Letter to a Dissenter*, pp. 2–4; Anon., *The New Test … Examined by the Old Test of Truth and Honesty* (1687), pp. 5–6; Gilbert Burnet, *Six Papers* (1687), pp. 10, 12; Maurice, *Antithelemite*, p. 23.

181 For such claims see, e.g., Halifax, *Letter to a Dissenter*, p. 16.

182 Halifax, *Letter to a Dissenter*, pp. 5–8. Similar claims were made in 1672: Bate, *Declaration of Indulgence*, p. 90. Addresses of thanks were mocked in Anon., *To the King's Most Excellent Majesty, the Humble Address of the Atheists, or the Sect of the Epicureans* (1688).

183 Halifax, *Letter to a Dissenter*, pp. 8–9, 14.

184 Burnet, *Six Papers*, pp. 13 (benefices), 23.

185 Burnet, *Six Papers*, pp. 9, 15, 21. On the Scottish Indulgence, see Clare Jackson, *Restoration Scotland, 1660–1690: Royalist Politics, Religion, and Ideas* (Woodbridge, 2003), pp. 160–1.

through the experience of James's reign, they were created in an atmosphere redolent of Reformation assumptions.

DISSENTERS, CHURCH COURTS, AND THE SUPREMACY

A not insignificant number of Dissenters were willing to praise the supremacy when it offered them relief. This was not a purely reactive phenomenon, but also a proactive pushing of monarchs towards indulgence. Even during phases of intolerance, therefore, some nonconformists continued to use the supremacy as an anticlerical or antiprelatical tool to erode Anglican authority. Ideological opposition to what would later be dubbed 'priestcraft' has been recognised as part of an early English Enlightenment, but this historiography has largely overlooked a jurisdictional argument about episcopal usurpation of sovereign rights through canon law and church courts.[186] This claim had Tudor roots. The Elizabethan puritan William Stoughton, as well as William Prynne in the 1630s, argued that ecclesiastical jurisdiction should take place in the name of the king, not the clergy. Restoration complaints about prelatical usurpation of supremacy stemmed not only from nonconformists, but also from Marvell, Locke, and Shaftesbury: conformists sympathetic to Dissent. One of the most prominent contributors to detailed legal analysis which questioned the legitimacy of ecclesiastical jurisdiction was the idiosyncratic Anglican minister Edmund Hickeringill.[187] Couching their cases in a rhetoric of loyalty to supremacy, those who echoed the language (and cited the precedents) of earlier puritans sought to drive a wedge between the twinned forces of Church and crown.

This private *quo warranto* campaign targeted the whole structure of ecclesiastical courts with their lay officials and canon law as neither found in scripture nor legally warranted by Tudor statutes. As such, it looked back to the Edwardian statute ordering episcopal courts to use 'no other Seale of Jurisdiction but wherin his Maj*est*ies armes be ingraven' to show that spiritual as well as temporal jurisdiction flowed from the king.[188] Prynne indicted prelates erecting an 'absolute, irregular, Papall and Episcopall

[186] Not discussed, for example, in Goldie, 'Priestcraft'; briefly mentioned in Andrew Swatland, *The House of Lords in the Reign of Charles II* (Cambridge, 1996), p. 164.

[187] J. L. C. McNulty, 'An Anticlerical Priest: Edmund Hickeringill (1631–1708) and the Context of Priestcraft' (MPhil. thesis, University of Cambridge, 1998), esp. ch. 4.

[188] 'Vestigia veritas', in Henry Care, *A Perfect Guide for Protestant Dissenters, in Case of Prosecution Upon Any of the Penal Statutes Made Against Them* (1682), 2nd pag., pp. 19–20; Edmund Hickeringill, *The Test or Tryal of the Goodness & Value of Spiritual-Courts, in Two Queries*, 2nd edn (1683), pt I, p. 3; pt II, p. 6.

Iurisdiction of their owne … to tread your Majesties Ecclesiasticall Iurisdiction … under their feet'. By using their own names and seals, they 'stamp and coyne the Kings Ecclesiasticall proces, (as much his by Law as his coyne)', and thus could be resisted by parishioners.[189] His case was both facilitated and flawed by the uncertainty over whether the 1547 statute remained in force. Hickeringill insisted that the statute, ostensibly repealed by Mary, had been revived when James I repealed Mary's legislation. If the Church of England wanted to claim its courts and canons were the king's courts (as it often did), there was 'all the reason in the World' for Edward's law, enacted under a good protestant sovereign (not the essentially papist Henry VIII).[190] Francis Fullwood's counter-attack on Hickeringill and Henry Care posited not only that the statute *was* repealed, but also that bishops, despite issuing writs in their own names, always believed that their jurisdiction derived from the king, for they would not foolishly risk *praemunire* by denying it.[191] Whereas Hickeringill claimed the Edwardian statute was still in force, Care argued it ought to be revived. Fullwood noted that Charles I's judges had declared that ecclesiastical process in the bishops' own names was legitimate. Hickeringill retorted that High Commission had intimidated the judiciary.[192] Why might not a Protestant supreme head wear a Protestant face in his own courts?[193]

This mode of argument had, at least ostensibly, a practical purpose; insofar that if a court could not prove its authority, a case could be removed to the temporal courts on a writ of prohibition, or even incur the threat of *praemunire*. Hickeringill noted how Edward Lake (chancellor of Lincoln diocese, and author of a tract calling for the revival of *ex officio* process) had been complained of when he refused to absolve a petitioner.[194] Hickeringill's own actions when cited into Doctors Commons exemplified such defiant questioning of the court's jurisdiction: refusing

[189] William Prynne, *A Breviate of the Prelates Intollerable Usurpations*, 3rd edn (Amsterdam, 1637), pp. 245 (qu.), 80–1 (qu.), 114–18, 215–16, 230, and the appended 'Briefe Instructions'.

[190] Hickeringill, *Test or Tryal*, pt I, passim, qu. p. 21; H. Cary, *The Law of England: Or, A True Guide for all Persons Concerned in Ecclesiastical Courts* (n.p., n.d.), pp. 11–13. Care later referred to 'Cary's' pamphlet as his own, written in 1664: *English Liberties* (1680), p. 157.

[191] Francis Fullwood, *Leges Angliæ: The Lawfulness of Ecclesiastical Jurisdiction in the Church of England* (1681), pp. 21–40 (bishops: p. 29).

[192] Hickeringill, *Test or Tryal*, pt II, p. 8; pt I, passim (p. 10 on High Commission); Fullwood, *Leges Angliæ*, pp. 31–5. Edmund Hickeringill, *A Vindication of the Naked Truth* (1681), p. 16, noted that these were the same judges condemned by parliament for their opinion in Hampden's Case.

[193] Hickeringill, *Vindication of the Naked Truth*, p. 34.

[194] Edmund Hickeringill, *The Naked Truth, the Second Part* (1681), p. 25; see *CSPD, May to Sept. 1672*, pp. 536–9 (30 Aug. 1672); Edward Lake, *Memoranda: Touching the Oath Ex Officio, Pretended Self-Accusation and Canonical Purgation* (1662).

to remove his hat until the court admitted it was founded on royal authority, citing Henrician statutes against it.[195] This reflected Care's advice on how to evade prosecution. Continually barraging church courts with the need to certify their rightful legality was, Care insisted, an obligation under the Oath of Supremacy.[196] His true purpose was revealed in his dictum that there was not only a legal advantage at stake, but also the enjoyment of 'the trouble and vexation you put them [courts] to, by quarrelling at there [*sic*] Authority and Jurisdiction'.[197]

If a careful exposition of ecclesiastical process maximised the potential for prohibitions, a more damaging assertion was that the whole juridical structure was guilty of *praemunire*. This case used Henrician laws to deny the legality not only of ecclesiastical courts, but also of the canon law used within them. Yet it also manipulated those statutes or exploited their ambiguities to suggest that parliamentary ratification of canons was required. The idea of a *reformatio legum ecclesiasticarum* was a mockery, since no pre-Reformation canon was compatible with royal authority. Convocation might now sit if it pleased, Hickeringill wrote, but only the sovereign authority of the king-in-parliament could enact religious laws (here anticlericalism approached whiggery).[198] What was a loyal subject to do, since denial of the authority of a synod provoked excommunication, but denial of imperial supremacy incurred *praemunire*?[199] 'What are the Spiritual Courts good for? … Are they not good at acting in defiance of the Statutes of this Realm? And have they not always been good at that?'[200] But while men were entrapped by 'Cobweb-Canons' and 'Lime-twig-Laws', the prelatical emperor had no legal clothes: episcopal authority was a 'blazing Wisp of Straw' unless confirmed by statute.[201] When defining *praemunire*, Care crucially included any English court which usurped common law jurisdiction, whether 'the court of *Rome*, or any Ecclesiastick Court within the Realm'. Citing legal precedents, he admitted that some Civil lawyers contended that this had changed with Henrician supremacy, but remained unconvinced. He accordingly firmly subordinated ecclesiastical courts to common law prohibitions.[202]

[195] Edmund Hickeringill, *News from Doctor's Commons* (1681), pp. 2–3; Edmund Hickeringill, *Scandalum magnatum* (1682), p. [70] (mispag. 58).
[196] Cary, *Law of England*, pp. 5, 129–30.
[197] Cary, *Law of England*, p. 10.
[198] Hickeringill, *Vindication of the Naked Truth*, pp. 17, 25.
[199] Hickeringill, *Naked Truth, the Second Part*, pp. 2–4.
[200] Hickeringill, *Naked Truth, the Second Part*, p. 26.
[201] Hickeringill, *Scandalum magnatum*, pp. 52, 50.
[202] Cary, *Law of England*, ch. 7, pp. 47 (qu.), 54; Care, *English Liberties*, p. 163; Anon., *The Case and Cure of Persons Excommunicated* (1682, perhaps by Care), p. 36. See above, p. 70.

For Hickeringill, to make the clergy 'buckle and stoop, and thrust the Hierarchy and holy Pastoral head under a Lay-girdle' was vital to securing royal supremacy.[203] His embitterment led him to exalt royal authority to dangerous heights. He rejected Fullwood's claim that the clergy must retain the Keys, for those who

> can open the Church-doors to let his Majesty in, can also (*whilst they have the keeping of the Keys*) upon displeasure, lock him out … I would advise his Majesty as Head of the Church, and Governour thereof, to *keep the Keys* of the Church in *his Pocket*, or hang them *under his Girdle.*

Hickeringill's passion pushed him on to heterodox ground, asking what laws

> exclude this purely Spiritual power of the Keys from the Supremacy of our Kings, if our Kings, (like good King *David*,) or wise King *Solomon* should have a mind to be *Ecclesiastes*? … our Kings at their Coronations, have *at the same time* been ordained Clergymen, they are no more excluded (*then*) by our Laws from the power of the Keys then Mr. *Archdeacon* [Fullwood] or the Pope himself.[204]

Hickeringill's apparent attribution of spiritual power to kings was radical, but his anxiety about *iure divino* rhetoric overthrowing monarchs was shared by the chief patrons of the Country and whig movements. Shaftesbury reported Wharton asking the bishops in the Lords whether *iure divino* bishops could excommunicate their sovereign, 'which they Evading to answer, and being press'd by some other Lords, said they never had done it', whereupon Halifax dryly remarked that they had been too beholden to the crown since the Reformation to do it.[205]

The idea that royal jurisdiction was being usurped by church courts complemented the wider case that imperial supremacy was under attack from bishops. In a long letter of June 1682 to the Anglican minister John Cheyney, Richard Baxter worried that arguments for the necessity of the magistrate impugned the pre-Constantinian church. That emperor himself had told his bishops he was outside the church: '*Over it, but not essentiall* to it in the strict & exact proper sence'.[206] Yet, as William Lamont has shown, Baxter's distaste for Christian magistracy in the late 1670s

[203] Hickeringill, *Naked Truth, the Second Part*, p. 5.

[204] Hickeringill, *Vindication of the Naked Truth*, pp. 3–4. Edmund Hickeringill, *Reflections on a Late Libel, Intituled, Observations on a Late Famous Sermon, Intituled, Curse ye Meroz* (1680), p. 16, offered the Hobbesian idea that the Bible was the Word of God per se; but that royal intervention was needed to make it *canonical* (a law).

[205] Anon. [Anthony Ashley Cooper, first Earl of Shaftesbury?], *A Letter from a Person of Quality to his Friend in the Country* (1675), p. 25.

[206] Baxter, *Correspondence*, no. 1109 (3 June 1682); see Catherine Nunn's *ODNB* entry on Cheyney, which suggests he harboured sympathy towards Presbyterians.

and early 1680s was atypical of his career.[207] For Baxter, as for Prynne, the Church erred in jettisoning her old godly bishops and the imperialist language of John Foxe and John Bale. In one letter he wrote that the Tudors had understood what powers ought to be given to godly magistrates, the sovereign Moses superior to the high priest Aaron. Popery, whether on the 'Italian' (papal) or 'French' (conciliar) model, was 'the denying or obscuring [sovereign power], and confining church power to the sacerdotal'. The godly magistrate needed protection from 'French papists': the episcopal conciliarists Dodwell, Sherlock, and Heylin.[208] Baxter might seem here to be in agreement with men like Louis du Moulin, who wrote to him in 1670 that '*all Church-power is Popery*, which motto if it would serve for my everlasting condition I would have it put upon my tombe ... This *Papismus*, Popery or Church-power is the grand mystery of iniquity.'[209] But Baxter thought du Moulin's radical Erastianism dangerously demolished clerical authority: his own aim was for the monarch to support and enforce religious discipline.[210] The church before Constantine was not pure, but unworthy of Christian magistracy attained in its maturity; after its coming of age, pious kings ruled priests while being guided by godly advisors.[211] Instead of confining royal divinity, Baxter wanted kings to use their swords against popery; only if they misused their powers by surrendering to a foreign jurisdiction could they unking themselves.[212] Baxter's adherence to a Foxean view of Constantine inaugurating the millennium seemingly increased over time; whilst in his separatist phase he grumbled that the emperor was over-generous in exalting clerical power, he later claimed that Constantine had rescued the church from its nadir.[213]

Baxter agreed with Hickeringill, Care, and Marvell that clergy, not princes, cause persecution, schism, and wars. 'They cry up the Prince like an Angel so long as he will be their *Executioner*.'[214] Marvell's history

[207] William M. Lamont, *Richard Baxter and the Millennium: Protestant Imperialism and the English Revolution* (1979), p. 17 and passim.

[208] Lamont, *Baxter*, pp. 264, 12–13, 63–4 (qu.), 105, 131.

[209] Baxter, *Correspondence*, no. 796 (from Louis du Moulin, *c*. Mar. 1670); see du Moulin's comments (letter no. 778, *c*. Aug. 1669?) on toleration as preferable to comprehension, and a likelier way to ruin the church hierarchy.

[210] Baxter, *Correspondence*, no. 783 (to Louis du Moulin, 21 Sept. 1669); Lamont, *Baxter*, pp. 133, 161, 162, 167, 187.

[211] Lamont, *Baxter*, pp. 69, 305.

[212] Lamont, *Baxter*, pp. 235, 92–3. He nevertheless rebuked John Humfrey for coming too close to resistance theory: Lamont, *Baxter*, pp. 93, 223–24; see Baxter, *Correspondence*, no. 766 (to Humfrey, ? early 1669).

[213] Lamont, *Baxter*, pp. 13–14, 240–1, 263.

[214] Care, *English Liberties*, p. 94 (qu.); Baxter, *Correspondence*, nos. 857 (to Edward Fowler, 7 Oct. 1671), 964 (pref. to *Catholick Theologie*, 1675), 1017 (to Thomas Long, 26 July 1678); Hickeringill,

of the decay of Christianity in the fourth century was not of the decline of bishops owing to court religion, but rather of the corruption of imperial monarchy by crafty prelates who 'crept at first by Court-insinuations and flattery into the Princes favour, till those generous Creatures suffered themselves to be backed and ridden by them'. Clergymen dared not openly challenge the prince, yet became 'Independent upon the Prince, and sometimes absolute over the Prince'. For, Marvell explained, they eventually 'thought the Magistrate scarce worthy to be trusted with it [persecution] longer, & a meer Novice at it, and either wrested it out of his hands, or gently eased him of that and his other burdens of Government'.[215] For Care, the clergy were akin to ivy, ascending by '*Intertwisting* their *own* Interest' with that of the royal oak, yet eventually eating into and killing it.[216] He complained that Charles II was encouraged to withdraw his indulgence(s) by prelates who 'grutch him the exercise of his Right'. For Care, nonconformists were far more loyal to the supremacy than bishops, for Dissenters 'acknowledge their *Soveraign* to be both *King and Priest*: *A King* as he is *Supream Head of the Government*; a *Priest* as the *Supream Head of the Church*'.[217] Shaftesbury as well as his amanuensis, Locke, insisted that clergy preached temporal absolutism in exchange for support for *iure divino* episcopacy by monarchs blind to its dangers. Indeed, 'less then this the Bishops could not offer in requital to the Crown for parting with its Supremacy, and suffering them to be sworn to equal with it self'.[218]

On occasion, these musings on clerical subversion of supremacy were translated into plans for positive action, as shown in three papers written by or for the Earl of Shaftesbury in the early 1670s.[219] One provided a series of reflections on the powers which Tudor supremacy involved, citing laws which remained 'in their full force and Vigor' in Shaftesbury's time. Supremacy included the ability to reform canon law, to issue

Scandalum magnatum, p. 41; Hickeringill, *Test or Tryal*, pt 1, p. 16; Cary, *Law of England*, pp. 59–60; Care, *Perfect Guide*, p. 1.

215 Andrew Marvell, 'A Short Historical Essay, Touching General Councils, Creeds, and Imposition in Religion', in *Mr Smirke; Or, The Divine in Mode* (1676), pp. 67–8. Marvell would not, however, entrust a heathen magistrate with judging the truth: p. 6. 'Independent upon …': Edmund Hickeringill, *The Third Part of Naked Truth* (1681), p. 5.

216 Henry Care, *Draconica: Or, An Abstract of all the Penal Laws Touching Matters of Religion*, 2nd edn (1688), p. 20 (qu.); Care, *English Liberties*, p. 93. Royal oak: Charles hid in an oak tree after his escape from the battle of Worcester (1651).

217 Care, *Perfect Guide*, p. 9.

218 Anon. [Shaftesbury?], *Letter*, pp. 1, [34] (qu., mispag. 32).

219 On their date and authorship see John Locke, *An Essay Concerning Toleration*, ed. J. R. Milton and Philip Milton (Oxford, 2006), pp. 148–52.

injunctions to regulate the church, and to act as 'the vltimate Judge of Heresy'.[220] Shaftesbury outlined how 'w*ha*tsoever the B*isho*p of Rome could lawfully doe ... is now legally instated in the King'.[221] He repeatedly emphasised how Henrician statutes created a supremacy inhering in the king, which meant that 'All Jurisdicc*i*on Eccl*esiast*ical as well as Secular is derived from him', citing 1 Edw. VI c. 2 as further evidence for this. Although this did not mean that the king personally exercised jurisdiction, it did allow the monarch to grant such authority to anyone he chose, laity as well as clergy. Bishops held authority only 'by dependance and delegacy' from the crown, and Shaftesbury drove home the notion that this included 'exco*mmun*ications, suspensions and deprivations'. 'The Jurisdicc*i*on Sp*irit*uall ascribed to the King or Queen in ... 26 Hen 8:c.1. and 1 Eliz. c.1 involves the Jurisdicc*i*on of exco*mmun*icac*i*on ... if not exercised by Himselfe and His Vicegerent and other Com*missio*ners Lay Persons ... yet so established in the King as to appoint when, and in w*ha*t matters the Clergy ... shal execute or not execute it.'[222]

A shorter paper similarly emphasised that ecclesiastical jurisdiction was not 'in *th*e Clergie but magistracy; and in them (whether Clergie or not) to whom the supream magistrate would impart itt'. It sarcastically reminded the bishops that they could hardly object to lay exercise of such authority, since they themselves used lay chancellors and officials in their church courts. Shaftesbury argued that 'church' included lay worshippers, not just the clergy, unconsciously echoing St German.[223] Both this paper and the longer one cited Thomas Cromwell's vicegerency in spirituals of the 1530s as an example of delegation of ecclesiastical jurisdiction to a layman. A third paper developed the example into a fully-fledged call to revive Cromwell's office. Shaftesbury urged Charles to 'some signall act' to reassert his ecclesiastical supremacy, thwarted by parliaments and prelates. His justifications for this combined an appeal to Charles's baser instincts (a vicegerential visitation would extract lots of money from the Church) with an appeal to godly rule. A vicar-general could purge the Church of the scandals of nepotism, bad appointments, lack of discipline, and failure to fulfil the duties of hospitality and charity. One might suspect that Shaftesbury's motives had much more to do with the chance 'to chastise, in a Legall and plausible [popular] way that Clergy; which hath so much opposed [Charles's] conduct of late; and to reduce them into such a condition that they shall rather allay then augment for the

220 TNA, PRO 30/24/6B/427, qu. fos. 1r, 3r. 221 TNA, PRO 30/24/6B/427, fo. 4v.
222 TNA, PRO 30/24/6B/427, fos. 1r–2r. 223 TNA, PRO 30/24/6B/430.

future any discontentm*ents* in his Parliament', but it is significant that he added a godly gloss of this fulfilling the king's 'duty in reforming the Church'.[224]

Did Shaftesbury have himself in mind? He wrote to the Earl of Carlisle in 1675 that 'a great office with a strange name is preparing for me'. Vicegerent Shaftesbury seems incredible given the then hegemony of the Anglican royalist Earl of Danby (although the Venetian ambassador suggested that Charles was trying to widen his political options).[225] But if Shaftesbury never presided over the subjugation of the clergy, he and his associates did continue their campaign in printed works. The anticlerical as well as anti-absolutist animus of *A Letter from a Person of Quality* is often overlooked, despite it being one of the most famous of proto-whig texts.[226] It fulsomely rejected any threat of *imperium in imperio*, the only safe religious organisation being Independency or one 'that ownes an entire dependency on [government], and is but a branch of it'. Churchmen's authority and their exercise thereof derives only 'from the *King as head of the Church*, and from *God* as through him, as all his other Officers'.[227] Shaftesbury or his pen-man reiterated a recurring case for bishops as state servants. Marvell insisted that Constantine correctly thought he could 'make' and 'unmake' bishops just as he could 'his other Lay-Officers'.[228] Even Hickeringill's loyalist sermon of 1680, *Curse ye Meroz*, argued that kings and laws 'Ordain' and 'constitutes' the 'only true Christian Bishops, Priests and Deacons' in exactly the same way as judges, and that the king 'may deprive all of them equally'. Whatever *iure divino* pretences might be asserted, the 'open Administration' of such powers was 'from the Civil Authority alone'.[229]

By asserting that bishops had royal consent to exercise their jurisdictional authority, conformists argued that ecclesiastical law was not a threat to the supremacy. Fullwood deemed church laws to be 'aptly and rightly

224 TNA, PRO 30/24/6B/429.

225 *Calendar of State Papers Venetian, 1673–1675*, pp. 348–50 (1 Feb. 1675); cf. Locke, *Essay Concerning Toleration*, p. 151, in which Milton is more sceptical (and speaks of episcopal 'apoplexy' at the thought).

226 Although it is recognised by Mark Goldie, 'Danby, the Bishops, and the Whigs', in Tim Harris, Paul Seaward, and Mark Goldie, eds., *The Politics of Religion in Restoration England* (Oxford, 1990).

227 Anon. [Shaftesbury?], *Letter*, p. 24. He held Danby's 'no alteration' oath to be '*the greatest attempt that had been made against the King's Supremacy since the Reformation*' (p. 24).

228 Marvell, 'Essay on Councils', in *Smirke*, p. 64 (first pag., irregular pagination).

229 Edmund Hickeringill, *Curse ye Meroz, Or the Fatal Doom, in a Sermon Preached in Guildhall Chappel … 9 May 1680*, 4th edn (1680), pp. 22–3, 32. See Hickeringill, *News*, p. 7, on bishops as 'the *Kings creatures*'.

called The *Kings Ecclesiastical Laws of England*'.[230] As was shown earlier,[231] history could be used to demonstrate imperial control of ecclesiastical courts from time immemorial in an absolutist, not just constitutionalist, way. Fullwood employed this case to argue for a common-law based monarchical, not statutory, supremacy. Reception of canon law by custom or statute domesticated it; attacking church courts obliquely derogated from monarchical powers.[232] In the golden age before popish usurpations, spiritual jurisdiction was 'twisted and Interwoven … wrapt in the very Bowels of the *Civil* [law] … *intimately* wrought into the Temporal Law and Government'. Priests had then not only upheld order but also taken their rightful place in royal counsels. 'The mouth of the Priest was an Oracle to the People, and the mouth of the Bishop was an Oracle to the King and the Commonwealth.'[233] Christian emperors never made canons without episcopal consent and wielded the Keys in a purely political way, without immediate spiritual power. 'The *King* is a Priest in *tanto* [many things] not in *Toto* [all things].'[234]

Fullwood's assertion of a jurisdictional but not priestly supremacy responded to the strongly anticlerical twist of some Dissenting attacks on ecclesiastical jurisdiction. This was the radical edge of Dissenting imperialism, which in its most anticlerical mode appears in tune with emerging 'Enlightenment' ideals. Those enunciating such ideas were, however, using Reformation language of godly rule, *praemunire*, and prelacy as well as the proto-Enlightenment sense of priestcraft. The rose-tinted spectacles through which Restoration nonconformists viewed the pre-Civil War, or pre-Stuart, polity, distorted history into a story of stranger churches outside the bounds of uniformity, of monarchs tolerant of diversity, tacitly conniving at peaceful departures from episcopal rigour. Such a picture was chimerical, but its image of a godly prince exercised a powerful sway a century later. Dissenters must be desperate, Simon Patrick jibed in 1669, to clutch at assertions that the king tacitly indulged them. They had once sought to limit royal power by law; now they stooped to the supremacy. 'Then … you thought yourselves able to make the King bow to *you*; and now your Weakness forces You to worship *him*.'[235]

[230] Fullwood, *Leges Angliæ*, sig. [A5]v. [231] See Chapter 2, pp. 115–16.
[232] Fullwood, *Leges Angliæ*, pp. 51–6, 75–6, sig. [A5]r.
[233] Fullwood, *Leges Angliæ*, pp. 48–9.
[234] Francis Fullwood, *A Dialogue Betwixt Philautus and Timotheus* (1681), p. 10; Fullwood, *Leges Angliæ*, sig. A4v.
[235] Patrick, *Continuation*, p. 54; see pp. 47–57.

CHAPTER 5

Anticlericals and 'Erastians': the spectre of Hobbes

Nonconformists who sought to use the supremacy to restrain or even abolish bishops were often more antiprelatical than anticlerical. They saw godly clergy as having a role in the church (however organised) and some of them clung to the possibility of a godly bishop. Other theorists were more vehemently anticlerical, perceiving sedition coming from Catholic, Presbyterian, *and* episcopal sources. These men bemoaned 'priestcraft', a word which captured fears about the socio-cultural as well as political power of the clergy.[1] The warriors in this anticlerical campaign included some of the most prominent thinkers in seventeenth-century England: John Selden, Thomas Hobbes, John Harrington, and John Locke. It is, therefore, no surprise that when discussing religious ideas, intellectual historians of the period have been prone to write the history of heterodoxy and unbelief.

The word usually employed to describe men who sought to subordinate all priestly power to the state is 'Erastian'. It is a term not wholly inappropriate, but it is dangerously slippery. Erastus himself attacked aggressive excommunication in sixteenth-century Heidelberg, triggering a heated debate with Theodore Beza.[2] Although Erastianism in its purest form thus opposed excommunication being used against the state or without state sanction, Erastus's writings did not subjugate the church to a secular magistrate. He opposed excessive use of the discipline, but left Heidelberg when a Lutheran elector dismantled it in 1576.[3] But as John Neville Figgis showed over a century ago, in 1640s England 'Erastian' came to be applied to those who did wish the state to control the church.[4] In fact, the Civil

[1] See Mark Goldie, 'Priestcraft and the Birth of Whiggism', in Nicholas Phillipson and Quentin Skinner, eds., *Political Discourse in Early Modern Britain* (Cambridge, 1993). 'Preistis craft' was used in 1589: Thomas Nash, *Mar-Martine* (1589), sig. A3v.

[2] He had originally challenged George Withers' claim that ministers must 'excommunicate every Sinner (including Princes as well)': Erastus Evans, *Erastianism* (1933), p. 29.

[3] Evans, *Erastianism*, p. 33.

[4] J. Neville Figgis, 'Erastus and Erastianism', *Journal of Theological Studies*, 2 (1901), pp. 66–101.

War and Interregnum writers who made such claims were Erastians in the pure sense too, concerned that Presbyterian clergy were using excommunication in a way uncontrolled by the law. Thus, as Chapter 1 showed, the Long Parliament and the Westminster Assembly argued over which of them should decide which offences warranted excommunication, and whether those expelled could appeal to common law courts or parliament to review their punishments. Such wrangles frustrated and emasculated the imposition of Presbyterianism in England.

Another underlying link between many of those termed 'Erastians' was their interest in Hebraic scholarship, a theme whose interstices scholars have been understandably reluctant to penetrate. Erastus explained how 'the consideration of the Jewish republic and Church did not a little help me'. John Selden offered a detailed account of natural law in the Hebrew commonwealth. The Erastian clergyman John Lightfoot wrote works on Hebraic worship and told the Westminster Assembly that Israelite excommunication was 'of a civil import'.[5] We might note here too the philosemitism of that early eighteenth-century warrior against priestcraft, John Toland. Hobbes and Locke are the exceptions to the rule.[6]

'Erastian' might, therefore, be justifiably applied to both those who saw the supremacy as involving a godly magistrate *and* those who controlled the church via a secular state. Historiographical use of 'Erastian' often (confusingly) blurs this distinction. English defenders of the royal supremacy were normally the former. Given the ambiguities of the term, this chapter is not entitled 'the question of Erastianism'. Either version of the term is inappropriate to the writers it describes, for it explores how, in the hands of men like Hobbes, an anticlerical version of the royal supremacy not only reduced the sacerdotal status of the clergy, but also inflated the monarch into a priestly king, quite contrary to the normal defence of supremacy as jurisdictional. Erastus did not consecrate the monarch, and the defence of a sacerdotal supremacy ought not to be called an Erastian argument, although we will find writers beginning to muddle the two positions. The 1640s Erastian Thomas Coleman insisted that he did not want to grant parliament power to ordain the clergy.[7] Conversely, the

[5] Erastus, quoted in Evans, *Erastianism*, p. 44; Alex F. Mitchell and John Struthers, eds., *Minutes of the Sessions of the Westminster Assembly of Divines* (Edinburgh, 1874), p. 440.

[6] Johann P. Sommerville, 'Hobbes, Selden, Erastianism, and the History of the Jews', in G. A. J. Rogers and Tom Sorell, eds., *Hobbes and History* (2000); Nabil I. Matar, 'John Locke and the Jews', *Journal of Ecclesiastical History*, 44 (1993), pp. 45–62, at pp. 49, 57–61. For Harrington, see Mark Goldie, 'The Civil Religion of James Harrington', in Anthony Pagden, ed., *The Languages of Political Theory in Early-Modern Europe* (Cambridge, 1987), p. 208.

[7] See above, p. 77.

1650s writer Theophilus Brabourne looks 'Erastian' in many ways: concerned about excommunication, he criticised Presbyterian and episcopal forms of clerical authority. Brabourne noted that many 'say, that I am an *Erastine*, but they are such as know not the opinion of *Erastus*'. In contrast to the wider Civil War meaning of Erastianism as civil control of the church, Brabourne emphasised the Christian nature of the magistrate. Since 'a Christian king is an Ecclesiasticall person', the censures he imposed were 'no civill, but Christian, Ecclesiasticall, and Chu[r]che authority'.[8] Like Hobbes, he defended this by drawing on the classic case for supremacy, that the church was the commonwealth.[9] Brabourne, like Hobbes, seemed ambivalent about whether sovereignty was royal or parliamentary, so long as it restrained the power-seeking tendencies of clergy – of whatever persuasion.[10] And both argued that, if bishops really were necessary, they were *iure humano* and that the king consecrated them. 'If *Moses* did consecrat the High-Priest, may not our King consecrat an inferiour Bishop?'[11]

Similarly, Hobbes's sovereign governs religion, but that government is priestly not civil. The importance of the theistic, theological, and, most recently, ecclesiological aspects of Hobbes's thought are now well recognised.[12] If the sincerity of Hobbes's profession of Christian belief is unverifiable, his investigation of religious doctrines and ecclesiastical power is now agreed to be significant, at minimum to secure the Hobbesian state – albeit with a lingering implication that Hobbes cannot be sincere if his religion helped his political project. While many agree on the significance of Hobbes's interpretation of religion, scholars remain fundamentally divided on how to describe his theology and ecclesiology. Thus Richard Tuck and Jeffrey Collins see *Leviathan* as advocating Independency, an argument which Johann Sommerville denies.[13]

[8] Theophilus Brabourne, *A Defence of the Kings Authority and Supremacy*, 2nd edn (1660), pp. 4–5; Theophilus Brabourne, *The Second Part of the Change of Church-discipline* (1654), pp. 54, 20; Theophilus Brabourne, *A Reply to the indoctus doctor edoctvs* (1654, printed in Brabourne, *Second Part of the Change*), p. 78.

[9] Brabourne, *Second Part*, pp. 21, 43.

[10] On sovereignty: Brabourne, *Second Part*, sig. A2r; on clergy, see the subtitles to Brabourne, *Second Part* and Brabourne, *Defence of the Kings Authority*.

[11] Theophilus Brabourne, *Sundry Particulars Concerning Bishops* (n.p., 1661), pp. 8, 12; see also Theophilus Brabourne, *An Humble Petition … Tending to the Refining of the Booke of Common-Prayer* (1661); and *An Appendix to my Humble Petition* (n.p., 1661).

[12] Jacqueline Rose, 'Hobbes among the Heretics?', *Historical Journal*, 52 (2009), pp. 493–511.

[13] Richard Tuck, 'The "Christian Atheism" of Thomas Hobbes', in Michael Hunter and David Wootton, eds., *Atheism from the Reformation to the Enlightenment* (Oxford, 1992); Jeffrey R. Collins, *The Allegiance of Thomas Hobbes* (Oxford, 2005); Johann Sommerville, 'Hobbes and Independency', *Rivista di storia della filosofia*, 59 (2004), pp. 155–73.

A. P. Martinich depicted a Calvinist Hobbes attacked by a rising Arminian clique, and noted the use of Hobbesian language by 'respectable latitudinarians' such as Stillingfleet and Tillotson.[14] Whilst Martinich placed Hobbes *too* close to the supremacist tradition (as the final part of this chapter shows, latitudinarians were not always deemed 'respectable'), Hobbes as Henrician-Elizabethan-Jacobean supremacy theorist has also been supported by Patricia Springborg and Franck Lessay.[15] By contrast, while Collins sees Hobbes as 'the apogee of England's Erastian tradition', he ultimately dismisses such similarities as 'rhetorical', masking a civil religion: 'Hobbes's humanism trumps his Protestantism'.[16] Such debates are further complicated because Hobbes's ecclesiology was far from static. Tuck sees *Leviathan* as a sharp contrast to what he deems the episcopalian language of *De cive*, a claim denied by Sommerville and by Lodi Nauta.[17]

The following account draws on but also inverts prior studies by using Hobbes to explore the supremacy, not reading the Reformation to contextualise Hobbes. It newly extends our understanding by paying attention to Hobbes's Restoration works, still relatively unexplored terrain, but a rich source for Hobbes's ecclesiological pronouncements. It argues that Hobbes did have a subversive view of the supremacy from the early 1640s, a view made increasingly explicit between each of *The Elements of Law*, *De cive*, and *Leviathan*, *and* that this trend continued after 1660. Whilst care is needed when reading Hobbes's casuistical claims of lifelong royalism, his Restoration tracts provide a particularly rich seam of Hobbesian supremacism. It is true that many churchmen promoted to high office at the Restoration were on record against Hobbes to a remarkable degree; yet he still spoke out against them – his notorious cowardice was never intellectual. But the chronology of Hobbes's post-1660 writings is revealing: 1662, as the church was being settled; and especially the late 1660s and early 1670s – the 'Cabal' era when the clergy was at its

[14] A. P. Martinich, *The Two Gods of Leviathan: Thomas Hobbes on Religion and Politics* (Cambridge, 1992), pp. 284 (qu.), 333–4, 273, 37.

[15] Patricia Springborg, '*Leviathan*, the Christian Commonwealth Incorporated', *Political Studies*, 24 (1976), pp. 171–83, at p. 171; Franck Lessay, 'Hobbes's Protestantism', in Tom Sorell and Luc Foisneau, eds., *Leviathan after 350 Years* (Oxford, 2004), p. 272; Patricia Springborg, 'Thomas Hobbes and Cardinal Bellarmine: Leviathan and "The Ghost of the Roman Empire"', *History of Political Thought*, 16 (1995), pp. 503–31, at p. 514 (although not mentioning supremacy explicitly). Another useful discussion is Mark Whitaker, 'Hobbes's View of the Reformation', *History of Political Thought*, 9 (1988), pp. 45–58.

[16] Collins, *Allegiance of Thomas Hobbes*, pp. 15, 36, 57.

[17] Tuck, 'Christian Atheism'; Sommerville, 'Hobbes and Independency'; Lodi Nauta, 'Hobbes on Religion and the Church Between the *Elements of Law* and *Leviathan*: A Dramatic Change of Direction?', *Journal of the History of Ideas*, 63 (2002), pp. 577–98; Collins, *Allegiance of Thomas Hobbes*, p. 130, n. 73.

most vulnerable and when the case for 'magisterial Independency' was revived.[18] In these years Hobbes revised and added to the Latin version of *Leviathan*, defended himself against Bishop Bramhall, discussed the nature of common law, sketched the history of heresy, had his *Historia ecclesiastica* transcribed, and penned *Behemoth*. Hobbes published only in his maturity, but his productivity in his final decades was astonishingly high.

Hobbes's works bridge Tudor and Jacobean ideas of supremacy and proto-Enlightenment attacks on priestcraft. His pronunciations on church and state were enunciated in the language of royal supremacy, excellently evidencing the supremacy as a peculiarly English addition to Bodin's marks of sovereignty, whether located in monarchs or revolutionary regimes. As he put it in the 1620s, 'the Supremacy in matters Ecclesiastical ... is one of the chiefest guides of a Commonwealth'.[19] What form of ecclesiology Hobbes preferred is impossible to answer definitively, but he clearly could live with *iure humano* versions of episcopacy and Independency, and rejected papacy, Presbyterianism, and *iure divino* episcopacy. Hobbes's definition of the church, his account of royal ecclesiastical powers, and his anticlerical polemic all echoed and subverted prior accounts: he, like others, shaped his own conception of supremacy under the guise of defending it. The bitterness of condemnations of Hobbes stemmed not least from the way he undermined orthodoxy by claiming to participate in it.[20] And the Hobbesian threat grew in the Restoration because it seemed to some members of the church that such ideas were infiltrating the clergy. As the final section of this chapter shows, the rediscovery of Archbishop Cranmer's writings allowing a

[18] Compare Collins, *Allegiance of Thomas Hobbes*, who (pp. 85–6) does not note this antiprelatical phase of Charles's government; and wrongly suggests (pp. 274, 110) that Independency was always separatist after 1660; compare Chapter 4 above. This is peculiar since Collins has elsewhere noted ('The Restoration Bishops and the Royal Supremacy', *Church History*, 68 (1999), pp. 549–80) the conflict between crown and episcopate. He mentions the importance of Hobbes's post-1660 works (p. 59), but reads them as insincere (p. 2), and states that Hobbes's political theorising 'essentially ended' in the 1650s (p. 1).

[19] Thomas Hobbes, 'A Discourse on the Beginning of Tacitus', in Noel B. Reynolds and Arlene W. Saxonhouse, eds., *Thomas Hobbes: Three Discourses* (Chicago, 1995), p. 50. When 'king' is used below, one must assume Hobbes would apply this to any sovereign.

[20] As Jon Parkin insightfully comments in 'Hobbism in the Later 1660s: Daniel Scargill and Samuel Parker', *Historical Journal*, 42 (1999), pp. 85–108, at pp. 107–8; see also Jon Parkin, *Science, Religion and Politics in Restoration England: Richard Cumberland's De legibus naturae* (Woodbridge, 1999), pp. 6, 17, 11; Noel Malcolm, '*Leviathan*, the Pentateuch, and the Origins of Modern Biblical Criticism', in Sorell and Foisneau, eds., *Leviathan after 350 Years*, pp. 247–8; Mark Goldie, 'The Reception of Hobbes', in J. H. Burns and M. A. Goldie, eds., *The Cambridge History of Political Thought, 1450–1700* (Cambridge, 1991), pp. 596, 600.

sacerdotal supremacy worsened the Hobbes problem. Negotiating honest historical scholarship, due respect for Cranmer, the need to defend the supremacy, and the imperative to distance the church from Hobbism raised a series of questions haunted not by the ghost of Thomas Erastus, but by the spectre of Thomas Hobbes.

CONSECRATING THE MONARCH

Although its implications were broadcast more explicitly after the Restoration, Hobbes's account of supremacy was founded before 1660 and, indeed, before *Leviathan*.[21] 'As soon as one knows what a *Church* is, one knows immediately who should have government of Christians' Hobbes wrote in *De cive*.[22] Bishop Bramhall's argument that Hobbes's absolute equation of church and commonwealth was unique seems accurate, but (deliberately) downplayed Hobbes's proximity to Anglican rhetoric.

Hooker's language of church and polity as 'one and the selfsame multitude' is a useful comparator.[23] *De cive* insisted that *civitas* and *ecclesia* 'are exactly the same thing under two names', both materially ('the same Christian men') and formally ('the legal authority to summon them is also the same').[24] The crucial distinction was that Hooker was a realist and Hobbes a nominalist. So, for the Tudor theorist, church and commonwealth were 'names which import thinges really different', having distinct 'properties and actions', 'qualities and functions', albeit 'accidentes' of the same 'subject'.[25] For Hobbes, temporal and spiritual are 'but two words ... to make men see double, and mistake their *Lawfull Soveraign*'.[26] England is 'called a *Civill State*, for that the subjects of it are *Men*; and a *Church*, for that the subjects thereof are *Christians*'. He reiterated the idea in the 1668 appendix to *Leviathan*.[27] *De cive* and *Leviathan* recognised the diverse meanings of *ecclesia*: a gathering of citizens, the Elect (the *ecclesia* (church/kingdom) to come, of which Christ is the head), or those who

21 Thomas Hobbes, *An Answer to a Book Published by Dr Bramhall, Late Bishop of Derry, Called the Catching of the Leviathan* (1668, publ. 1682), p. 70. On proximity, see J. P. Sommerville, '*Leviathan* and its Anglican Context', in Patricia Springborg, ed., *The Cambridge Companion to Hobbes's Leviathan* (Cambridge, 2007), which I read after drafting the original version of this chapter.

22 Thomas Hobbes, *On the Citizen*, ed. Richard Tuck and Michael Silverthorne (Cambridge, 1998), p. 246. This work is cited henceforth as *De cive*.

23 *LEP*, VIII.i.2 (p. 319). 24 Hobbes, *De cive*, p. 221.

25 *LEP*, VIII.i.5; VIII.i.2 (pp. 325, 319–20).

26 Thomas Hobbes, *Leviathan*, ed. Richard Tuck, rev. edn (Cambridge, 1996), p. 322.

27 Hobbes, *Leviathan*, pp. 321–2; Thomas Hobbes, 'Thomas Hobbes: 1668 Appendix to *Leviathan*', trans. and ed. George Wright, *Interpretation*, 18 (1991), pp. 323–413, at p. 370.

profess Christ (not necessarily sincerely).[28] Hobbes stressed ecclesial *legality* derived from sovereign summons.[29]

A further point of comparison is with Henrician 'branch theory' of universal Christianity jurisdictionally divided into national churches. The 'King's Book' of 1543 argued that national churches, 'as they be distinct in places, so they haue distinct ministers & diuers heades in earth, gouernours, and rulers'. The 'Bishops' Book' of 1537 declared that particular 'partes, porcions, or membres' of the universal church were 'all equall in power and dignitie', none enjoying headship or sovereignty over the others.[30] *Leviathan* portrayed the papacy as the '*Ghost* of the deceased *Romane Empire*'; *De cive* described the fissuring of that empire into 'individual commonwealths' which 'were so many *Churches*' on whose consent Rome's authority rested.[31] The appendix to the Latin *Leviathan* moved smoothly from branch theory into royal supremacy:

> There are as many catholic churches as there are heads of churches. And there are as many heads of churches as there are Christian kingdoms and commonwealths. For in every land (*regio*), the prince of the Christians of that land is the head of his subjects, independent of another head on earth. Thus there are as many visible churches as there are heads of churches.[32]

This claim is shot through with Henrician language of *imperium*, the sovereign independence of individual monarchs in their own dominions. Hobbes echoed Stephen Gardiner's claim that it was a logical imperative for the head of the polity to head the local (English) branch of the church, since church and polity constituted the same people. 'Shall he not beinge called the headde of the realme of Englande be also the headde of the same men whan they are named the churche of Englande?' Gardiner asked, and Hobbes concurred.[33]

On to such language Hobbes grafted a theory of personation and representation. It is not excessively reductionist to say that Hobbes's justification of royal supremacy consisted of branch theory plus personation.

[28] Hobbes, *Leviathan*, pp. 320–1; Hobbes, *De cive*, pp. 219–20.

[29] Hobbes, *Leviathan*, p. 321; Hobbes, *De cive*, pp. 220–1.

[30] *A Necessary Doctrine and Ervdition for any Christen Man* (1543, citing STC 5168), fo. 15v; *The Institvtion of a Christen Man* (1537, citing STC 5164), fo. 14v.

[31] Hobbes, *Leviathan*, p. 480; Hobbes, *De cive*, p. 222.

[32] Hobbes, 'Appendix', p. 370.

[33] Stephen Gardiner, 'The Oration of True Obedience', in *Obedience in Church and State: Three Political Tracts by Stephen Gardiner*, ed. Pierre Janelle (Cambridge, 1930), pp. 93–5: 'Shall the termynge of wordes … turne the nature of the thinges them selues vp side downe?'; Hobbes, *Leviathan*, pp. 321–2.

Historians have debated Hobbes's developing theory of persons in secular terms, leaving aside his ecclesiastical account (separate from the theological application to the Trinity).[34] But personation was, importantly, developed in the 1642 edition of *De cive* for the church, and only fully explained apropos the state in the 1647 edition, and enlarged in *Leviathan*. Inanimate objects do things only when personated, *Leviathan* explained, listing 'Church' as the first example. But the concept that something inanimate needs 'personality' to act begins to do its theoretical work in chapter 17 of *De cive*. Here the universal church is not 'a *person*' and 'does not therefore do or make anything', 'not a *single person*, of which it could be said that it has *done, decreed, decided, excommunicated, absolved*'.[35] When in *Leviathan* Hobbes attacks Bellarmine, he stresses that there was no universal polity whose corporate body the pope could bear. France, Spain, Venice, and England are 'severall [individual] Bodies of Christians; that is to say severall Churches' represented by

> their severall Soveraigns ... whereby they are capable of commanding and obeying, of doing and suffering, as a naturall man; which no Generall or Universall Church is, till it have a Representant; which it hath not on Earth.[36]

In chapter 16 of *Leviathan*, Hobbes's first extensive account of civil personation, 'a Multitude of men, are made *One* Person, when they are by one man, or one Person, Represented'. 'For it is the *Unity* of the Representer, not the *Unity* of the Represented, that maketh the Person *One*.' But this had already been stated in *De cive*: a church is '*one*, and capable of the functions of a *person*, not because it has unity of doctrine [the represented], but because it has unity of authority [the representer] to summon Synods and assemblies of CHRISTians'. For 'otherwise it is merely a crowd, and several distinct *persons*, however much they agree in belief'. The makers of the state in *Leviathan* 'submit their Wills, every one to his [sovereign] Will'. And in *De cive* 'the commonwealth whose will is contained in his [sovereign] will, is the very thing which we call a *church*'.[37] One

[34] Quentin Skinner, 'Hobbes and the Purely Artificial Person of the State', repr. in *Visions of Politics*, vol. III, *Hobbes and Civil Science* (Cambridge, 2002); David Runciman, *Pluralism and the Personality of the State* (Cambridge, 1997), ch. 2; Gianni Paganini, 'Hobbes, Valla and the Trinity', *British Journal for the History of Philosophy*, 11 (2003), pp. 183–218. Patricia Springborg, '*Leviathan*, the Christian Commonwealth Incorporated', is the nearest to an ecclesial account, although p. 171 still refers to personation and the Trinity.

[35] Hobbes, *Leviathan*, p. 113; qu. Hobbes, *De cive*, pp. 228, 230 (the index to Tuck's edition lists only 'person, civil'). It is not present in *The Elements of Law*.

[36] Hobbes, *Leviathan*, p. 397.

[37] Hobbes, *Leviathan*, pp. 114, 120; Hobbes, *De cive*, p. 229. The need for 'the consent of every one of that Multitude in particular' would outlaw papacy.

correspondent tellingly described Hobbes's view of Elizabeth I as 'the person of the state, and of its Church, being its sole representative'.[38]

Hobbes radically collapsed any distinction between the members, form, or rulers of church and commonwealth. The sovereign bears the person of the state when doing 'political' acts, and of the church for 'religious' ones. That this theory is propounded in *De cive* suggests the potential radicalism of that text: whenever Hobbes says 'church', he means the sovereign. When the 'state' acts, really the sovereign does; when the 'church' decrees, its supreme head pronounces; as Hobbes later explicitly told Bramhall, 'without the Head the Church is mute'.[39] Since Hobbes's royal supremacy enveloped the church, it naturally involved supreme sacerdotal as well as jurisdictional powers.

Hobbes depicted a supreme head whose powers wavered between ecclesial orthodoxy (regarding synods and church courts) and subversion (a radically sacerdotal supremacy incorporating priestly officiating, prophecy, and determining scriptural canonicity). The extent to which Hobbes was aware of prior literature on the supremacy is hard to ascertain, but he certainly employed its language. Chapter 40 of *Leviathan* described the various recensions of God's covenant with the Israelites' sovereign representatives. Insisting that the head of the polity (whether king or priest)[40] wielded both spiritual and temporal power, Hobbes stressed kingly power over priests after the rejection of God's personal rule. Solomon had deposed the high priest, 'which is a great mark of Supremacy in Religion'; he dedicated and consecrated the Temple: 'another great mark of Supremacy in Religion'. Josiah dispatched men of the Law: 'another mark of the Supremacy in Religion'; and apportioned land to tribes: 'is not this full Power, both *temporall* and *spirituall*?'[41] Hobbes baited the clergy by reminding them that the canons of 1604 described Old Testament kings as models for English monarchs.[42] The only alternative locus of spiritual power was in the prophets, but Hobbes subjugated prophets to kings. Hezekiah and Josiah had heard Isaiah and Hulda, but would anyone say Isaiah was 'supreme Head of the Church', or that Hulda 'had the Supreme

[38] Thomas Hobbes, *Correspondence*, ed. Noel Malcolm (2 vols., Oxford, 1994), no. 121 (from François du Verdus, 12/22 Mar. 1657): 'la persone de l'etat et de son eglise et la represente seule'.

[39] Hobbes, *Answer to Bramhall*, pp. 74–5.

[40] Hobbes, *Leviathan*, p. 328. Hobbes, *De cive*, p. 198, argued that *de facto* authority lay in the prophets, *de iure* in the high priests after the death of Joshua.

[41] Hobbes, *Leviathan*, p. 329.

[42] Thomas Hobbes, *A Dialogue Between a Philosopher and a Student, Of the Common Laws of England*, ed. Alan Cromartie, in Thomas Hobbes, *Writings on Common Law and Hereditary Right*, ed. Alan Cromartie and Quentin Skinner (Oxford, 2005), p. 115.

authority in matter of Religion; which I thinke is not the opinion of any Doctor'?[43]

In his insistence on the exclusively royal right to summon councils and ratify canons, Hobbes proposed no more than Henry VIII had done. The *Historia ecclesiastica* berated the insolence of the pope calling a synod without princely permission, whilst *Leviathan* noted the need for imperial reception of papal canons until Charlemagne's time. Apostolic synods counselled, not commanded: 'they could not deliberate [remove the natural right to judge for oneself] what others should do, unless their Assembly had had a Legislative Power; which none could have but Civil Soveraigns'.[44] The pre-Constantinian clergy were perfectly able to meet voluntarily, but such assemblies were not 'a synod with authority to decide, whose decrees it was unjust not to obey'.[45] Hobbes was not stretching the supremacy. The Twenty-First of the Thirty-Nine Articles stated that no general council could impose its decrees without royal assent. According to the Henrician Act for the Submission of the Clergy, royal ratification was required to translate canons into laws. Hobbes duly argued the same. In the *Dialogue*, the Philosopher explains that kings, not churchmen, make canons into laws, and clergy are guilty of *praemunire* if their doctrines derogate from royal power.[46] Hobbes condemned Bramhall's assertion that the church might assemble without sovereign permission as 'taking away of the Kings Supremacy in causes Ecclesiastical'.[47]

Hobbes's worries about the dangers of independent clerical jurisdiction exercised by synods and church courts were far from unique. His *Dialogue* on the common laws intervened in the legal debate over whether the ecclesiastical courts of post-Reformation England can commit *praemunire*. The Philosopher asks whether a plea entered at Lambeth against a case decided at Westminster is *praemunire*, and the Lawyer answers yes. The Philosopher replies in the vein of Thomas Ridley, Richard Cosin, and John Cowell: the Reformation made the court the king's. Should 'any simple Man' undergo the drastic penalties of *praemunire* when he just 'mistakes his right Court'? The Lawyer insists, with Edward Coke, that the courts are still foreign despite the Submission of the Clergy. The

43 Hobbes, *Leviathan*, p. 331.

44 Thomas Hobbes, *Historia ecclesiastica*, ed. Patricia Springborg et al. (Paris, 2008), lines 1629–30, see also line 757; Hobbes, *Leviathan*, pp. 421, 362 (qu.).

45 Hobbes, 'Appendix', p. 385.

46 Hobbes, *Dialogue*, p. 115; pp. 19–20 had a conformist emphasis: because ratified by the king, canons *are* English laws. See, similarly, Thomas Hobbes, *Behemoth*, ed. Paul Seaward (Oxford, 2010), pp. 119–20.

47 Hobbes, *Answer to Bramhall*, pp. 71–2.

Philosopher (Hobbes himself?) flatly rejects the notion that 'Alia Curia' means 'per aliam Legem' or 'ad aliud Examen': suing a case is not asking the pope for a bishopric, and the statute 'doth not distinguish Courts otherwise than into the Courts of the King, and into the Courts of the Forraign States, and Princes'.[48]

Hobbes needled his Anglican opponents by stressing their convergence. He jibed at Bramhall that they agreed that 'Supream Judicature in matter of Religion' was best placed 'in the Head of the Church, which is the King'. 'But because his Lordship knew not how to deduce it, he was angry with me because I did it.'[49] Hobbes's account of public worship was typical in approaching an Anglican view while demurring at crucial points. The 'property' of public worship is 'to be *Uniforme*', and 'natural reason' prescribes uniformity for 'Commonwealths as wholes, each of which is one person'.[50] *Leviathan*'s language of 'natural' versus 'arbitrary' worship reconfigured rather than contradicted prior distinctions between actions commanded in scripture and those left 'indifferent'. But the latter are determined by the sovereign, not the clergy.[51]

Yet Hobbes inflamed churchmen by empowering monarchs to judge scripture and prophecy and granting them priesthood. Not only ecclesiastical canons but also the scriptural canon is subject to sovereign determination of its content and, in the Hobbesian world of radical subjectivity, its meaning as well. Hobbes never philologically undermined the New Testament in the way he did the Old, but his seemingly generous admission that divines 'did not … falsifie the Scriptures' was followed by an extremely backhanded compliment. 'If they had had an intention so to doe, they would surely have made them more favorable to their power over Christian Princes, and Civill Soveraignty, than they are.'[52] *De cive* stated God's Word is right reason. But after stressing the meaning not the letter of the textual canon, it demands 'a canonical interpreter' with the 'legal responsibility' to determine disputes 'by explicating *God's Word* in actual judgements'. The authority of this '*interpreter of scripture* and *supreme judge* of all *doctrines*' should be 'as strongly upheld as the authority of those who approved scripture itself as the canon of faith in

[48] Hobbes, *Dialogue*, pp. 106–110; see also p. 43. *Aliam legem* and *aliud examen* were Coke's glosses: see above, p. 70.

[49] Hobbes, *Answer to Bramhall*, p. 62.

[50] Hobbes, *Leviathan*, p. 252; Hobbes, *De cive*, p. 181.

[51] Hobbes, *Leviathan*, pp. 249, 253; Hobbes, *De cive*, p. 177 (p. 181 has natural versus conventional). Locke's early writings make a similar move: Jacqueline Rose, 'John Locke, "Matters Indifferent", and the Restoration of the Church of England', *Historical Journal*, 48 (2005), pp. 601–21.

[52] Hobbes, *Leviathan*, p. 266.

the first place'.[53] Yet for Hobbes only the sovereign can wield such power. His conflation of church and commonwealth, which follows this passage, emptied his clerical rhetoric of substantive content. Such insistence grew bolder over time. In *Leviathan*, 'the authority of the Church' 'maketh a Book Canonicall', but the church is the sovereign, so 'those Books only are Canonicall … which are established for such by the Soveraign Authority'.[54] The *Answer* to Bramhall even more explicitly linked a theory of personation to sovereign determination of scriptural canonicity. 'If this Authority be in the Church of *England*, then it is not any other than the Authority of the Head of the Church, which is the King.'[55]

Hobbes consistently subordinated individual prophecies to sovereign allowance. The Seventy Elders 'Prophecyed as Moses would have them: otherwise they had not been suffered to Prophecy at all'. When Bramhall protested, Hobbes denied that sovereigns could 'make' prophecies 'true or false', but reiterated their right to prohibit public teaching of them 'whether false or true'.[56] Hobbes leapt from the question of 'who is the Soveraign Prophet' to 'who is next under Christ our Supream Head and Governor'. In a heated paragraph he asked Bramhall who ought to judge doctrine:

> Shall a private Lay-man … No man ever thought that … Shall a Synod of *Presbyterians* … No; For most of the *Presbyters* in the Primitive Church were undoubtedly subordinate to Bishops, and the rest were Bishops. Who then? A Synod of Bishops? Very well … But … who shall call them together? The King. What if he will not? Who should Excommunicate him … who shall send forth a Writ of *Significavit*?[57]

The only logical location for ecclesiastical authority was in the king.

Most radically, Hobbes propounded a sacerdotal supremacy. Whereas prior polemicists were keen to prove that ecclesiastical supremacy did not mean kings ordained priests or administered communion, *Leviathan* exploded such distinctions.[58] In chapter 42, 'Of Power Ecclesiasticall', Hobbes explained how, by baptism alone, 'Christian Kings have Power, to execute all manner of Pastoral function': preaching, baptism, giving communion, ordaining priests, consecrating buildings. Only the constraints

[53] Hobbes, *De cive*, pp. 175, 218–19 (qu. 219).

[54] Hobbes, *Leviathan*, pp. 266, 260; cf. Thomas Hobbes, *The Elements of Law*, ed. Ferdinand Tönnies, 2nd edn, intro. M. M. Goldsmith (1969), pp. 58–9, where the church makes the canon.

[55] Hobbes, *Answer to Bramhall*, p. 74. See also Hobbes, *Behemoth*, p. 176; Hobbes, *Leviathan*, pp. 307, 326, 355–6.

[56] Hobbes, *Leviathan*, pp. 296 (qu.), 326–7; Hobbes, *De cive*, pp. 195–6; Hobbes, *Answer to Bramhall*, p. 60.

[57] Hobbes, *Answer to Bramhall*, pp. 61–2. *Significavit*: a writ to arrest an excommunicated person.

[58] Hobbes, *Elements of Law*, p. 167, gave a pretty strong hint.

of time led them to delegate such matters to the clergy. Hobbes manipulated the Israelite exemplars which the Church of England used to uphold supremacy, matter-of-factly outlining Solomon having 'not only the right of Ecclesiasticall Government; but also of exercising Ecclesiasticall Functions', blessing his people and consecrating the Temple.[59] When, following this, Hobbes trumpeted the 'Right Politique, and Ecclesiastique' of Christian sovereigns to 'all manner of Power over their Subjects, that can be given to man, for the government of mens externall actions, both in Policy, and Religion', his marginal gloss announced 'the Civill Soveraigne if a Christian, is head of the Church in his own Dominions'. He furthermore declared such powers to be 'incident to all Soveraigns, whether Monarchs, or Assemblies'.[60] After 1660, he did not retreat, but had the temerity to claim that royal sacerdotal power was the original intention of the Elizabethan Settlement, 'almost all' ministers in 1559 believing that supremacy and sacerdotal monarchy went together. Elizabeth's Injunctions declared she would *exercise* no greater a supremacy than Henry or Edward, but she imposed no limits on her successors.[61] *Mr Hobbes Considered* (1662) blithely supposed that its target, the Presbyterian John Wallis, might have disliked Hobbes's 'Attributing to the Civil Soveraign all Power *Sacerdotal*' – a pretty safe supposition. 'This perhaps may seem hard when the Soveraignty is in a Queen', Hobbes mused. 'But it is [hard] because you are not subtile enough to perceive, that though *Man* be *male* and *female, Authority* is not.'[62]

Hobbes deployed evidence used to support jurisdictional supremacy to uphold his own sacerdotal version, which even his anticlerical disciples questioned.[63] Solomon's deposition of Abiathar was frequently cited to show kings might punish rebellious priests; Hobbes argued it showed kings might 'Ordaine, and Deprive Bishops'. Uzzah, struck down for touching the Ark, normally exemplified excessive (although well-intentioned) lay intervention. Hobbes emphasised David's displeasure at

59 Hobbes, *Leviathan*, pp. 374–7 (qu. 374, 377).

60 Hobbes, *Leviathan*, pp. 377–8; see also Hobbes, *Elements of Law*, p. 167.

61 Hobbes, 'Appendix', p. 386. In the Latin *Leviathan*, Hobbes argued that Elizabeth had not performed sacerdotal actions because of her gender but, in so doing, firmly tied the supremacy to priestly actions: see the addition to ch. 42 in Thomas Hobbes, *Leviathan: With Selected Variants from the Latin Edition of 1668*, ed. E. M. Curley (Indianapolis, 1994), pp. 371–2; see also Hobbes, *Correspondence*, no. 108, at p. 416 (from du Verdus, 22 Dec. 1656 / 1 Jan. 1657).

62 Thomas Hobbes, *Mr Hobbes Considered in his Loyalty, Religion, Reputation, and Manners by Way of Letter to Dr Wallis* (1662), pp. 48–9; quoted by Skinner, 'Artificial Person', p. 198, in a secular context.

63 Hobbes, *Correspondence*, nos. 108, 121 (from du Verdus, 22 Dec. 1656 / 1 Jan. 1657 and 12/22 Mar. 1657).

the death of Uzzah.[64] *Behemoth* blamed lack of priesthood for kings losing headship of the church to the pope. To rectify such errors, Hobbes invoked the sense of *episcopus* as overseer, asserting that amongst heathens '*Episcopus* was a name common to all Kings'. Since Christian bishops are only 'Christian[s] indued with Power to gouerne the Clergy, it follows that euery Christian King is not only a Bishop, but an Arch-Bishop, and his whole Dominion his Diocese'. Imposition of hands at baptism changes a royal 'Bishop' already overseeing the clergy to 'a Christian Bishop'.[65] Against Bramhall, Hobbes stressed that though 'the Bishop Consecrates', 'the King both makes him Bishop and gives him his Authority. The Head of the Church not only gives the power of Consecration, Dedication, and Benediction, but may also exercise the Act himself if he please'.[66]

As Hobbes collapsed any distinction between the church and commonwealth, he radicalised the orthodox account of their congruity. Granting power to kings over synods, canons, and church courts was acceptable; over the canonicity of scripture, prophets, and sacerdotal functions deeply subversive. To Hobbes, the logic of the supremacy inexorably pointed in this radically sacerdotal direction. Is not the king 'supreme shepherd of his people? And can't a king create assistant shepherds?' asks one interlocutor in the *Historia ecclesiastica*.[67] *Leviathan* explained how power ecclesiastical was transferred by imposition of hands before Christian sovereigns,[68] but a tectonic shift occurred when emperors converted. Once Christian, a monarch as supreme pastor ordains his clergy in the same way as he appoints mayors of towns; for clergy, like magistrates, judges, and military commanders, are 'but his Ministers'.[69] Hobbes's clergy wield ministerial, never magisterial, powers. Publicly they must endorse the sovereign; their function is to teach subjects obedience.[70] Hobbes made monarchs priests and clergy civil servants without any supernatural functions, seeing sacraments not (as Anglicans did) as 'visible signs of invisible grace' but, in politically inspired language, 'solemne oathes … of our Alleageance'. His description of baptism as 'the Sacrament of Allegeance' is a significant formulation if, as has been suggested, Hobbes was familiar with the Jacobean Oath of Allegiance literature.[71]

[64] Hobbes, *Leviathan*, pp. 394, 263. [65] Hobbes, *Behemoth*, pp. 123–4.

[66] Hobbes, *Answer to Bramhall*, pp. 80–1.

[67] Hobbes, *Historia ecclesiastica*, lines 1809–12.

[68] Hobbes, *Leviathan*, p. 339. [69] Hobbes, *Leviathan*, pp. 372–4 (qu. 373).

[70] Hobbes, *Answer to Bramhall*, p. 4; Hobbes, *Dialogue*, p. 12.

[71] Hobbes, *Leviathan*, pp. 286, 347; Linda Levy Peck, 'Constructing a New Context for Hobbes Studies', in Howard Nenner, ed., *Politics and the Political Imagination in Later Stuart England*

CIVILISING THE CLERGY

Hobbes's location of temporal and spiritual authority in a single sovereign advantageously allowed kings to control the clergy, but problematically permitted clerical meddling in politics. His Old Testament examples of unified sovereignty located both powers in the high priest, and he admitted that the king either had to take sole authority or, in effect, cede his government to the pope.[72] A virulent defence against the dangers of priestcraft was a necessary ideological imperative as well as, for Hobbes, an enjoyable exercise.

Before turning to the ways in which Hobbes attacked specific manifestations of clerical power, it is worth dwelling on his plangent criticisms of priestly politicking in general. Hobbes's readers enlisted him as an ally in the polemic against what would come to be known as 'priestcraft'. John Davies's preface to the purportedly unauthorised publication of *Of Libertie and Necessitie* in 1654 presented Hobbes attacking theological disputations, which created religious parties and erupted into civil wars.[73] Hobbes and his avid French disciple, François du Verdus, exchanged complaints about the clerical kingdom of darkness, while the Deist Charles Blount depicted Hobbes as loftily above priestly criticisms.[74]

Hobbes's *Historia ecclesiastica*, published posthumously in 1688, provided a litany of the ills of priestcraft (although he never used the word). Written between the late 1650s and early 1670s, it condemns priestly status, of whatever theological persuasion, as morally and politically corrupting. Heathen priests are as guilty as Christian ones; indeed Christianity spread because of popular disaffection with clerical vices.[75] Political troubles result from theological disputations; priests use populist rhetoric to undermine monarchs. Hobbes praises Ergamenes, the king of Ethiopia who slaughtered his priests in order to prevent sedition, not only in the *Historia*, but also in *Behemoth*, where 'A' reflects that executing a thousand preachers might have prevented a hundred thousand deaths in the Civil Wars.[76] Ergamenes even appears in the first of Hobbes's *Ten Dialogues of*

(Rochester, NY, 1997), pp. 173–4; Springborg 'Hobbes and Bellarmine', p. 514; Collins, *Allegiance of Thomas Hobbes*, pp. 23–5. Lessay, 'Hobbes's Protestantism', pp. 276–7, notes Hobbes's atypicality.

[72] Hobbes, *Leviathan*, pp. 327, 385, 396, 402.

[73] John Davies, preface to Hobbes, *Of Libertie and Necessitie* (1654); Collins, *Allegiance of Thomas Hobbes*, p. 182, notes Hobbes's possible complicity in the publication.

[74] See Hobbes, *Correspondence*, nos. 201 (from Charles Blount, 1678), 78, 168, 170, and passim (from du Verdus, 26 Mar. / 5 Apr. 1656, 24 July / 3 Aug. 1664; 19/29 Aug. 1664).

[75] Hobbes, *Historia ecclesiastica*, lines 785–6, 1359–60.

[76] Hobbes, *Historia ecclesiastica*, lines 203–213; Hobbes, *Behemoth*, p. 231.

Natural Philosophy, which describes the priestly astrology extant before true (Hobbesian) philosophy.[77] The mirror-image of Ergamenes was Phocas, whose grant of power to the pope epitomised the supine kingship which permitted the rise of priestly power.[78] Hobbes echoed accounts that blamed clericalism on over-generous monarchs.[79] His hyperbolically negative colouring of the Constantinian and Nicene era (imperial indulgence rewarded with clerical sedition) was complemented by his insistence on the early infiltration of the church by ambition, philosophical quibbles, and 'heresy'. This dramatically contrasted with the patristic shift in seventeenth-century Anglican attitudes.[80]

Sometimes Hobbes turned from attacking priestcraft in general to popery and Presbyterianism specifically. Popes had seduced emperors into granting them powers, encouraging popular sedition.[81] The early pages of *Behemoth* detailed the papal origins of the distinction of spiritual and temporal, papal usurpation helped by pernicious doctrines like priestly celibacy and Aristotelian philosophy.[82] But Presbyterian ministers equally clawed at power. 'What haue we then gotten by our deliuerance from the Pope's tyrranny, if these petty men succeed in the place of it?'[83] When Hobbes wrangled with the Presbyterian professor John Wallis over mathematics in 1656, he harped on Erastian themes.[84] Wallis and his ilk perpetuated popery by wanting 'to uphold the Authority of a Church, as a distinct thing from the Common-wealth'.[85] In 1662 Hobbes renewed his attack on Wallis's 'crime' of subverting supreme headship by changing

77 Thomas Hobbes, *Decameron physiologicum: Or, Ten Dialogues of Natural Philosophy* (1678), p. 5.

78 Hobbes, *Historia ecclesiastica*, lines 1523–4; lazy kings: line 876. See Hobbes, 'Appendix', p. 371.

79 Hobbes, *Historia ecclesiastica*, lines 1189–90.

80 This shift is detailed above in Chapter 3. Springborg, 'Heresy and the *Historia ecclesiastica*', pp. 559, 561, also notes Hobbes's relationship to it. The end of Rymer's preface to the *Historia ecclesiastica* (p. 601) claimed Hobbes's adherence was to the apostolic, pre-Nicene age; although cf. *Leviathan*, p. 418, on problems 'almost from the time of the Apostles'.

81 Hobbes, *Historia ecclesiastica*, lines 1187–90, 2030–2, 1755–6.

82 Hobbes, *Behemoth*, pp. 123–9. Hobbes was fascinated with the bizarre idea of priestly celibacy being a prelatical plot to debar the king from his rightful sacerdotal role. *De cive*, p. 247, bemoaned the political disadvantages of princes lacking priesthood, 'a great bond of civil obedience'; *Leviathan*, p. 477, complained that if the king becomes a priest he cannot marry and secure the succession; if he remains a layman, he is subjected to the clergy; see also *Historia ecclesiastica*, lines 1801–8.

83 Hobbes, *Behemoth*, p. 343.

84 This was Hobbes's stimulus, not incidental: *Correspondence*, no. 112 (to Samuel Sorbière, 29 Dec. 1656); Thomas Hobbes, *Six Lessons to the Professors of the Mathematiques* (1656); Thomas Hobbes, *Stigmai Ageometrias ... or Markes of the Absurd Geometry, Rural Language, Scottish Church-Politicks and Barbarismes of John Wallis* (1657).

85 Hobbes, *Six Lessons*, p. 60. Henry Stubbe and Thomas Barlow encouraged this view: *Correspondence*, nos. 96–8 (from Stubbe, 25 Oct. and 9 Nov. 1656), 109 (from Barlow, 23 Dec. 1656); see also no. 91 (from Stubbe, 7 Oct. 1656).

liturgy and church government without permission, for all such external worship should be 'judged by those to whom God has committed the ordering of Religion; that is, to the Supream Governors of the Church, that is, in *England*, to the King'.[86]

Even during the Cromwellian Interregnum, Hobbes had the royal supremacy in mind, in 1657 invoking 'the authority of the Christian Soveraign Christs immediat Vicar and supream Governour of all Persons and Judge of all causes both spiritual and temporal in his own Dominions'.[87] If this echoed the ecclesiastical policy of the 'magisterial Independents', Hobbes also made favourable remarks about some sort of emasculated episcopacy. He displayed a remarkable concern in 1656 to prove *Leviathan* had not attacked Anglicans: he had written a 'Vindication of the Church of *England*', allowed their clergy to 'escape'.[88] There was no political imperative to take this line in the mid 1650s, unless the absence of episcopal persecution altered priorities. Hobbes ridiculed Wallis's insistence that ministers preach *ex officio* as 'very unlike' to English laws, which made ministers 'by the Supream Authority of the Common-Wealth'. Hobbes would, by contrast, permit the 'gentle terms' of successive imposition of hands as an aid to the ministry, so long as this was not 'too rude' by excluding the civil sovereign.[89]

To analyse Hobbes's 'sincerity' when discussing episcopacy, especially after 1660, is difficult. It is, therefore, important to distinguish between different forms of that institution: high-church *iure divino* episcopacy, flatly rejected by Hobbes, versus *iure humano* bishops authorised by the state, to whom he seems more favourable. Hobbes fought against churchmen who defended a catholic ecclesiology, which he condemned as potentially subverting royal supremacy. Such ideas flourished from the Laudian era through the Interregnum and into the Restoration; Hobbes challenged a dominant rhetoric. But his critique needs careful placement within the *heterogeneous* spectrum of Anglican opinion: church government determined by civil decree was occasionally supported from Elizabeth's Archbishop Parker to Stillingfleet and Tillotson (labelled Hobbist) during the Restoration.

Nevertheless, bishops as well as popes had wheedled monarchs into ceding authority. *Behemoth* depicted bishops blithely nodding through Henry

[86] Hobbes, *Mr Hobbes Considered*, pp. 14, 36. The use of supreme 'governor' is atypical of Hobbes.
[87] Hobbes, *Stigmai*, p. 18.
[88] Hobbes, *Six Lessons*, pp. 62–3. Cf. *Correspondence*, no. 112 (to Sorbière, 29 Dec. 1656 / 12 Jan. 1657): written against 'all the ecclesiastics of England'.
[89] Hobbes, *Stigmai*, p. 17.

VIII's Act of Supremacy as a means to claim *iure divino* power directly.[90] In passages prudently deleted from the printed Restoration editions, Hobbes suggested that episcopal subversion of monarchy fuelled demands for the abolition of bishops in 1641.[91] At the time of the Root and Branch Petition, Hobbes confided to Cavendish that an unpopular church government could be changed, despite commenting that men wrongly blamed the institution for the faults of individual bishops.[92] The final chapter of *Leviathan* surveyed the benefits which the pope *and other clergy* accrued from their 'kingdom of darkness'. 'In effect' the Reformation returned ecclesiastical power to royal hands, 'saving that they, by whom the Kings administred the Government of Religion, by maintaining their imployment to be in Gods Right, seemed to usurp, if not a Supremacy, yet an Independency on the Civill Power'. Yet this was a misleading impression: 'they but seemed to usurpe it, in as much as they acknowledged a Right in the King, to deprive them of the Exercise of their Functions at his pleasure'. Elizabethan bishops retained the phrase 'iure divino' and so were 'thought to demand' their powers immediately of God, but their exercise of the same was 'in Right of the Queen'.[93] The authors of darkness were, ultimately, Roman Catholic and Presbyterian clergy. Nevertheless, Hobbes wanted to prevent the use of *iure divino* language by bishops to prevent them 'sliely slip[ping] off the Collar of their Civill Subjection'.[94] The safest bishops were those who were clearly royal servants.

Hobbes's distinctions of, and preferences between, different modes of episcopacy were occasionally made explicit. 'All Bishops', he explained, 'are not in every point like one another'. Those 'content to hold their Authority from the Kings Letters Patents … have no cause to be angry with Mr *Hobbes*'. It was the demand for more, for something *iure divino* ('they know not what'), which irked Hobbes, since those who stressed imposition of hands and consecration, deeming their authority to be immediately *iure divino*, bypassed the king. 'The Pastorall Authority of Soveraigns only is *de Jure Divino*, that of other Pastors is *Jure Civili*.'[95] In a tract of 1662 Hobbes professed amazement at attacks on him for basing church authority 'wholly upon the Regal Power'.[96] He stridently

[90] Hobbes, *Behemoth*, pp. 132, 290, 180–1.

[91] Hobbes, *Behemoth*, p. 224, cf. pp. 231–2 and 214 on the insincerity of Presbyterian claims of episcopal subversion of monarchy.

[92] Hobbes, *Correspondence*, no. 37 (to William Cavendish, third earl of Devonshire, 23 July 1641).

[93] Hobbes, *Leviathan*, pp. 475, 479. [94] Hobbes, *Leviathan*, p. 374.

[95] Hobbes, *Mr Hobbes Considered*, p. 45; Hobbes, *Leviathan*, p. 374.

[96] Thomas Hobbes, *Seven Philosophical Problems, and Two Propositions of Geometry* (1662, publ. 1682), sig. A2v.

declared himself 'for all that believe the King only, and without sharers, to be the Head of all the Churches within his own Dominions'.[97] But the ambiguity of church*es*, and Hobbes's endorsement of 'such an Episcopacy as is now in *England*' were slippery in 1662, when uniformity was being re-established. Hobbes's defence of a supremacy independent of parliamentary statute ('the King … without sharers') would have authorised prerogative dispensation with the Act of Uniformity. His justification of episcopacy as the most 'commodious'[98] means of royal government of English Christians bespoke an indifferency to ecclesiological form, though one which might be receptive to *iure humano* episcopacy.

Although civilising the clergy was qualitatively different to the *iure humano* tradition, Hobbes was able to defend himself by bringing the two ideas together, especially when anathematising the Anglo-papalist strains detectable in bishops such as Bramhall. Against Bramhall, Hobbes could portray himself as a good scriptural Protestant supremacist challenging a scholastic and Romish bishop whose doctrine 'smells of Ambition and encroachment of Jurisdiction, or Rump of the *Roman* Tyranny', undermining sovereign rights, 'heaving at the Kings Supremacy'.[99] Hobbes invoked the rhetoric of submission to royal authority in order to justify his dissent from clerical power, offering his obedience to the church, not every theologian thereof; to the 'Supream Pastor, which is the King', not to 'inferior Pastors' – mere bishops![100] Hobbes's ecclesiology may be summarised in a single angry sentence. 'The best government in Religion is by Episcopacy, but in the King's Right, not in their own.'[101]

HUNTING HOBBISTS

After 1662, the Church may have been a greater threat to Hobbes than Hobbes was to the Church. The restoration of a narrow and intolerant establishment marked the triumph of priestcraft. Some churchmen nevertheless saw Hobbist ideas infiltrating not only court wit and libertinism but also the clergy. If Hobbes was a scoundrel, Hobbism in the clergy was a scandal. The publication of a manuscript which appeared to show that the archiepiscopal father of the Reformation, Thomas Cranmer, had toyed with the idea of a priestly monarch, exasperated high churchmen.

[97] Hobbes, *Mr Hobbes Considered*, p. 45. [98] Hobbes, *Mr Hobbes Considered*, p. 44.
[99] Hobbes, *Answer to Bramhall*, pp. 32, 41, 126 (qu.), 75 (qu.).
[100] Hobbes, *Answer to Bramhall*, pp. 108–9, 118 (qu.), 81–2 (qu.).
[101] Hobbes, *Answer to Bramhall*, p. 105.

Labelling those who publicised the manuscript Hobbists was a useful polemical strategy.[102]

In April 1540 Henry VIII had reviewed doctrine and ceremonies by means of collating written opinions from divines of varying shades of belief, opinions which would be reprised in the *Necessary Doctrine for a Christen Man* of 1543.[103] The commission on doctrine, chaired by Cranmer, considered seventeen 'questions' on the definition, nature, and necessity of sacraments.[104] Questions nine to fourteen discussed the status of bishops and priests and who had power to make them.[105]

The ninth question put to the divines was 'whether the apostles lacking a higher power, as in not having a christian king among them, made bishops by that necessity, or by authority given them by God'. Cranmer's response, the longest he made to any of the questions, showed a remarkable distaste for the pre-Constantinian church,[106] which was 'constrained of necessity' to appoint ministers by common consent. This reply, unique in its pejorative connotations, included the atypical claim that God committed to kings 'the whole cure of all their subjects, as well concerning the administration of God's word for the cure of souls [as civil matters]'. Bishops, priests, and vicars were akin to officers of state, appointed in similar ways by kings; consecration was an optional ceremony, conferring no greater grace on ecclesiastical than on civil office. The extremism of Cranmer's response is evidenced by comparison to those who argued not for *iure divino* apostolic ordination, but by those who stated that Christian princes, had they existed, would have nominated bishops.[107]

102 On the manuscript and the debate, see Diarmaid MacCulloch, *Thomas Cranmer: A Life* (New Haven, 1996), pp. 276–80; John Marshall, 'The Ecclesiology of the Latitude-Men, 1660–1689: Stillingfleet, Tillotson, and "Hobbism"', *Journal of Ecclesiastical History*, 36 (1985), pp. 407–27; J. A. I. Champion, *The Pillars of Priestcraft Shaken: The Church of England and its Enemies, 1660–1730* (Cambridge, 1992), pp. 88–90.

103 MacCulloch, *Cranmer*, pp. 276–7.

104 An original is extant in BL, Cotton Cleopatra Ev, no. 3, fos. 36ff. The whole was reprinted in Gilbert Burnet, *The History of the Reformation of the Church of England, the First Part, of the Progress Made in it During the Reign of K. Henry the VIII* (1679), appx, pp. 201–44. Cranmer's responses are available from John Strype, *Memorials of … Thomas Cranmer* (3 vols., Oxford, repr. 1848–53), I.417–23; Thomas Cranmer, *Miscellaneous Writings and Letters*, ed. John Edmund Cox (Cambridge, 1846), pp. 115–17; partly printed in Edward Stillingfleet, *Irenicum* (1660), pp. 391–3. A full list of the divines is given in Burnet, *History of the Reformation, Part I*, p. 289. I quote Cranmer's responses from Cox's edition, and other divines' from Burnet's.

105 Strype, *Cranmer*, I.424–8, prints the king's responses to the answers; no responses are extant for questions nine to fourteen; see I.417n. for a comment on dating.

106 As commented by MacCulloch, *Cranmer*, p. 280.

107 Cranmer, *Writings*, p. 116; Burnet, *History of the Reformation, part I*, appx, pp. 220–3.

This issue was raised again in the thirteenth and fourteenth questions, about whether a Christian monarch who had conquered infidels could, clergy being absent, preach and ordain; and whether divine law forbade a king making clergy 'if it so fortuned that all the bishops and priests of a region were dead'. Cranmer's even conceiving such a situation appeared new. The bishop of Rochester commented he had 'never read these cases, neither in Scripture, nor in the Doctors'.[108] Cranmer's own brief replies were uncompromising. To the first: monarchs 'ought indeed' to preach and ordain; to the second: 'it is not forbidden by God's law'. His fellow divines wavered, some arguing that in necessity kings could act in such ways.[109] Cranmer's divergence was thus not so much in the bare idea of royal ordinations as in his matter-of-fact treatment thereof, never viewing it as an emergency. The period of innovation constrained by necessity was, for him, that of the apostolic era; sacerdotal monarchy seemed the norm.

Questions ten, eleven, and twelve dealt with the relative powers of episcopacy and presbytery. Cranmer's account of consecration as an *iure humano* ceremony conflicted with his colleagues' insistence on imposition of hands at minimum. In response to the question of whether 'only a bishop, may make a priest', Cranmer responded that 'princes and governors' might do so

> by the authority of God committed to them, and the people also by their election: for as we read that bishops have done it, so christian emperors and princes usually have done it; and the people, before christian princes were.

Again this departed from a milder account by some others of how magisterial consent to consecrations was needed. Rochester said only bishops could ordain, but warned that 'no Bishop being subject to a Christian Prince, may either give Orders or Excommunicate, or use any manner of Jurisdiction, or any part of his Authority, without Commission from the King, who is Supreme Head of that Church whereof he is a Member'.[110]

Cranmer thus undermined bishops from below (only civil promotion elevating them over priests) and from above (by a sacerdotal supremacy), doubly damning him in the eyes of some Restoration churchmen. But others laid bare his views. Edward Stillingfleet's reconciliatory manoeuvres publicised Cranmer's opinions at the very moment of the Restoration.

[108] Burnet, *History of the Reformation, part I*, appx, p. 232.
[109] Cranmer, *Writings*, p. 117; Burnet, *History of the Reformation, part I*, appx, pp. 232–6.
[110] Cranmer, *Writings*, p. 117; Burnet, *History of the Reformation, part I*, appx, pp. 226–31 (qu. 226).

Irenicum argued that divine law decreed church government necessary, but left its form indifferent, determinable by the civil magistrate. Chapter 8, which claimed that Reformed divines had held church-polity to be mutable, began by quoting Cranmer's 'ascribing the particular Form of Government in the Church to the determination of the Supreme Magistrate'. The archbishop 'instrumental in our Reformation' did not think episcopacy 'a distinct order from Presbytery of Divine Right' but 'a prudent constitution of the Civil Magistrate for the better governing in the Church'.[111] Stillingfleet, mistakenly dating the manuscript to 1547, did not comment on sacerdotal supremacy, and his appendix of 1662 refuting charges of Erastianism did not discuss the manuscript.[112]

The potential explosiveness of Stillingfleet's discovery went unrecognised until John Durel's defence of the Church, published in 1669. Durel found the views expressed in the manuscript 'incredible' and 'amazing', for 'in this Cranmer clearly thinks as Erastus'.[113] Was the document – never cited by puritans, nor Foxe, nor other historians – genuine? Furnished with a transcription, Durel noted that Cranmer had subscribed not only his own paper but also that of 'Leighton' (Richard Layton, who expressed less Erastian sentiments than the archbishop), and condemned Stillingfleet for omitting this fact.[114] Durel pardoned Cranmer's sentiments as part of an excusable, though excessive, reaction against papalism. Past errors were clear, future truth obscure: 'no-one should be surprised' that Cranmer 'erred in some matters concerning ecclesiastical regiment'.[115] But Durel's judiciousness was not disinterested. A leading figure in the French stranger church in London, he constantly encouraged what one contemporary called an 'Anglo-Gallicane' style.[116] To recruit Cranmer for the episcopal side was vital to such an enterprise.

The full manuscript, providing the opinions of others as well as Cranmer, was printed only in 1679, in Gilbert Burnet's *History of the*

111 Stillingfleet, *Irenicum*, p. 393.

112 His misdating derived from his discovery of the manuscript together with plans for canon law reform: Stillingfleet, *Irenicum*, p. 386, relying on Foxe; Edward Stillingfleet, *A Discourse Concerning the Power of Excommunication in a Christian Church, by Way of Appendix to the Irenicum* (1662).

113 John Durel, *Sanctæ ecclesiæ Anglicanæ … vindiciæ* (1669), pp. 326–7: 'mira mihi, & quasi incredibilia', 'in iis enim plane cum *Erasto* sentit *Cranmerus*'.

114 Durel, *Sanctæ ecclesiæ Anglicanæ*, p. 328.

115 Durel, *Sanctæ ecclesiæ Anglicanæ*, pp. 327–8: '*Cranmerum* eo tempore licet animum ad Reformationem propensum haberet multis tamen adhuc erroribus circa ipsam doctrinam mancipatum fuisse; Unde nemo mirabitur si circa Ecclesiasticum Regimen aliquid quoque erraverit', 'in via errorum se diu ambulasse cognoscebant, sed rectam viam nondum repererant'.

116 Quoted in Vivienne Larminie, 'John Durel', *ODNB*.

Reformation.[117] Dating the manuscript to 1539/40, Burnet explained how the Henrician Reformation had often proceeded by collating written opinions of divines on set questions. In the main body of his book, over a hundred pages away from the source, Burnet admitted that Cranmer had 'some singular opinions' about 'Ecclesiastical Offices', but insisted that these 'were not established as the Doctrine of the Church, but laid aside as particular conceits of his own, and it seems that afterwards he changed his opinion'. By later subscribing the *Necessary Doctrine for a Christen Man*, Cranmer endorsed a view 'directly contrary to those opinions set down in these Papers'.[118]

Burnet's apparent care to balance evidence with reassurance was not appreciated by the high churchman Simon Lowth, who launched an attack on him, Stillingfleet, and those within the Church of England who reduced episcopacy's status relative to both presbyters and monarchs. Discrediting the manuscript (but not its author) vindicated 'our Church from Erastianism, and [shows] that her Reformation did not enstate all Church-Power'.[119] Lowth suggested that the manuscript was either copied or presented erroneously. He repeatedly rebuked Burnet for not making it clearer that Cranmer had subscribed Layton's paper as well as his own.[120] Dismissing the manuscript as a private opinion, he suggested (echoing Durel) that the Henrician Reformation had toyed with several ideas before deciding which to adopt officially. Why focus on Cranmer when in the same document eight other divines had stated that royal supremacy did *not* mean sacerdotal power?[121] Lowth nevertheless distorted the debate by comparing Cranmer's responses with those of the archbishop of York – more uncompromising than the majority.[122]

Lowth's text evinced an almost desperate denial of any ideas of sacerdotal supremacy. Selden and 'his great Master *Erastus*'[123] passed their errors, via Hobbes's account of clergy as civil servants, to men *inside* the Restoration Church: Stillingfleet and Tillotson. Yet this dangerous mistake originated

[117] Burnet, *History of the Reformation, part I*, appx, p. 201, stated the manuscript was from Stillingfleet; he was not granted access to the Cotton manuscripts (see Champion, *Pillars of Priestcraft Shaken*, p. 32).

[118] Burnet, *History of the Reformation, part I*, p. 289.

[119] Simon Lowth, *Of the Subject of Church-Power* (1685), sig. A4v.

[120] Lowth, *Church-Power*, sig. [A7]v, p. 486; also Simon Lowth, *A Second Letter to Dr Burnet* (1684), pp. 3–5; Simon Lowth, *A Letter to Edw. Stillingfleet* (1687 (licensed 19 July 1686)), pp. 60–2 (citing Durel).

[121] Lowth, *Church-Power*, pp. 487–9.

[122] E.g. he was one of only two to flatly deny royal powers to ordain if no clergy existed: Burnet, *History of the Reformation, part I*, appx, p. 234.

[123] Lowth, *Church-Power*, pp. 191 (qu.), 193.

in the 'Whimsical Brains of some one or two'. The Thirty-Nine Articles had denied the 'sinister Consequences' which had been affixed to the early Elizabethan supremacy, 'particularly that the King was declared a Priest, impower'd to administer in Divine Service'.[124] The orthodox Church of England thought sacerdotal power neither held by nor even deriving from the prince, who 'is in himself neither Bishop nor Pastor, can neither officiate in the high Affairs of Salvation, nor ordain, substitute and depute others to do it'. Constantine was called a bishop, but this had reference purely to external governance, not sacred functions.[125]

While Burnet's first response to Lowth defended the integrity of the manuscript and his edition thereof,[126] his second reply finally paid attention to the opinions of those other than Cranmer. Layton and Thomas Robertson, whose papers Cranmer signed, argued that the exercise of clerical functions needed magisterial consent, 'which is all that most Erastians plead for' and 'that in Cases of Necessity Princes may make both Bishops and Priests, and I know few Erastians that plead for more'. Burnet smugly stated that only his new evidence of Cranmer's endorsing the *Necessary Doctrine* prevented Presbyterians and Erastians citing him.[127] Both sides were, therefore, beginning to conflate sacerdotal supremacy with Erastianism.

In an epistle dedicatory dated 1 June 1685, Stillingfleet briefly refuted Lowth. He mentioned the Cranmer manuscript very little, wearily saying the debate over it had grown stale.[128] Whilst Stillingfleet had indeed written in 1679 that 'he would not have said' 'many things' in *Irenicum* if writing it again,[129] Lowth's response offered a lengthy diatribe of disbelief that Stillingfleet was sufficiently ecclesiologically orthodox (i.e. as episcopalian as Lowth). Had Stillingfleet repented, he would not have sent a 'vagrant, illegitimate Script', undated and lacking provenance, to Burnet for publication. Citing Durel's list of writers who would undoubtedly have employed the document against the church had they known of it, Lowth added venomously 'how came Mr *Hobbs* not to find it out?'[130] Lowth printed parallel passages from the manuscript and *Leviathan*,

124 Lowth, *Church-Power*, pp. 137, 432.
125 Lowth, *Church-Power*, pp. 62 (qu.), 67, 137.
126 Gilbert Burnet, *A Letter from Gilbert Burnet … to Mr Simon Lowth* (1685), pp. 2–5; Gilbert Burnet, *A Letter Occasioned by the Second Letter to Dr Burnet* (1685), pp. 5–6.
127 Burnet, *Letter Occasioned by the Second Letter*, pp. 4–5.
128 Edward Stillingfleet, *A Sermon Preached at a Publick Ordination at St Peter's Cornhill, March 15th 1684/5* (1685), ep. ded., sig. [b2]r–v.
129 Edward Stillingfleet, *Several Conferences Between a Romish Priest, a Fanatick Chaplain, and a Divine of the Church of England* (1679), p. 148.
130 Lowth, *Letter to Edw. Stillingfleet*, pp. 57–8.

since 'you' (attributing Cranmer's views to Stillingfleet) 'and Mr *Hobbs* so exactly jump together'.[131] Whereas the first half of Lowth's *Letter* had criticised Stillingfleet for undermining episcopacy, the second half shifted to attacking sacerdotal supremacy. 'Now you place in [the king] the whole Priesthood … [so] not that the King may govern the Church by a parity, or imparity of Officers; but that he may govern it without any, or consecrate whom he please.'[132] As if, Lowth scorned, consecration was but a *iure humano* ceremony – exactly the view which Cranmer implied.[133]

In 1687 new polemicists reiterated rather than reignited the debate. Robert Grove, arguing for Stillingfleet, invoked the heated debates on Henrician supremacy to excuse Cranmer's attributing 'as much to the King, as ever had been usurped by the *Pope*', and added that veneration of the early reformer did not bind men to follow his private, uncertain, and later abandoned view.[134] Replying to Grove, Samuel Grascome reiterated Lowth's condemnation of Stillingfleet[135] and Burnet for printing a document 'fitter for the Fire than for the Press … to scandalize our Reformation [and] expose the greatest Prelate that was concerned in it'. Restoration churchmen could hardly welcome a manuscript 'which Sacrificeth their whole Order to the pleasure of the Magistrate, or the *Mobile*, and actually degrades them into the Rank of Presbyters'.[136] It is unsurprising to discover that, after 1689, Grove became a Revolution bishop and Grascome a nonjuror.

Significantly, Restoration high churchmen like Lowth and Grascome did not simply jettison Cranmer. Not only was such a response impossible once his ideas had openly circulated, but the importance of Reformation history to Restoration praxis was so fundamental that it still mattered if, over a century earlier, Cranmer had said that bishops were presbyters and monarchs were priests. The manuscript had to be discredited and Cranmer reclaimed as an episcopal divine. The polemic also exposed fissures within the Church: those like Lowth and Grascome feared nonconformists and Hobbes himself less than 'Men of Latitudinarian and Erastian Principles' *inside* the Church.[137] Naturally, high churchmen endeavoured to discredit their irenic counterparts by associating them with figures such as Hobbes,

[131] Lowth, *Letter to Edw. Stillingfleet*, pp. 43–6 (qu. 43).
[132] Lowth, *Letter to Edw. Stillingfleet*, pp. 47 (qu.), 25–6, 29–31.
[133] Lowth, *Letter to Edw. Stillingfleet*, p. 32; Cranmer, *Writings*, pp. 116–17.
[134] Robert Grove, *An Answer to Mr Lowth's Letter to Dr Stillingfleet* (1687), pp. 30 (qu.), 33.
[135] Samuel Grascome, *A Letter to a Friend in Answer to a Letter* (1688), pp. 14–15, 21, 24.
[136] Grascome, *Letter to a Friend*, pp. 17, 8. [137] Grascome, *Letter to a Friend*, p. 6.

often quite unjustly.[138] Such strategies were understandable when used by those who firmly believed the 'worst of *Hereticks*' to be those 'that arise among ourselves'.[139] More incredible is the continuation of this debate under James II, when there were more pressing threats to the Church. An Erastian or Hobbist view of the supremacy was calamitous, but combined with a Catholic monarch it could be catastrophic.

138 Marshall, 'Latitude-Men'. 139 Lowth, *Letter to Edw. Stillingfleet*, p. 13.

CHAPTER 6

Catholics and Anglicans: James II and Catholic supremacy

To be a Catholic in seventeenth-century England was to court opprobrium, social exclusion, and political suspicion. While in practice Englishmen co-existed with their Catholic neighbours, they feared and reviled the vaguer bogeyman of the papist. The spectre of popery haunted British kings and it twice derailed Stuart monarchs, in the mid-century Civil Wars and in the Revolution of 1688. If Charles I had lost his kingdoms because he was thought to have countenanced creeping crypto-Catholicism at court, and Charles II had been rocked by the Exclusion Crisis partly over fears of a popish successor, what chance did a dedicated overtly Catholic king have? James's vow upon his accession to 'preserve the government in Church and State as it is by law established' might have provided limited reassurance when the nation called to mind similar early promises by the previous Catholic monarch, Mary I.[1] From the incense burned at the Mass which James attended nine days after his accession Protestant nostrils imbibed no holy aroma, but rather the acrid whiff of Smithfield flames.

James was undoubtedly committed to improving the status of his co-religionists, although J. R. Jones and John Miller have seen this as providing security for Catholic worship and rights (in James's language, 'establishment') rather than aiming at a Catholic national church ('entire establishment'), at least in James's own lifetime.[2] This project, ambitious enough for any late seventeenth-century king, was made more difficult by James's authoritarian instincts and lack of political sensitivity. Like his father, James fundamentally failed to understand his subjects' sentiments, which meant that they perceived him to be establishing despotic

[1] In 1553 Mary had proclaimed that she would refrain from coercing her people into Catholicism until a parliament repealed Protestant legislation; the extent of Catholic restoration thus surprised some.

[2] J. R. Jones, 'James II's Revolution: Royal Policies, 1686–92', in Jonathan I. Israel, ed., *The Anglo-Dutch Moment* (Cambridge, 1991), pp. 54–5; John Miller, *James II* (1979), p. 126.

Francophile popery, whether or not he actually intended to. Like his father, James stretched his prerogative and exploited legal ambiguity and loopholes rather than totally ignoring the law. Similarly, both kings' unwillingness to even pretend to listen to unwelcome counsel alienated men into opposing them. Ironically, James's concern to avoid Charles I's fate meant that he obstinately refused to make concessions even when a more flexible posture might have helped his designs. Even Miller, who led the revisionist march to rehabilitate James, admits that the king was unable to comprehend the depth of English anti-popery.[3] Reflexive distrust of popery meant that James's offers, whether to uphold the Anglican Church or to tolerate Dissent, were treated with suspicion. The king did much to strengthen this. Incapable of discerning the difference between opposition and rebellion, he did not comprehend that Anglican ideas of obedience contained large religious caveats. He offered indulgence to Dissenters, but only grudgingly accepted the Huguenot refugees for whom nonconformists felt sympathy; James had an account of French persecution burned by the hangman and issued a *quo warranto* against the Huguenot church in London. By late 1688 James had irrevocably alienated most sections of society as well as – perhaps crucially – his Dutch son-in-law by his adherence to Louis XIV.

Contrary to popular perception, James's Catholic kingship did not mean subservience to the papacy: a Gallican model of royal sway over the church under the pope's spiritual primacy attracted him. But the implementation of his plans recalled Henry VIII's England as much as Louis XIV's France. Steve Pincus has recently emphasised the Gallican nature of James's vision for a restored Catholic church, calling James's programme 'Catholic modernity'. Pincus challenges the revisionist scholarship which rehabilitated James as a moderate tolerationist king whose willingness to countenance Dissent provoked Anglican opposition and a conservative revolution.[4] Instead, he sees James as committed to a 'modern' French Catholicism independent of papal control, intolerant, with a 'modern' state apparatus. However, what Pincus calls 'identity politics' still prevailed under James. An ideology of intolerance, re-Catholicising a Protestant nation by force if need be, was a classic Counter-Reformation mentality. If anyone had novel notions in the late seventeenth century about forging political alliances independently of religious commitments,

[3] Miller, *James II*, p. 68.
[4] Steve Pincus, *1688: The First Modern Revolution* (New Haven, 2009), esp. chs. 5–7.

it was Innocent XI, not James.[5] A degree of independence from papal meddling in a country's Catholicism was an aim not only of Louis XIV and James II, but also of Mary I, Philip II, and numerous Catholic kings. Moreover, although Pincus labels James's Francophile tendencies Gallican, he does not specify what type of Gallicanism he has in mind. James's sovereign prerogatives looked rather unlike the ways in which, according to Anthony Brown, Anglo-Irish Gallicanism had developed in the seventeenth century: dualist, tolerationist, and desperate to prove Catholic loyalty. Serenus Cressy, John Austin, and Peter Walsh occasionally cited French practice, but their concerns arose out of autocthonous debates over the Oath of Allegiance of 1606 and the clash between the Irish Catholic Confederates and the papal nuncio in the 1640s.[6] Thus Cressy modelled various oaths of allegiance for Catholics on the English state oaths, calling kings 'Supreme Governors over the persons of all their Subjects and in all causes even Ecclesiastical wherein their Civil authority is mixed'. Walsh's toleration of two religions matched the French situation between 1594 and 1685, but not that of James's own era.[7] Furthermore, even French Gallicanism was no unified entity. Jotham Parsons's description of sixteenth- and early seventeenth-century Gallicanism charts its origins in humanist readings of history carried out by a particular class of jurists, the *gens du roi*, in the *parlements*. These men, who had no equivalent in England, sought to limit papal involvement in the church in order to stabilise the monarchy after the wars of religion, emphasising their institutional and constitutional role as guarantors of custom, justice, and stability, a theory that collapsed under Richelieu and the *Frondes*.[8] James's regime, and Pincus's account of it, show no knowledge of these multiple Gallican models, all arguably more up to date than James's mentality.

James's policy was neither 'Catholic modernity', nor Enlightened freedom of religious choice. Instead, he used Tudor means to his religious ends, crushing the Anglican Church and helping Catholics and Dissenters through exploiting the royal supremacy. James did not need, and did not use, foreign models of Catholic Reformation, for his English prerogatives sufficed. As this chapter will show, discussions of James's

5 Eoin Devlin, 'English Encounters with Papal Rome in the Late Counter-Reformation, *c.*1685 – *c.*1697' (Ph.D thesis, University of Cambridge, 2010).

6 Anthony J. Brown, 'Anglo-Irish Gallicanism, *c.*1635 – *c.*1685' (Ph.D. thesis, University of Cambridge, 2004).

7 Brown, 'Anglo-Irish Gallicanism', p. 123 and chs. 5–6.

8 Jotham Parsons, *The Church in the Republic: Gallicanism and Political Ideology in Renaissance France* (Washington, 2004).

policies delved into the interstices of English law, English sovereign prerogatives, and English history. While this study conceives of tory Anglican opposition (which itself contained many strands) as important to James's downfall, it does not seek to downplay the roles of whigs or Dutch forces. Considering the relationship between the supremacy and the episcopate naturally tends to explain how and why Anglican-royalists were alienated, although, as Mark Goldie points out, their 'Anglican Revolution' was distinct from the later Williamite one.[9] This chapter steps outside the historiographical debates in which revisionists have rehabilitated royal policies and questioned whether James's overthrow was really a 'sensible', bloodless, but whig-inspired revolution. It shows how debate over James's religious policy discussed Tudor-Stuart statutes and the models of Thomas Cromwell and the High Commission, and did so using the language of *praemunire* and Reformation discourse about obeying God before man.

'James II managed to be both papal and caesaro-papal; his Anglican opponents took care to be neither.'[10] In 1685, sovereign papist Erastianism, or papist caesaropapism, was something that the English had not experienced for over a century. This chapter therefore first considers the way in which James and the political elite negotiated the idea of a Catholic supreme governor. What would happen to the Chapel Royal? Would a Catholic king appoint bishops in the Church of England? Could such a king be called supreme governor of the Church? Secondly, it considers ecclesiological debates between Anglicans and Catholics, showing that these generally continued (albeit with greater frequency and urgency) Carolean claims. If the idea of popish sedition was downplayed under a Catholic sovereign, the Church of England continued to offer a model of episcopal independence from both popes and kings. The chapter then turns to two more 'practical' interactions between the king and the Church: James's Ecclesiastical Commission and the trial of the Seven Bishops, considering arguments about the powers and limits of the royal prerogative which drew on precedents and models specifically related to prior uses of supremacy. In James's reign, the issues of royal, parliamentary, Dissenting, and episcopal relationships came together. For all concerned, the role of the supremacy in the afterlife of the English Reformation was an important key to the ecclesiological politics of Jacobite kingship.

[9] Mark Goldie, 'The Political Thought of the Anglican Revolution', in Robert Beddard, ed., *The Revolutions of 1688* (Oxford, 1991).

[10] Goldie, 'Anglican Revolution', p. 136.

PAPIST CAESAROPAPISM

Disquiet over the prospect of a Catholic head of the church was not confined to whigs and radicals in the decade before James's succession. Whilst the pursuit of Exclusion was the most notorious attack on James, it was far from the only solution sought in the Restoration Crisis of 1678 to 1682. Indeed, limiting York's ecclesiastical powers had been proposed in 1677 in a bill introduced into the Lords by Archbishop Dolben to prevent a Catholic monarch appointing bishops and securing a Protestant education for such a ruler's children. Within forty days of the death of Charles (and all future monarchs), the archbishops and bishops were to meet and tender an oath against transubstantiation to each other. At least nine of them would then, within two weeks, tender that oath to the monarch (or to the regent of a monarch younger than fourteen) and certify the response in chancery. A king who refused to deny transubstantiation would be rendered incapable of appointing prelates; instead, a committee of bishops would nominate three candidates from whom the monarch could choose one. In default of any such choice within thirty days, the first nominee would be appointed. Prelates who failed to comply would lose their sees. Children of a Catholic king would be educated between the ages of seven and fourteen by the two archbishops and the bishops of London, Durham, and Winchester, who would also approve their officials after they were fourteen.[11] This plan would have radically restricted the ecclesiastical supremacy of a Catholic monarch and would have placed a significant amount of patronage, lay as well as ecclesiastical, in the hands of the clergy. It also, perhaps crucially, failed to provide for the (not unlikely) scenario of royal defiance of the clergy, and what happened if king and clergy nominated two different bishops.

Fourteen Lords dissented from this bill, and it caused consternation amongst MPs when debated on 20 and 27 March. The bill's supporters claimed it secured Protestantism while maintaining the royal prerogative (for the king still retained some role in appointments). Its opponents denounced it as a priestly usurpation of the supremacy which was constitutionally invalid as well as repugnantly sacerdotalist. What if the bishops were popish? If not, what happened if the king chose a different bishop entirely? As Harbottle Grimston pointed out, if the bishops were not

[11] HMC, *Ninth Report*, pt II, appx, pp. 81–2; *LJ*, XIII.48, 51, 75; Andrew Marvell, *An Account of the Growth of Popery and Arbitrary Government* (1677), pp. 89–100.

appointed by the king, 'they are all in a *praemunire*'.[12] Underlying this legally accurate point – the statute 25 Henry VIII c. 20 made it *praemunire* to refuse to consecrate a royal nominee – lay an anticlerical sentiment. For some MPs, enduring an episcopalian supremacy was even worse than suffering a Catholic one.

That it was bishops and Anglican royalists who first sought to protect their Church from James was prophetic of his reign. Between late 1678 and early 1681 Charles repeatedly promised parliament that he would consider means to secure Protestantism, short of excluding his brother. Although in November 1678 he wanted to protect the power and just rights of any successor, by April 1679 he offered to 'limit and circumscribe' such a successor's authority. He even declared himself open to such suggestions at the start of the Oxford Parliament of 1681.[13] Charles was most forthcoming in spring 1679 about the possibility of a way to 'distinguish a Papist from a Protestant Successor'. A Catholic king would be obliged to grant ecclesiastical benefices to 'pious and learned Protestants' and appoint Protestant JPs. Parliament, which was to contain no Catholic MPs or Lords, would sit for 'a competent time' upon Charles's death and it would choose privy councillors and judges. It or its nominees would appoint army and naval officers. Such proposals, whether coming from Charles or from MPs, could attract those wary of Exclusion, but were frequently deemed unworkable in a number of ways. Who would determine that a successor was popish? Such a test was 'the most impracticable thing imaginable'.[14] Were such limitations, a 'crown manacled', consistent with the English constitution and with the Oaths of Allegiance and Supremacy? '[The] Nature of our Government is quite contrary to any Expedient. The King names all the Counsellors, Judges, and Bishops, and what manner of King would you make him, by limiting him?'[15] That this position could be held by both Hugh Boscawen, who favoured Exclusion, and those who opposed it, such as Littleton, shows the complexity of alignments. In January 1681 Finch suggested that parliament should appoint privy councillors and make their advice

12 Grey, *Debates*, IV.284–96, 318–26 (qu. 285) (20, 27 Mar. 1677); Mark Goldie, 'Danby, the Bishops and the Whigs', in Tim Harris, Paul Seaward, and Mark Goldie, eds., *The Politics of Religion in Restoration England* (Oxford, 1990), pp. 83–90.

13 Grey, *Debates*, VI.172, VII.158 (qu.), 348, 433, VIII.147, 234–5 (9 Nov. 1678, 30 Apr. 1679, 21 Oct., 9 Nov., 15 Dec. 1680, 4 Jan. 1681).

14 Grey, *Debates*, VII.253 (qu.), 162 (11 May, 30 Apr. 1679).

15 Grey, *Debates*, VII.257, 238, 412–13 (10, 11 May 1679, 2 Nov. 1680). 'Expedient' was the contemporary term for limitations.

binding on the king, a claim rejected by the Exclusionist Birch as contrary to the prerogative.[16]

Exclusion was perhaps *less* radical than limitations that warped the powers of a personal monarchy. Exclusion might also provide a clearer solution to the succession crisis than limitations, for nobody had an acceptable answer to what happened if the king defied the limits. Could such a king be resisted? Was it not an offence to call the king a papist and resist his officials?[17] In a proleptic question in November 1678, Sir George Hungerford (who favoured Exclusion) challenged Secretary Coventry's proposed ban on dispensations for Catholics by asking who could resist them if issued.[18] A Catholic king might summon his fellow-religionists to the Lords and overturn laws limiting him. Limitations, Boscawen argued in May 1679, 'look like gold, but are leaf-gold when you touch them'.[19]

By autumn 1680 these problems led many MPs to think Exclusion the only expedient, although the Lords tried drafting another bill. This stated that parliament would be summoned for six months within thirty days of James's accession and that all ecclesiastical appointments in the royal gift would be 'conferred and presented by direction of the said two Houses of Parliament' to Protestants. James, whose exemption from the Second Test Act would be repealed, could not veto any bills for Protestantism. He could not make civil, ecclesiastical, or military appointments without parliament's consent. Thus far the bill appeared similar to its predecessors. But it also contained mechanisms for overcoming some of their difficulties. Any soldiers appointed by the king alone could be resisted, and were dubbed traitors. When not sitting, parliament would appoint forty-one men to fill offices, and ratify those appointments when it reconvened. The remit of those forty-one men was later expanded to include governance of Irish and foreign policy; and the Lords proposed banishing James until Charles's death. The bill was lost when parliament was dissolved.[20]

Long before James became king, therefore, parliament had discovered the constitutional difficulties of meddling with the royal prerogative. As Francis Winnington bitterly reflected, 'it is easy to argue, that we are

16 Grey, *Debates*, VIII.274 (6 Jan. 1681).

17 Grey, *Debates*, VII.161–2 (12 May 1679); referring to 13 Chas. II c. 1 and 17 Chas. II c. 2.

18 Grey, *Debates*, VI.262 (22 Nov. 1678).

19 Grey, *Debates*, VI.253, VII.259 (qu.) (21 Nov. 1678, 11 May 1679). James was advised that he could not dispense with the Second Test Act: J. P. Kenyon, *Robert Spencer, Earl of Sunderland, 1641–1702* (1958), p. 166.

20 Mark Knights, *Politics and Opinion in Crisis, 1678–81* (Cambridge, 1994), p. 88; HMC, *House of Lords, 1678–88*, pp. 220–2 (qu.); HMC, *Ormonde*, V.502.

inevitably ruined if there be a Popish Successor, but it is hard to say what will save us'.[21] It appeared that Protestants would have to rely on James not abusing his prerogative. But could a Catholic king fulfil his duty to God and to his Protestant people? Would James reject the royal supremacy and subject England to papal control – or would he exploit his ecclesiastical prerogative to undermine the established Church?

James's view of the relative authorities of the king, the pope, and the Church of England was indicated by his attitude to his title of supreme governor of the Church of England. James was not part of that Church, so how could he be its head? The last Catholic monarch, Mary I, had vehemently rejected the title of supremacy – albeit using its powers where they helped her – actions which opened up a multitude of legal problems with writs which omitted her title before parliament had repealed Henrician legislation.[22] In James's accession proclamation he was 'defender of the faith, &c' (although 'etc' was omitted when Garter King of Arms proclaimed his titles at his coronation), the same formula he used when dispensing the Catholic John Massey from taking the state oaths before his degree.[23] However, this omission of 'supreme governor' might not have been very striking, for etceteration was by now common practice. Edward VI and Mary I used 'supreme head' in their accession proclamations. Elizabeth I used 'etc'. James I used neither supreme governor nor etc, whilst his sons reverted to 'etc'. Etceteration was in fact first used in a treaty between Henry VIII and Charles V, as a compromise between English insistence on the use of the title and Spanish opposition to it.[24] If James II did not use 'supreme governor', he was capable of coming pretty near it. In a warrant to Archbishop Sancroft licensing building work in Lambeth churchyard, James (or his ministers) spoke of 'our supreme authority royal and plenitude of power ecclesiastical, as supreme patron of the archiepiscopal see of Canterbury and supreme ordinary in all cases [*sic*] ecclesiastical'.[25] James – however his subjects saw him – was no supine papalist: he would govern his own Catholic church of England without excessive meddling from Rome. If he disdained the

[21] Grey, *Debates*, VII.250 (11 May 1679). [22] See above, p. 44.

[23] *London Gazette*, no. 2009; Francis Sandford, *The History of the Coronation of … James II* (1687), p. 122 (but cf. title page, which has etc); Samuel Weller Singer, ed., *The Correspondence of Henry Hyde* (2 vols., 1828), II.472.

[24] Paul L. Hughes and James F. Larkin, eds., *Tudor Royal Proclamations* (3 vols., New Haven, 1964–9), I.381, II.3, 99; Paul L. Hughes and James F. Larkin, eds., *Royal Proclamations of King James I, 1603–1625* (Oxford, 1973), p. 2; James F. Larkin, ed., *Royal Proclamations of King Charles I, 1625–1646* (Oxford, 1983), p. 2; *A Proclamation of Both Houses of Parliament* (1660); J. J. Scarisbrick, *Henry VIII* (1968), pp. 439–40.

[25] *CSPD, Jan. 1686 – May 1687*, pp. 126–7 (7 May 1686).

title of supreme governor, he was certainly not above using its powers. As his reign progressed, he found these increasingly useful, as he realised that he needed not just to woo Dissenters with a tolerationist stance but also to crush Anglican resistance by jurisdictional force.

James had triumphed over Exclusion, but in 1685 there were significant obstacles to a Catholic, and Catholicising, regime. Popular antipopery was a large cultural obstacle to James's desire to liberate his co-religionists – a barrier which was put in James's mind annually by his failure to suppress (by order in Council) the 5 November celebrations of England's deliverance from popish plots.[26] There were also more precise legal snares which could entrap him and his government, especially that of *praemunire* (undermining royal jurisdiction), an offence which carried some of the heaviest penalties short of death. Since James never even attempted to repeal *praemunire* legislation, it remained illegal to receive or send emissaries to or from Rome, and even to possess Catholic books or spread devotional aids.[27] The papal representative Ferdinando D'Adda waited for months between arriving in England and being formally received at Court. When he was, the Duke of Somerset refused to participate because receiving a papal nuncio was *praemunire*. Somerset reportedly told the king that, if James was above the law, he was not, and that a preemptive pardon would not indemnify him from prosecution.[28] When the City government feasted D'Adda, Roger Morrice thought them guilty of *praemunire*.[29] He made similar criticisms of the unchallenged accession of the Jesuit Petre to the Privy Council in November 1687; whilst Evelyn reported that Sancroft, Halifax, Clarendon, and Nottingham told the king in late October 1688 that conciliar acts in the presence of Catholics were *praemunire* (perhaps a sign of growing Anglican defiance in late 1688).[30] James's ambassador to Rome, the Earl of Castlemaine, was also acting illegally – Lord Chancellor Jeffreys took out a pardon as a precaution against later prosecution for countenancing the embassy. Castlemaine's formal reception by the pope was put off while the terms of

26 *EB*, P654, Q73, Q193–4.

27 13 Eliz. c. 2 (high treason to put papal bulls in ure, *praemunire* to import or receive *Agnus Deis*); 23 Eliz. c. 1 (treason to seduce subjects to Rome); 3 & 4 Jac. I, c. 5 (a fine of 40 shillings per Catholic book possessed).

28 *EB*, Q160, see also P499, P629 (arrival mid Nov. 1685, reception July 1687); Gilbert Burnet, *The History of the Reign of King James the Second* (Oxford, 1852), p. 214; Andrew Barclay, 'The Impact of King James II on the Departments of the Royal Household' (Ph.D thesis, University of Cambridge, 1994), pp. 152–3. Thomas Bruce, second Earl of Ailesbury, also avoided the reception.

29 *EB*, Q194; *The Diary of John Evelyn*, ed. E. S. De Beer (6 vols., Oxford, 1955), IV.563.

30 *EB*, Q200; Evelyn, *Diary*, IV.602–3. All (except perhaps Halifax) were tories.

James's submission to Rome were negotiated; Rome reportedly demanded the recognition of papal supremacy and payment of First Fruits; James eventually admitted the pope's spiritual fatherhood, but refused to countenance papal appointments of bishops or the payment of taxes to Rome. Castlemaine's formal reception finally took place nearly a year after he arrived in Rome.[31]

The difficulties of a supreme governor who was technically in breach of *praemunire* laws symbolised the problems of papist caesaropapism. But if James and his ministers could be 'praemunired' because of their contact with Rome, so too could Anglican bishops for defying the wishes of their royal head. When James left the archbishopric of York vacant, and when he deprived Scottish and suspended English bishops, fears of him issuing dispensations to Catholics to become bishops within the established Church grew. In fact, James went no further than appointing Anglicans whom he thought would support his policies, such as Nathaniel Crewe at Durham, Thomas Sprat at Rochester, and Samuel Parker at Oxford. But there is evidence that the Anglican hierarchy expected a sharper attack. Archbishop King of Dublin asserted that a *praemunire* charge for refusing to consecrate a Catholic bishop was so evil as to be void *ipso facto*,[32] but this was of rather limited practical value. Sancroft took more detailed counsel from his tory legal advisor Roger North on whether he could refuse to consecrate a Catholic bishop without being convicted of *praemunire*.[33]

What North later described as a 'full and particular discourse'[34] began with a lengthy preliminary account of *praemunire* as an unusual legal process, which required even peers (who would be tried by a common jury) to appear in person on a specific day on pain of forfeiture. The consequences of conviction were severe: loss of lands and goods, indefinite imprisonment, and being put out of the king's pleasure (which, until 1564, allowed

[31] For English perceptions of Castlemaine's failure, see Burnet, *History*, pp. 188–91; *EB*, P528, P534, P550, Q19, esp. Q234; but cf. Devlin, 'English Encounters'.

[32] Goldie, 'Anglican Revolution', p. 130.

[33] North acted as Sancroft's advisor on several contentious issues during James's reign. Having himself voted against the dispensing power in the 1685 parliament, he noted that he 'studied the point, collected all the law I could find about it, found seasonable distinctions to reconcile the umbrages some passages in the law books had given to it' and revised his paper for the archbishop. He also wrote on the Ecclesiastical Commission (see below). Sancroft would, North said, write out such papers in his own hand – and many of them are extant both in the British Library and in the Bodleian's Tanner collection. His service did not cease after the Revolution, when as chancellor he kept the archbishop's courts and issued his writs in his name as before, taking no notice of 'a supposed deprivation', refusing to see or act for Tillotson. Augustus Jessop, ed., *The Autobiography of the Hon. Roger North* (1887), pp. 181, 121–3, 113–14. On North's later reflections, see Goldie, 'Anglican Revolution', p. 116.

[34] Jessop, ed., *Autobiography*, p. 122.

anyone to murder the convict). Listing the acts and cases governing *praemunire*, North noted the post-Reformation debate over whether it applied to English ecclesiastical courts. The Jacobean Civilian Thomas Ridley had argued not: the ban on appealing to Rome or 'any other court' from the king's (27 Edw. III st. 1 c. 1) referred to times when the papacy was based outside of Rome, not to English courts. But this was not how the judges had seen it. '*Th*e Eccl*esiastical* Courts of all Sorts incur p*rae*munire, if they entertain Suits bare-fac'd, *tha*t are of Com*mon* Law Jurisd*icio*n.'[35] North then turned to specific instances of *praemunire*, revealing his particular concern by only ever discussing one case: 25 Henry VIII c. 20, which made archiepiscopal refusal to consecrate a king's nominee to a bishopric *praemunire*. Firstly, he charted its Tudor repeal and counter-repeal to show it was still in force, according to the judges in 1607. Secondly, he argued that if the consecration was carried out other than as the Ordinal required, the archbishop had breached the Acts of Uniformity but not committed *praemunire*, for the nominee still became a bishop so long as the substantial elements had been carried out. These substantial aspects did *not* include the state oaths, which ought to be administered but were 'no p*ar*t of *th*e Substance of *th*e Consecr*acio*n'. However, the archbishop was not obliged to continue with the consecration if the nominee refused to take the oaths or to conform to a non-substantial part of the liturgy. And this was not *praemunire*, for the Henrician statute referred to consecration in '<due> Form'. What if the king dispensed with the bishop elect's need to swear the oaths? North felt this was not possible, just as the king could not dispense with a judge's oath, for both judge and bishop were officers, whose duties were 'indispensable' (literally, impossible to dispense). But he refused to say whether *Godden* v. *Hales* had changed this. It was not impossible that the judgment could be applied to more groups than to soldiers, although they provided a different type of service to bishops, who had another 'Interest'.[36]

In the final analysis, North refused to definitively pronounce on what Sancroft should do, this being 'a Matter of Conscience, & Discreti*on*, more *tha*n Law'. If *praemunire* were not a possible charge, then he would advise the archbishop to allow a case to be brought in King's Bench, for the court's decision would be a 'Discharge in omni Foro'. But the risks of *praemunire* were simply too great – 'none will be p*ro*secuted in this kind, but will be convicted'. The Henrician statute would offer little help

[35] Bodl., Tanner MS 459, fos. 74r–91r, qu. fo. 79v. [36] Ibid., fos. 82r–84r.

to the defendant, who would be able to cite only the Act of Uniformity's penalties in favour of his refusal to consecrate. But since these were overridden by the dispensation, the case would have small chance of succeeding. North concluded that it was 'more adviseable to p*ro*ceed, than not', albeit with the caveat that extra-legal considerations might compel a different conclusion. They, he concluded with relief, were not for him to judge.[37] He then went back a stage in the process of appointing a bishop, to the point where a cathedral chapter assembled to 'elect' their prelate (naturally they always chose the royal nominee). There had been a suggestion that when the dean received the king's *congé*, he was obliged to summon the prebends on pain of *praemunire* – but that if they did not come, they were guilty only of canonical disobedience and could avoid electing a new bishop for a limited penalty. But North rejected this, thinking the whole chapter might be held liable. Instead he thought the *congé* needed to be delivered to the prebends in chapter session, so that if no chapter was summoned, they were irregular and liable to be deprived, but not guilty of *praemunire*. The king might issue a *mandamus* to summon the chapter; any refusal to meet would then be subject to common law penalties but not *praemunire*. Signs of the Church's desperation at negotiating its Catholic head were emerging here: North admitted that he offered only 'Thrids [i.e. threads] to hang upo*n*', not a reliable defence.[38] Such dilemmas might soon be impossible to avoid, for there were rumours that the London prebends would use such strategies to avoid electing a new bishop if Compton, at that time suspended, were to be deprived.

James held back from nominating any Catholic bishops to Anglican sees, although he gave the revenues from vacant Church of Ireland livings to Catholic priests and he allowed the convert to Catholicism Edward Sclater to keep the income from his living, substituting a curate.[39] His attitude to court worship was a similar mixture of the offensive and the discreet. The centre of monarchical devotional practice, the Chapel Royal, might have seemed an obvious target for James's Catholicising policy. James quickly seized the chance to openly attend Catholic worship and he erected a Catholic chapel royal. But his appointment of Catholic religious servants was in contrast to what Andrew Barclay has shown to be a predominantly Protestant court.[40] Initially, James was keen 'to avoid all

[37] Ibid., fo. 84r–v. [38] Ibid., fos. 84v–85r.

[39] Pincus, *1688*, p. 163; W. A. Speck, *James II* (Harlow, 2002), p. 102; Edward Vallance, 'Edward Sclater', *ODNB*.

[40] This and the following paragraphs draw largely on Barclay, 'Impact of King James II'; for his general conclusions, see also Andrew Barclay, 'James II's "Catholic" Court', *1650–1850*, 8 (2003), pp. 161–71. Barclay sees this (two parallel established churches) as a possible model for James's kingdom: 'Impact of James II', p. 115.

reasonable cause of complaint' by continuing the Protestant chapel 'in its splendour and order', and insisting that his clerk of the closet, Nathaniel Crewe, unseal the privy oratory which Crewe had shut. This contrasted with James's surprisingly overt Catholic devotions at his ducal oratory. As was traditional, his courtiers escorted him to worship, but they remained in the antechamber – only later did James begin to encourage them to join him.[41]

In parallel with the trends of his reign, James began to act more forcefully against the Anglican chapel in 1686 and 1687. At Windsor he took over the Anglican chapel, leading the staunchly Anglican Evelyn to bemoan the loss of 'the late kings glorious Chapell, now seiz'd on by the Masse-priests'. This may have been no more than a practical measure: the Windsor closet was simply too small for the king. More ominous was the use of Catholic priests and rites when touching for the king's evil.[42] In late 1687 James dismissed his almoner, Bishop Turner, in favour of Cardinal Howard (whose place was *de facto* filled by Bishop Leyburne), a rare direct replacement of an Anglican by a Catholic. James also removed William Holder, sub-dean of the Chapel Royal, from his place as sub-almoner, perhaps to make way for Edward Petre.[43] Petre was Clerk of the Closet of James's largest Catholic prestige project, his ostentatious new chapel at Whitehall. This theatre of conspicuous Catholic consumption had been planned as early as 1685, was constructed in 1686, and expanded in 1687. James ordered a fine altarpiece in white marble with veined pilasters, and had his chapel furnished by the best artists: Grinling Gibbons and Arnold Quellin, and painted by Antonio Verrio. The ceiling was embellished with 8132 leaves of gold and a huge altarpiece was constructed including a Nativity scene and four statues, which James was still paying for as late as October 1688, the dying days of his regime. Evelyn could hardly believe that 'I should ever have lived to see such things in the K. of Englands palace, after it had pleased God to enlighten this nation'.[44] Although the rest of his court underwent financial retrenchment, James found money for his chapel, spending £3,983, half as much again as the Anglican Chapel Royal received (£2,600). His patronage repeated that for Charles II's new chapel constructed at Windsor in 1680–2, although Charles's was decorated with carvings in white natural wood and depicted Easter and healing miracles. Charles paid Verrio £1,050 for painting the walls and ceilings, James £1,250. Charles paid over £1,000 to Gibbons and £1,132 for

[41] Barclay, 'Impact of James II', pp. 105–6, 109.
[42] Evelyn, *Diary*, IV.518; Barclay, 'Impact of James II', p. 110.
[43] Barclay, 'Impact of James II', pp. 113–14. [44] Evelyn, *Diary*, IV.534–5.

gilding, but repaired the organ (£100) where James had to purchase a new one (£1,100).[45]

The Anglican Chapel Royal symbolised the presence and yet absence of its supreme head by maintaining its staff, services, and obsequies to a now empty throne. Princess Anne, James's Chamberlain Mulgrave, his Clerk of the Closet, and Protestant household attended, but the throne was left vacant. Yet the Chapel played a more than symbolic role, with sermons by leading preachers unafraid to challenge popery. In 1686 Bishop Frampton preached on the need for constancy in affliction, applying this to the Church; in 1687 John Tillotson attacked apostasy to Rome and 'magnified those who … choose rather to be God's favourites than the King's'. Evelyn described Anne, a host of nobles, and a crowd rushing to hear Bishop Ken in 1687 denounce the superstitious and persecuting scribes and Pharisees who preferred tradition to scripture, a reference which everyone – according to Evelyn – understood.[46] It was, again, Ken who preached in April 1688 on the calamity of the true Judean church under Babylon, urging patient submission to tyranny before God would revive the true religion. Ken painted himself as a prophet, fearing none but God, with a divine duty to speak – whether or not the court wanted to hear his words. He told how the true church was held captive under the Babylonians (Catholics) and their allies the Edomites (the Dissenters) who revolted from Judah. There was little courting of Dissenters here; instead they were told to reconcile themselves to the true church.[47] And Ken described, precisely and concisely, the Anglican attitude to James when he explained how the Jews were:

> To subject their persons to the Babylonish government, but not to prostitute their consciences to the Babylonish idolatry, whensoever the commands of God, and of the king of Babylon, stood in competition. To have then obeyed the king, had not been allegiance but apostasy. In such cases, the true Israelites would always be martyrs, but never rebels.[48]

Ken preached the virtues of repentance and submission to ill-fortune, apt topics for a Passion Day sermon – and especially apt for his own

[45] H. M. Colvin et al., eds., *The History of the King's Works*, vol. v (1976), pp. 287–93, 326. Similarly, James made do with worshipping in the gallery at Holyrood until his accession, after which he restored the Abbey Church, which was then sacked in the Revolution. Charles A. Malcolm, *Holyrood* (1937), pp. 141–4.

[46] *The Diary of Thomas Cartwright, Bishop of Chester* (1843), p. 44 (qu.); Evelyn, *Diary*, iv.503, 541.

[47] Thomas Ken, 'A Sermon Preached at Whitehall upon Passion Sunday [1688]', in *Prose Works*, ed. James Thomas Round (1838), pp. 176, 180, 186. The sermon was posthumously published and probably preached *memoriter*.

[48] Ken, 'Sermon', p. 198.

church's situation. As a reward for patient suffering, the Judeans were rescued by God, who freed them (but not the Edomites) from Babylon, crushing their opponents to leave them in splendour.[49] Ken disclaimed explicitly mapping any of these groups on to current ones – he hardly needed to – except Judah, the model for the Church of England's 'fervent prayers and tears'.[50]

Ken's prophetic models won over their kings. Micah, whom the 'assistance of God's spirit made ... wonderfully successful', was able, however, to speak directly to his king in person. That monarch, Hezekiah, 'liked the preacher the better, for the conscientious discharge of his prophetic duty'. Ken had little hope of such outcomes with James, though in the quasi-public court pulpit he blamed not the monarch but evil talemongers who misrepresented preachers to a king 'in whose royal candour a faithful preacher might be secure'.[51] Underlying Ken's sermon was Anglican outrage at being denied their rightful access to the royal presence, particularly that privileged access to the king's conscience which could be gained in the Chapel Royal. There was also a particular bitterness in the galling rhetoric of Ken, usually deferential, and who would become one of the mildest of the nonjurors. The previous year, James, without notifying the bishop, had employed Ken's cathedral seat, Bath Abbey, to touch for the king's evil using Henrician Catholic rites, prefacing the ceremony with a proselytising sermon. Ken refused to wage a public war over this, instead preaching the following Sunday on the advantages of charitably lending the Catholics the Abbey in order that more people could be cured – thus depriving his opponents of a victory.[52] In what should have been the more secluded space of the Chapel Royal, he could afford a ninety-minute harangue – even if, as Evelyn's account proved, the public squeezed in if they could. To his monarch's face he was even blunter. When James's 'royal candour' manifested itself in a summons to the royal closet, the bishop was hardly cowed, telling the king that 'if his Majesty had not neglected his own duty of being present', unfair accusations would not have been made.[53] Ken had some experience in rebuking kings, for he had refused (with success) to house Charles II's mistress, Nell Gwyn, when that king came to visit in 1683. And within a few weeks, he would help lead the opposition to reading James's Second Declaration of

[49] Ken, 'Sermon', pp. 198, 200–2. [50] Ken, 'Sermon', pp. 203–4.

[51] Ken, 'Sermon', pp. 177–8, 203.

[52] E. H. Plumptre, *The Life of Thomas Ken*, 2nd rev. edn (2 vols., 1890), 1.279–80.

[53] Plumptre, *Life*, 1.288–93; William Hawkins, *A Short Account of the Life of ... Thomas Ken* (1713), pp. 17–18.

Indulgence, a document which was declaimed in the Anglican Chapel Royal, but only by a choirboy.[54]

ANGLICANS VERSUS CATHOLICS

The torrent of literature which renewed arguments between Catholics and Anglicans during James's reign has never been fully analysed by historians. The present study leaves aside the significant proportion of this which engaged with doctrinal questions, instead focusing on the ecclesiological aspects of the quarrel. As will be shown, the anti-papal case was put more forcefully by the Church as its polemical attention was drawn away from Dissent and towards Rome. But the fundamentals of the argument were well-established, continuing themes from Charles II's reign and before. Furthermore, even if James had a Gallican understanding of his ecclesiastical authority, that point was lost on Anglicans, whose claims were targeted at popes.

Two strands of argument were directed at Catholics before 1685. The first was their dubious loyalty: that they could never be trustworthy subjects – or perhaps subjects at all – of English Protestant sovereigns. A wealth of texts, sermons, and images propounded such claims, but a work of 1675 by the high-church theorist and future nonjuror Henry Dodwell provides a good example. *Some Considerations of Present Concernment; How Far the Romanists May be Trusted by Princes of Another Perswasion* rejected any notion that the Court of Rome (papal temporal claims) could be detached from the Church of Rome (papal spiritual authority). 'Out of Councils, there is not as much as a Notion of the *Church* of *Rome* contradistinct from the *Court*, and acting independently on [*sic*] it.'[55] Whereas many defenders of the royal supremacy had sought to show a tradition of immemorial royal independence of monarchs and cited examples of kingly defiance of medieval popes, Dodwell ironically inverted this to argue that medieval England was subservient to Rome's decrees. King John had submitted to the pope, the canons of the Fourth Lateran Council on transubstantiation had been received.[56] Dodwell thus rhetorically inflated the dangers of allowing any leeway to English Catholics, who would consider

[54] William Marshall, 'Thomas Ken', *ODNB*; Evelyn, *Diary*, IV.577–8, 584; HMC, *Le Fleming*, p. 210.

[55] Henry Dodwell, *Some Considerations of Present Concernment; How Far the Romanists May be Trusted by Princes of Another Perswasion* (1675), pp. 293 (qu.), 20, 288, 303.

[56] Dodwell, *Some Considerations*, pp. 182–3, 15–16. On Catholic obligations to believe this, see Isaac Barrow, *A Treatise of the Pope's Supremacy*, in *Theological Works*, ed. Alexander Napier, vol. VIII (Cambridge, 1859), pp. 35, 38.

themselves bound to submit to papal decisions if they conflicted with royal orders. He also showed a classic Reformation concern in the example he picked to illustrate Catholic threats: that of Thomas Becket, the target of Henrician attack. Dodwell argued for over a hundred pages that Catholics were obliged to believe Becket a saint, and thus to think his defiance of the king exemplary. It is notable that Dodwell twice insisted that Becket was not wrong *per se* to defend the church's rights against an intrusive monarch, merely that he had overreacted and trespassed on royal authority.[57] Having demonstrated the danger of Catholic principles, the second half of Dodwell's book was devoted to showing that kings could never be so certain of the personal loyalty of Catholics to trust that their piety would override their seditious teachings. He struggled to find a formula by which this might be secured, eventually suggesting one which would reject any possible deposing power, promised by the clergy in a council which they believed could defy the pope and a general council – almost an impossibility, although he also thought that some small favours, gradually doled out, would foster more loyalty.[58] Nothing symbolised better the mental block on the idea of Catholic loyalism than Dodwell's comment that, insofar as individual Catholics were obedient, they were Protestants.[59]

In another work of 1676, Dodwell switched to the second strand of anti-papal rhetoric: the attack on papal supremacy as justifying the separation of the Church of England from Rome. It is telling that it was this, not his earlier work, which was reprinted in 1688. The depiction of Catholics as dangerous insurrectionists did not befit the new circumstances of James's reign. From 1685 to 1688 the danger was not Catholic sedition, but supine sovereign surrender to Rome's dictates. Thus the second strand of anti-papal argument, papal usurpation of 'all the ancient constitutions, privileges, and liberties of Churches' (rather than of kings), intensified.[60] The depiction of the English Church as reviving the pristine primitive ecclesiology of ante-papal Christianity had been useful to earlier theorists, since it neatly converted Reformation into restoration. Rooted in Interregnum thought,[61] it was perpetuated after 1660 by Isaac Barrow, William Cave,

57 Dodwell, *Some Considerations*, pp. 54–5, 100; see also p. 403 and pp. 34–146 on Becket.

58 Dodwell, *Some Considerations*, pp. 390–5, 418.

59 Dodwell, *Some Considerations*, p. 407. See also, on papal deposing, Barrow, *Pope's Supremacy*, pp. 20–5, 34.

60 Barrow, *Pope's Supremacy*, p. 46 (qu.); William Sherlock, *A Vindication of Some Protestant Principles of Church-Unity and Catholick-Communion* (1688), p. 11; William Cave, *A Dissertation Concerning the Government of the Ancient Church by Bishops, Metropolitans, and Patriarchs*, ed. Henry Cary (Oxford, 1840, first publ. 1683), p. 360.

61 See Chapter 1, pp. 83–7.

and William Sherlock. It was expressed fulsomely under Charles II, but its great advantage under James was that it allowed a defence of English episcopal rights against the pope and silent sidelining of the royal supremacy. It also had implications for that supremacy.

Barrow divided his massive attack on papal supremacy, posthumously printed in 1680, into seven 'suppositions' made by Catholics: Peter's primacy, derivable by others; that Peter was bishop of Rome, and remained there until his death; that his successors at Rome thus had an *iure divino* supremacy, that this had been continually held, and was immutable. Some writers never got past the biblical exegesis necessary to demolish the first supposition. Many granted Peter to be unique in his worth, in repute, perhaps (though Barrow disliked this) in 'order'; some were amenable to Rome inheriting these characteristics – at least while its bishops were pious and orthodox.[62] But, as Cave noted, this meant 'a primacy of order … not an universal, monarchical, uncontrollable power and supremacy … Is there no difference between precedency and supremacy, between dignity and dominion?'[63] With regard to jurisdiction, all the apostles were equal. When Christ told Peter He would build His church 'upon this rock', when he ordered Peter to 'feed my sheep', when he gave him the Keys, Peter represented all the apostles and thus all bishops (Matt. 16:18–19, John 21:17). 'All the Apostles were *Heads*, *Rectors*, and *Pastors* of the *universal Church*, and … the *whole World* was their *Diocess*.'[64] Barrow expended page after page after page showing that the rights of the bishops of Rome were held by each and every later bishop, and that popes usurped nineteen types of sovereignty from bishops and/or emperors.[65]

The case for apostolic equality, a staple of anti-papal argument since the Reformation, was immeasurably strengthened by the Anglican belief that such a model had been practised in the early church. The evidence drawn from this loomed far larger in seventeenth-century accounts than in those of the Tudor period. Indeed, it is no exaggeration to say that Restoration churchmen's ecclesiological hero was Cyprian, the third-century African bishop who had upheld orthodoxy and denounced schism, but also acted with respect for and yet independently of Rome. Was the third-century African church free of Rome's meddling? So too

62 Barrow, *Pope's Supremacy*, pp. 66, 76, 144, and, on order, pp. 71–2; Sherlock, *Church-Unity*, p. 44 (order in the sense of speaking in turn); Cave, *Dissertation*, pp. 371, 387, 442.

63 Cave, *Dissertation*, p. 387; Barrow, *Pope's Supremacy*, p. 78; [Nicholas Stratford?], *A Discourse of the Pope's Supremacy* (1688), pp. 5, 55, 28.

64 [Stratford?], *Discourse of the Pope's Supremacy*, pp. 116 (qu.), 6–20; Barrow, *Pope's Supremacy*, pp. 113, 221.

65 Barrow, *Pope's Supremacy*, pp. 427–635.

was the seventeenth-century English. The African church 'and accordingly, every national church, has an inherent power of determining all causes that arise within itself'. Rome's dictates to Cyprian's province were 'so solemnly denied, so stiffly opposed, not by two or three, but by two or three hundred bishops'. And at this time, Anglicans proclaimed, the British Church was also free, independent for six hundred years. Edward Stillingfleet defended Henry Spelman's portrayal of British bishops defending their rights, just like Cyprian.[66] Although Cave cited the myth of British Christianity being as old as King Lucius, he did not do so in order to show the royal supremacy, but as one-upmanship on Rome: Britain was Christian in AD 37, before Peter was within sniffing distance of Rome. Stillingfleet thought Lucius existed, but was sceptical of his correspondence with Eleutherius – yet said this was superfluous. He could prove Christianity was preached in Britain by no less a person than St Paul.[67]

When they ceased pursuing Paul's footsteps upon England's pleasant pastures and mountains green and turned to patristic scholarship, Anglicans found countenance for their ecclesiology in Cyprian's *De unitate ecclesiae* and epistles (especially his fifty-second) of the early 250s. Drawing on such texts, they depicted every individual bishop participating in and upholding the orthodoxy and unity of the church. These prelates together made up 'one bishop' as each possessed equal and entire power in his own province. 'Episcopus unus est, cuius a singulis in solidum pars tenetur', wrote Cyprian, a dictum almost precisely (if necessarily more verbosely) translated by William Sherlock in 1688, who wrote of the universal church as 'one Bishoprick' which is

> divided into parts, into particular Dioceses, and every Bishop has a part of this Universal Bishoprick, which he has in *solidum*; that is, he has his part to govern with the fulnes and plentitude of the Episcopal power, without any Superior authority, or Jurisdiction over him.[68]

The attribution of *plenitudo potestatis*, that most papal of powers, to every bishop, was vital to the church. 'All bishops, as such, stand upon a common level', wrote Cave, and 'every bishop, as such, is, in a sense, intrusted with the care and solicitude of the universal church, and though for

[66] Edward Stillingfleet, *Origines Britannicae* (1685), pp. 364, 101; Cave, *Dissertation*, pp. 435–40 (qu. 435–6).

[67] Cave, *Dissertation*, p. 437; Stillingfleet, *Origines*, pp. 39–48, 58–67 (with a clear Protestant impulse to show a Pauline rather than Petrine foundation for faith).

[68] Sherlock, *Church-Unity*, p. 35; Cyprian, *The Lapsed; The Unity of the Catholic Church*, trans. Maurice Bévenot (1957), p. 47 (a dictum importantly present in both versions of the text).

conveniency limited to a particular charge, may yet act for the good of the whole'.[69] Cave had in mind the expulsion of heretical bishops from the communion of the faithful, carried out not by popes as supreme pastors but by the correction of other bishops. Correspondingly, the recognition of a bishop as the true bishop of his province was carried out by other bishops writing to him as such, rather than by papal confirmations ('so few, so late, so lame, so impertinent'[70]). The church's unity was constituted by an episcopal network, linked not by councils but by letters communicatory. The Restoration Church's view of episcopacy was not conciliar but collegial.[71] Writers did not speak of general councils but of 'several confederations of Bishops' (Barrow), 'a kind of mutual consociation' (Cave), and the episcopal college and 'consenting multitude of many Bishops' (Sherlock, citing Optatus and Cyprian's fifty-second epistle).[72]

This model offered mutual support and counsel, not hierarchy and jurisdiction.[73] The particular churches that were tied into the church universal by their episcopal heads did, however, have a hierarchical principle. 'The Universal Church is unorganized as to the whole, though made up of organized parts ... particular National Churches [are] Organized Bodies', wrote Sherlock.[74] This was not a departure from Cyprian's model, for that bishop had stood firm against schismatic deacons and presbyters, criticising his colleagues for employing his clergy without his permission.[75] Thus the Cyprianic case neatly refuted Dissenting or Presbyterian claims for freedom from or a devolution of authority within a particular church. It was expressed not only in works against Dissenters, but also in those refuting Catholics, since one claim levelled against the English Church was its hypocrisy in justifying its own separation from Rome whilst refuting Dissenting separatism. Clagett's defence of the Reformation as within the English Church's 'just Power' made his book useful to reprint in 1686. Anglican separation from Rome was carried out by a 'Competent Authority', and was no separation; it was rather a quarrel between two separate churches, not a schism within one church.[76] It was also more justified because regarding doctrinal fundamentals not *adiaphora*. As Sherlock noted, there was a need for uniform decency within a single church, but there was no catholic decency.[77] When Christ spoke to Peter,

[69] Cave, *Dissertation*, pp. 388, 453. [70] Barrow, *Pope's Supremacy*, p. 522.

[71] For a direct denial of Anglican conciliarism, see Sherlock, *Church-Unity*, pp. 22–4, 54–6.

[72] Barrow, *Pope's Supremacy*, p. 381; Cave, *Dissertation*, p. 375; Sherlock, *Church-Unity*, p. 36.

[73] Sherlock, *Church-Unity*, pp. 20, 68. [74] Sherlock, *Church-Unity*, p. 76.

[75] Cyprian, *Letters*, ed. G. W. Clarke (4 vols., New York, 1984), II. 15.

[76] William Clagett, *The Difference of the Case Between the Separation of Protestants from the Church of Rome and the Separation of Dissenters from the Church of England* (1683, repr. 1686), pp. 6, 42, 17.

[77] Clagett, *Difference of the Case*, pp. 24–5; Sherlock, *Church-Unity*, pp. 100–1.

The Unity he made him the Pattern of, was not that of the universal, but of particular Churches; he promised to build his Church upon *one*, to shew that in every particular Church he would have but *one* ... the Bishops as Successors of St *Peter*, are this Principle of Unity, and the Foundation, every one in his own Church, upon which all the rest depend.[78]

A 'complete and entire' i.e. jurisdictionally self-sufficient Church of England could oblige Dissenters to conform in a way that Rome could never do. Within a diocese, within England, obedience was due to the bishop, the 'Supream Governour' in his own see.[79]

Employing the language of royal supremacy to describe bishops or, as an anonymous tract of 1688 did, apostles as 'supreme heads', signalled a shift towards the episcopal more than royal foundations of the Church.[80] The royal supreme governor did not disappear in Anglican attacks on the papacy, but he was sidelined. Barrow's description of imperial convening of and presidency in synods, for example, was deployed to deny papal rights over councils rather than to prove royal ones. Sherlock was even more dismissive, admitting that councils advised Christian emperors, but therefore seeing them as civil not ecclesiastical meetings.[81] Similarly, although writers spoke of a national church, they hardly saw this as constituted by its supreme governor. Sherlock described the consent of particular churches to unite in forming a provincial or national church, but argued that this corporation was not a political body: 'Combinations ... for Communion, not for Government'. Thus a constitutive regent head was 'not essential to the Notion of a National Church', and indeed, even being a national church was optional.[82] For Sherlock, Dissenters from Anglican worship broke the rules decreed by a Cyprianic episcopate and would be schismatics even were the Book of Common Prayer not obligatory by statute law.[83] Clagett, too, spoke of a national church making common rules in convocation, which only thereafter became laws through monarchical motion. In his model, the national church acted for itself and the laws of the land only 'bind the Consciences' to obey 'something more', merely an extra tie of obedience.[84] Even more than Cyprian's prelates might 'the Bishops of a whole Christian Kingdom confederate together to order Church matters Independently upon the See of *Rome*'.[85] The Reformation story was a tale of episcopal recovery and use of ancient

[78] [Stratford?], *Discourse of the Pope's Supremacy*, p. 66.
[79] Sherlock, *Church-Unity*, pp. 80, 51, 103.
[80] [Stratford?], *Discourse of the Pope's Supremacy*, p. 44.
[81] Barrow, *Pope's Supremacy*, pp. 442–64; Sherlock, *Church-Unity*, pp. 52–3.
[82] Sherlock, *Church-Unity*, pp. 20, 17–18, 50. [83] Sherlock, *Church-Unity*, p. 103.
[84] Clagett, *Difference of the Case*, pp. 18–19. [85] Clagett, *Difference of the Case*, p. 7.

prelatical liberties, not monarchical breaking of Roman chains. Dodwell bluntly stated that defenders of the English Reformation cited law only to refute the notion that these changes went against royal will.[86]

If there was a present-day positive place for the supremacy in protecting episcopally driven reform, there was a darker role that kings had played in ecclesiastical history. Their grants disrupted episcopal equality by facilitating the rise of Rome. Cave and Barrow described the sordid origins of Romish supremacy in papal 'trucking and bartering' with quarrelling bishops and kings, special privileges gained by 'crafty suggestions ... at opportune times from easy and unwary Princes procured' and iced over with false *iure divino* rhetoric.[87] Worry about clever exploitation of naive monarchical devotion pervaded Anglican minds in the 1680s. But they turned this history to good effect, for if emperors had 'erected' papal authority, it could be 'dejected' by their successors. And with the collapse of the Roman empire, those successors were individual monarchs. 'Whatever power was granted by human authority, by the same may be revoked; and what the Emperor could have done, each Sovereign power may now do for itself.'[88] Thus Barrow neatly implied a far more positive account of royal supremacy and national churches. If he did not quite say *rex in regno suo est imperator*, he certainly suggested he was thinking of it in his description of how, as Christendom divided into 'many parcels', so too there were 'correspondingly ... distinct ecclesiastical governments, independent of each other' – *episcopus in dioecese sua est papa*! Each monarch might then change bishoprics in his own sphere, but should also uphold religious uniformity (a slightly different explanation from Sherlock's and Clagett's for the existence of national churches).[89] Sherlock said civil grants of extra jurisdiction that disrupted episcopal equality were no 'pure Ecclesiastical Authority'. But he later saw such 'mixt Authority' as 'very fitting' and 'convenient' to give to archbishops. Even better, it prevented any papal power, for there was no universal monarch to grant such a worldwide ecclesiastical jurisdiction.[90]

Historians have detected the unlikelihood of James surrendering his ecclesiastical prerogatives to the pope; his subjects were not so sanguine. While for some writers papal supremacy was the key barrier to accepting

86 Henry Dodwell, 'An Answer to Six Queries', in *Two Short Discourses Against the Romanists* (1676; repr. 1688), p. 113.
87 Barrow, *Pope's Supremacy*, pp. 45–6 (qu.), 425, 418 (qu.); Cave, *Dissertation*, pp. 460–2.
88 Barrow, *Pope's Supremacy*, pp. 398, 640.
89 Barrow, *Pope's Supremacy*, pp. 340 (qu.), 399, 733, 748.
90 Sherlock, *Church-Unity*, p. 73.

so Roman a Catholicism, for others opposition to James was rooted in doctrinal doubts. 'I may be contented to be oppressed in my Christian Liberties, I can never be contented to be damned.'[91] Very few Anglicans, however, proved to be contented with either situation. It was not just their monarch's toleration of idolatry but his particular targeting of Anglican hegemony which highlighted the caveat of Anglican 'Subjection and Obedience in all things, saving their Common Christianity'.[92] Intellectual polemic against Rome was renewed more than created after 1685; what was novel was the need to respond to royal policies which actively manifested the dangers of papist Erastianism.

A NEW CROMWELL? THE ECCLESIASTICAL COMMISSION VERSUS THE CHURCH

Staunching the plethora of anti-papal polemic which issued forth from Anglican presses and pulpits became an urgent necessity for James's government, but it was difficult to ask bishops to suppress defences of their Church. Authority might normally flow from the king to his archbishops, and thence to bishops, archdeacons, and parish clergy. But when the episcopate disagreed with a royal order to the extent that they were willing to defy it, or not to pass it on, the system broke down. James thus needed to find a way of bypassing the ecclesiastical hierarchy or disciplining it from outside. Three interlinked Reformation precedents proved particularly useful for his purposes: Thomas Cromwell's vicegerency in spirituals of the later 1530s and its descendant, the High Commission of Elizabethan and early Stuart times, which was, in effect, Cromwell's office held by several people. Ironically, the legislation of England's Protestant Josiah, Edward VI, would also prove an inspiration to the Catholic James.

Rumours that the king was seeking ways to impose his authority on the Anglican clergy were current in July 1686, when Morrice reported talk of the appointment of a new vicar general – perhaps Sunderland or Jeffreys – although he thought a collective commission more likely.[93]

[91] Sherlock, *Church-Unity*, p. 11 (qu.); for the first view, see Dodwell, 'An Account of the Fundamental Principle of Popery', in *Two Short Discourses*, sig. A5r.

[92] Clagett, *Difference of the Case*, p. 7.

[93] *EB*, P560, P562, cf. the terse shorthand note at P566: 'no vicar general'. Burnet thought it a strategy by Jeffreys to regain influence: *State Trials*, XI.1127n.; cf. Angus Macintyre, 'The College, King James II, and the Revolution, 1687–1688', in Laurence Brockliss, Gerald Harriss, and Angus Macintyre, eds., *Magdalen College and the Crown* (Oxford, 1988), p. 45, who attributes the idea to either Jeffreys or Sunderland. *EB*, Q87, commented on the Commission and Court factions.

From August 1686 until autumn 1688 the Commission oversaw some of the highest profile clashes of church and state during James's rule.[94] The Commission's patent, issued on 8 July 1686, authorised it to 'exercise use occupy & execute under Us all manner of Iurisdictions priviledges & preheminences in any wise ~~belonging~~ touching or concerning any spirituall or Ecclesiasticall Iurisdiction within this Our Realme … and to visit, reforme redresse Order Correct and amend all such abuses Offences Contempts & Enormities whatsoever which by the Spirituall or Ecclesiasticall Laws of this Our Realme can or may lawfully be reformed, Ordered, redressed, Corrected, restrayned or amended'. It was to enquire after transgressions and to 'order Correct reforme & Punnish by Censures of the Church', and punish clergy 'by suspending or depriving them from all promotions Eccl*esiast*icall & from all Functions in the Church, & to inflict such other punishment or Censures upon them, according to the Eccl*esiast*icall Lawes of this Realme'. The Commissioners were to enquire into incest, adultery, marital problems, and all 'great Crymes' in church law. They were to examine, correct, and if need be write anew statutes for universities, cathedral churches, and ecclesiastical foundations. Originally they were charged with examining any suspects, but this was deleted when the Commission was renewed on 19 November. Those defying the Commission were to be punished 'by excommunication, Suspention, Deprivacion or other Censures Eccl*esiast*icall'.[95] Although the patent said nothing explicitly about preaching, James announced to the Privy Council that he had created the court 'for the p*re*vention of Indiscreet Preaching'.[96]

Archbishop Sancroft refused to join the Commission, using ill health as a thinly disguised excuse for his dislike of it. Roger North's memo 'Of not sitting upo*n* *th*e King's Com*m*ission' weighed up the duty to serve the king against the risk of acting illegally. Natural law required service to be given to the monarch. 'But *the*n *tha*t Service req*ui*r'd must not be ag*ain*st Law … To sitt upo*n* Com*missio*ns ag*ain*st Law is a dangerous th*in*g.' Remember Empson and Dudley, executed by Henry VIII for their service to his father. Remember Edward Coke, who refused to sit on James I's High Commission. And if Coke held James I's Commission to be illegal, so must James II's be too.[97] Despite almost half the Commission being made up of Protestants – the Earl of Rochester, Bishop Crewe of Durham, and Bishop Sprat of Rochester – this was felt to be no security

94 The exceptions were *Godden* v. *Hales* and the trial of the Seven Bishops.

95 TNA, SP 44/337, pp. 68–74.

96 TNA, PC 2/71, p. 300.

97 Bodl., Tanner MS 460, fo. 82r–v (qu. 82r).

against Catholicising policies.[98] When it was thought that Sancroft had been summoned, Morrice reported panic, but the primate may have been prepared.[99] North recorded writing 'a paper or discourse upon the high commission', which Sancroft kept ready to deliver to the Commission in case he was cited before it, to claim that the Commission was null by common law. In contrast to later historians who have seen the archbishop as passive during James's reign, North thought this a 'stout regular opposition', which put the Commission off citing the primate.[100] North denied that Elizabeth's High Commission had ever punished a bishop, and least of all prosecuted the archbishop of Canterbury, who had always been tried when necessary by his peers in parliament.[101]

James in effect delegated part of his ecclesiastical prerogative to the Commission. As Morrice claimed, its members were given 'all the power that Soveraignity can depute, and all that Plenitudo Potestatis that is invested in the King as Supream'. When its powers were extended in November 1686, Morrice described the Commissioners gaining 'greater plenitude of power … before they had only Episcopall power, now they have Spirituall power'.[102] Burnet condemned the Commission as a 'stretch of the supremacy so contrary to law … assumed by a king, whose religion made him condemn all that supremacy that the law had vested in the crown'.[103] North complained that even Henrician trials had not been overseen 'in an arbitrary way by Lay men'. No High Commission had tried Wolsey, none had been created when the whole clergy fell into *praemunire*.[104] But although the targeting of conformist Anglicans was novel, the Commission was recognised as far from an unprecedented embodiment of supremacy. Morrice thought its patent 'much after the forme of the Commission given to the Lord Cromwell in Hen*ry* the 8ths time, with all such powers as the High Commissioners formerly had', dubbing it the 'Septem-Virate Vicaracy'. Tellingly, one of its members, Thomas Cartwright, invariably referred to 'the high commissioners' in his diary.[105]

98 *EB*, P581. Bishop Cartwright of Chester was added later, for the Magdalen College case; Burnet thought Cartwright and Parker (who, perhaps significantly, never sat) were the two bishops most likely to ruin the Church: see *State Trials*, XI.1148n.

99 *EB*, P627.

100 Jessop, ed., *Autobiography*, pp. 121–2; see also John Gutch, *Collectanea curiosa* (2 vols., Oxford, 1781), I.xxxix.

101 Bodl., Tanner MS 460, fos. 67v–68r, 70v.

102 *EB*, P651, Q11. Morrice's meaning is unclear.

103 *State Trials*, XI.1127n.

104 'A short view of the Dispensing Power in relation to Acts of Parlament', Bodl., Tanner MS 460, fos. 61r–70v, at fos. 65r–67r (qu. 65r).

105 *EB*, P573, P577; Cartwright, *Diary*, pp. 53, 10, 48.

Reformation precedent made the Commission less indubitably 'contrary to law' than the whig Burnet thought.

Although the nature and purposes of Cromwell's vicegerency remain obscure, it may well have been to discipline the bishops and impose on them more forcefully a sense of their being servants of their royal supreme head.[106] The Edwardian Act insisting that all ecclesiastical courts act in the king's name and use seals displaying the royal arms was evidenced in Edwardian episcopal seals, which bore the royal arms, supported by a lion and unicorn, and, importantly, a closed imperial crown. Their legends began with 'sigillum regiae maiestatis ad causas ecclesiasticas', followed by the particular officer of the diocese.[107] This was a significant move away from the pre-Reformation episcopal seals, which depicted mitred bishops blessing their flocks; although, as sigillographers have shown, later sixteenth-century seals showed preaching bishops and scriptural scenes.[108]

Elizabethan episcopal seals removed the images and legends emphasising royal authority. The Edwardian tradition was not lost, however, for it was echoed in the High Commission described in the Act of Uniformity of 1559. Until 1576 individual members of the Commission used their own seals, but thereafter 'for the better credit and more manifest notice of your doings in the execution of this our commission' they switched to employing

> a seal engraved with the rose and the crown over the rose, and the letter E before and the letter R after the same, with a ring or circumference about the same seal, containing as followeth: Sigil*lum* Comiss*ariorum* Reg*inae* Ma*jestatis* ad Caus*as* Ecclesiast*icas*.[109]

The late Tudor and early Stuart High Commission disciplined recalcitrant clergy, and it did so as a body composed of a mixture of lay and clerical members. By 1640, its actions had infuriated several groups in society.

106 S. E. Lehmberg, 'Supremacy and Vicegerency: A Re-Examination', *English Historical Review*, 81 (1966), pp. 225–35; F. Donald Logan, 'Thomas Cromwell and the Vicegerency in Spirituals: A Revisitation', *English Historical Review*, 103 (1988), pp. 658–67; Margaret Bowker, 'The Supremacy and the Episcopate: The Struggle for Control, 1534–1540', *Historical Journal*, 18 (1975), pp. 227–43.

107 For examples, see David H. Williams, *Catalogue of Seals in the National Museum of Wales, vol. II* (Cardiff, 1998), p. 17; Sir William Blackstone, 'A Letter … to the Honourable Daines Barrington, Describing an Antique Seal; with Some Observations on its Original, and the Two Successive Controversies which the Disuse of it Afterwards Occasioned', *Archæologia*, 3 (1775), pp. 414–25, at pp. 414–16, 425 (p. 416 suggests many were destroyed under Mary); M. C. J., 'Seal of the Commissary of the Deanery of Arustley', *Archaeologia Cambrensis*, 5th ser., 1 (1884), pp. 228–31; David H. Williams, 'Catalogue of Welsh Ecclesiastical Seals as known down to 1600 AD', *Archaeologia Cambrensis*, 133 (1984), pp. 100–35; and 134 (1985), pp. 162–89, at pp. 166–7 and plate xviii.

108 Williams, 'Welsh Ecclesiastical Seals', p. 107.

109 G. W. Prothero, ed., *Select Statutes and Other Constitutional Documents Illustrative of the Reigns of Elizabeth and James I* (Oxford, 1913), pp. 239–40.

Puritans hated its enforcement of Prayer Book conformity and, in the 1630s, Laudian ceremony. Common lawyers detested its *ex officio* process and they questioned its legal standing. In 1641, parliament abolished High Commission. It was so disliked that when ecclesiastical jurisdiction was restored in 1661, the erection of High Commission or 'some such like court' was banned.[110]

This lengthy digression into pre-Reformation seals and statutes is necessary to show how the legal position of an ecclesiastical commission was extremely muddled by 1685.[111] Those who wished to argue against such a body pointed to the Act of 1661. For men such as Edward Stillingfleet, this statute was especially useful because it upheld 'ordinary' (episcopal) jurisdiction and church courts, but left them free from 'extraordinary' (royal) meddling. Parliament had created the possibility of a high commission in 1559, and parliament a century later had got rid of this. But James and his supporters were not indisputably acting illegally. The 1661 statute contained a clause saving the rights of the royal supremacy. Furthermore, the 1559 statute had 'declared' and not 'created' the Commission, warranted under letters patent by the royal prerogative independently of parliament. Most powerfully, those arguing thus could point to Coke's judgment in Caudrey's Case. Using the absolutist strain in his common law mind, Coke had insisted that the Commission was part of the immemorial royal prerogative, not a novelty created in 1559, for the Elizabethan Act of Uniformity was 'not a statute introductory of a new law, but declaratory of the old ... so that if that Act had never been made, it was resolved by all the Judges, that the King or Queen of England for the time being may make such an ecclesiastical commission'.[112] So James's supporters argued in the 1680s. And, with an urgent need to impress royal ecclesiastical authority on a body of recalcitrant bishops, James's new Ecclesiastical Commission turned to an old seal. The letters patent for the Commission ordered that

> for the better Creditt, and more manifest notice of your doing in the Execution of this Our Commission Our pleasure & Comandment is, That to your Letters Missive, Provisoes, Decrees, Orders, & Judgem*en*ts ... [you] shall cause to be put & afixed a seale Engraven with the Rose & Crowne, & the Letter J and Figure 2 before, & the Letter R. after the same, with a Ring or Circumference about the same seale, containing as it followeth Sigillum Commissar*iorum* Regiae Majestatis ad Causas Ecclesiasticas.[113]

[110] 13 Chas. II st. 1 c. 12. See above, p. 69.

[111] On lawyers' uncertainty about the status of the Commission see *EB*, P593–4.

[112] 77 Eng. Rep. 9–10, 5 Co. Rep. 8a–b.

[113] TNA, SP 44/337, p. 74 (and see Anon., *The History of King James's Ecclesiastical Commission* (1711), pp. 7–8). This almost precisely followed the wording of the 1576 Commission. James's regime's

James's commission was not a modern French Catholic body. It was created through the authority and in the tradition of Tudor equivalents. Discussion of it looked back to sixteenth-century debates and argued about Reformation precedents. It answered the call of Francis Knollys in the 1590s, of William Prynne in the 1640s, and of the Earl of Shaftesbury in the 1670s for the appointment of a new vicar-general to discipline the clergy.[114] And it embodied James's strategies for dismantling Anglican hegemony. Like Charles I, James was successful to a point because he stretched rather than unambiguously overshot his prerogative. Like his father, he pushed it too far.

The Commission's negative reputation was shaped by three cases: those of Henry Compton, bishop of London, the University of Cambridge, and Magdalen College, Oxford.[115] Such high-profile cases, especially those of Magdalen College and Bishop Compton, provided the main stimuli to polemic about the Commission. But it is important to remember that these were not the only matters which fell under its remit. J. P. Kenyon has emphasised the Commission's less inflammatory work on marriage and divorce suits.[116] Even cases akin to those of Magdalen and Compton did not have the same outcomes. Some were perhaps fortunate in that pressure of time and business meant their cases were dropped. The governors of Charterhouse Hospital refused to admit Andrew Popham as a pensioner without his taking the oaths from which the king had dispensed him. Jeffreys pressed James's dispensation, but was outnumbered by opponents, primarily Danby, who announced 'that power of Dispenceing he thought to be illegall, and the Judges opinions in [Hales's] Case he found to be thought unwarrantable by the Lawes of England, and by the generallity of the best Lawyers'. A phalanx of loyalists – Sancroft, Ormonde, Halifax, Craven, Danby, Nottingham, and Compton – signed a petition to the king, Ormonde protesting that 'an Act of Parliament is not so slight a thing but that it deserves to be considered'. Despite the threat of *quo warranto*, the Charterhouse case was never referred to the Commission.[117] Furthermore, the Commission was occasionally defeated.

awareness of the value of earlier attacks on the clergy is shown in its writing to John Phelps/Archer/Debois for information on his activities as Clerk to the Rump Parliament's Committee for Ecclesiastical Affairs: *CSPD, Jan. 1686 – May 1687*, pp. 330–1.

114 Knollys: BL, Add. MS 48064, fo. 95r; Prynne and Shaftesbury: see above, pp. 194–201.

115 *State Trials*, XI.1123–66, 1315–40, XII.1–112.

116 J. P. Kenyon, 'The Commission for Ecclesiastical Causes, 1686–1688: A Reconsideration', *Historical Journal*, 34 (1991), pp. 727–36.

117 Anon., *History*, pp. 22–5; Danby, qu. in *EB*, Q49; Ormonde, qu. in Anthony Quick, *Charterhouse* (1990), p. 25.

When the Catholic Baron Petre asserted his family's right to nominate to fellowships they had endowed at Exeter College, the College struck back by pleading that fellowships were freehold property and thus outside the Commission's ecclesiastical jurisdiction. In January 1687, Jeffreys denounced Exeter's petition (the same plea as Magdalen's) as a libel against the Commission's jurisdiction. But on 17 February the Commission dismissed the case.[118]

However, these escapes from the Commission's jurisdiction did not make the best polemical headlines. Compton, Cambridge, and Magdalen did. Compton was a constant torment to James, having vehemently defended the Protestant education of the royal princesses in the 1670s and mounted an attack on the dispensing power in the parliament of 1685. Compton was both a popular bishop (something his trial exacerbated) and an aristocratic one, his nephew being the Earl of Northampton.[119] He was cited after refusing to suspend the London preacher John Sharp, who had preached an anti-Catholic sermon in answer to an anonymous letter, thus breaking James's 'Directions to Preachers', which had banned anti-Catholic polemic. Compton's letter to James explained that he could not suspend Sharp without due process, but that the preacher had agreed to remain silent, a response which to the authoritarian James looked like rank insubordination.[120] Compton attacked the Commission on several fronts. His lawyers were uncertain whether statutes abolishing High Commission saved enough of the supremacy to legitimate James's new Commission. On 7 August Compton was 'ready to run all hazards ... and thought it was best to demur to the jurisdiction of the court'. But the next morning his counsel, Sir John Maynard, worried that this was 'somewhat dangerous' as it might be held to treasonably impugn the supremacy (he was willing to accept Compton's demurrer as 'a tender nice point'). In any case, the Commission refused to let him see their warrant.[121] Compton condemned the suit as retrospective, Sharp's case having occurred before

[118] *EB*, Q33, Q45, Q61, Q72–3; Q229 implied Magdalen should have used this argument. His account also shows (Q44) that Sancroft managed to insert his own nominee to the headship of Christ Church before James's (rumoured to be Dryden); and that Balliol College successfully petitioned the king to be allowed to choose its own master (Q181).

[119] Cases always seemed to attract crowds (see *State Trials*, XI.1325, XII.34; and Anon., *An Impartial Relation of the Illegal Proceedings Against St Mary Magdalen Colledge in Oxon*, 2nd edn (1689), p. 43), but Compton was savvy enough to arrive with a phalanx of doctors of divinity and nobility: *EB*, P601, P613.

[120] Ironically, Sharp was reinstated after petitioning the king himself: *EB*, Q46.

[121] *State Trials*, XI.1157; *EB*, qu. P593–4, P603; see also P601, P608, P642; P620 reports James saying that 'if the Court have no good foundation in Law then they that advised it must pay the reckoning, but if it have then the Bishop of London must'.

the Commission was created. Protesting loyalty to the royal supremacy, he yet insisted that only the archbishop and his suffragans could try a bishop 'by all the law in the Christian church in all ages, and by the particular law of this land'.[122] Finally, he pleaded compliance with the duty to *rescribere et reclamere principi* when ordered to execute an illegal act.[123] Three members of the Commission (Rochester, Herbert, and Sprat) initially opposed Compton's suspension. Although James pressured his brother-in-law into changing sides, Compton's sentence was sealed, but not signed.[124] Compton's defeat was not a clear victory for James, since the legality of the Commission remained contested. Furthermore, Compton's popularity may have fuelled antagonism to the Commission, uniting groups against royal policies. Morrice had 'never known of late yeares ... so universall an Interest of Churchmen, Trimmer and Dissenters' joining a cause. Compton had 'the whole body of the Kingdome for [his] defence and support ... [even] all the Dissenters'.[125]

The Commission's second major case was that of John Peachell, the Vice-Chancellor of the University of Cambridge, for refusing a degree to Alban Francis, a Benedictine monk whose need to take the oaths James had dispensed with. The University's ability to exclude Francis was limited by Joshua Basset, the new Catholic master of Sidney Sussex, who was able to block a grace from the University's convocation against granting the degree.[126] The case came before the Commission in late April 1687, thus overlapping with the beginning of Magdalen's troubles and the enlargement of the Commission's remit. Peachell argued that it was a breach of trust not to tender the oaths – whilst royal nominees in the past had not *taken* them, none had actively *refused* them – that a degree was no ecclesiastical matter, and that the Commission's legality was dubious.[127] University representatives appeared before the Commission on 30 April, but sentencing was delayed whilst the king was consulted. Morrice reported stories that the Court wanted a test case, akin to that of Hales,

[122] *State Trials*, XI.1160 (qu.); Henry Compton, *An Exact Account of the Whole Proceedings Against ... Henry Lord Bishop of London* (1688), pp. 16–19 (p. 19 has 'by the most Authentique and Universal Ecclesiastical Laws').

[123] *State Trials*, XI.1161 (qu.); Compton, *Exact Account*, p. 23. See also 'A Syllogism in Defence of *the* B*isho*p of London, in *the* high Com*m*ission', Bodl., Tanner MS 460, fo. 79r.

[124] *State Trials*, XI.1128n.; *EB*, P621–2; Edward Carpenter, *The Protestant Bishop: Being the Life of Henry Compton, 1632–1713, Bishop of London* (1956), pp. 96–7.

[125] *EB*, P602, P613.

[126] *State Trials*, XI.1321; for Basset, see Mark Goldie, 'Joshua Basset, Popery, and Revolution', in D. E. D. Beales and H. B. Nisbet, eds., *Sidney Sussex College Cambridge* (Woodbridge, 1996).

[127] *State Trials*, XI.1326–8, 1337–8.

brought to prove the legality of the Declaration of Indulgence. By the middle of May he heard that visitations of the universities were likely.[128]

The third prominent attack on the Anglican establishment by the Ecclesiastical Commission was the case of Magdalen College, Oxford.[129] When President Clerke died on 24 March 1687, the Fellows and their Visitor, Peter Mews, bishop of Winchester, moved swiftly to try to prevent the intrusion of a Catholic head. A royal mandate to elect Anthony Farmer, a Catholic convert of seemingly infinite dissoluteness, arrived on 5 April; on the ninth the Fellows unsuccessfully protested to James that Farmer could not be elected as he was not a member of Magdalen or New College as their statutes required. On 15 April they elected John Hough president, justifying this by citing their duty in conscience to obey their oaths which, they told a deputation of the Ecclesiastical Commission, bound them not to seek or use any dispensation from their statutes. Henry Fairfax, the senior Fellow, also entered a plea against the authority of the Commission and demanded a copy of the libel; he was removed from court while protesting that the election was not an ecclesiastical matter.[130]

It was unclear whether the special deputation of Commissioners sitting in Magdalen acted as a branch of the Commission or as Visitors of the College. Whilst the king as supreme visitor could not be defied, the Fellows argued that he still had to follow due process according to statute:

> no Commissioners can be authorized by the Crown to proceed in any Commission under the Great Seal or otherwise, but according to Law; in Spiritual Causes by the Canon Law; in Temporal by the other Laws and Statutes of the Land … *Magna Charta* provides for our Spiritual Liberties, as well as our Temporal.[131]

[128] *EB*, Q111, Q129.

[129] This paragraph draws on *State Trials*, XII.1–112; Anon., *Impartial Relation*; J. R. Bloxam, *Magdalen College and King James II, 1686–1688* (Oxford, 1886); Brockliss, Harris, and Macintyre, eds., *Magdalen College*; Anon., *History*, pp. 30–52. Macintyre, 'College, King James II, and the Revolution', p. 31n., attributes *An Impartial Relation*, the early 1688 official account by the College, to the Vice-President, Charles Aldworth; others to Fairfax or Smith. I cite from the 2nd edn of 1689, which added 'Four Queries' justifying allegiance to William III. Morrice, ever a fan of Sir John Maynard, attributed Magdalen's success to his pleading, snidely commenting that the University of Cambridge had been defeated because they had snubbed Maynard's offer of assistance: *EB*, Q105, Q147, Q151.

[130] See esp. Anon., *Impartial Relation*, pp. 8–9, 12–13; Macintyre, 'College, King James II, and the Revolution', pp. 45–7.

[131] Anon., *Impartial Relation*, pp. 27–9 (qu. p. 29); *State Trials*, XII.25–6.

Hough, exhorted to give up the keys to the President's lodgings, insisted that his freehold was subject only to the Westminster courts. Edward Herbert and Bishop Sprat thought his election regular. Jeffreys, Crewe, Wright, and Cartwright showed remarkable ignorance of their own power when proposing to incapacitate the Fellows from ecclesiastical promotions 'if this Court can doe it'.[132] Fairfax meanwhile insouciantly entered a plea resting on the royal insistence that consciences were not to be forced – James's Declaration of Indulgence had been issued only a day before his mandate to elect Farmer.[133] Sarcastic references to a 'Magdalen College conscience' later circulated.[134]

In December 1687, with Magdalen's case 'the Common Talk of the Town', the Dissenter Henry Care set out to prove the legality of the Commission.[135] He cited Caudrey's Case to argue that the 1559 Act of Supremacy was declaratory, not introductory, and therefore that statutes could not limit the ecclesiastical prerogative. As a commission had been possible before the Elizabethan Act of Uniformity, it might be created even if the relevant clause of that Act was repealed. Care nonetheless asserted that 13 Chas. II c. 12 only banned commissions from *ex officio* process, fining, and jailing.[136] North's paper for Sancroft of 'A*nim*adu*er*sions upon *the* Vindic*ati*on of *the* Eccl*esiast*icall Com*missio*n' counter-asserted that *any* equivalent of High Commission had been outlawed. Only ordinary ecclesiastical powers had been restored.[137] But Care saw James as 'Supreme Ordinary' of the Church, and he snidely commented that correcting 'Debauched and Persecuting' clerics was 'not a Destroying [the Church], but rather an using proper methods to preserve and secure it'.[138] Had not common lawyers attributed to the king powers that popes had held? 'There hath been such a vulgar Notio*n*', North admitted, 'but amongst Dablers only: no com*m*on Lawyer will affirm it.' Tudor statutes had given kings only powers *lawfully* exercised before.[139] Popes dispensed,

132 *State Trials*, XII.32; Anon., *Impartial Relation*, p. 41; Bodl., Rawlinson MS D365, fo. 23r–v.

133 *State Trials*, XII.37; Anon., *Impartial Relation*, p. 48. Fairfax was being tried separately because of his refusal to join the Fellows in electing before they had repeatedly petitioned the king. His query had been raised earlier, with an uncertain reply: Bloxam, *Magdalen College*, p. 21. Morrice (*EB*, Q151) was amazed that the quiet Fairfax showed so much daring.

134 Macintyre, 'College, King James II, and the Revolution', p. 61.

135 Henry Care, *A Vindication of the Proceedings of His Majesties Ecclesiastical Commissioners* (1688), p. 1 (licensed 21 Dec. 1687); Henry Care, *The Legality of the Court Held by His Majesties Ecclesiastical Commissioners Defended* (1688).

136 Care, *Legality*, pp. 8–12; Care, *Vindication*, pp. 5–19 (pp. 9–16 do not exist).

137 'A*nim*adu*er*sions upon *the* Vindic*ati*on of the Eccl*esiast*icall Com*missio*n': Bodl., Tanner MS 460, fos. 25r–32v, at fo. 25r.

138 Care, *Legality*, pp. 2, 29; Care, *Vindication*, p. 34.

139 Bodl., Tanner MS 460, fo. 26r–v; against Care, *Vindication*, pp. 42, 44–5.

said Care, kings might too; even with statutes in ecclesiastical matters, if not with *mala in se*. And if national statutes were dispensable, surely college ones were, since colleges, as spiritual and ecclesiastical corporations, were cared for by the supreme head. Magdalen's case was 'feeble', 'vain and ludicrous', its Fellows could not be obliged by their statutes when the king dispensed with the obligation of such laws; no college statute was indispensable.[140] Folly, North replied; all laws were equally binding.[141]

Harping on his favourite theme, Care declared the Commission 'more Legal than the Bishops Courts; *This* is in the KING's Name, Theirs in their Own Names only'.[142] Only royal clemency saved church courts from the consequences of their audacity in running ecclesiastical process in their own names. 'As the Old *Puritans* did imagin, their Courts were Illegal, their Bishops Premunir'd.'[143] North initially replied that early Stuart judges had confirmed ecclesiastical jurisdiction; he then struck this out, before stating that they declared proof of the repeal of Edward's law.[144] Care insisted that Compton's primary duty should have been obedience to his supreme governor. Drawing on Lyndwood's compilation of canon law, Care claimed Sharp's error was a manifest fact, so Compton needed only to sentence, not to judge, him. Compton's quibbling over the fact of the crime was 'a very manifest Mistake', since the king had already satisfied himself of the fact, and 'the Bishop is bound to Obey, if Commanded by the Supreme Ordinary'.[145] North thought this 'manifestly false' since 'neither by Canon-Law, nor any other in *th*e World (be *th*e people barbarous, or civil) can a Man be punished w*i*thout Hear*ing* him'. Excommunications and deprivations could be incurred *ipso facto*, but not suspensions.[146]

Care reminded the church of the surprisingly significant amount of clemency it had enjoyed from a king who would not 'go so Far, as Justly He might'.[147] History clearly evidenced royal ability to legislate on rites without parliamentary sanction. James, whose supremacy was as ample as any of his ancestors', might enforce subscription to liberty of conscience, far preferable to decreeing ceremonial rigour.[148] Alternatively, he might

140 Care, *Vindication*, pp. 44–5, 47–8, 49 (qu.), 57–8 (qu.).
141 Bodl., Tanner MS 460, fo. 28r.
142 Care, *Vindication*, p. 19. For this obsession, see above, pp. 194–6.
143 Care, *Vindication*, pp. 59–60.
144 Bodl., Tanner MS 460, fos. 29v–30r, 31v–32r.
145 Care, *Vindication*, pp. 26–34 (qu. pp. 28, 34).
146 Bodl., Tanner MS 460, fo. 25v. North's initial note to find out which law Care could mean was struck out; on fo. 26r he mentioned parliamentary attainder as the single exception.
147 Care, *Vindication*, pp. 3 (qu.), 74; Care, *Legality*, p. 30.
148 Care, *Legality*, pp. 17–23, 24, 35.

(especially if provoked by opposition) employ the supremacy to change all ceremonies to Catholic ones.[149] Not even parliament could stop this, Care declared, in a ringing endorsement of personal royal *imperium*

> as the KING, by the Fulness of His Ecclesiastical Power can, *without a Parliament*, make what Laws He please for the Government of the Clergy; in like manner, The *Power of the KING*, in Matters Ecclesiastical, is too ample to be *limited by an Act of Parliament*.[150]

But North distinguished acting 'without' and acting 'against' parliament. The king might decide matters not yet decreed; he could not arbitrarily change settled laws. He might dispense with canons, but that was no legislative power. To suspend laws sanctioned by parliament would constitute legislation, but this would be illegal. 'Canons are not to be made w*i*thout *th*e Concurrence of a Convocation, no more *the*n Laws w*i*thout a parl*iamen*t: w*hi*ch consists w*i*th *th*e Supremacy; For *tha*t is allow'd in *th*e Temporalitie also, & yet doth not implie a sole Legislature.'[151]

The Dissenter Care might have inflated the royal prerogative in order to justify an Ecclesiastical Commission which would quash Anglican hegemony. But defences of James's actions from men within the Church of England also existed. Nathaniel Johnston was a royal physician who would remain loyal to James after 1689, exploiting 'Country' sentiment to gain support for Jacobitism. During James's reign he defended *The Excellency of Monarchical Government* (1686) and denied that James planned to seize back church lands. He was granted access to public records in the Tower by the government, presumably in order to aid his propaganda. *The King's Visitatorial Power Asserted* defended his sovereign's rights over Magdalen in particular and the church in general. Licensed on 23 July 1688, this was the last gasp of James's regime, emerging just before the king rapidly changed his policies in the autumn of 1688 in an attempt to woo Anglican royalists again.[152] Johnston, like Care, praised the 'great Clemency' of James, who might have summarily proceeded in a harsher way against Magdalen. James, as supreme ordinary, supreme visitor, held sway over all subordinate bodies politic within his realm. No corporation, Johnston said menacingly, was exempt from *quo warranto*

149 Care, *Vindication*, pp. 75–6. 150 Care, *Vindication*, p. 41.

151 Bodl., Tanner MS 460, fos. 26v, 31r (qu.).

152 *CSPD, Jan. 1686 – May 1687*, p. 367; Mark Goldie, 'Nathaniel Johnston', *ODNB*. This states that his *Excellency of Monarchical Government* (1686) was the last absolutist text before the Revolution; in church politics his 1688 book wins this prize. See also Goldie, 'Anglican Revolution', p. 106. Johnston wrote part of his book a while before it was printed: see *The King's Visitatorial Power Asserted* (1688), sig. [A4]r. CUL, J.10.14 is Johnston's presentation copy to Halifax.

process, especially not universities, over which post-Reformation monarchs exercised a 'more Despotical Authority' than other corporations.[153] All of the rights of Oxford University derived from its royal founder, King Alfred.[154]

Admitting that the supremacy was only a jurisdictional, not sacerdotal, power, Johnston nevertheless thought that with regard to 'outward Regiment', monarchs did 'whatever the Pope *de Jure*, if not *de facto* could or did do' – a definition astonishingly wide.[155] Beyond the universities, kings had invested bishops and seized their temporalities; they had separated ecclesiastical from temporal courts. They had decreed which pope was to be obeyed during schisms and authorised legatine visitations.[156] Since post-Reformation kings abrogated papal bulls and punished men observing them, they unquestionably could do the same with college statutes.[157] Tudor monarchs reformed and counter-reformed the universities to suit their individual religious convenience. Edward VI radically altered statutes, lectures, even terms ('a Reformation being designed by the King, there was no place in the University for the Unconformable'); Mary and Pole reversed his alterations, changed all over again by Elizabeth. Charles I had dispensed with statutes at Emmanuel College, Cambridge, even in the face of protests from Fellows.[158] Not only college rules but also academic personnel were subject to supremacy. In 1552 Walter Haddon, future defender of the Elizabethan Settlement, had only gained the presidency of Magdalen when royal pressure forced the incumbent's resignation.[159] In 1631 Oxford's statutes were changed without even 'the formality of a Visitation', since kings dispensed with and altered statutes 'either by themselves in their Closets, or by their Commissioners'.[160] Parliament had only wielded visitatorial rights in 1647, when it also exercised sovereignty.[161]

Johnston impatiently insisted that the public trust held by the king allowed him to override the authority of the local episcopal visitor especially where, as in Magdalen's case, the bishop was a party in the case. The Fellows had sworn to uphold the College's statutes, but this duty was

[153] Johnston, *Visitatorial Power*, pp. 11 (qu.), 255–6, 161 (qu.).
[154] Johnston, *Visitatorial Power*, pp. 129–32.
[155] Johnston, *Visitatorial Power*, pp. 157–8, 145 (qu.), 10.
[156] Johnston, *Visitatorial Power*: popes, p. 145; bishops: pp. 148 (invested their baronies, not their orders), 155; courts: pp. 156–7; legates: pp. 153–4.
[157] Johnston, *Visitatorial Power*, pp. 183, 187–8.
[158] Johnston, *Visitatorial Power*, pp. 206–13 (qu. 208), 246, 347–51.
[159] Johnston, *Visitatorial Power*, pp. 341–5. For the controversial presidential election at Magdalen in 1589, see Stephen Wright, 'Nicholas Bond', *ODNB*.
[160] Johnston, *Visitatorial Power*, pp. 249, 335.
[161] Johnston, *Visitatorial Power*, p. 254.

trumped by their obligation to the royal supremacy. The Fellows' recalcitrance was but one step from open rebellion, for according to the *Digest* a mandate from an emperor required only a ready obedience, and their defiance warranted 'just Chastisement'.[162] *Qua* supreme ordinary, the king could punish their contempt without normal judicial process – as the Fellows well knew. 'You could not be ignorant of the Kings being your Supreme Ordinary by the Antient Common Law of this Land, of which the *Statutes* [of the realm] are not *Introductory* but *declaratory*.'[163] For Johnston, the fact that college statutes could not inhibit the dispensing power of the royal donor represented in microcosm the fact that parliament could not limit the royal prerogative. Had not the judges fully justified the dispensing power, a necessary adjunct of sovereignty to deal with imperfect human laws?[164]

Those who defended the Commission tended, like Care and Johnston, to emphasise the personal supremacy of the king. Many who opposed it offered a constitutionalist case stressing parliamentary limitations on the royal prerogative. Such arguments were proposed by the whig lawyer Robert Washington, the low-church anti-Catholic divine Edward Stillingfleet, and the anonymous 'Philonomus Anglicus'. Although their opposition was couched in preponderantly constitutionalist tones, it was possible to find caveats within absolutist *imperium* to defend the Church from the Commission. The Oxford high-church don Jonas Proast made such a case by using the tory idea of royal *concessio*, gracious self-limitation. Proast based his defence of Magdalen College, dedicated to Hough in October 1688, on the oath to the college statutes not contravening the supremacy 'as so limited by the King Himself'. Kings were bound to observe the concessions of their forebears, which counted as their own acts, for the king never dies.[165] Monarchs might condescend to enter covenants with their subjects: express and solemn or 'tacit & presumptive'. The latter existed regarding Magdalen. Kings had silently assented to (not opposed) Magdalen's oath, so they could not dispense with it later. And the presumption must be that college founders and kings would always uphold college statutes to protect learning.[166] If statutes could not be

162 Johnston, *Visitatorial Power*, pp. 294, 304–8, 314–15 (qu.).
163 Johnston, *Visitatorial Power*, pp. 10, 3, 57, 104–5 (qu.).
164 Johnston, *Visitatorial Power*, pp. 243, 260–9.
165 Jonas Proast, 'A Brief Defense of the Society of St Mary *Magdalen* College in *Oxford*': Bodl., Tanner MS 338, fos. 302r–311r, at fos. 303r, 305r–306r. North made similar comments: Bodl., Tanner MS 460, fo. 27r.
166 Bodl., Tanner MS 338, fos. 307r–308v. Here Proast contrasted the canonist claim that kings could 'irritate' (make void) the oath with Protestant denials that mortals could dispense with oaths (fo. 310r–v).

dispensed with, still less could they be abolished, except by the legislative power of king-in-parliament.[167] Here Proast slid towards arguing for mixed rather than self-limiting monarchy.

That alternative case, of limited rather than self-limiting kingship, was used by the other pamphleteers who denounced the Commission, either in 1688 or in the aftermath of the Williamite Revolution.[168] Philonomus Anglicus described how kings were heads of the realm and church, but were 'bound by the Laws of the Realm in the exercise of their Jurisdiction'. Washington drew the ecclesiological parallel. 'The *Ancient Ecclesiastical Supremacy* of the Kings of this Realm, was no *personal Prerogative*.'[169] The whig jurist, like the tory lawyer North, was aghast at the idea that kings exercised the same powers as popes. When Johnston asserted that kings could do all that popes *de facto* or *de jure* might do, Washington quickly replied that kings' spiritual jurisdiction was law-governed.[170] In denying a purely monarchical, personal, supremacy, all these writers looked to history to support their arguments. Anglo-Saxon monarchs had, they insisted, undertaken ecclesiastical governance through their great councils. 'The whole Fabrick of the *English Saxon Church* was built upon Acts of Parliament.'[171] This had not been disrupted in 1066, for medieval kings too ruled as mixed rather than mere monarchs, their ecclesiastical sovereignty shared with parliament. Both Washington and Stillingfleet claimed that Archbishop Anselm directed his appeal against his deprivation to parliament. 'Our Kings Antient Ecclesiastical Jurisdiction', concluded Philonomus, 'was not a Personal Supremacy, separate and distinct from the States of the Realm [but …] in the King encompassed with Peerage and Cominalty.'[172]

Such generic claims about the supremacy of king-in-parliament were also applied to ecclesiastical commissions in particular. Stillingfleet found no evidence in history for the prerogative power to appoint a commission

[167] Bodl., Tanner MS 338, fo. 309v.

[168] Washington and Stillingfleet published in 1689, but Stillingfleet had drafted some of his tract by the middle of Jan. 1688: *EB*, Q228. Philonomus published before 23 July 1688, since Johnston refuted his 'Ignorant Assertion': *Visitatorial Power*, p. 202. Goldie, 'Anglican Revolution', p. 111, downplays constitutionalist opposition to James (although cf. pp. 118–20), but this seemed to be a strong element of opposition to the Ecclesiastical Commission.

[169] Philonomus Anglicus, *A Letter to the Author of the Vindication of the Proceedings of the Ecclesiastical Commissioners* ('Eleutheropolis' [Oxford], 1688, citing Wing L1728), p. 8; Robert Washington, *Some Observations upon the Ecclesiastical Jurisdiction of the Kings of England with an Appendix in Answer to Part of a Late Book Intitled, The King's Visitatorial Power Asserted* (1689), p. 8.

[170] Johnston, *Visitatorial Power*, p. 145; Washington, *Observations*, pp. 164–5.

[171] Washington, *Observations*, p. 20. [172] Philonomus, *Letter*, p. [15] (mispag. 16).

exercising extraordinary jurisdiction over first instance cases and inflicting ecclesiastical censures.[173] Thus the 1559 statute must have introduced such authority anew. And if so, it was repealed in 1641 and that repeal confirmed in 1661. Did the clause saving the supremacy negate this? No proviso, Philonomus and North declared, could be held to invalidate the rest of the statute.[174] Washington thought that the best argument James's Ecclesiastical Commission could cite was the precedent of Thomas Cromwell's vicegerency. Yet he stated that even that delegation was not exercised in the first two years of Henry's supremacy, but only after the 1534 Act of Supremacy granted Henry powers of visiting and correcting. That act, repealed under Mary, was never revived.[175] Washington argued that every facet of the supremacy inhered in parliament as well as the crown: allowance of papal bulls, of legates, of canons; elections of bishops, deprivations thereof, erecting and endowing new sees; judging whom to accept as pope during schisms.[176] The division of spiritual and temporal courts was authorised by parliament (a division which Philonomus said the king could 'neither enlarge nor abridge').[177] No king could subject the realm to foreign power by his sole authority, for he was bound by the laws to defend it: Edward I told the pope's nuncio he could not collect papal taxes without parliament's authorisation; no monarch dared dispense with acts of provisors until authorised by parliament; James I's judges told him he could not alter the ecclesiastical laws.[178] Against foreign usurpations the royal supremacy was a formidable power, but within the realm it ran in the normal channels of the temporal prerogative, through the king *and his courts*. 'A *Personal Supremacy*' was a 'Fiction', 'without any warrant from *Antiquity*, *Law*, or *History*'.[179]

If the laws were immutable, the king could not dispense with them. The third chapter of Stillingfleet's attack on the Ecclesiastical Commission offered an account of the limits of royal dispensing with any statute, not just college ones. Dispensing, the preacher concluded, was more than merely administering or interpreting a law. If a law was intrinsically

[173] Edward Stillingfleet, *A Discourse Concerning the Illegality of the Late Ecclesiastical Commission* (1689), p. 9. (Literally extra-ordinary, i.e. outside ordinary jurisdiction exercised by bishops and church courts.)

[174] Philonomus, *Letter*, p. 18; Bodl., Tanner MS 460, fo. 25r. Stillingfleet claimed that the proviso intended to show that ordinary ecclesiastical jurisdiction was compatible with the supremacy.

[175] Washington, *Observations*, pp. 135–7. [176] See above, pp. 112–15.

[177] Washington, *Observations*, pp. 239–40, 282–3; Philonomus, *Letter*, p. 14.

[178] Washington, *Observations*, pp. 215–16, 186–7, 226–7, 170–8.

[179] Washington, *Observations*, pp. 237–8, 284–5 (qu. 285), 242, 259; pp. 196–9 conflated the Oath of Supremacy and medieval oaths to defend the laws.

bad (*malum in se*), it was simply void. If the king could dispense anything which was *malum prohibitum*, what security was there for any law? Stillingfleet argued that the king could not dispense with a law the intent of which was to ban certain men from serving the monarch (i.e. the Tests' ban on Catholics).[180] And he crossly argued that all the limits on dispensing outlined by lawyers like Vaughan in *Thomas* v. *Sorrell* ought to apply even more stringently to the Church. Kings could not dispense nuisances, but were highways more important than religion? If they could not dispense from monopolies, why was the religious monopoly of the Church of England seemingly the only exception to this? And if a dispensation was not possible when a particular individual was damaged, why did the law care more for one man than the whole public, disadvantaged if Catholicism was introduced?[181]

At best delayed, and at worst thwarted, when dispensing individuals by Anglican intransigence, and perhaps emboldened by the judicial decision in favour of his dispensing power in *Godden* v. *Hales*, James raised the stakes in 1688. He ordered his reissued Declaration of Indulgence to be read from every Anglican pulpit. In so doing, he united the country against him and he did so under the most unlikely leadership of all, the episcopate of the Church of England.

THE KING VERSUS THE BISHOPS

When James ordered that his Second Declaration of Indulgence be read from every Anglican pulpit, he provoked the denouement of the conflict between episcopal and monarchical concepts of supremacy. For the Church of England to defend itself against Catholicism, the suspending power, and prerogative attacks on its rights was far from new. But the number and prestige of those who defied James over reading the Declaration, and the range of arguments on which they drew, epitomised how supremacy and episcopacy could come into direct conflict. The tensions which had existed between the two for much of the Restoration now turned into open warfare. Many churchmen refused to read the Declaration, the London clergy protested, and seven bishops, including the Archbishop of Canterbury, presented James with a petition begging him to excuse them from endorsing the Declaration. The king responded

180 Stillingfleet, *Discourse*, pp. 33–5. See, similarly, Bodl., Tanner MS 460, fo. 64r.

181 Stillingfleet, *Discourse*, pp. 40–2. For *Thomas* v. *Sorrell*, see above, p. 92. It is unlikely that a lawyer could have made this argument: 'damage' was specific to an individual.

with fury, eventually prosecuting the Seven Bishops for seditious libel in Kings Bench.[182]

James was far from devoid of support. Many tracts berated the Seven Bishops – and indeed other recalcitrant bishops and clergy – for the disobedience to their king which exposed the hollowness of their 'threadbare paradox/Passive Obedience'.[183] To baulk at the Declaration was held to signify an unwillingness to tolerate Dissenters, especially (Care said) given the willingness of clergy to read contentious royal orders such as the Book of Sports.[184] Frequently the denunciation of the apparent hypocrisy of Anglican loyalty when really tested slid into specific claims about the supreme head of the Church being the best judge of what his clergy should read. Care reminded churchmen that the king was their supreme ordinary, to whom they owed canonical obedience. One anonymous pamphleteer reminded the Bishops that Henry VIII would have prosecuted them for *praemunire* for such defiance – and carefully computed the cost of this to Henrician bishops as a staggering £118,840.10d. And after their trial *Melinus inquirendum* bemoaned how kings, as supreme as popes and ordained at their coronations, had to subordinate their will to the Church's wishes.[185] Care scorned the notion that reading the Declaration was an act of assent to it, or that churchmen might petition the king against his decision. 'A Bishop's private Opinion may be warrant enough for him to speak when he is requir'd, but not to reprove a Prince upon pretence of Duty.'[186] Nor did these writers deem such assent to endorse an act against divine law. The supine bishop of Hereford, Herbert Croft, took refuge in such notions when he insisted that the Declaration might contravene parliament's view of the laws, but was not *malum in se*. Croft argued that, by comparison,

[182] Jeffreys suggested a trial in King's Bench to avoiding his sitting in judgement on the bishops in the Ecclesiastical Commission. James altered the charge from scandalous to seditious libel: William Gibson, *James II and the Trial of the Seven Bishops* (Houndmills, Basingstoke, 2009), pp. 106, 121.

[183] *The Paradox*, lines 3–4 and *The Church of England's Glory*, line 74, in George deF. Lord, gen. ed., *Poems on Affairs of State*, vol. IV., ed. G. M. Crump (New Haven, 1968), pp. 225, 233; Anon., *A Sober Answer to a Scandalous Paper* (1688), pp. 8–9, 13; Anon., *The Countrey-Ministers Reflections on the City-Ministers Letter* (1688), pp. 1, 3; Henry Care, *An Answer to a Paper Importing a Petition* (1688), pp. 27–8.

[184] Anon., *The Countrey-Ministers Reflections*, p. 3; W. E., *Melinus inquirendum* (1688), p. 2; Anon., *An Answer to the City-Conformists Letter* (1688), pp. 6–7; Care, *Answer to a Paper*, p. 30.

[185] Anon., *Sober Answer*, p. 7; W. E., *Melinus inquirendum*, p. 3; Andrew Poulton, *An Answer to a Letter from a Clergyman in the City* (1688), p. 6; Care, *Answer to a Paper*, p. 13; Anon., *The Clergy's Late Carriage to the King* (1688), p. 2.

[186] Care, *Answer to a Paper*, p. 15.

he could not obey a royal order to read a Catholic homily.[187] But most Anglicans felt that the step from reading the Declaration to promoting Catholicism was indiscernible.

Once churchmen had erased any distinction between reading the Declaration and assenting to it,[188] they then turned to argue that its contents were illegal by both human and divine law. This two-pronged rhetoric was common to the high-church Oxford divine Jonas Proast and the London latitudinarian Edward Fowler. According to Morrice, Fowler was crucial in encouraging the London clergy to oppose reading the Declaration. Fowler's reasons partly rested on the appearance that compliance would produce: scandalising[189] the people, annoying parliament, earning the contempt of Catholics and Dissenters, and setting a poor example.[190] Clearly the clergy (and their king, if he really did think their endorsement of the Declaration was important as more than a test of obedience) still felt themselves to wield significant cultural influence in the polity. But there were other reasons for 'preferring Suffering before a base Compliance', and Fowler found it hard to say whether conscience or prudence weighed greater in these.[191] Reading the Declaration was 'a *sinfull* approbation' of a thing 'evill in it selfe'. 'Shall our mouths proclaime a Lisence [*sic*] for Idolatry and all errours, a transcendency of Prerogative above Law?' Feeling toleration to be *malum in se* rendered any endorsement of it wrong, as well as constitutionally illicit.[192] Morrice's account states that he told Fowler (although from the account it appears more as if Fowler told him) that the Declaration was neither legal nor honest, although parts were both. Furthermore, it was 'most heynously criminall to publish the Princes private Will and pleasure against his Legall and introtrolable Will, and that in such a fundamentall point as the Dispensing power is that overthrows the very Constitution of the

187 Herbert Croft, *A Short Discourse Concerning the Reading His Majesties Late Declaration* (1688), pp. 6, 9. Croft made his argument even more unpalatable with a Hobbesian citation of Naaman bowing to an idol (pp. 12–13). On the potentially unauthorised publication of this, see *EB*, Q266 (cf. Goldie, 'Anglican Revolution', p. 120, n. 50, which says Croft retracted it).

188 E.g. Anon., *A Letter from a Clergy-man in the City … Containing his Reasons for Not Reading the Declaration* (1688), pp. 2–3, 5; cf. Care, *Answer to a Paper*, p. 29 (2nd pag.) The first is sometimes wrongly attrib. to Halifax; Gibson, *Trial of the Seven Bishops*, p. 100, suggests William Sherlock.

189 Scandal in the ecclesiastical sense: unjust offence to brethren.

190 *EB*, Q255–6.

191 *EB*, Q256. Fowler clearly felt that clergy who refused would lose their places; he never mentions any risk of *praemunire* prosecutions.

192 *EB*, Q257 (my emphasis).

Government'.[193] This constitutionalist strain, already seen in some of the responses to the Ecclesiastical Commission, was reiterated in the London clergy's final paper, which denounced the Declaration as 'founded upon such a Dispensing power as may at pleasure set aside all Lawes Ecclesiasticall and civill [which] appeares to us illegal, and did so to the Parliament in 1672'. The fear of civil as well as ecclesiastical laws being undermined echoed the worries expressed by parliament in 1663 and 1673. However, references to the temporal laws being undermined were deleted in the Bishops' petition. This adapted its language to describe dispensing as 'often declared illegal in parliament' rather than an act which 'appeares to us illegal'. Conversely, while the London clergy's paper mentioned only the 1672 parliament, the Bishops' petition added references to 1662 and, most provocatively, 1685. Both the paper and the petition disavowed dislike of Dissenters, but the Bishops alone took care to protest their obedience and the Anglican tradition of loyalty.[194]

It might be unsurprising to find a divine like Fowler, who sympathised with nonconformity and had close contacts with the Dissenter Morrice, proffering a constitutional case. It is even more revealing, therefore, that such language formed part of the Seven Bishops' argument at their trial. This might have grown out of a desire to enter an 'award of parliament' plea based on parliament's resolutions that Declarations of Indulgence were illegal, but the likelihood of such being allowed was small.[195] Instead, the Bishops constructed a varied case, in their petition and at their trial, which justified their defiance on the grounds of conscience and counsel, the privilege of peers and the liberty of the subject, the duties of magistrates, and the limitations of the royal prerogative.

When presenting the petition to James, Bishop White of Peterborough protested, 'Sir, you allow liberty of conscience to all mankind: the reading this Declaration is against our conscience.' His primate's planned speech for their trial – never in fact given – similarly emphasised that 'when all his Majesty's subjects had liberty of conscience, those who had most pretence [claim] to it should not be the only persons to whom it is denyed'.[196] This

[193] *EB*, Q258. The references to the clergy in the first person plural, their obedience to their metropolitan, and to their maintenance of the Real Presence, signal an Anglican author. Cf. Roger Thomas, 'The Seven Bishops and their Petition, 18 May 1688', *Journal of Ecclesiastical History*, 12 (1961), pp. 56–70.

[194] *EB*, Q259–60. (Since the parliamentary debates took place in the spring of 1663 and 1673, contemporaries dated them a year earlier, as the year began on 25 Mar.) On the changes, see Thomas, 'Bishops and their Petition'; for the text of the Bishops' petition see Gutch, *Collectanea*, I.336–7.

[195] *EB*, Q270. [196] Gutch, *Collectanea*, I.339, 368.

epitomised the way in which the bishops simultaneously claimed common rights with other subjects and religious groups, and yet still perceived themselves to be a special established church, which thus had '*most*' claim to be heard. One account of Holloway's judgment at the Bishops' trial had the judge stating that the petition was no libel, since it was presented from 'conviction of Conscience'.[197] Conscience was more a useful echo of James's own rhetoric than any true conversion to an ideal of freedom of conscience – as the Bishops probably felt that they could invoke conscience because theirs were truly ordered, correct, consciences.[198] Similarly, the attempt by their legal counsel to claim the rights of subjects to delay entering a plea at their trial – an endeavour which largely failed – sat uneasily with the repeated citations of peers' privilege of freedom from arrest.[199] Much as these invocations may have appeared legal quibbling, episcopal peerage was an argument which was put to greater effect in Sir Robert Sawyer's speech, which stated that all peers had a duty to uphold the laws, an idea which Sancroft would have repeated.[200]

The general warrant of prelates *qua* peers to uphold the law echoed in a further argument, which presented all bishops as magistrates who had a right to query the enforcement of an act which they felt to be illegal. Just as Compton had regarding James's order to suspend Sharp, so at the Bishops' trial Somers cited 'the law of all civilized nations', *rescribere principi*, and Creswell Levinz argued that even a constable might petition a JP against carrying out an illegal order.[201] This line of defence was further intensified by stressing the specific duty of ecclesiastical magistrates to uphold laws on religion. Levinz and Sawyer cited the Elizabethan Act of Uniformity which urged all bishops in God's name to uphold uniformity; more vaguely, Sawyer insisted that the Seven Bishops' petition was 'an act they did, and do conceive they might lawfully do with relation to their ecclesiastical polity, and the government of their people as bishops'. Both he and Sancroft's speech paired the obligations of prelates to the laws and the bishops to Protestantism. The archbishop planned to argue that

He always esteemed it his duty, as a Prelate, not only to do his utmost endeavour to conserve the profession of the reformed religion amongst us, but to promote the honour and interest of the Church, and to oppose, as far as lawfully

[197] Anon., *An Account of the Proceedings at Westminster-Hall* (1688), p. 2; *State Trials*, XII.426 has 'could not in conscience give obedience'.
[198] Goldie, 'Anglican Revolution', p. 125.
[199] *State Trials*, XII.205, 220–23, 267–8 (peers); 241 (subjects).
[200] *State Trials*, XII.361; Gutch, *Collectanea*, I.346, 364.
[201] *State Trials*, XII.397 (qu.), 394.

he could, all that tended to her ruine, and struck at her safety … and as a Peer of the Realm he thought himself likewise under very great obligations, not only not to betray the laws himself, but also to transmit them to posterity.[202]

But what actions counted as lawful protest in a society which lacked any concept of a loyal opposition? The early modern alternative to this notion was the concept of counsel, a means to freely express opinion when invited, to criticise royal ideas in a constructive manner. Counsel was fundamental to the Bishops' defence against the specific charge against them, that of seditious libel. Much of the prosecution's case (at least before it was derailed by the attack on the suspending power) focused on proving that they had published their petition, which according to the prosecution constituted sedition rather than counsel because it had not been invited by the king. The Bishops had therefore to prove that they had not broken the unwritten rules of counsel, which stated that freedom of speech *once invited* should not be held against the giver, and they did so by insisting that their supreme head had an obligation to hear ecclesiastical counsellors. Sancroft's draft speech was most explicit 'that as all his brethren, the Bishops of this Church, so he more eminently, were counsellors to the King by their office, in matters ecclesiasticall, as the temporal Peers were of his counsell in lay matters, and his judges in matters of law'. Bishop Lloyd of St Asaph also argued that Sancroft 'by his place is Counsellor to his Majesty and … ought to be advised with in all things belonging to the Church'. Although their speeches were not given, their legal counsel did have time to echo their sentiments, as in Finch's comment that they had 'more than an ordinary call' to correct the king's mistaken notion of his ecclesiastical prerogative.[203] The language of counsel similarly echoed in the general debate about whether the petition could really be seditious, if presented humbly and in 'the privatest way that could be'.[204]

All these claims rested, fundamentally, on the notion that suspending was illegal – or at least that its legality was so uncertain that there was justifiable warrant for querying an order to read (endorse) it from the pulpit. The concept of reading the Declaration being *malum in se* was overtaken at the trial by parliamentary objections to suspending. Of the Bishops' counsel, Sawyer had opposed James issuing writs dispensing Catholics and Levinz had been dismissed in 1686, possibly for opposing dispensing. Sir Francis Pemberton had refused to act as counsel to

[202] *State Trials*, XII.392–3, 364, 359 (qu.), 361; Gutch, *Collectanea*, I.363–4.

[203] Gutch, *Collectanea*, I.364, 371; *State Trials*, XII.369. It is noteworthy that the bishops could invoke counsel whereas the London clergy did not.

[204] *State Trials*, XII.358; Anon., *Account of the Proceedings*, p. 1 (qu.).

Arthur Godden and thought the degree awarded by Cambridge to the Catholic Alban Francis was illegal. Sir Henry Pollexfen and John Somers had long been whigs. Thus James united men who had acted on opposing sides in the last years of Charles II. The prosecution of the Bishops was completely derailed when the defence read out a series of parliamentary declarations (concluding with that of 1685) that universal dispensing was illegal, thus reinforcing the citation of parliament's rejection of Declarations of Indulgence in 1663 and 1673 in the petitions of the Bishops and the London clergy.[205] Attorney-General Powys and Solicitor-General Williams countered by insisting that the petition was still seditious, not least because of the power of the royal ecclesiastical prerogative, declared in rather than introduced by statutes, and therefore not bound by parliament (especially parliamentary declarations rather than acts).[206] Serjeant Trinder stated that the king, as supreme ordinary, had supreme ecclesiastical authority, and thus could dispense – not least because of the 1559 Act of Uniformity and many statutes containing clauses saving the supremacy. Serjeant Baldock added that this meant that the Seven Bishops and their fellow prelates were 'bound' to dispatch the Declaration 'by virtue of their obedience, and not to examine more'.[207] But the Bishops convinced not only the jury but also Judge Powell, who stated that he could 'not remember, in any case in all our law (and I have taken some pains upon this occasion to look into it) that there is any such power in the king'; i.e. to question dispensing was not libellous. Judge Holloway could not think the petition seditious or libellous.[208] For James, such a manifest error rendered a man incapable of remaining one of His Majesty's judges; Holloway and Powell lost their places on 2 July.

In late summer 1688 it might have seemed that the Bishops and their Church had won their battle with the king. Sir John Reresby described the cheers at the trial as 'a little rebellion in noise though not in fact'.[209] Celebrated in the streets of London, in pamphlets, and in a series of engravings, episcopal defence of the Church of England seemed to earn endorsement from a wide variety of English Protestants. The Bishops, too, might have felt that they had achieved their aim of disobeying a royal order 'with all the duty in the world'.[210] The person who clearly did not reach any such conclusion was James. Criticism of the Bishops continued

[205] *State Trials*, XII.374–94; Gutch, *Collectanea*, I.337.
[206] *State Trials*, XII.412–14, 399. [207] *State Trials*, XII.420, 418.
[208] *State Trials*, XII.426–7. [209] Quoted in Gibson, *Trial of the Seven Bishops*, p. 133.
[210] Gutch, *Collectanea*, I.371. On the engravings, see Goldie, 'Anglican Revolution', pp. 133–4; and p. 123 on the recollection of Marian persecution.

after their trial not only in ephemeral tracts which fulminated against episcopal defiance of supremacy, but also in government circles. The king ordered the Ecclesiastical Commission 'to enquire who obeyed the king's order for reading the king's late declaraci*o*n for liberty of conscience & what ministers refused'.[211] As James's regime hung in the balance between late summer and autumn of 1688, it might have appeared that Anglicans had reconciled their paradox of passive obedience whilst winning a victory against the supremacy, that prelacy had vanquished *praemunire*. James's refusal to recognise this lost him his final support, leaving him helpless against William's invasion. That five of the Seven Bishops became nonjurors, refusing to endorse the new regime, is, however, telling. The Dutch descent was disastrous for James, but it was also a resounding defeat for Anglican royalism.

[211] Quoting Bodl., Rawlinson MS D365, fo. [31]r–v; *EB*, Q282 (which says the king was also worried about 'makeing of Bonefires'), Q286–7; Burnet, *James II*, p. 270; Goldie, 'Anglican Revolution', p. 134, mentions the threat of *praemunire*.

Conclusion

Between the Act of Appeals in 1533 and the Revolution of 1688, the royal supremacy moved from underpinning the ideology of the monarchical and episcopal 'establishments' to undermining them. When Henry VIII broke with Rome, he sought an immediate solution to a pressing problem: the need for a divorce and an heir. His method of doing so seemingly increased the power of English kings to unprecedented heights. Supremacy was created in the 1530s to justify the jurisdictional independence of the English Church from Rome and enhance the judicial, ecclesiastical, and fiscal authority of the crown. In making the monarch supreme governor of the Church, it reflected the early modern assumption that membership of the polity and of the national church went hand in hand. In many ways, that assumption still prevailed in Restoration England. To reject papal authority was a patriotic act in 1688, just as it was in 1588.

Yet the supremacy forged for monarchical empowerment turned out to be rather more complex than its creators imagined. Supremacy was the juridical embodiment of that pervasive early modern English mentality, anti-popery. As such, it could support a powerful ecclesiastical prerogative and a Protestant episcopal establishment. But, like anti-popery, it shifted over time to providing a language by which to critique insufficiently godly kings and churchmen. The use of statute law to enforce Henrician supremacy allowed Restoration parliaments to claim a right to check royal Declarations of Indulgence, while its Tudor use to purge ungodly clergy inspired later Dissenters to wield it against high-church prelates. Like anti-popery, therefore, supremacy was a widely shared political language which meant very different things to different users of it. Indeed, the prevalence and persistence of both of these rhetorics may have derived from their helpful ambiguity. They could apparently unite the nation while implicitly excluding certain groups from membership of it. The difference between 1588 and 1688 was that Elizabeth gained loyalty for opposing the dark forces of popery; James II was deposed for inviting them in.

The different versions of supremacy which were suggested between 1530 and 1660 set up a variety of precedents for Restoration writers to follow. The Reformation was not merely an important historical event, but a whole framework in which the politics of religion took place. The royal supremacy provides a reminder of the continuing importance of polemical religious history in the later seventeenth century. History was still 'entangled in the tendrils of ideology'. Indeed, it became *increasingly* polarised between low- and high-church accounts of Reformation.[1] Because the Reformation was not secure from Catholic attack, its integrity and legality – indeed, its necessity – had to be repeatedly defended. The entrenched Catholic strategy of attacking Henry VIII's motives for the break with Rome and denouncing the illegitimacy of a church headed by a layman forced Anglicans to defend the supremacy. The fierce debates over whether Cranmer had endorsed a sacerdotal supremacy, and whether the Edwardian Episcopal Elections Act remained in force, demonstrate how the Reformation was not just a historical question, but provided precedents for contemporary policies. These affected the writing of history. The need for a precise understanding of the wording of statutes, injunctions, and canons, and of their repeal and counter-repeal, increased the importance of accurately reproducing historical documents: legal demands as well as historical scholarship impelled the editing of sources. This book has shown, too, that the interpretation of Reformation supremacy was not confined to the pages of church history. It echoed in parliamentary debates on indulging nonconformity, in Archbishop Sancroft's concerns about *praemunire*, in James II's pursuit of Catholicisation through his Ecclesiastical Commission, and in the church courts which prosecuted Dissenters and the maverick pastor Hickeringill. The nature of Reformation was a legal as well as historical question, intensifying its political import.

Consideration of the relationship between church and state shows the importance of Reformation history. Yet it also reminds us that this was just one of many types of history needed to negotiate ecclesiological politics. Polemicists invoked Israelite, Anglo-Saxon, and patristic history as well. The first was important to Erastians, who presented the unity of the Hebrew church-state as a model for England. If the commonwealth and

[1] J. A. I. Champion, *The Pillars of Priestcraft Shaken: The Church of England and its Enemies, 1660–1730* (Cambridge, 1992), pp. 40 (qu.), 92.

church of God's chosen people were both governed by the Sanhedrin, should not their Christian successors follow the same divinely warranted path? The Civil War debate on excommunication, and the argument over whether the Old Testament evidenced God's preference for monarchy or republicanism, stimulated attention both to the Old Testament and to rabbinical commentary on it.[2] Especially powerful in the 1640s, this history lessened in intensity after the Civil Wars – the Restoration lacked a Selden. Secondly, Anglo-Saxon history was pursued to substantiate the claim that civil and ecclesiastical courts were not separate bodies before 1066. Historians have documented the rise of feudal and medieval history in the seventeenth-century debate on the origins of parliament, but the complementary interest in Gothic ecclesiastical history warrants further investigation. Third, and most important, was the centrality of patristic scholarship to Restoration churchmen. This was not wholly new, but the Fathers took on a novel importance. Quantin has shown how this developed in doctrinal debate;[3] this book has demonstrated its impact on ecclesiology. That story might be further extended into the political sphere, regarding the history of early Christian passive obedience, most dramatically evidenced in the 1680s debate over Samuel Johnson's *Julian the Apostate*. The historical genre (naturally) absent is classical history; interest in the Greek and Roman worlds was a republican pursuit which the thinkers studied in this book were less urgent in refuting than they were in suppressing Catholic and Calvinist resistance theory.[4] To Restoration thinkers on religion and politics, imperial Christian Rome was more important than pagan republican Rome. And if, for Anglican churchmen, Cyprian now pushed Constantine aside, Cicero did not feature at all. We find a long Reformation, but no long Renaissance.

The royal supremacy strikingly demonstrates the poverty of a secular paradigm for understanding early modern political thought. Those who wrote on supremacy were interested in how royal prerogative powers could be used to uphold their vision of godliness. Those discontented with the policies their supreme governors were pursuing were often unwilling to have recourse to resistance theory. It was suggested in the 1550s and experimented with in the 1640s – but that very experiment made men wary of

[2] Eric Nelson, *The Hebrew Republic: Jewish Sources and the Transformation of European Political Thought* (Cambridge, MA, 2010).

[3] Jean-Louis Quantin, *The Church of England and Christian Antiquity* (Oxford, 2009).

[4] I have outlined elsewhere the Restoration interest in tracing the history of seditious *religious* ideas: 'Robert Brady's Intellectual History and Royalist Antipopery in Restoration England', *English Historical Review*, 122 (2007), pp. 1287–1317.

trying it again. Furthermore, most of the time English authors were grappling not with ungodly tyrants but with recalcitrantly godly kings. They did not seek to resist rulers, but to channel royal authority to its 'proper' godly ends. In these circumstances, absolutism was far from being a simple creed of unthinking obedience. As this study has shown, Anglicans had to keep a careful and precarious balance between upholding nonresistance and criticising kings who abused their supremacy to tolerate other denominations. Royal headship of the Church shored up passive obedience. But it also encumbered the king with extra responsibilities to be godly, and opened up an arena in which subjects could advise him on how to rule.

Discussion of royal ecclesiastical prerogative involved expertise in more than just theology. It also required legal knowledge. This study reminds us of the danger of marginalising the role of lawyers in political thinking. The importance of St German, Coke, Bagshaw, Hale, and North provides a constant reminder of how political argument was infused with legal language, as polemicists had to penetrate and adjudicate the interstices of statutes, canons, proclamations, and injunctions. The ambiguities and permutations of Tudor *imperium* made it problematic to pin down, but also advantageously opened up a space for exploitation. Supremacy, like Reformation, could be tweaked to serve an individual's own purpose. Supremacy, like Reformation, was simultaneously a singular and a plural entity. It was an arena for argument, allowing widely divergent interpretations, but nevertheless with some rules and boundaries of engagement. This was an arena in which political thought interacted with political action. Supremacy is a constant reminder of the symbiotic relationship between policy and polemic. Dissenters, for example, pushed Charles towards indulgence, and they responded when he offered it.

This book has explored how ideological claims which had been proposed as *ex post facto* justifications for particular acts could, over time, take on a life of their own. The deeds of Henry VIII and his successors were implemented to solve *their* problems, but over time their policies, and defences of them, sprouted quasi-independent afterlives. Those afterlives evolved in the circumstances of monarchical willingness to subvert the episcopal establishment by indulging Catholics and Dissenters – circumstances which made the period between 1660 and 1688 a distinct one. After 1660, MPs and lawyers were willing to admit a role for the royal prerogative and accept clauses saving the supremacy in statutes. But when monarchs sought to bypass penal laws with prerogative dispensations, many MPs grew angry. They, like Restoration churchmen, had to negotiate due respect for supremacy with somehow restraining it. As the prevailing tendency in the Restoration Church towards a more catholic ecclesiology increased, the limits of supremacy were enunciated more clearly than they had been before the Civil Wars. That trend was not merely a result of a belief in *iure divino* episcopacy, but a necessary defence when monarchs sought to use their supremacy to indulge Dissenters and Catholics. Nevertheless, when kings threw their prerogative weight behind the Church, Anglican royalism flourished.

Against the alliance of Church and crown, Dissenters might have looked to parliament. But given the staunch Anglicanism of much of the Commons, nonconformists turned to royal aid for relief from prosecution. Dissenting praise for supremacy complicated the relationship between civil and religious liberty, checking any simple proclivity amongst nonconformists towards constitutional monarchy. And, given royal wishes to indulge rather than comprehend those outside the Church (in order to benefit Catholics), Dissenters were forced towards separation and away from a national church. Nevertheless, there was a lingering preference, especially amongst Presbyterians, for retaining a national church. Richard Baxter's criticism of the established Church was not that it was established but that it was – in the words of his Elizabethan forebears – 'but halfly reformed'. Godly kingship provided a chance for full reformation. Baxter, like the majority of Dissenters who sought to use the supremacy to restrain persecutory prelacy, wanted to support a godly pastoral ministry. But this mode of argument could extend to full-scale anticlericalism. In the hands of men like Hobbes and Hickeringill, supremacy was mobilised against clericalism of any variety. They fought the early battles of their war against priestcraft with Reformation (and medieval) weapons like *praemunire*. Thus the long Reformation almost imperceptibly became the early Enlightenment.

Early Enlightenment thinkers focused on the need to dismantle clerical authority. John Toland, Matthew Tindal, and Sir Robert Howard found plenty of English *infame* to be crushed. But the early Enlightenment campaign against priestcraft was familiar territory to those instrumental in earlier conflicts against *imperium in imperio*.[5] Edmund Hickeringill is a telling example, since his anticlerical campaign stretched from the 1680s to the 1700s – from *praemunire* to priestcraft. This suggests how a long story can be traced of the extension of *praemunire* from its application to

[5] Mark Goldie, 'Priestcraft and the Birth of Whiggism', in Nicholas Phillipson and Quentin Skinner, eds., *Political Discourse in Early Modern Britain* (Cambridge, 1993).

popes in the fourteenth century, to Catholic bishops under Henry VIII, to high-church prelates in the seventeenth century, and to all clergy from the 1690s onwards. This diffusion was paralleled by a historical narrative of the decline of pure apostolic clergy into corrupt courtly prelates, whose politicking subverted the civil state. For Edward Fox in the 1530s, this was a story of Catholic error; for William Prynne in the 1630s, of godly bishops degenerating into lordly prelates; for Andrew Marvell in the 1670s, of general clerical decay. Thomas Hobbes told a similar story in his *Historia ecclesiastica*, which when translated in 1722 included the word 'priestcraft'.[6] This was an editorial interpolation, although Hobbes surely understood the concept. Since the roots of the priestcraft problem could be located in the Constantinian era, it was feasible to link it to Nicene bickering over the definition of the Trinity, a route which Hobbes took, and which led in heretical directions. But it was not a necessary result of distaste for priestcraft: theologically orthodox lawyers could be vehemently anticlerical. Thus, while early Enlightenment ideas could arise from Spinozist materialism,[7] or from Bayle's scepticism, the above suggests how it might also develop from within learned traditions – in this case, a legal power (*praemunire*) turned against the church-state which had created it. Royal supremacy provides an example of the phenomenon described by Noel Malcolm, where 'ideas which may not in themselves have had … radical force' nevertheless 'supplied some of the components' or 'prompted some of the questions' of radical thinking.[8] Even if theological heterodoxy was the source of the radical Enlightenment, historians should not diminish the subversive nature of the cry of priestcraft. To dismantle the socio-cultural power of the clergy and to purge politics of priestly involvement challenged the very foundations of the early modern church-state.

However fascinating they are to modern scholars – still seemingly more intrigued by the seeds of unbelief and heterodoxy than the persistence of belief and orthodoxy – early Enlightenment thinkers were a minority. In the 1690s the Church had to negotiate what the Williamite revolution implied for relationships between bishops, kings, and parliaments. The politics of supremacy did not vanish in 1689. The nonjuring schism

[6] Thomas Hobbes, *Historia ecclesiastica*, ed. Patricia Springborg et al. (Paris, 2008), lines 976–7, 1168–78; Thomas Hobbes, *A True Ecclesiastical History* (1722), pp. 77, 93–4.

[7] As suggested by Jonathan Israel, most prominently in *Radical Enlightenment: Philosophy and the Making of Modernity, 1650–1750* (Oxford, 2001).

[8] Noel Malcolm, 'Hobbes, Ezra, and the Bible: The History of a Subversive Idea', in Malcolm, *Aspects of Hobbes* (Oxford, 2002), p. 398.

highlighted earlier divisions within the Restoration Church. Theorists of *iure humano* episcopacy accepted positions in the new establishment: John Tillotson became archbishop of Canterbury, Edward Stillingfleet played a prominent role in defending the jurors. On the other side, Henry Dodwell led the nonjuring critique of the Williamite clergy. Although intellectual positions did not translate into political ones in any simple way – a striking number of opponents of James II's Catholicising programme located the true Anglican Church at St Germain, not Hampton Court – the Revolution converted differing theories about episcopacy and supremacy into conflict. Older divergent views of supremacy were also reiterated after 1689. Edward Welchman's tract of 1701 provided an account which would have been recognisable to sixteenth-century churchmen.[9] In 1706, Matthew Tindal prefaced his *Rights of the Christian Church* with a lengthy account of the history of supremacy, endorsing Robert Washington's, and thus ultimately Christopher St German's, location of it in crown-in-parliament. He stated that Anne had 'no power in Ecclesiasticals except by the Laws of the Land, and can't divest her self of any part of it without Consent of Parliament'.[10] Yet Tindal combined this with a critique of priestcraft – clergy should be elected, not consecrated – and repeatedly used Lockean language of fiduciary clerical power and toleration.

Nevertheless, the politics of supremacy did change after 1689. Debate on supremacy arose when it was useful for an immediate political need, and over time those needs changed. Post-Revolution kings might still be presented as godly rulers, to shore up their providentially sanctioned legitimacy against Jacobite dynastic threats, or to present them as defenders of European Protestantism, or to urge moral reformation.[11] Nevertheless, while the rhetoric of godly kingship survived in royal image-making, the changing nature of godly rule was signalled by the decline of detailed dissection of Reformation canons, statutes, and legal precedents. As the nonjuring debate became less clamorous, monarchical appointment and deprivation of bishops was less discussed. After 1717, when convocation was suppressed, arguments over royal or parliamentary ratification of canons fell away. The need for Dissenters to advocate supremacy also

[9] Edward Welchman, *The Regal Supremacy in Ecclesiastical Affairs Asserted* (1701).

[10] Matthew Tindal, *The Rights of the Christian Church* (1706), pp. ix, lxxxi. Dmitri Levitin, 'Matthew Tindal's "Rights of the Christian Church" (1706) and the Church–State Relationship', *Historical Journal* (forthcoming), considers these themes in detail.

[11] See Hannah Smith, *Georgian Monarchy: Politics and Culture, 1714–1760* (Cambridge, 2006), ch. 1, at p. 38, explicitly stating that Old Testament prophetical figures were not mapped on to Georgian kings; Tony Claydon, *William III and the Godly Revolution* (Cambridge, 1996), pp. 231–2, and *passim* the description of this as propaganda.

decreased, as religious pressures impelling them to exploit supremacy altered. The 'Act of Toleration' was restricted, and its survival was far from guaranteed in its first decades of life. But it did change debate about toleration from one about royal dispensing and indulgence to, for example, occasional conformity. Before 1689, conformists angrily rejected the idea of Dissenters being allowed to miss church; afterwards, they crossly rebuked those who took Anglican communion merely to qualify themselves to hold civil office. Furthermore, the Act entrenched the mentality of a new generation of Dissenters to seek toleration outside the Church, rather than further reformation of a national establishment. By decisively placing decisions on toleration in parliament's hands, it answered the question of the dispensing power. Thus, after 1689, because supremacy's utility as a weapon in issues of political and religious policy diminished, discussion of it necessarily declined. Arguments over church and state did continue, but required less attention *specifically* to *supremacy.*

As this book has argued, that diminution should not be read back into the era before 1688. Studying the royal supremacy highlights some important aspects of Restoration England. Religion and politics were closely entwined, but alignments rapidly shifted between Anglican royalism and puritan whiggery on the one hand, and Dissenting supremacism and Anglican restraints on supremacy on the other. For this reason, crucial changes in the relationship between crown and parliament, and developments such as toleration, were halting and sporadic. The Civil Wars could not be forgotten, but the memory of them made many MPs wary of asserting too much authority, and divided men over whether denominational diversity needed to be crushed or accepted. As royal policies quickly shifted between persecution and indulgence, asserting the prerogative and then backing down in the face of parliamentary opposition, those debating the supremacy had to respond. And so they did: in print, in scribal treatises, in speeches, in letters, and in sermons. Despite the burgeoning mass of printed debate, argument took place in a broader arena than that of print culture. Discourse about supremacy provided all sorts of men with a chance to express discontent with part of the establishment whilst claiming to obey another part of it – a sort of loyal opposition. Indeed, given the way in which kings themselves proved willing to undermine the established Church, it is hard to speak of a united 'establishment'.

Attitudes to supremacy were a complex combination of an individual's reading of history, their idea of the nature of the church, and the political circumstances during which they wrote. Restoration circumstances constantly interacted with a complex and ambivalent Reformation legacy. Restoration writers could not agree on who held supremacy and for what purposes. They looked to history to solve their problems, but history could not do so, because Tudor *imperium* was too multivalent to decide later arguments. Yet the ambiguities within the Henrician Reformation came to the fore slowly. For many decades the contradictory strands which made up supremacy coexisted. They were only retrospectively discovered when later kings, parliaments, churchmen, and Dissenters found it useful to unpick them. Henry's legacy was not *the* royal supremacy, but a whole range of *supremacies*, all interpreted in conflicting ways by the different groups which the English Reformation had spawned. The weapon which William Prynne's book showed Charles II grasping to support the Church was truly a double-edged sword.

Bibliography

PRIMARY SOURCES

MANUSCRIPT SOURCES

Bodleian Library, Oxford

Clarendon 87
Rawlinson D365
Tanner 36
Tanner 44
Tanner 271
Tanner 338
Tanner 459
Tanner 460

British Library, London

Additional 21099
Additional 32523
Additional 48064
Cotton Cleopatra Ev
Lansdowne 61
Stowe 424

The National Archives, London

PC 2/71
PRO 30/24/6B/427
PRO 30/24/6B/429
PRO 30/24/6B/430
SP 6/2
SP 6/8
SP 12/1
SP 12/221/23
SP 16/437/58

SP 29/67/31
SP 29/67/36
SP 29/70/13
SP 29/72/12
SP 29/274 pt 1 / 31
SP 29/319/220
SP 29/319/221
SP 29/319/222
SP 44/337

The Queen's College, Oxford

MS 280
MS 289

University Library, Cambridge

Mm 6.62

LEGAL CASES

75 Eng. Rep. 734, 2 Plowden 493 (*Grendon* v. *Bishop of Lincoln*, 1573)
77 Eng. Rep. 1, 1 Co. Rep. 1 (*R.* v. *Cawdrey*, 1593)
78 Eng. Rep. 750, Cro. Eliz. 500 (*Austen* v. *Twynne*, 1595)
82 Eng. Rep. 84, Jones W. 158 (*Evans and Kiffins* v. *Askwith*, 1625)
84 Eng. Rep. 906, 3 Keb. 607 (*R.* v. *Tayler*, 1675)
86 Eng. Rep. 781, 1 Mod 124 (*Manby* v. *Scott*, 1663)
89 Eng. Rep. 63, Freeman KB 85 (*Thomas* v. *Sorrell*, 1674)
89 Eng. Rep. 1050, 2 Shower KB 475 (*Godden* v. *Hales*, 1686)
90 Eng. Rep. 318, Comberbach 21 (*Godden* v. *Hales*, 1686)
124 Eng. Rep. 1098, Vaugh. 330 (*Thomas* v. *Sorrell*, 1674)

PRINTED PRIMARY SOURCES: CALENDARS AND REFERENCE WORKS

Brown, Rawdon, ed., *Calendar of State Papers Venetian, 1534–1554* (1873)
Calendar of State Papers Venetian, 1555–1556 (1877)
Bruce, John, et al., eds., *Calendar of State Papers, Domestic, of the Reign of Charles I* (23 vols., 1858–97)
Firth, C. H., and Rait, R. S., eds., *Acts and Ordinances of the Interregnum* (1911)
Green, M. A. E., et al., eds., *Calendar of State Papers, Domestic, of the Reign of Charles II* (28 vols., 1860–1947)
Hinds, Allen B., ed., *Calendar of State Papers Venetian, 1673–1675* (1947)
Howell, Thomas, and Cobbett, William, *A Complete Collection of State Trials* (34 vols., 1809–28)

Journals of the House of Commons
Journals of the House of Lords
Royal Commission on Historical Manuscripts, *Calendar of the Manuscripts of the House of Lords, 1678–1688* (1887)
Calendar of the Manuscripts of the Marquess of Ormonde, vol. v (1908)
Calendar of the Manuscripts of S. H. Le Fleming (1890)
Eighth Report (1881)
Ninth Report (1884)
Seventh Report (1879)
Twelfth Report (1889)
Stamp, A. E., ed., *Calendar of Patent Rolls, 1553–1554* (1937)
Statutes of the Realm (11 vols., 1810–28)

PRINTED PRIMARY SOURCES

An Account of the Proceedings at Westminster-Hall (1688)
Act Asserting His Majesties Supremacy (Edinburgh, 1669)
Advice to Protestant Dissenters Shewing 'tis their Interest to Repeal the Test (1688)
An Answer to the City-Conformists Letter (1688)
An Answer to a Late Pamphlet, Intituled, The Judgment and Doctrine of the Clergy of the Church of England (1687)
Assheton, William, *Toleration Disapprov'd and Condemn'd* (1670)
Atkyns, Sir Robert, *An Enquiry into the Power of Dispensing with Penal Statutes* (2nd edn, 1689)
Atwood, William, *The Lord Chief Justice Herbert's Account Examin'd* (1689)
An Aunswere to the Proclamation of the Rebels in the North (1569)
Aylmer, John, *An Harborowe for Faithfull and Trewe Subiectes* (Strasbourg [London], 1559)
Bacon, Francis, *The Essayes or Counsels, Civill and Morall*, ed. Michael Kiernan (Oxford, 1985)
Bacon, Matthew, *A New Abridgement of the Law*, 7th edn (8 vols., 1832)
Bagshaw, Edward, *A Just Vindication of the Questioned Part of the Reading* (1660)
Mr Bagshaw's Speech in Parliament February the Ninth, 1640 (1641)
Two Arguments in Parliament (1641)
Baillie, Robert, *Letters and Journals, 1637–62*, ed. D. Laing (3 vols., Edinburgh, 1841–2)
Baker, J. H., ed., *The Reports of Sir John Spelman* (2 vols., 1977–8)
Bancroft, Richard, *A Sermon Preached at Paules Crosse the 9 of Februarie 1588* ([1589])
Tracts Ascribed to Richard Bancroft, ed. Albert Peel (Cambridge, 1953)
Barlow, Thomas, *The Original of Kingly and Ecclesiastical Government* (1681)
Barrow, Henry, *A Petition Directed to Her Most Excellent Maiestie* (S.I., 1591)
Barrow, Isaac, *A Treatise of the Pope's Supremacy*, in *Theological Works*, ed. Alexander Napier, vol. VIII (Cambridge, 1859)
Baxter, Richard, *The Difference Between the Power of Magistrates and Church-Pastors* (1671)

Sacrilegious Desertion of the Holy Ministery Rebuked, and Tolerated Preaching of the Gospel Vindicated (1672)
Bilson, Thomas, *The Perpetval Gouernement of Christes Chvrch* (1593)
Bisbie, Nathaniel, *Unity of Priesthood Necessary to the Unity of Communion in a Church* (1692)
Blackstone, William, 'A Letter … to the Honourable Daines Barrington, Describing an Antique Seal; with Some Observations on its Original, and the Two Successive Controversies which the Disuse of it Afterwards Occasioned', *Archæologia*, 3 (1775), pp. 414–25
Bond, Maurice F., ed., *The Diaries and Papers of Sir Edward Dering Second Baronet, 1644 to 1684* (1976)
B. P., *A Modest and Peaceable Letter Concerning Comprehension* (1668)
Brabourne, Theophilus, *An Appendix to my Humble Petition* (n.p., 1661)
A Defence of the Kings Authority and Supremacy, 2nd edn (1660)
An Humble Petition … Tending to the Refining of the Booke of Common-Prayer (1661)
A Reply to the indoctus doctor edoctvs (1654, printed in Brabourne, *Second Part of the Change*)
The Second Part of the Change of Church-discipline (1654)
The Second Vindication of my First Book of the Change of Discipline (1654)
Sundry Particulars Concerning Bishops (n.p., 1661)
Bramhall, John, *The Consecration and Succession of Protestant Bishops Justified* (Gravenhagh, 1658; repr. London, 1664)
A Replication to the Bishop of Chalcedon (1656)
Schisme Garded and Beaten Back (Gravenhagh, 1658)
Works (5 vols., Oxford, 1842–5)
Bray, Gerald, ed., *The Anglican Canons, 1529–1947* (Woodbridge, 1998)
Bray, Gerald, ed., *Documents of the English Reformation* (Minneapolis, 1994)
Bridge, William, Burroughes, Jeremiah, Goodwin, Thomas, Nye, Philip, and Simpson, Sidrach, *An Apologeticall Narration* (1643)
Bridges, John, *A Defence of the Government Established in the Church of England for Ecclesiasticall Matters* (1587)
The Supremacie of Christian Princes (1573)
Brown, Thomas, *Heraclitus ridens redivivus* (1688)
Browne, Thomas, *Some Reflections on a Late Pamphlet, Entituled A Vindication of their Majesties Authority to Fill the Sees of the Deprived Bishops* (1691)
Browning, Andrew, ed., *Memoirs of Sir John Reresby* (Glasgow, 1936)
Brydall, John, *The Clergy Vindicated* (1679)
Burnet, Gilbert, *The History of the Reformation of the Church of England, the First Part, of the Progress Made in it During the Reign of K. Henry the VIII* (1679)
The History of the Reign of King James the Second (Oxford, 1852)
A Letter from Gilbert Burnet … to Mr Simon Lowth (1685)
A Letter Occasioned by the Second Letter to Dr Burnet (1685)
Six Papers (1687)
Byfield, Adoniram, *A Brief View of Mr Coleman* (1645)

Care, George, *A Reply to the Answer of the Man of no Name* (1685)

Care, Henry, *Animadversions on a Late Paper Entituled A Letter to a Dissenter* (1687)

An Answer to a Paper Importing a Petition (1688)

Draconica: Or, an Abstract of all the Penal Laws Touching Matters of Religion, 2nd edn (1688)

English Liberties (1680)

The Law of England: Or, a True Guide for all Persons Concerned in Ecclesiastical Courts (n.p., n.d.)

The Legality of the Court Held by His Majesties Ecclesiastical Commissioners Defended (1688)

A Perfect Guide for Protestant Dissenters, in Case of Prosecution Upon Any of the Penal Statutes Made Against Them (1682)

A Vindication of the Proceedings of His Majesties Ecclesiastical Commissioners (1688)

Carleton, George, *Ivrisdiction Regall, Episcopall, Papall* (1610)

Cartwright, Thomas, *A Second Admonition to the Parliament* ([Hemel Hempstead?], 1572)

The Second Replie … against Maister Doctor Whitgiftes Second Answer ([Heidelberg], 1575)

[Cartwright, Thomas], *The Diary of Thomas Cartwright, Bishop of Chester* (1843)

The Case and Cure of Persons Excommunicated (1682)

The Case of Sir Edward Hales (1689)

Catalogus variorum & insignium librorum instructissimarum bibliothecarum … (1678)

Cave, William, *A Discourse Concerning the Unity of the Catholick Church Maintained in the Church of England* (1684)

A Dissertation Concerning the Government of the Ancient Church by Bishops, Metropolitans, and Patriarchs, ed. Henry Cary (Oxford, 1840; first publ. 1683)

A Serious Exhortation (1683)

Cecil, William, *The Execution of Iustice in England* (1583)

Clagett, William, *The Difference of the Case Between the Separation of Protestants from the Church of Rome and the Separation of Dissenters from the Church of England* (1683; repr. 1686)

The Clergy's Late Carriage to the King (1688)

Coke, Edward, *The Fourth Part of the Institutes of the Lawes of England*, 4th edn (1669)

The Third Part of the Institutes of the Lawes of England, 4th edn (1669)

Coleman, Thomas, *A Brotherly Examination Re-Examined* (1645)

Hopes Deferred and Dashed (1645)

Male dicis maledicis (1646)

Compton, Henry, *An Exact Account of the Whole Proceedings Against … Henry Lord Bishop of London* (1688)

[Cooper, Anthony Ashley, first Earl of Shaftesbury?], *A Letter from a Person of Quality to his Friend in the Country* (1675)

Corbet, John, *A Discourse of the Religion of England* (1667)
A Second Discourse of the Religion of England (1668)
Cosin, Richard, *An Apologie for Svndrie Proceedings by Iurisdiction Ecclesiasticall* (1593)
The Countrey-Minister's Reflections on the City-Minister's Letter to his Friend (1688)
Cranmer, Thomas, *Miscellaneous Writings and Letters*, ed. John Edmund Cox (Cambridge, 1846)
Croft, Herbert, *A Short Discourse Concerning the Reading His Majesties Late Declaration* (1688)
Cyprian, *The Lapsed; The Unity of the Catholic Church*, ed. Maurice Bévenot (1957)
Letters, ed. G. W. Clarke (4 vols., New York, 1984)
Of the Unity of the Church, trans. John Fell (Oxford, 1681)
Dalison, William, *Les reportes des divers special cases* (1689)
De Beer, E. S., ed., *The Diary of John Evelyn* (6 vols., Oxford, 1955)
A Dialogve Betwene a Knyght and a Clerke (1533)
A Discourse for Taking off the Tests and Penal Laws about Religion (1687)
Dodwell, Henry, *A Defence of the Vindication of the Deprived Bishops* ('1695' [1697])
The Doctrine of the Church of England, Concerning the Independency of the Clergy on the Lay-Power ('1697' [1696])
Some Considerations of Present Concernment; How Far the Romanists May be Trusted by Princes of Another Perswasion (1675)
Two Short Discourses Against the Romanists (1676; repr. 1688)
Donne, John, *Sermons*, ed. George R. Potter and Evelyn M. Simpson (10 vols., 1953–62)
Dryden, John, *The Hind and the Panther* (1687), in *Works*, vol. III, ed. H. T. Swedenberg, Earl Miner, and Vinton A. Dearing (Berkeley, 1969)
Du Moulin, Louis, *The Power of the Christian Magistrate in Sacred Things* (1650)
Durel, John, *Sanctæ ecclesiæ Anglicanæ … vindiciæ* (1669)
Dyer, James, *Cy ensouont ascuns novel cases* (1585)
[Edward VI], *K. Edward VI His Own Arguments Against the Pope's Supremacy* (1682)
Eedes, Richard, *Six Learned and Godly Sermons* (1604)
Episcopal Government and the Honour of the Present Bishops Proved Necessary to be Maintained (Dublin, 1679)
Eusebius, *Life of Constantine*, ed. Henry Wace and Philip Schaff (Oxford, 1905)
Facsimile of the Original Manuscript of The Book of Common Prayer Signed by Convocation December 20th, 1661, and Attached to the Act of Uniformity, 1662 (1891)
Falkner, William, *Christian Loyalty*, 2nd edn (1684)
Libertas ecclesiastica, 2nd edn (1674)
Two Treatises … to Which are Annexed, Three Sermons (1684)
Fell, Philip, *Lex talionis: Or, the Author of Naked Truth Stript Naked* (1676)

Ferne, Henry, *A Compendious Discourse* (1655)

Of the Division Between the English and Romish Church Upon the Reformation (1652)

A Few Sober Queries Upon the Late Proclamation for Enforcing the Laws Against Conventicles (1668)

Fiennes, Nathaniel, *A Second Speech … Touching the Subject's Liberty* (1641)

Vindiciae veritatis (1654 (written 1646–8))

Finch, Henry, *Nomotexnia* (publ. 1613, written *c.*1585)

Foster, Elizabeth Read, ed., *Proceedings in Parliament, 1610* (2 vols., New Haven, 1966)

Foxe, Edward, *The True Dyfferens Between the Regall Power and the Ecclesiasticall Power*, trans. Henry Lord Stafford (1548)

Fullwood, Francis, *A Dialogue Betwixt Philautus and Timotheus* (1681)

Humble Advice to the Conforming and Non-Conforming Ministers and People (1673)

Leges Angliæ: The Lawfulness of Ecclesiastical Jurisdiction in the Church of England (1681)

Toleration Not to be Abused, Or, a Serious Question Soberly Debated, and Resolved Upon Presbyterian Principles (1672)

Gailhard, Jean, *The Controversie Between Episcopacy and Presbytery* (1660)

Gardiner, Stephen, *De vera obedientia oratio*, in Pierre Janelle, ed., *Obedience in Church and State: Three Political Tracts by Stephen Gardiner* (Cambridge, 1930)

Gauden, John, *A Pillar of Gratitude* (1661)

Gillespie, George, *Male audis* (1646)

Nihil respondes (1645)

A Sermon Preached Before … the House of Lords … 27 August 1645 (1645)

Godolphin, John, *Repertorium canonicum; Or, an Abridgement of the Ecclesiastical Laws of this Realm, Consistent with the Temporal* (1678)

Goldie, Mark, Harris, Tim, Knights, Mark, McElligott, Jason, Spurr, John, and Taylor, Stephen, eds., *The Entring Book of Roger Morrice* (6 vols., Woodbridge, 2007)

Goodwin, William, *A Sermon Preached Before the King … August 28 1614* (Oxford, 1614)

Grascome, Samuel, *A Letter to a Friend in Answer to a Letter* (1688)

Grey, Anchitell, *Debates of the Honourable House of Commons* (10 vols., 1763)

Grove, Robert, *An Answer to Mr Lowth's Letter to Dr Stillingfleet* (1687)

Gutch, John, *Collectanea curiosa* (2 vols., Oxford, 1781)

Haddon, Walter, *A Dialogue Agaynst the Tyrannye of the Papistes* (1562)

A Sight of the Portugall Pearle, trans. Abraham Hartwell (1565)

Hale, Matthew, *Historia placitorum coronae* (2 vols., 1736)

The Judgment of the Late Lord Chief Justice Sir Matthew Hale, Of the Nature of True Religion, the Causes of its Corruption, and the Churches Calamity by Mens Additions and Violences, with the Desired Cure (1684)

Pleas of the Crown (1678)

'Reflections by the Lrd Cheife Justice Hale on Mr Hobbes his Dialogue of the Lawe', printed in W. S. Holdsworth, *A History of English Law*, vol. v (1924), pp. 499–513

The Royal Supremacy (n.d.)

Hammond, Henry, *Of the Power of the Keys* (1647)

Of Schisme (1653)

A Vindication of the Dissertations Concerning Episcopacie (1654)

Hartley, T. E., ed., *Proceedings in the Parliaments of Elizabeth I* (3 vols., 1981–95)

Hawkins, William, *A Short Account of the Life of ... Thomas Ken* (1713)

Hayward, John, *Of Supremacie in Affaires of Religion*, 2nd edn (1624)

Henning, Basil Duke, ed., *The Parliamentary Diary of Sir Edward Dering, 1670–1673* (New Haven, 1940)

[Henry VIII], *An Epistle of the Most Myghty & Redouted Prince Henry the VIII ... to all Christen Princes* (1538)

Herbert, Edward, *A Short Account of the Authorities in Law ... in Sir Edward Hales his Case* (1688)

Hickeringill, Edmund, *Curse ye Meroz, Or the Fatal Doom, in a Sermon Preached in Guildhall Chappel ... 9 May 1680*, 4th edn (1680)

The Naked Truth, the Second Part (1681)

News from Doctor's Commons (1681)

Reflections on a Late Libel, Intituled, Observations on a Late Famous Sermon, Intituled, Curse ye Meroz (1680)

Scandalum magnatum (1682)

The Test or Tryal of the Goodness & Value of Spiritual-Courts, in Two Queries, 2nd edn (1683)

The Third Part of Naked Truth (1681)

A Vindication of the Naked Truth (1681)

Hickes, George, *An Apologetical Vindication of the Church of England* (1687)

His Majesties Declaration ... December 26 1662 (1662)

The History of King James's Ecclesiastical Commission (1711)

Hobbes, Thomas, *An Answer to a Book Published by Dr Bramhall, Late Bishop of Derry, Called the Catching of the Leviathan* (1668; publ. 1682)

Behemoth, ed. Paul Seaward (Oxford, 2010)

On the Citizen, ed. Richard Tuck and Michael Silverthorne (Cambridge, 1998)

Correspondence, ed. Noel Malcolm (2 vols., Oxford, 1994)

Decameron physiologicum: Or, Ten Dialogues of Natural Philosophy (1678)

The Elements of Law, ed. Ferdinand Tönnies, 2nd edn, intro. M. M. Goldsmith (1969)

Historia ecclesiastica, ed. Patricia Springborg et al. (Paris, 2008)

Leviathan, ed. Richard Tuck, rev. edn (Cambridge, 1996)

Leviathan: With Selected Variants from the Latin Edition of 1668, ed. E. M. Curley (Indianapolis, 1994)

Of Libertie and Necessitie (1654)

Mr Hobbes Considered in his Loyalty, Religion, Reputation, and Manners by Way of Letter to Dr Wallis (1662)
Seven Philosophical Problems and Two Propositions of Geometry (1662; publ. 1682)
Six Lessons to the Professors of the Mathematiques (1656)
Stigmai Ageometrias … or Markes of the Absurd Geometry, Rural Language, Scottish Church-Politicks and Barbarismes of John Wallis (1657)
'Thomas Hobbes: 1668 Appendix to *Leviathan*', trans. and ed. George Wright, *Interpretation*, 18 (1991), pp. 323–413
A True Ecclesiastical History (1722)
Writings on Common Law and Hereditary Right, ed. Alan Cromartie and Quentin Skinner (Oxford, 2005)
Hooke, Richard, *The Bishop's Appeale* (Newcastle, 1661)
Hooker, Richard, *The Folger Library Edition of the Works of Richard Hooker*, gen. ed. W. Speed Hill (7 vols., Cambridge, MA, 1977–98)
Horne, Robert, *An Answeare … to a Booke Entituled, The Declaration of Svche Scruples …* (1566)
Howes, John, *A Sermon Preached at the Assizes at Northampton, August the 9th 1669* (1670)
Hughes, Paul L., and Larkin, James F., eds., *Royal Proclamations of King James I, 1603–1625* (Oxford, 1973)
Tudor Royal Proclamations (3 vols., New Haven, 1964–9)
Humfrey, John, *A Case of Conscience* (1669)
A Defence of the Proposition (1668)
The Obligation of Human Laws Discussed (1671)
A Proposition for the Safety and Happiness of the King and Kingdom Both in Church and State (1667)
Hunt, Thomas, *The Honours of the Lords Spiritual Asserted* (1679)
Mr Emmerton's Marriage with Mrs Bridget Hyde Considered (1682)
Hussey, William, *A Plea for Christian Magistracie* (1645)
An Impartial Relation of the Illegal Proceedings Against St Mary Magdalen Colledge in Oxon, 2nd edn (1689)
Iniunctions geven by the Quenes Maiestie (1559)
The Institvtion of a Christen Man (1537)
James VI and I, *Political Works*, ed. Charles Howard McIlwain (Cambridge, 1918)
Jansson, Maija, ed., *Proceedings in the Opening Session of the Long Parliament, House of Commons*, vol. 1 (Rochester, NY, 2000)
Two Diaries of the Long Parliament (Gloucester, 1984)
Jessop, Augustus, ed., *The Autobiography of the Hon. Roger North* (1887)
Jewel, John, *An Apologie or Aunswer in Defence of the Church of England* (1562)
The Apology of the Church of England, trans. Edmund Bohun (1685)
A Defense of the Apologie of the Churche of Englande (1571)
A Sermon Preached Before Q. Elizabeth (1641)
J. J., *Flagellum poeticum: Or, a Scourge for a Wilde Poet* (1672)

Johnston, Nathaniel, *The King's Visitatorial Power Asserted* (1688)
Jones, Henry, *A Sermon Preached at the Consecration of … Ambrose Lord Bishop of Kildare … June 29 1667* (Dublin, 1667)
Jordan, W. K., ed., *The Chronicle and Political Papers of King Edward VI* (1966)
The Judgment and Doctrine of the Clergy of the Church of England Concerning … Dispensing with the Penal Laws (1687)
Keeble, N. H., and Nuttall, Geoffrey F., eds., *Calendar of the Correspondence of Richard Baxter* (2 vols., Oxford, 1991)
Ken, Thomas, 'A Sermon Preached at Whitehall upon Passion Sunday [1688]', in *Prose Works*, ed. James Thomas Round (1838)
Kettlewell, John, *Of Christian Communion, to be Kept on in the Unity of Christ's Church* (1693)
The King's Dispensing Power Explicated and Asserted (1687)
To the King's Most Excellent Majesty, The Humble Address of the Atheists, or the Sect of the Epicureans (1688)
Lake, Edward, *Memoranda: Touching the Oath Ex Officio, Pretended Self-Accusation and Canonical Purgation* (1662)
Laney, Benjamin, *Five Sermons, Preached before His Majesty at Whitehall* (1669)
Langbaine, Gerald, *Episcopall Inheritance* (Oxford, 1641)
Larkin, James F., ed., *Royal Proclamations of King Charles I, 1625–1646* (Oxford, 1983)
Latimer, Hugh, *The Fyrste Sermon of Mayster Hughe Latimer which he Preached before the Kynges Maiest[ie]* (1549)
A moste faithfull Sermon (1550)
The Seconde[-Seventh] Sermon … Preached before the Kynges Maiestie (1549)
Laud, William, *Works* (7 vols., Oxford, 1847–60)
Lee, Matthew Henry, ed., *Diaries and Letters of Philip Henry* (1882)
L'Estrange, Roger, *An Answer to a Letter to a Dissenter* (1687)
Two Cases Submitted to Consideration (Edinburgh, 1687)
A Letter to the Author of the Vindication of the Proceedings of the Ecclesiastical Commissioners ('Eleutheropolis' [Oxford], 1688)
A Letter from a Clergy-man in the City … Containing his Reasons for Not Reading the Declaration (1688)
A Letter of the Presbyterian Ministers in the City of London, presented the first of Jan. 1645 (1668)
Lever, Thomas, *A Sermon Preached the Thyrd Sondaye in Lent* (1550)
Lightfoot, J. B., *The Apostolic Fathers, Part II: St Ignatius, St Polycarp* (3 vols., 1889)
Lloyd, John, *A Treatise of the Episcopacy, Liturgies, and Ecclesiastical Ceremonies of the Primitive Times* (1660)
Lloyd, William, *Considerations Touching the True Way to Suppress Popery* (1677)
An Historical Account of Church-Government (1684)
Locke, John, *An Essay Concerning Toleration*, ed. J. R. Milton and Philip Milton (Oxford, 2006)
Political Essays, ed. Mark Goldie (Cambridge, 1997)

Two Treatises of Government, ed. Peter Laslett (Cambridge, 1988)
Lockyer, Nicholas, *Some Seasonable and Serious Queries upon the Late Act against Conventicles* (1670)
London Gazette, no. 2009 (1685)
Lord, George deF., gen. ed., *Poems on Affairs of State: Augustan Satirical Verse, 1660–1714* (7 vols., New Haven, 1963–75)
Lowth, Simon, *A Letter to Edw. Stillingfleet* (1687)
A Second Letter to Dr Burnet (1684)
Of the Subject of Church-Power (1685)
Loyalty and Nonconformity (1669)
Lynne, Walter, *A most necessarie Treatise, declaring the Beginning and Ending of all Poperie* (1548)
Marprelate, Martin, *Hay any Work for Cooper* ([Coventry, 1589])
Oh read ouer D. John Bridges ([East Molesey, Surrey, 1588])
Theses Martinianae ([Wolston, 1589])
Marvell, Andrew, *An Account of the Growth of Popery and Arbitrary Government* (1677)
The Poems and Letters of Andrew Marvell, ed. H. M. Margoliouth, 3rd edn (2 vols., Oxford, 1971)
The Rehearsal Transpros'd and the Rehearsal Transpros'd the Second Part, ed. D. I. B. Smith (Oxford, 1971)
'A Short Historical Essay, Touching General Councils, Creeds, and Imposition in Religion', in *Mr Smirke; Or, the Divine in Mode* (1676)
Matthew, Simon, *A Sermon made in the Cathedrall Churche of Saynt Paule at London, the XXVII day of June, Anno 1535* (1535)
Maurice, Henry, *The Antithelemite, Or An Answer to Certain Quæries by the D[uke] of B[uckingham]* (1685)
The Minister's Reasons for his not Reading the Kings Declaration, Friendly Debated (1688)
Mitchell, Alex F., and Struthers, John, eds., *Minutes of the Sessions of the Westminster Assembly of Divines* (Edinburgh, 1874)
Morison, Richard, *A Lamentation ... what Ruyne and Destruction cometh of Seditious Rebellyon* (1536)
Muller, J. A., ed., *The Letters of Stephen Gardiner* (Cambridge, 1933)
Nash, Thomas, *Mar-Martine* (1589)
A Necessary Doctrine and Ervdition for any Christen Man (1543)
A New Test of the Church of England's Loyalty (1687)
The New Test ... Examined by the Old Test of Truth and Honesty (1687)
Nowell, Alexander, *The Reprovfe of M. Dorman ... continued* (1566)
Nye, Philip, *The Best Fence against Popery: Or, A Vindication of the Power of the King in Ecclesiastical Affairs* (1670, 1686)
The King's Authority in Dispensing with Ecclesiastical Laws, Asserted and Vindicated (1687)
The Lawfulness of the Oath of Supremacy and Power of the Civil Magistrate in Ecclesiastical Affairs and Subordination of Churches thereunto (1662)

Ochino, Bernando, *A Tragoedie or Dialoge of the Vniuste Vsurped Primacie of the Bishop of Rome*, trans. John Ponet (1549)
Owen, John, *Correspondence*, ed. Peter Toon (Cambridge, 1970)
Indvlgence and Toleration Considered (1667)
A Peace-Offering in an Apology and Humble Plea for Indulgence and Liberty of Conscience (1667)
Truth and Innocence Vindicated (1669)
Unto the Questions Sent Me Last Night (1659)
Works, ed. William H. Goold (16 vols., 1965–8)
Parker, Samuel, *A Defence and Continuation of the Ecclesiastical Politie* (1671)
A Discourse of Ecclesiastical Politie (1670 [1669])
A Discourse in Vindication of Bp Bramhall and the Clergy of the Church of England from the Fanatick Charge of Popery (1673)
Religion and Loyalty (2 vols., 1684–5)
A Reproof to the Rehearsal Transprosed (1673)
Patrick, Simon, *An Appendix to the Third Part of the Friendly Debate* (1670)
A Continuation of the Friendly Debate (1669)
A Friendly Debate Between a Conformist and a Non-Conformist, 5th edn (1669)
A Further Continuation and Defence, or, a Third Part of the Friendly Debate (1670)
Pearson, John, *Vindiciae epistolarum S. Ignatii* (Cambridge, 1672)
Peirce, Edmund, *The English Episcopacy and Liturgy Asserted* (1660)
Penn, William, *Considerations Moving to a Toleration and Liberty of Conscience* (1685)
Good Advice to the Church of England, Roman Catholick, and Protestant Dissenter (1687)
The Great and Popular Objection Against the Repeal of the Penal Laws (1688)
A Perswasive to Moderation to Dissenting Christians (1685)
The Reasonableness of Toleration and the Unreasonableness of Penal Laws and Tests (1687)
Som Free Reflections upon Occasion of the Public Discourse about Liberty of Conscience (1687)
Penry, John, *Th'Appellation of Iohn Penri, vnto the Highe Court of Parliament* ([La Rochelle, 1589])
A Briefe Discouery of the Vntrvthes and Slanders (against the Trve Gouernement of the Church of Christ) ([Edinburgh], 1590)
An Hvmble Motion with Svbmission ([Edinburgh], 1590)
A Treatise wherein is manifestly proved ... ([Edinburgh, 1590])
Pepys, Samuel, *Diary*, ed. Robert Latham and William Matthews (11 vols., 1970–83)
Perrinchief, Richard, *A Discourse of Toleration* (1668)
Indulgence Not Justified: Being a Continuation of the Discourse of Toleration (1668)
Pett, Peter, *A Discourse Concerning Liberty of Conscience* (1661)
The Obligation Resulting from the Oath of Supremacy to Assist and Defend the Pre-eminence or Prerogative of the Dispensative Power (1687)
Pierce, Thomas, *A Vindication of the King's Sovereign Rights* (1683)

Plumptre, E. H., *The Life of Thomas Ken*, 2nd rev. edn (2 vols., 1890)

Popple, William, *A Letter to Mr Penn with his Answer* (1688)

Poulton, Andrew, *An Answer to a Letter from a Clergyman in the City* (1688)

A Proclamation of Both Houses of Parliament (1660)

Prothero, G. W., ed., *Select Statutes and Other Constitutional Documents Illustrative of the Reigns of Elizabeth and James I* (Oxford, 1913)

Prynne, William, *A Breviate of the Prelates Intollerable Usurpations*, 3rd edn (Amsterdam, 1637)

An Exact Chronological Vindication and Historical Demonstration of our British, Roman, Saxon, Danish, Norman, English Kings Supreme Ecclesiastical Jurisdiction (1665)

Independency Examined, Vnmasked, Refuted (1644)

Trvth Trivmphing over Falshood (1645)

A Vindication of Foure Serious Questions ... touching Excommunication and Suspention [sic] from the Sacrament of the Lords Supper (1645)

Reynolds, Noel B., and Saxonhouse, Arlene W., eds., *Thomas Hobbes: Three Discourses* (Chicago, 1995)

Robbins, Caroline, ed., *The Diary of John Milward, Esq., Member of Parliament for Derbyshire, September, 1666 to May, 1668* (Cambridge, 1938)

Rolle, Samuel, *A Sober Answer to the Friendly Debate* (1669)

Rudd, Anthony, *A Sermon Preached at the Covrt at Whitehall before the Kings Maiesty ... the 13 of May 1604* (1604)

St German, Christopher, *The Addicions of Salem and Byzance* (1534)

An Answere to a Letter (1535)

Doctor and Student, ed. T. F. T. Plucknett and J. L. Barton (1974)

A Treatise Concernynge Diuers of the Constitucyons Prouiynciall and Legantines (1535)

A Treatise Concernynge the Diuision Between the Spirytualtie and Temporaltie, in Thomas More, *Complete Works*, vol. IV, ed. J. B. Trapp (New Haven, 1979)

A Treatise Concernynge Generall Councilles, the Byshoppes of Rome, and the Clergy (1538)

A Treatyse concerninge the Power of the Clergye and the Lawes of the Realme (n.d.)

Sandford, Francis, *The History of the Coronation of ... James II* (1687)

Saravia, Hadrian, *Of the Diuerse Degrees of the Ministers of the Gospell* (1592)

Savile, George, marquess of Halifax, *A Letter to a Dissenter* (1687)

A Seasonable Discourse Shewing the Unreasonableness and Mischeifs of Impositions in Matters of Religion (1687)

A Second Letter to a Member of the Present Parliament, Against Comprehension (1668)

Seignior, George, *God, the King, and the Church* (1670)

Sherlock, William, *A Letter to Anonymus* (1683)

A Vindication of a Passage in Dr Sherlock's Sermon Preached before the Honourable House of Commons, May 29 1685 (1685)

A Vindication of Some Protestant Principles of Church-Unity and Catholick-Communion (1688)

[Sherman, Thomas?], *Upon His Majesties Late Declarations for Toleration and Publication of War Against the Hollander* (1672)
Short Reflections on a Pamphlet Entituled, Toleration Not to be Abused (1672)
Shute, Giles, *A New Test in Lieu of the Old One* (1688)
Singer, Samuel Weller, ed., *The Correspondence of Henry Hyde* (2 vols., 1828)
A Sober Answer to a Scandalous Paper (1688)
Spalding, Ruth, ed., *The Diary of Bulstrode Whitelocke, 1605–1675* (Oxford, 1990)
A Speech Touching Toleration in Matters of Religion (1668)
Speed, John, *The History of Great Britaine* (1614)
Starkey, Thomas, *An Exhortation to the People* (1536)
Stephens, Jeremiah, *An Apology for the Ancient Right and Power of the Bishops to Sit and Vote in Parliaments* (1660)
Stillingfleet, Edward, *An Answer to Several Late Treatises* (1673)
An Answer to Some Papers Lately Printed (repr. Dublin, 1686)
The Council of Trent Examin'd and Disprov'd (1688)
A Discourse Concerning the Illegality of the Late Ecclesiastical Commission (1689)
A Discourse Concerning the Power of Excommunication in a Christian Church, by Way of Appendix to the Irenicum (1662)
Irenicum ('1661' [1660])
The Mischief of Separation, 3rd edn (1680)
Origines Britannicae (1685)
The Reformation Justify'd, 2nd edn (1674)
A Sermon Preached on the Fast-Day at St Margaret's Westminster, Novemb. 13 1678, in *Ten Sermons* (1697)
A Sermon Preached at a Publick Ordination at St Peter's Cornhill, March 15th 1684/5 (1685)
Several Conferences Between a Romish Priest, a Fanatick Chaplain, and a Divine of the Church of England (1679)
Ten Sermons (1697)
The Unreasonableness of Separation (1681)
A Vindication of their Majesties Authority to Fill the Sees of the Deprived Bishops (1691)
Stoughton, William, *An Abstract of Certain Acts of Parliament* (1583)
[Stratford, Nicholas?], *A Discourse of the Pope's Supremacy* (1688)
Strype, John, *Memorials of … Thomas Cranmer* (3 vols., Oxford, repr. 1848–53)
Stubbe, Henry, *A Further Iustification of the Present War Against the United Netherlands* (1673)
Sutcliffe, Matthew, *A Treatise of Ecclesiasticall Discipline* (1591)
Swinnerton, Thomas, *A Litel Treatise Ageynste the Mutterynge of some Papistis in Corners* (1534)
A Mustre of Scismatyke Byshoppes of Rome (1534)
A Third Dialogue Between Simeon and Levi (1688)
Thomas, William, *A Speech … Concerning the Right of Bishops Sitting and Voting* (1641)

Thorndike, Herbert, *A Discourse of the Forbearance or the Penalties which a Due Reformation Requires* (1670)
A Discourse of the Right of the Church in a Christian State (1649)
Just Weights and Measures (1662)
A Letter Concerning the Present State of Religion Amongst Us (1656)
Theological Works (6 vols., Oxford, 1844–56)
Two Discourses (Cambridge, 1650)
Tillotson, John, *The Protestant Religion Vindicated from the Charge of Singularity and Novelty* (1680)
Tindal, Matthew, *The Rights of the Christian Church* (1706)
The Toleration Intolerable (1670)
Tomkins, Thomas, *The Inconveniences of Toleration* (1667)
A Treatise Provynge … the Byshops of Rome had Neuer Ryght to any Supremitie within this Realme (1534)
The True Interest of the Legal English Protestants (1687)
Tunstall, Cuthbert, *A Sermon of Cvthbert Bysshop of Duresme made vpon Palme Sondaye last past* (1539)
Tunstall, Cuthbert, and Stokesley, John, *A Letter written … vnto Reginald Pole* (1540)
Udall, Ephraim, *The Bishop of Armaghes Direction, Concerning the Lyturgy and Episcopall Government* (repr. 1660)
Udall, John, *A New Discovery of Old Pontificall Practises* (printed 1643)
Udall, Nicholas, ep. ded. to *The First Tome … of the Paraphrases of Erasmus* (1551)
Ussher, James, *The Reduction of Episcopacie* (1660)
Vaughan, Edward, ed., *The Reports and Arguments of that Learned Judge Sir John Vaughan* (1677)
Villiers, George, duke of Buckingham, *A Short Discourse upon the Reasonableness of Men's Having a Religion* (3rd edn, 1685)
Vindiciæ libertatis evangelii: Or, a Justification of our Present Indulgence, and the Acceptance of Licenses (1672)
Washington, Robert, *Some Observations upon the Ecclesiastical Jurisdiction of the Kings of England with an Appendix in Answer to Part of a Late Book Intitled, The King's Visitatorial Power Asserted* (1689)
W. E., *Melinus inquirendum* (1688)
Welchman, Edward, *The Regal Supremacy in Ecclesiastical Affairs Asserted* (1701)
A Second Defence of the Church of England (1698)
Whitelocke, Bulstrode, *The King's Right of Indulgence in Spiritual Matters, with the Equity thereof, Asserted* (1688)
Whitgift, John, *An Answere to a certain Libell intituled, An Admonition to the Parliament* (1573)
The Defense of the Aunswere to the Admonition against the Replie of T[homas] C[artwright] (1574)
Wild, Robert, *A Letter from Dr Robert Wild to his Friend Mr J.J. upon Occasion of His Majesty's Declaration for Liberty of Conscience* (1709)
Wilde, John, *The Impeachment Against the Bishops* (1641)

Wilkins, David, ed., *Concilia Magnae Britanniae et Hiberniae* (4 vols., 1737)
Wilson, John, *Jus regium coronae* (1688)
W. K., *An English Answer to the Scotch Speech, Shewing the Intolerableness of Tolleration* (1668)
Wolseley, Charles, *Liberty of Conscience the Magistrates Interest* (1668)
Liberty of Conscience Upon its True and Proper Grounds Asserted & Vindicated (1668)
Womock, Laurence, *An Answer to the Gentleman's Letter to his Friend* (1680)
Anti-Boreale (1662)
The Associators Cashier'd (1683)
Pulpit-Conceptions, Popular-Deceptions (1662)
The Religion of the Church of England More Sound, More Safe, More Primitive and Catholick than that of Rome (1648, repr. 1679)
The Religion of the Church of England the Surest Establishment of the Royal Throne (1673)
Sober Sadnes (Oxford, 1643)
Suffragium Protestantium (1683)
The Verdict upon the Dissenters Plea (1681)
Yale, D. E. C., ed., *Lord Nottingham's Chancery Cases* (2 vols., 1957 and 1961)

SECONDARY WORKS

PUBLISHED

Abernathy, George R., jr, 'Clarendon and the Declaration of Indulgence', *Journal of Ecclesiastical History*, 11 (1960), pp. 55–73
'The English Presbyterians and the Stuart Restoration, 1648–1663', *Transactions of the American Philosophical Society*, n.s., 55 (1965), number 2
Albion, 25 (1993), pp. 237–77, 565–651 (special issues on Plumb and parties)
Alford, Stephen, *Kingship and Politics in the Reign of Edward VI* (Cambridge, 2002)
Appleby, David, *Black Bartholomew's Day: Preaching, Polemic, and Restoration Nonconformity* (Manchester, 2007)
Armitage, David, *The Ideological Origins of the British Empire* (Cambridge, 2000)
Ashcraft, Richard, *Revolutionary Politics and Locke's Two Treatises of Government* (Princeton, 1986)
Aston, Margaret, *The King's Bedpost* (Cambridge, 1993)
Baker, J. H., 'The Common Lawyers and the Chancery: 1616', *The Irish Jurist*, n.s. 4 (1969), pp. 368–92
Monuments of Endlesse Labours: English Canonists and Their Work, 1300–1900 (1998)
Barclay, Andrew, 'James II's "Catholic" Court', *1650–1850*, 8 (2003), pp. 161–71
Barnard, Leslie W., 'The Use of the Patristic Tradition in the Late Seventeenth and Early Eighteenth Centuries', in Richard Bauckham and Benjamin Drewery, eds., *Scripture, Tradition and Reason* (Edinburgh, 1988)

Bate, Frank, *The Declaration of Indulgence, 1672: A Study in the Rise of Organised Dissent* (1908)

Beddard, Robert, 'The Church of Salisbury and the Accession of James II', *Wiltshire Archaeological and Natural History Magazine*, 67 (1972), pp. 132–48

'Sheldon and Anglican Recovery', *Historical Journal*, 19 (1976), pp. 1005–17

'Vincent Alsop and the Emancipation of Restoration Dissent', *Journal of Ecclesiastical History*, 24 (1973), pp. 161–84

Bennett, Gareth Vaughan, 'Patristic Tradition in Anglican Thought, 1660–1900', *Oecumenica* (1971–2), pp. 63–85

Birdsall, Paul, '"Non Obstante": A Study of the Dispensing Power of English Kings', in Carl Wittke, ed., *Essays in History and Political Theory in Honour of Charles Howard McIlwain* (Cambridge, MA, 1936)

Blayney, Peter, 'William Cecil and the Stationers', in Robin Myers and Michael Harris, eds., *The Stationers' Company and the Book Trade, 1550–1990* (Winchester, Hants., 1997)

Bloxam, J. R., *Magdalen College and King James II, 1686–1688* (Oxford, 1886)

Bosher, Robert S., *The Making of the Restoration Settlement: The Influence of the Laudians, 1649–1662* (1951)

Bowker, Margaret, 'The Supremacy and the Episcopate: The Struggle for Control, 1534–1540', *Historical Journal*, 18 (1975), pp. 227–43

Boyer, Richard E., *English Declarations of Indulgence, 1687 and 1688* (The Hague, 1968)

Brooks, Christopher W., *Law, Politics and Society in Early Modern England* (Cambridge, 2008)

Browning, Andrew, *Thomas Osborne, Earl of Danby* (3 vols., Glasgow, 1951)

Buckroyd, Julia, 'The Dismissal of Archbishop Alexander Burnet, 1669', *Records of the Scottish Church History Society*, 18 (1973), pp. 149–55

Buranelli, Vincent, *The King & the Quaker: A Study of William Penn and James II* (Philadelphia, 1962)

Cargill Thompson, W. D. J., 'Sir Francis Knollys' Campaign Against the *Jure Divino* Theory of Episcopacy', in C. Robert Cole and Michael E. Moody, eds., *The Dissenting Tradition* (Athens, OH, 1975)

Carpenter, Edward, *The Protestant Bishop: Being the Life of Henry Compton, 1632–1713, Bishop of London* (1956)

Champion, J. A. I., *The Pillars of Priestcraft Shaken: The Church of England and its Enemies, 1660–1730* (Cambridge, 1992)

Chapman, Alister, Coffey, John, and Gregory, Brad, eds., *Seeing Things Their Way: Intellectual History and the Return of Religion* (Notre Dame, 2009)

Christie, W. D., *A Life of Anthony Ashley Cooper, First Earl of Shaftesbury* (2 vols., 1871)

Churchill, E. F., 'Dispensations under the Tudors and Stuarts', *English Historical Review*, 34 (1919), pp. 409–15

'The Dispensing Power of the Crown in Ecclesiastical Affairs', *Law Quarterly Review*, 38 (1922), pp. 297–316, 420–34

'The Dispensing Power and the Defence of the Realm', *Law Quarterly Review*, 37 (1921), pp. 412–41

Claydon, Tony, *William III and the Godly Revolution* (Cambridge, 1996)

Coffey, John, *Persecution and Toleration in Protestant England, 1558–1689* (Harlow, 2000)

Politics, Religion and the British Revolutions: The Mind of Samuel Rutherford (Cambridge, 1997)

Colclough, David, *Freedom of Speech in Early Stuart England* (Cambridge, 2005)

Collins, Jeffrey R., *The Allegiance of Thomas Hobbes* (Oxford, 2005)

'The Restoration Bishops and the Royal Supremacy', *Church History*, 68 (1999), pp. 549–80

Collinson, Patrick, 'If Constantine, then also Theodosius: St Ambrose and the Integrity of the Elizabethan *Ecclesia Anglicana*', *Journal of Ecclesiastical History*, 30 (1979), pp. 205–29

The Elizabethan Puritan Movement (Oxford, 1967)

The Religion of Protestants: The Church in English Society, 1559–1625 (Oxford, 1982)

Colvin, H. M., et al., eds., *The History of the King's Works*, vol. v (1976)

Cornwall, Robert D., 'The Search for the Primitive Church: The Use of Early Church Fathers in the High Church Anglican Tradition, 1680–1745', *Anglican and Episcopal History*, 59 (1990), pp. 303–29

Cromartie, Alan, *The Constitutionalist Revolution* (Cambridge, 2006)

Sir Matthew Hale, 1609–1676: Law, Religion and Natural Philosophy (Cambridge, 1995)

Cross, Claire, *Church and People: England, 1450–1660*, 2nd edn (Oxford, 1999)

The Royal Supremacy in the Elizabethan Church (1969)

Davies, Julian, *The Caroline Captivity of the Church: Charles I and the Remoulding of Anglicanism, 1625–1641* (Oxford, 1992)

De Krey, Gary S., *London and the Restoration, 1659–1683* (Cambridge, 2005)

'Reformation in the Restoration Crisis, 1679–1682', in Donna B. Hamilton and Richard Strier, eds., *Religion, Literature, and Politics in Post-Reformation England, 1540–1688* (Cambridge, 1996)

Dixon, Dennis, '*Godden* v. *Hales* Revisited – James II and the Dispensing Power', *Journal of Legal History*, 27 (2006), pp. 129–52

Duffy, Eamon, *Fires of Faith: Catholic England under Mary Tudor* (New Haven, 2009)

Duffy, Eamon, and Loades, David, eds., *The Church of Mary Tudor* (Aldershot, 2006)

Edie, Carolyn A., 'The Irish Cattle Bills: A Study in Restoration Politics', *Transactions of the American Philosophical Society*, n.s., 60 (1970), number 2

'Revolution and the Rule of Law: The End of the Dispensing Power, 1689', *Eighteenth-Century Studies*, 10 (1977), pp. 434–50

'Tactics and Strategies: Parliament's Attack upon the Royal Dispensing Power, 1597–1689', *American Journal of Legal History*, 29 (1985), pp. 197–234

Elton, G. R., 'The Evolution of a Reformation Statute', *English Historical Review*, 64 (1949), pp. 174–97

Evans, Erastus, *Erastianism* (1933)

Figgis, J. Neville, 'Erastus and Erastianism', *Journal of Theological Studies*, 2 (1901), pp. 66–101

Fincham, Kenneth, '"According to Ancient Custom": The Return of Altars in the Restoration Church of England', *Transactions of the Royal Historical Society*, 6th ser., 13 (2003), pp. 29–54

Ford, Alan, 'Criticising the Godly Prince: Malcolm Hamilton's *Passages and Consultations*', in Vincent P. Carey and Ute Lotz-Heumann, eds., *Taking Sides? Colonial and Confessional Mentalités in Early Modern Ireland* (Dublin, 2003)

Foxcroft, H. C., *The Life and Letters of Sir George Savile, Bart, First Marquis of Halifax* (2 vols., 1898)

Gibson, William, *James II and the Trial of the Seven Bishops* (Houndmills, Basingstoke, 2009)

Goldie, Mark, 'The Civil Religion of James Harrington', in Anthony Pagden, ed., *The Languages of Political Theory in Early-Modern Europe* (Cambridge, 1987)

'Danby, the Bishops and the Whigs', in Tim Harris, Paul Seaward, and Mark Goldie, eds., *The Politics of Religion in Restoration England* (Oxford, 1990)

'A Darker Shade of Pepys: The *Entring Book* of Roger Morrice' (Friends of Doctor Williams's Library, 61st Annual Lecture, read 25 Oct. 2007, publ. 2009)

'The Hilton Gang and the Purge of London in the 1680s', in Howard Nenner, ed., *Politics and the Political Imagination in Later Stuart Britain* (Rochester, NY, 1997)

'John Locke and Anglican Royalism', *Political Studies*, 31 (1983), pp. 61–85

'Joshua Basset, Popery, and Revolution', in D. E. D. Beales and H. B. Nisbet, eds., *Sidney Sussex College Cambridge* (Woodbridge, 1996)

'The Political Thought of the Anglican Revolution', in Robert Beddard, ed., *The Revolutions of 1688* (Oxford, 1991)

'Priestcraft and the Birth of Whiggism', in Nicholas Phillipson and Quentin Skinner, eds., *Political Discourse in Early Modern Britain* (Cambridge, 1993)

'The Reception of Hobbes', in J. H. Burns and M. A. Goldie, eds., *The Cambridge History of Political Thought, 1450–1700* (Cambridge, 1991)

'The Revolution of 1689 and the Structure of Political Argument', *Bulletin of Research in the Humanities*, 83 (1980), pp. 473–564

Roger Morrice and the Puritan Whigs (Woodbridge, 2007)

'Sir Peter Pett, Sceptical Toryism and the Science of Toleration in the 1680s', in W. J. Sheils, ed., *Persecution and Toleration* (Oxford, 1984)

'The Theory of Religious Intolerance in Restoration England', in Ole Peter Grell, Jonathan I. Israel, and Nicholas Tyacke, eds., *From Persecution to Toleration: The Glorious Revolution and Religion in England* (Oxford, 1991)

'Toleration and the Godly Prince in Restoration England', in John Morrow and Jonathan Scott, eds., *Liberty, Authority, Formality: Political Ideas and Culture, 1600–1900* (Exeter, 2008)

Goldie, Mark, and Spurr, John, 'Politics and the Restoration Parish: Edward Fowler and the Struggle for St Giles Cripplegate', *English Historical Review*, 109 (1994), pp. 572–96

Green, Ian, 'Career Prospects and Clerical Conformity in the Early Stuart Church', *Past and Present*, 90 (1981), pp. 71–115

The Christian's ABC: Catechisms and Catechizing in England, c.1530–1740 (Oxford, 1996)

The Re-Establishment of the Church of England, 1660–1663 (Oxford, 1978)

Greenslade, Stanley L., 'The Authority of the Tradition of the Early Church in Early Anglican Thought', *Oecumenica* (1971–2), pp. 9–31

The English Reformers and the Fathers of the Church (Oxford, 1960)

Gunther, Karl, and Shagan, Ethan H., 'Protestant Radicalism and Political Thought in the Reign of Henry VIII', *Past and Present*, 194 (2007), pp. 35–74

Guy, John, *Christopher St German on Chancery and Statute* (1985)

'The Elizabethan Establishment and the Ecclesiastical Polity', in Guy, ed., *The Reign of Elizabeth I* (Cambridge, 1995)

'The "Imperial Crown" and the Liberty of the Subject: The English Constitution from Magna Carta to the Bill of Rights', in Bonnelyn Young Kunze and Dwight D. Brautigam, eds., *Court, Country and Culture* (Rochester, NY, 1992)

'The Rhetoric of Counsel in Early Modern England', in Dale Hoak, ed., *Tudor Political Culture* (Cambridge, 1995)

'Scripture as Authority: Problems of Interpretation in the 1530s', in Alistair Fox and John Guy, eds., *Reassessing the Henrician Age* (Oxford, 1986)

'Thomas Cromwell and the Intellectual Origins of the Henrician Revolution', in Guy, ed., *The Tudor Monarchy* (1997)

'Thomas More and Christopher St German: The Battle of the Books', in Alistair Fox and John Guy, eds., *Reassessing the Henrician Age* (Oxford, 1986)

'Tudor Monarchy and its Critiques', in Guy, ed., *The Tudor Monarchy* (1997)

Guy, John, ed., *The Reign of Elizabeth I: Court and Culture in the Last Decade* (Cambridge, 1995)

Harris, Tim, 'What's New About the Restoration?' *Albion*, 29 (1997), pp. 187–222

Harris, Tim, Seaward, Paul, and Goldie, Mark, eds., *The Politics of Religion in Restoration England* (Oxford, 1990)

Headley, John M., 'Borromean Reform in the Empire? *La Strada Rigorosa* of Giovanni Francesco Bonomi', in John M. Headley and John B. Tomaro, eds., *San Carlo Borromeo: Catholic Reform and Ecclesiastical Politics in the Second Half of the Sixteenth Century* (Cranbury, NJ, 1988)

Henning, Basil Duke, *The House of Commons, 1660–1690* (3 vols., 1983)

Hirst, Derek, 'Making all Religion Ridiculous: Of Culture High and Low: The Polemics of Toleration, 1667–1673', *Renaissance Forum*, 1 (1996) (www.hull.ac.uk/renforum)

Holdsworth, W. S., *A History of English Law*, vol. v (1924)
'Sir Matthew Hale', *Law Quarterly Review*, 39 (1923), pp. 402–26
Horwitz, Henry, *Parliament, Policy and Politics in the Reign of William III* (Manchester, 1977)
'Protestant Reconciliation in the Exclusion Crisis', *Journal of Ecclesiastical History*, 15 (1964), pp. 201–17
Revolution Politicks: The Career of Daniel Finch, Second Earl of Nottingham, 1647–1730 (Cambridge, 1968)
Houston, Alan, and Pincus, Steve, 'Introduction: Modernity and Later-Seventeenth-Century England', in Houston and Pincus, eds., *A Nation Transformed: England After the Restoration* (Cambridge, 2001)
Israel, Jonathan, *Radical Enlightenment: Philosophy and the Making of Modernity, 1650–1750* (Oxford, 2001)
Jackson, Clare, *Restoration Scotland, 1660–1690: Royalist Politics, Religion, and Ideas* (Woodbridge, 2003)
Jacob, James R., *Henry Stubbe, Radical Protestantism and the Early Enlightenment* (Cambridge, 1983)
Jones, David Martin, *Conscience and Allegiance in Seventeenth Century England: The Political Significance of Oaths and Engagements* (Rochester, NY, 1999)
Jones, J. R., 'James II's Revolution: Royal Policies, 1686–92', in Jonathan I. Israel, ed., *The Anglo-Dutch Moment* (Cambridge, 1991)
'Political Groups and Tactics in the Convention of 1660', *Historical Journal*, 6 (1963), pp. 159–77
Jones, Norman L., *Faith by Statute: Parliament and the Settlement of Religion, 1559* (1982)
Kenyon, J. P., 'The Commission for Ecclesiastical Causes, 1686–1688: A Reconsideration', *Historical Journal*, 34 (1991), pp. 727–36
Robert Spencer, Earl of Sunderland, 1641–1702 (1958)
Knights, Mark, '"Mere Religion" and the "Church State" of Restoration England: The Impact and Ideology of James II's Declarations of Indulgence', in Alan Houston and Steve Pincus, eds., *A Nation Transformed: England after the Restoration* (Cambridge, 2001)
Politics and Opinion in Crisis, 1678–81 (Cambridge, 1994)
Representation and Misrepresentation in Later Stuart Britain (Oxford, 2005)
Lacey, Douglas R., *Dissent and Parliamentary Politics in England, 1661–1689* (New Brunswick, NJ, 1969)
Lake, Peter, *Anglicans and Puritans? Presbyterianism and English Conformist Thought from Whitgift to Hooker* (1988)
'"The Monarchical Republic of Queen Elizabeth I" (and the Fall of Archbishop Grindal) Revisited', in John F. McDiarmid, ed., *The Monarchical Republic of Early Modern England* (Aldershot, 2007)
Lamb, John A., 'Archbishop Alexander Burnet, 1614–1684', *Records of the Scottish Church History Society*, 11 (1952), pp. 133–48
Lamont, William M., *Godly Rule: Politics and Religion, 1603–60* (1969)

Marginal Prynne, 1600–1669 (1963)

Richard Baxter and the Millennium: Protestant Imperialism and the English Revolution (1979)

Landon, Michael, *The Triumph of the Lawyers: Their Role in English Politics, 1678–1689* (Alabama, 1970)

Lathbury, Thomas, *A History of the Convocation of the Church of England*, 2nd edn (1853)

Lee, Maurice, jr, *The Cabal* (Urbana, IL, 1965)

Lehmberg, S. E., 'Supremacy and Vicegerency: A Re-Examination', *English Historical Review*, 81 (1966), pp. 225–35

Lenthall, F. Kyffin, 'A List of the Names of the Members of the House of Commons that advanced Horse, Money, and Plate for Defence of the Parliament, June 10, 11, and 13, 1642', *Notes and Queries*, 1st ser., 12 (1855), pp. 358–60

Lessay, Franck, 'Hobbes's Protestantism', in Tom Sorell and Luc Foisneau, eds., *Leviathan after 350 Years* (Oxford, 2004)

Levitin, Dmitri, 'Matthew Tindal's "Rights of the Christian Church" (1706) and the Church–State Relationship', *Historical Journal* (forthcoming)

Loades, D. M., 'The Last Years of Cuthbert Tunstall, 1547–1559', *Durham University Journal*, n.s. 35 (1973), pp. 10–21

The Oxford Martyrs (1970)

Lockwood, Shelley, 'Marsilius of Padua and the Case for the Royal Ecclesiastical Supremacy', *Transactions of the Royal Historical Society*, 6th ser., 1 (1991), pp. 89–119

Logan, F. Donald, 'Thomas Cromwell and the Vicegerency in Spirituals: A Revisitation', *English Historical Review*, 103 (1988), pp. 658–67

McAdoo, H. R., *The Spirit of Anglicanism* (1965)

MacCulloch, Diarmaid, 'The Myth of the English Reformation', *Journal of British Studies*, 30 (1991), pp. 1–19

Thomas Cranmer: A Life (New Haven, 1996)

Tudor Church Militant: Edward VI and the Protestant Reformation (1999)

Macintyre, Angus, 'The College, King James II, and the Revolution, 1687–1688', in Laurence Brockliss, Gerald Harriss, and Angus Macintyre, eds., *Magdalen College and the Crown* (Oxford, 1988)

McLaren, Anne, *Political Culture in the Reign of Elizabeth I* (Cambridge, 1999)

Malcolm, Charles A., *Holyrood* (1937)

Malcolm, Noel, *Aspects of Hobbes* (Oxford, 2002)

'*Leviathan*, the Pentateuch, and the Origins of Modern Biblical Criticism', in Tom Sorell and Luc Foisneau, eds., *Leviathan after 350 Years* (Oxford, 2004)

Maltby, Judith, *Prayer Book and People in Elizabethan and Early Stuart England* (Cambridge, 1998)

Marshall, John, 'The Ecclesiology of the Latitude-Men, 1660–1689: Stillingfleet, Tillotson, and "Hobbism"', *Journal of Ecclesiastical History*, 36 (1985), pp. 407–27

Marshall, Peter, 'Papist as Heretic: The Burning of John Forest, 1538', *Historical Journal*, 41 (1998), pp. 351–74

Martinich, A. P., *The Two Gods of Leviathan: Thomas Hobbes on Religion and Politics* (Cambridge, 1992)

Matar, Nabil I., 'John Locke and the Jews', *Journal of Ecclesiastical History*, 44 (1993), pp. 45–62

Matthew, H. C. G., and Harrison, Brian Howard, eds., *The Oxford Dictionary of National Biography* (61 vols., Oxford, 2004)

Mayer, Thomas F., *Reginald Pole: Prince and Prophet* (Cambridge, 2000)

M. C. J., 'Seal of the Commissary of the Deanery of Arustley', *Archaeologia Cambrensis*, 5th ser., 1 (1884), pp. 228–31

Miller, John, 'Charles II and his Parliaments', *Transactions of the Royal Historical Society*, 5th ser., 32 (1982), pp. 1–23

James II, rev. edn (1989)

'James II and Toleration', in Eveline Cruickshanks, ed., *By Force or by Default? The Revolution of 1688–1689* (Edinburgh, 1989)

Popery and Politics in England, 1660–1688 (Cambridge, 1973)

Milton, Anthony, *Catholic and Reformed: The Roman and Protestant Churches in English Protestant Thought, 1600–1640* (Cambridge, 1995)

Morrill, John, 'Between Conventions: The Members of Restoration Parliaments', *Parliamentary History*, 5 (1986), pp. 125–32

'A British Patriarchy? Ecclesiastical Imperialism under the Early Stuarts', in Anthony Fletcher and Peter Roberts, eds., *Religion, Culture and Society in Early Modern Britain* (Cambridge, 1994)

'The Church in England, 1642–9', in John Morrill ed., *Reactions to the English Civil War, 1642–1649* (London and Basingstoke, 1982)

Mullet, Charles F., 'Religion, Politics, and Oaths in the Glorious Revolution', *Review of Politics*, 10 (1948), pp. 462–74

Murdock, Graeme, 'The Importance of being Josiah: An Image of Calvinist Identity', *Sixteenth Century Journal*, 29 (1998), pp. 1043–59

Nauta, Lodi, 'Hobbes on Religion and the Church Between the *Elements of Law* and *Leviathan*: A Dramatic Change of Direction?', *Journal of the History of Ideas*, 63 (2002), pp. 577–98

Nelson, Eric, *The Hebrew Republic: Jewish Sources and the Transformation of European Political Thought* (Cambridge, MA, 2010)

Nenner, Howard, *By Colour of Law: Legal Culture and Constitutional Politics in England, 1660–1689* (Chicago, 1977)

Nobbs, D., 'Philip Nye on Church and State', *Cambridge Historical Journal*, 5 (1935), pp. 41–59

Oakley, Francis, 'Christian Obedience and Authority, 1520–1550', in J. H. Burns and Mark Goldie, eds., *The Cambridge History of Political Thought, 1450–1700* (Cambridge, 1991)

'Edward Foxe, Matthew Paris, and the Royal *Potestas Ordinis*', *Sixteenth Century Journal*, 18 (1987), pp. 347–53

Packer, John W., *The Transformation of Anglicanism, 1643–1660, with Special Reference to Henry Hammond* (Manchester, 1969)

Paganini, Gianni, 'Hobbes, Valla and the Trinity', *British Journal for the History of Philosophy*, 11 (2003), pp. 183–218

Parkin, Jon, 'Hobbism in the later 1660s: Daniel Scargill and Samuel Parker', *Historical Journal*, 42 (1999), pp. 85–108

Science, Religion and Politics in Restoration England: Richard Cumberland's De legibus naturae (Woodbridge, 1999)

Parry, J. P., and Taylor, Stephen, eds., *Parliament and the Church, 1529–1960* (Edinburgh, 2000; *Parliamentary History*, 19)

Parsons, Jotham, *The Church in the Republic: Gallicanism and Political Ideology in Renaissance France* (Washington, 2004)

Patterson, Annabel, *The Long Parliament of Charles II* (New Haven, 2008)

Peck, Linda Levy, 'Constructing a new Context for Hobbes Studies', in Howard Nenner, ed., *Politics and the Political Imagination in Later Stuart England* (Rochester, NY, 1997)

Pincus, Steve, *1688: The First Modern Revolution* (New Haven, 2009)

Plumb, J. H., *The Growth of Political Stability in England, 1675–1725* (Harmondsworth, 1967)

Pocock, J. G. A., *The Ancient Constitution and the Feudal Law* (Cambridge, 1957, reissued, 1987)

'A Discourse of Sovereignty: Observations on the Work in Progress', in Nicholas Phillipson and Quentin Skinner, eds., *Political Discourse in Early Modern Britain* (Cambridge, 1993)

Prior, Charles W. A., *Defining the Jacobean Church: The Politics of Religious Controversy, 1603–1625* (Cambridge, 2005)

Quantin, Jean-Louis, *The Church of England and Christian Antiquity* (Oxford, 2009)

Quehen, Hugh de, 'Politics and Scholarship in the Ignatian Controversy', *The Seventeenth Century*, 13 (1998), pp. 69–84

Quick, Anthony, *Charterhouse* (1990)

Ramsbottom, John D., 'Presbyterians and "Partial Conformity" in the Restoration Church of England', *Journal of Ecclesiastical History*, 43 (1992), pp. 249–70

Ratcliff, E. C., 'The Savoy Conference and the Revision of the Book of Common Prayer', in Geoffrey F. Nuttall and Owen Chadwick, eds., *From Uniformity to Unity, 1662–1962* (1962)

Ravitch, Norman, *Sword and Mitre: Government and Episcopate in France and England in the Age of Aristocracy* (The Hague, 1966)

Redworth, Glyn, *In Defence of the Church Catholic* (Oxford, 1990)

Rex, Richard, 'New Additions on Christopher St German: Law, Politics, and Propaganda in the 1530s', *Journal of Ecclesiastical History*, 59 (2008), pp. 281–300

Robbins, Caroline, 'Selden's Pills: State Oaths in England, 1558–1714', *Huntington Library Quarterly*, 35 (1971–72), pp. 303–21

Rodes, Robert E., jr, *Law and Modernisation in the Church of England: Charles II to the Welfare State* (Notre Dame, IN, 1991)

Lay Authority and Reformation in the English Church: Edward I to the Civil War (Notre Dame, IN, 1982)

Rose, Jacqueline, 'Hobbes among the Heretics?', *Historical Journal*, 52 (2009), pp. 493–511

'By Law Established: The Church of England and the Royal Supremacy', in Grant Tapsell, ed., *The Later Stuart Church* (Manchester, forthcoming)

'John Locke, "Matters Indifferent", and the Restoration of the Church of England', *Historical Journal*, 48 (2005), pp. 601–21

'Kingship and Counsel in Early Modern England', *Historical Journal*, 54 (2011), pp. 47–71

'Robert Brady's Intellectual History and Royalist Antipopery in Restoration England', *English Historical Review*, 122 (2007), pp. 1287–1317

'Royal Ecclesiastical Supremacy and the Restoration Church', *Historical Research*, 80 (2007), pp. 324–45

'The Ecclesiastical Polity of Samuel Parker', *The Seventeenth Century*, 25 (2010), pp. 350–75

Runciman, David, *Pluralism and the Personality of the State* (Cambridge, 1997)

Russell, Conrad, 'Parliament, the Royal Supremacy, and the Church', in J. P. Parry and Stephen Taylor, eds., *Parliament and the Church, 1529–1960* (Edinburgh, 2000; *Parliamentary History*, 19)

'Whose Supremacy? King, Parliament and the Church, 1530–1640', *Ecclesiastical Law Journal*, 4 (1996–7), pp. 700–8

Salmon, J. H. M., 'Catholic Resistance Theory, Ultramontanism, and the Royalist Response, 1580–1620', in J. H. Burns and Mark Goldie, eds., *The Cambridge History of Political Thought, 1450–1700* (Cambridge, 1991)

Scarisbrick, J. J., *Henry VIII* (1968)

Schochet, Gordon J., 'The Act of Toleration and the Failure of Comprehension: Persecution, Nonconformity, and Religious Indifference', in Dale Hoak and Mordechai Feingold, eds., *The World of William and Mary: Anglo-Dutch Perspectives on the Revolution of 1688–89* (Stanford, CA, 1996)

'John Locke and Religious Toleration', in Lois G. Schwoerer, ed., *The Revolution of 1688–1689: Changing Perspectives* (Cambridge, 1992)

'From Persecution to "Toleration"', in J. R. Jones, ed., *Liberty Secured? Britain Before and After 1688* (Stanford, CA, 1992)

Schwoerer, Lois G., 'The Transformation of the 1689 Convention into a Parliament', *Parliamentary History*, 3 (1984), pp. 57–76

Scott, Jonathan, *Algernon Sidney and the Restoration Crisis, 1677–1683* (Cambridge, 1991)

Seaton, A. A., *The Theory of Toleration under the Later Stuarts* (Cambridge, 1911)

Seaward, Paul, *The Cavalier Parliament and the Reconstruction of the Old Regime, 1661–1667* (Cambridge, 1989)

Shagan, Ethan H., *Popular Politics and the English Reformation* (Cambridge, 2003)

Shami, Jeanne, 'Kings and Desperate Men: John Donne preaches at Court', *John Donne Journal*, 6 (1987), pp. 9–23

Simon, Walter G., *The Restoration Episcopate* (New York, 1965)

Skinner, Quentin, *The Foundations of Modern Political Thought* (2 vols., Cambridge, 1978)

'Hobbes and the Purely Artificial Person of the State', repr. in *Visions of Politics*, vol. III, *Hobbes and Civil Science* (Cambridge, 2002)

'The Principles and Practice of Opposition: The Case of Bolingbroke versus Walpole', in Neil McKendrick, ed., *Historical Perspectives* (1974)

Visions of Politics, vol. I, *Regarding Method* (Cambridge, 2002)

Smith, David L., *Constitutional Royalism and the Search for Settlement, c. 1640–1649* (Cambridge, 1994)

Smith, Hannah, *Georgian Monarchy: Politics and Culture, 1714–1760* (Cambridge, 2006)

Sommerville, C. John, *The Secularization of Early Modern England: From Religious Culture to Religious Faith* (Oxford, 1992)

Sommerville, Johann P., 'Hobbes and Independency', *Rivista di storia della filosofia*, 59 (2004), pp. 155–73

'Hobbes, Selden, Erastianism, and the History of the Jews', in G. A. J. Rogers and Tom Sorell, eds., *Hobbes and History* (2000)

'*Leviathan* and its Anglican Context', in Patricia Springborg, ed., *The Cambridge Companion to Hobbes's Leviathan* (Cambridge, 2007)

'The Royal Supremacy and Episcopacy "Jure Divino", 1603–1640', *Journal of Ecclesiastical History*, 34 (1983), pp. 548–58

Spalding, Ruth, *The Improbable Puritan: A Life of Bulstrode Whitelocke, 1605–1675* (1975)

Speck, W. A., *James II* (Harlow, 2002)

Springborg, Patricia, '*Leviathan*, the Christian Commonwealth Incorporated', *Political Studies*, 24 (1976), pp. 171–83

'Thomas Hobbes and Cardinal Bellarmine: Leviathan and "The Ghost of the Roman Empire"', *History of Political Thought*, 16 (1995), pp. 503–31

Spurr, John, 'The Church of England, Comprehension and the Toleration Act of 1689', *English Historical Review*, 104 (1989), pp. 927–46

England in the 1670s (Oxford, 2000)

'The English "Post-Reformation"?', *Journal of Modern History*, 74 (2002), pp. 101–19

'"Latitudinarianism" and the Restoration Church', *Historical Journal*, 31 (1988), pp. 61–82

The Post-Reformation: Religion, Politics and Society in Britain, 1603–1714 (Harlow, 2006)

'Religion in Restoration England', in Lionel K. J. Glassey, ed., *The Reigns of Charles II and James VII & II* (Houndmills, Basingstoke, 1997)

The Restoration Church of England, 1646–1689 (New Haven, 1991)

'Schism and the Restoration Church', *Journal of Ecclesiastical History*, 41 (1990), pp. 408–24

'"A Special Kindness for Dead Bishops": The Church, History, and Testimony in Seventeenth-Century Protestantism', *Huntington Library Quarterly*, 68 (2005), pp. 313–34

'"A Sublime and Noble Service": John Evelyn and the Church of England', in Frances Harris and Michael Hunter, eds., *John Evelyn and his Milieu* (2003)

Starkie, Andrew, 'Gilbert Burnet's *Reformation* and the Semantics of Popery', in Jason McElligott, ed., *Fear, Exclusion, and Revolution: Roger Morrice and Britain in the 1680s* (Aldershot, 2006)

Stone, Lawrence, *Road to Divorce: England, 1530–1987* (Oxford, 1990)

Sutch, Victor D., *Gilbert Sheldon: Architect of Anglican Survival, 1640–1675* (The Hague, 1973)

Swatland, Andrew, *The House of Lords in the Reign of Charles II* (Cambridge, 1996)

Tapsell, Grant, 'Parliament and Political Division in the Last Years of Charles II, 1681–5', *Parliamentary History*, 22 (2003), pp. 243–62

'"Weepe Over the Ejected Practice of Religion": Roger Morrice and the Restoration Twilight of Puritan Politics', *Parliamentary History*, 28 (2009), pp. 266–94

Thomas, Roger, 'Comprehension and Indulgence', in Geoffrey F. Nuttall and Owen Chadwick, eds., *From Uniformity to Unity, 1662–1962* (1962)

'The Seven Bishops and their Petition, 18 May 1688', *Journal of Ecclesiastical History*, 12 (1961), pp. 56–70

Trisco, Robert, 'Carlo Borromeo and the Council of Trent: The Question of Reform', in John M. Headley and John B. Tomaro, eds., *San Carlo Borromeo: Catholic Reform and Ecclesiastical Politics in the Second Half of the Sixteenth Century* (Cranbury, NJ, 1988)

Troeltsch, Ernst, *The Social Teaching of the Christian Churches*, trans. Olive Wyon (2 vols., 1931)

Tuck, Richard, 'The "Christian Atheism" of Thomas Hobbes', in Michael Hunter and David Wootton, eds., *Atheism from the Reformation to the Enlightenment* (Oxford, 1992)

Tyacke, Nicholas, 'Arminianism and the Theology of the Restoration Church', in Simon Groenveld and Michael Wintle, eds., *The Exchange of Ideas* (Zutphen, 1994)

'Puritanism, Arminianism and Counter-Revolution', in Conrad Russell, ed., *The Origins of the English Civil War* (Basingstoke, 1975)

Tyacke, Nicholas, ed., *England's Long Reformation, 1500–1800* (1998)

Ullmann, Walter, 'This Realm of England is an Empire', *Journal of Ecclesiastical History*, 30 (1979), pp. 175–203

Ussher, Roland G., *The Rise and Fall of the High Commission* (Oxford, 1913)

Van Dam, Raymond, 'The Many Conversions of the Emperor Constantine', in Kenneth Mills and Anthony Grafton, eds., *Conversion in Late Antiquity and the Early Middle Ages* (Rochester, NY, 2003)

Walsham, Alexandra, *Charitable Hatred: Tolerance and Intolerance in England, 1500–1700* (Manchester, 2006)

Walters, Mark D., 'St German on Reason and Parliamentary Sovereignty', *Cambridge Law Journal*, 62 (2003), pp. 335–70

Whitaker, Mark, 'Hobbes's View of the Reformation', *History of Political Thought*, 9 (1988), pp. 45–58

Whiteman, Anne, 'The Restoration of the Church of England', in Geoffrey F. Nuttall and Owen Chadwick, eds., *From Uniformity to Unity, 1662–1962* (1962)

Williams, David H., *Catalogue of Seals in the National Museum of Wales, vol. II* (Cardiff, 1998)

'Catalogue of Welsh Ecclesiastical Seals as known down to 1600 AD', *Archaeologia Cambrensis*, 133 (1984), pp. 100–35; and 134 (1985), pp. 162–89

Witcombe, D. T., *Charles II and the Cavalier House of Commons, 1663–1674* (Manchester, 1966)

Worden, A. B., 'Toleration and the Cromwellian Protectorate', in William J. Sheils, ed., *Persecution and Toleration* (Oxford, 1984)

Yale, D. E. C., 'Hobbes and Hale on Law, Legislation and the Sovereign', *Cambridge Law Journal*, 31 (1972), pp. 121–56

UNPUBLISHED

Barclay, Andrew, 'The Impact of King James II on the Departments of the Royal Household' (Ph.D thesis, University of Cambridge, 1994)

Brown, Anthony J., 'Anglo-Irish Gallicanism, *c.*1635 – *c.*1685' (Ph.D thesis, University of Cambridge, 2004)

Devlin, Eoin, 'English Encounters with Papal Rome in the Late Counter-Reformation, *c.*1685 – *c.*1697' (Ph.D thesis, University of Cambridge, 2010)

Halcomb, Joel, 'Congregational Church Practice and Culture in East Anglia, 1642–1660' (MPhil. thesis, University of Cambridge, 2006)

Hampson, James E., 'Richard Cosin and the Rehabilitation of the Clerical Estate in late Elizabethan England' (Ph.D thesis, University of St Andrews, 1997)

McNulty, J. L. C., 'An Anticlerical Priest: Edmund Hickeringill (1631–1708) and the Context of Priestcraft' (MPhil. thesis, University of Cambridge, 1998)

Nicholson, Graham David, 'The Nature and Function of Historical Argument in the Henrician Reformation' (Ph.D thesis, University of Cambridge, 1977)

Powell, Hunter, 'The Last Confession: A Background Study of the Savoy Declaration of Faith and Order' (MPhil. thesis, University of Cambridge, 2008)

'Seeing Things their Way: Studying the History of Religious Ideas' (conference at Selwyn College, Cambridge, 1–3 July 2004)

Sommerville, J. P., 'Jacobean Political Thought and the Controversy over the Oath of Allegiance' (Ph.D thesis, University of Cambridge, 1981)

Whiteman, E. A. O., 'The Episcopate of Dr Seth Ward, Bishop of Exeter (1662 to 1667) and Salisbury (1667 to 1688/9), with Special Reference to the Ecclesiastical Problems of his Time' (DPhil. thesis, University of Oxford, 1951)

Index

Printed in Great Britain
by Amazon